Ernest Hemingway

SIX DECADES OF CRITICISM

Ernest Hemingway

SIX DECADES OF CRITICISM

Edited by
LINDA W. WAGNER

Michigan State University Press
1987

Printed in the United States of America

The paper used in this publication meets the minimum requirements of American National Standard for Information Sciences—Permanence of paper for printed materials ANSI 239.48–1984

Michigan State University Press
East Lansing, Michigan 48823-5202

Design and Production: Julie Loehr
Typesetting: The Copyfitters

Library of Congress Cataloging-in-Publication Data

Ernest Hemingway: six decades of criticism.

   Includes bibliographies and index.
   1. Hemingway, Ernest, 1899–1961—Criticism and interpretation.
I. Wagner, Linda W.
PS3515.E37Z58677   1987   813'.52   87-61766
ISBN 0-87013-250-4

To Paul Smith, James Nagel
and Jo August

Contents

vii

Introduction

ERNEST HEMINGWAY has been dead for twenty-six years, but the amount of criticism on him and on his work only increases. Readers remain intrigued with this modernist who was the apparent contradiction of the dedicated and isolated artist-at-work, this Hemingway who hunted big game in Africa, knew more about the Spanish bullfights than most aficionados, and patrolled the Cuban waters for Nazi activity in his own craft during World War II. Yet Hemingway the writer outlives the countless other personalities the man adopted throughout his life. In his finely written stories and novels, Hemingway brought the essence of the disillusioned yet enduring modern vision to millions of readers around the world.

The name *Hemingway* is synonymous with *writer*. People attempting to explain the writer's art, the writer's diligence, speak of Hemingway. They picture him standing at his writing board in the cool early mornings of Key West, or pausing with painstaking attention in the midst of writing dialogue in Ketchum, Idaho. They repeat his "iceberg theory"—that the writer may omit seven-eighths of what he knows, so long as what *does* show in his writing is the significant detail. They cite his maxims about writing, and about the writing life: "Writing, at its best, is a lonely life." "For a true writer each book should be a new beginning where he tries again for something that is beyond attainment." They quote his advice about the day-to-day practice of writing, the techniques of being a successful artist: "You write until you come to a place where you still have your juice and know what will happen next and you stop and try to live through until the next day when you hit it again." "What amateurs call a style is usually only the unavoidable awkwardnesses in first trying to make something that has not heretofore been made. Almost no new classics resemble other previous classics." "The most essential gift for a good writer is a built-in, shock-proof, shit detector. This is the writer's radar and all great writers have had it."[1] And, finally, they

1

turn to Hemingway for the inspiration to take up the writing life. As he answered the question, *Why does he write* in the *Paris Review* interview, "From things that have happened and from things as they exist and from all things that you know and all those you cannot know, you make something through your invention that is not a representation but a whole new thing truer than anything true and alive, and you make it alive, and if you make it well enough, you give it immortality."[2]

To make some new thing, some new art object, was the aim of the Modernist movement, for which Hemingway quickly became a spokesman. He was also an anomaly because much of the "new" writing early in the twentieth century did not find a wide audience. Obscurity and meaninglessness often resulted from extreme stylistic experiments, and the general public was more accustomed to mocking modernism than it was to championing it. Such was not the case with Hemingway. His careful selection of scenes and details, presented with little authorial interference, seemed simple. Hemingway's style was poetic, suggestive, open to a great many kinds of readings—but it conveyed its emotional insights clearly, and with sharp impact. Although his spare yet intense prose echoed that of Mark Twain, Stephen Crane, Sherwood Anderson, Ivan Turgenev, and Ezra Pound, it struck twentieth-century readers as original and genuine, which was exactly the effect Hemingway wanted. Like other modernists, he assumed that art lay in the *way* something was said. Style, form, and meaning were parts of an inseparable whole.

During the aftermath of the Great War, many traditional religious beliefs lost their force. Order and divine direction no longer characterized the world. In a changed situation, the task of the artist was to discover new meaning. As creative prophets, writers could hope to influence history. They also had a chance to make large sums of money. As national income rose from 59 billion dollars in 1920 to more than 87 billion in 1928, publishing burgeoned. The company of Alfred A. Knopf was established in 1915; Boni and Liveright in 1917; Harcourt Brace in 1919; and Viking in 1925. It was a heady time to begin a literary career.

Hemingway's identity had long been that of writer. After graduating from high school, he wrote for the Kansas City *Star*. Rather than considering himself a journalist, however, he termed himself a poet. Then he moved to the prose poems of *in our time*, the short sketches about bullfighting and war that Ezra Pound praised so highly. (Of the young Hemingway, Pound wrote that he was successful because he had been "applying the stricture against superfluous words to his prose, polishing, re-polishing, and eliminating, as can be seen in the clean hard paragraphs of the first brief *in our time*."[3]) Hemingway knew that he was here combining a desired "objectivity" with an authorial "selectivity" that conveyed exactly what he intended. It was no small accomplishment.

By the time Hemingway wrote *in our time*, followed by the 1925 *In Our Time*, which included a dozen full-length stories as well as the vignettes, he was a practiced writer. He was also a student of Pound, Gertrude Stein, Ford Madox Ford, James Joyce, and T. S. Eliot—and an expatriate. Leaving America after World War I had been difficult for Hemingway. He considered himself one of the best kinds of Americans: he mourned for his country more than he criticized it. But the origins of his alienation are clear. He was born in 1899, the first son and second child of a prominent Oak Park, Illinois, family. His father was a physician, given to bouts of depression even when Hemingway was small. His mother was an opera singer, voice teacher, and feminist. Both parents expected their children to excel, and Hemingway usually complied. He made good grades in school, wrote for the school newspaper and literary magazine, and participated in sports. With his father, he learned to hunt and fish. His older sister and his four younger siblings looked up to him; adults found his ingenuous manner and his convincing interest in them charming.

From the summer of his first birthday, Hemingway spent part of every year at the family cottage on Walloon Lake, near Charlevoix, Michigan. Summers there allowed him to explore rivers, lakes, and the wilderness—both with his father and alone, and, later, with Indian friends and lovers. Rowing across the lake with a storm coming up, fishing with friends, or hunting—some of his best writing draws on these early Michigan experiences, and on his sense of himself as an adventurer that grew from them. Early in his life, long before he went to Europe, Hemingway was eager for ways to escape the polite, effete, and curiously materialistic culture of his times.

After graduating from Oak Park High in 1917, Hemingway left home to work for the Kansas City *Star*, covering the hospital beat and some crime stories. Within a few months he was combining a personal storytelling style with a wry, almost slick, tone. He was a feature writer interested in character, rather than a reporter interested in events.

The next phase of Hemingway's education came in Europe, in the American Red Cross Ambulance Corps. Having served briefly in France, he was transferred to Italy, where in the summer of 1918 he was badly wounded in both legs. During his convalescence, first in Italian hospitals and then for a winter in Petosky, Michigan, he tried seriously to write—only to become further alienated from his family. By this time his father was irritable and depressed, near a breakdown, and his mother, who had assumed control of the household, was under financial pressures that Hemingway did not understand. Urged by his mother to go to work, he left for Chicago, where he worked on salary with the *Co-Operative Commonwealth* while writing short stories and poems that he tried, unsuccessfully, to publish. There he also met and, in 1921, married Hadley Richardson of St. Louis.

Shortly after their wedding, the Hemingways left for Paris. Hemingway wrote columns for the *Toronto Star* and played apprentice to the important modernists living in Paris. Their income was based on Hadley's inheritance and on Hemingway's writing. With Ezra Pound's encouragement, Hemingway in 1923 published *Three Stories and Ten Poems* with Robert McAlmon's Contact Press, followed the next year with *in our time* and in 1925 with the *In Our Time* that included stories as well as vignettes. This work was the culmination of Hemingway's word-by-word approach to style, through which he tried to endow prose with the density of poetry, making each image, each scene, serve several purposes. Both the metaphoric titles of his early stories—"The End of Something," about a broken romance and a decayed mill; "Cat in the Rain" in which a searching wife looks for a bedraggled cat as a love object; "Soldier's Home," a poignant study of a young veteran almost devastated by his family's inability to understand him—and the resonances that the stories acquire from the larger structure of the book, help to make *In Our Time* a masterful achievement. At age twenty-six, Hemingway suddenly acquired an enviable reputation.

When he wrote *The Sun Also Rises*, his first novel, in a brief period after he and Hadley had made a second trip to Pamplona to see the bullfights, he concentrated the many literary models he had absorbed into a work that was both thematically and technically revolutionary. Spare characterizations and taut relationships, drawn quickly in scenes at bars or over meals, serve a fast-paced plot line. Most readers praised *The Sun Also Rises* for its tight control of detail and its metaphorical richness; others criticized it for the immorality of its "lost" characters. The deeper stir that the 1926 novel created had to do with Hemingway's conception that his war-weary expatriates were re-defining heroism.

Emasculated by a war wound, Jake Barnes tries to help Lady Brett Ashley, the woman he loves, find happiness with other men. She finally decides to relinquish a young bullfighter-lover in order to save him from her jaded life. Purified by his mastery of the bullfight ritual, Pedro Romero lives an almost spiritual existence. Robert Cohn's poorly repressed competitiveness and insecurities make him arrogant, self-centered, and childish. To middle-class American readers, saddled with Prohibition and hounded by the desire to make money and be respectable, *The Sun Also Rises* was a complex and in some ways an offensive book. The wide range of critical opinion, heated critical opinion, testifies to the innate difficulty of the modernist text. Its apparent "simplicity" jars against an implicit elitism—these are wealthy characters, living a life of pleasure, even abandon. Without more didactic direction by the author, how are readers to measure the moral distance between a character like Robert Cohn and one like Jake Barnes, who on so many counts appear to be similar?

Although it was written sixty years ago, *The Sun Also Rises* still provokes controversy. So too does Hemingway's second novel, the 1929 *A Farewell to Arms*. In that text, as in the stories of *Men Without Women* (1927), Hemingway continued to explore the difficult truth of living in a war-torn and disillusioned culture. His characters illustrated, for the most part, a style of life described as "grace under pressure." In that code, his survivors mirror the honesty, the discipline, the restraint, and even something of the resonance that had come to mark his prose.

During the 1930s, Hemingway's art went through a period of transition. He wrote a great many non-fiction studies (*Death in the Afternoon, Green Hills of Africa*, countless columns for *Esquire* and other magazines), and only returned to writing novels later in the decade. When he published *To Have and Have Not* in 1937 and his play, *The Fifth Column* in 1938, readers were less than excited. The publication in 1940 of *For Whom the Bell Tolls* revived Hemingway's reputation, but readers recognized that Hemingway had left the highly polished style of his earlier work and had assumed a more rambling mode of narrative. The action that would have usually been reported from the outside was now handled in interior monologue or stream of consciousness style, as were some of Robert Jordan's sections in *For Whom the Bell Tolls*.

Whatever work Hemingway accomplished during the 1930s—and for the rest of his life—was written with more than the customary anguish and stress. Caught in the depression that seemed characteristic for his family, Hemingway struggled to maintain his life and art on the same energetic level he had achieved during his early years as a writer. Frequent accidents, plane crashes and other physical injuries took their toll as he grew more and more insistent that the modernist writer had to grow and change, had to remain versatile, and had to continue to "win." Given all his physical and psychological problems, it is not surprising that during his late years, Hemingway wrote comparatively little. Malcolm Cowley, the critic who was Hemingway's friend, recalls seeing him stand at his writing board from early morning till afternoon, seldom able to write at all.

Hemingway's last years were dominated not by writing but by his need to write. In 1950 he published *Across the River and into the Trees*, a paean to endurance and military hardihood that was denounced by critics. *The Old Man and the Sea* (1952) won the 1953 Pulitzer Prize for Fiction and led to Hemingway's being awarded the Nobel Prize for Literature a year later, but it too failed to match the quality of his earlier work. In 1960, he published a version of

The Dangerous Summer, an account of what would be his last visit to Spain for the bullfights. The posthumously published works—in 1964, *A Moveable Feast*, his memoir of the Paris years; in 1970, *Islands in the Stream*; and in 1986 *The Garden of Eden*—as well as other unfinished manuscripts, date from earlier times. They, too, fail in many ways to measure up to his best writing; and in each case, the question of changes made during the editing for publication remains troublesome. The crucial question of what Hemingway himself would have done with these partially finished manuscripts haunts the reader. Their publication, however, kept the mill of Hemingway criticism running at full speed for much of the quarter-century since the writer's suicide in 1961.

This collection opens with three recent essays that give new insight into some of Hemingway's personal life. Michael Reynolds' account of his family life during his boyhood is a segment of Reynolds' important biography, *The Young Hemingway*. Max Westbrook's essay on Hemingway's relationship with his parents after his return from World War I draws heavily on unpublished materials in the Humanities Center at the University of Texas (some hundreds of letters belonging to the Hemingway family). Scott Donaldson's assessment of Hemingway's friendship with John Dos Passos, a topic of speculation to critics as well as to friends of each of the writers, provides insight into the older Hemingway. The book then proceeds to essays that assess Hemingway's writing, particularly the novels most often taught. Each essay is either previously unpublished or is taken from journal sources that might be difficult for the general reader to obtain. No excerpts from books are included, nor is any material reprinted from my earlier collection, *Ernest Hemingway: Five Decades of Criticism*. This book attempts to provide a sense of the good earlier criticism, however, of which there has been a great deal. The reviews and essays by Nelson Algren, Paul Rosenfeld, C. Hugh Holman, John Wain, Dorothy Parker, William Faulkner, Claude McKay, and Malcolm Cowley illustrate the wealth of this earlier work. It also attempts to provide readings of Hemingway's work that will widen appreciation for it, that will enable readers to see richness in texts that have previously been limited by the criticism written about them. It also, perhaps most important, attempts to provide some indication of the newest directions in Hemingway criticism, those in gender-based approaches and those in manuscript study.

It now seems reasonable to divide Hemingway criticism in the mid-1970s— into that criticism written before the manuscripts of Hemingway's work were available to scholars at the John F. Kennedy Library, and that written after. Although collections of Hemingway materials are housed as well at the Lilly Library at Indiana University and at the National Humanities Center at Austin,

Texas, the primary collection is at the Kennedy Library. As Jo August, the first curator of that collection remembers, "Mary Hemingway started depositing papers in the Library in 1972. The first materials to arrive were about two feet of miscellaneous and fragmentary manuscripts. From that point until 1980, papers continued to arrive. . . from Mary Hemingway's New York apartment, her home in Ketchum, from Harvard's Houghton Library, and from Carlos Baker in Princeton. The bulk of the collection, however, came from two sources: Mary Hemingway's bank vault in New York, the contents of which Charles Mann and Philip Young listed in their Inventory, and from warehouse storage in New York. The papers arrived in boxes, trunks, filing cabinets, and shopping bags."[4]

On July 18, 1980, the Hemingway Room at the John F. Kennedy Library in Boston was officially opened. Before that time, the Hemingway materials were housed in a federal archives building in Waltham, Massachusetts. Between 1972, when the materials began to arrive and the move to the Kennedy in 1980, at least part of the large collection was accessible. Ms. August's account continues, describing that "manuscript materials were sent to the New England Document Conservation Center, where they were deacidified, and then repaired, separated, cleaned; and mylar encapsulated as necessary. Intensive preservation work was performed on the five very fragile scrapbooks kept by Grace Hall Hemingway from Ernest's birth until he was 18 years of age. The newspaper clipping scrapbooks were taken apart and the clippings were deacidified and encapsulated. Copy negatives were made of the over 10,000 still photographs, and the materials were placed in acid-free containers."[5] For the literary scholar, the most important part of the collection was the draft and manuscript material for countless stories and novels. Over 200 separate items relate to Hemingway's novels (including as a single item the 1147-page manuscript of *For Whom the Bell Tolls*); over 600 items relate to other of Hemingway's writing, published and unpublished.

Much of the criticism chosen for this collection has been informed by the study of these manuscripts. Some of the essays deal with the writer's craft and style, his revisions, the metamorphosis between early drafts and finished work. Other essays make less direct use of manuscript study, but approach the fiction anew because of materials in these several collections. Several other essays deal with the work that was published after Hemingway's death. Several others were first given at international Hemingway conferences, and three were originally published in the publications of the Hemingway Society, *The Hemingway Journal* and *The Hemingway Newsletter*, both housed at Ohio Northern University.

I am presently compiling a second *Reference Guide to Ernest Hemingway*, an annotated bibliography of all secondary materials published since the mid-1970s. (The first such guide appeared in 1977.) To read the quantity of essays and books published in the last decade is both impressive and exciting. Much of this recent criticism is as good as any criticism on Hemingway's work, leading the reader to new kinds of perceptions, new kinds of appreciations. It is the hope of the author that this collection will provide a beginning, a means of entry, into the study of Hemingway's writing. It is some of the best we have. As he said himself in 1937, "A writer's problem does not change. He himself changes, but his problem remains the same. It is always how to write truly and, having found what is true, to project it in such a way that it becomes a part of the experience of the person who reads it."[6] The best criticism verifies that complete experience—of reading and of then experiencing what has been read.

LINDA WAGNER
East Lansing, Michigan

1. *Conversations with Ernest Hemingway*, ed. Matthew J. Bruccoli (Jackson: University Press of Mississippi, 1986), p. 196; George Plimpton, "An Interview with Ernest Hemingway" *Paris Review*, 18 (1958), rpt. in *Ernest Hemingway: Five Decades of Criticism*, ed. Linda W. Wagner (East Lansing: Michigan State University Press, 1974), pp. 24, 32, 38.

2. Ibid., p. 38.

3. Ezra Pound, "Small Magazines," *The English Journal*, 19, No. 9 (November 1930), 700.

4. Jo August, "A Note on the Hemingway Collection," *Ernest Hemingway, The Papers of a Writer*, ed. Bernard Oldsey (New York: Garland Publishing, Inc., 1981), p. xxi.

5. Ibid.

6. Ernest Hemingway, "Fascism Is a Lie" in *Conversations with Ernest Hemingway*, p. 193.

I: Hemingway, The Life

HEMINGWAY'S HOME:
DEPRESSION AND SUICIDE

MICHAEL S. REYNOLDS

FATHERS AND SONS, a title Hemingway would later use ironically, were not always close in turn of the century Oak Park. The "boy problem," which ministers so loved to resolve, centered on the work ethic and role models. In Ernest's earliest years, his father needed no sermons to excite his sense of responsibility. Summers at Lake Walloon, Agassiz outings, fall bird hunts—wherever he could Clarence Hemingway cultivated a close relationship with his young son. In those years the Doctor was a progressive father, one who tried to be a friend and mentor. But when Ernest entered puberty and most needed his father, the Doctor began to succumb to a nervous condition, which Ernest, in his teens, could not understand.

As a boy, Ernest responded to all of his father's passions: natural history, fishing, hiking, hunting. But after 1912, the Doctor lost interest. He still loved the woods and the lake, but increasingly he loved them alone, shutting out his son. After his twelfth birthday, Ernest spent less and less time on the lake or in the hunting fields with his father. Dr. Hemingway gave up the Agassiz Club, donating the collection of stuffed birds and animals to the high school. Whatever father and son had shared was fixed in memory. What was left to share was embedded quite literally in Ernest's blood.[1]

In the summer of every year they had lived in a cottage that looked across Lake Walloon to his mother's farm. At the edge of the lake there was a boat dock, dry and grey in the sun, and the water shimmered and lapped in the shallows. Sometimes in the dark he and his sisters swam naked in the lake, but that was before the war when they were all much younger. Each summer Ernest saw less of his father. Each summer the Doctor left the lake earlier, coming back alone in

Reprinted with permission from *American Literature*, 57, No. 4 (December 1985), 600–10.

the fall to close up their cottage. Each summer the Doctor worried more about money. Each summer the Doctor's son was forced to assume more of his father's duties—fixing, digging, planting; the tedious chores his father loved so well and which Ernest detested. Then came the Great War, and in 1918 the young Hemingway spent his first summer away from the summer cottage. When he returned in 1919, everything had changed. It had been changing for some time, but he had not seen it.

That first year back from the war, Ernest had no patience for his father's problems, for he had immediate and long-range problems of his own: how to cope with the fears left him by his night wounding at Fossalta; what to do with the broken heart left him by the nurse in Milan; what to do with the rest of his life. In May 1919, as soon as it was warm at the lake, he slipped out of Oak Park, escaping alone to that last good country. Ernest would not see his brooding father again until late August when the Doctor came north to close up Windemere cottage. His sisters and mother agreed that two months by himself would be soothing for the Doctor's nerves, which for some time had been strained. His erratic shifts of mood—now gentle, now angry—pained and puzzled his children when they were younger. Now that his older daughters were of age, the Doctor's unpredictable behavior, still puzzling, became at times almost impossible to bear.

The woods and water about Windemere, the Pine barrens to the north, the Fox River, the Black—these places were Ernest's touchstones. There he had his closest friends—the local and summer people with whom he shared a freedom not found in Oak Park. Lake Walloon was the spawning ground that pulled at his genetic self. Over the years he watched his father lose the lake. The adult world of work, family, bills and responsibilities slowly eroded the pleasures of Windemere. If young Hemingway did not seem eager, that summer of 1919, to make plans for the future, perhaps it was because he knew that adults gave up such pleasures.

All that hot summer the Doctor treated his Oak Park patients and wrote daily, obsessive letters to his wife, numbering each and keeping carbon copies. Two of those letters—both originals and carbons—are missing from the family archives. From the existing evidence, it is clear that the Doctor's missing letters explained why he no longer would allow Ruth Arnold to live with the Hemingways. She could not even visit the house. Ruth, who first came to Grace as a voice student in 1907, had become a permanent fixture at North Kenilworth. The youngest daughter of a River Forest salesman, she was not overly bright, nor had she a promising voice, but she was sincere and hard working. Dominated at home by her older sisters—one a dress maker, the other a piano teacher—Ruth blossomed at the Hemingways. In 1908, she moved into North Kenilworth as a live-in student and part-time baby sitter and cook. She was thirteen years old, and she loved Grace with daughterly devotion. When Grace was away from Oak Park on her annual midwinter vacation or summering at Walloon, Ruth wrote her simple, loving letters; "Ever since I've known you, my soul has craved for the luxurious and more beautiful things in life—not so much for bodily comforts as for uplifting surroundings."[2]

On the Doctor's birthdays, Ruth gave him gifts, and her family once sent him a bouquet of asters. In the Hemingway tradition of nicknames, Ruth was called variously "Boofie" or "Bobs." Her letters to Grace were addressed: "Dearest Muv." Some summers she went to Walloon with the family; always she was one of the family, an older sister to the children and a confidante to Grace. By 1912, her voice was strong enough for a recital in Grace's music room, where she had the day to herself. In 1919, the Oak Park directory listed 600 North Kenilworth Avenue as Ruth's address. She was twenty-three years old, quiet, and physically attractive, and Grace's most admiring friend.

When the Hemingway children—first Leicester, then Marcelline and Sunny—wrote accounts of their home life, the name of Ruth Arnold did not appear. Oak Parkers all, the children knew better than to rattle the closet bones. Whatever the Doctor's reasons, the conflict festered during the hot summer in Oak Park. Ruth spent most of June and July at Windemere and Grace cottage. She returned to Oak Park on 2 August, arriving in the middle of the worst race riot in Chicago history. The trains, she said, were running late. All summer Ruth's unflagging devotion had supported Grace in her efforts to impose order at Windemere. Now Ruth was already homesick for Grace. "No distance," she said, "can separate my soul from the one I love so dearly."[3]

On her arrival in Oak Park, Ruth phoned Dr. Hemingway to assure him that Carol's brief sickness at the lake had cleared up and the family was well. Whatever else she said is lost to us, as is Dr. Hemingway's letter to his wife, written that very day. All we know is Grace's reply:

> Yours of Saturday and Sunday received last evening. Marcelline also had one from you which grieved her as much as mine grieved me because we both realize from those letters that you are no better for the 2 months rest from the family. I have so hoped and prayed that the quiet would help you to readjust your mental attitude and find yourself with God's help in relation to your family. If your mental attitude is really not a thing within your control, then you can count on me to help you all in my power, as long as I live. I will never fail you in trouble. I love you and grieve for you. However, the world is still wholesome and my dear blessed children with all their faults still need me and the dear faithful Ruth, who has given me her youth and her loyal service for these

many years, needs me. This is my platform. I shall desert none of you, for fancied wrongs on the part of anyone of the number. You are each one as dear to me as life, and no one in the world can ever take my husband's place unless he abdicates it to play at petty jealousy.[4]

Her husband's mind was clearly becoming more obsessed and erratic. Twice earlier in their marriage his "nervous condition" had become chronic; each time he had pulled himself together. This time he was pushing Grace right to the edge of her capacity to understand him.

As the summer waned into August, Marcelline was the first to return to Oak Park where her new job waited. There she found that her father had perversely spent his leisure time scraping, varnishing and painting her bedroom. No sooner had she arrived than she told him that she intended to move out of the house. The summer heat and his doctoring had done nothing to improve his "nervous condition." The idea of his first-born daughter leaving home only worsened matters. Marcelline wrote her mother that the Doctor was no better than when they had left him for the summer. "He is still excited and exacting but we all try to get along as well as possible."[5] "Dad tries to be nice, but his temperament does not allow him to see things as I do—and tho we get along beautifully on the surface, I feel a thousand miles away from his soul."[6]

Nothing Marcelline said quieted Grace's fears about her husband's precarious mind. The Doctor obsessively turned any conversation around until he could rant about Ruth Arnold. Marcelline could not bear to hear it. When Ruth called, Marcelline could not tell her why she was banned from the house. Instead she visited Ruth in the evening, not telling her father of their long walks together.

No more could Ruth understand the situation. When the girls arrived in Oak Park she immediately called Marcelline to say she would come over, only to be told that the Doctor would not allow it. Ruth pleaded with Grace: "Oh! dear what is the trouble now? You surely know, please tell me. If only my conscience were guilty I could ask to be forgiven, but I can't feel I am. . . . I have worked for and loved the Hemingway family so long that it seems impossible to cease going there."[7] She thanked God for giving Grace to her as an ideal, and she would have liked nothing better than to be with her that moment, brushing her hair or stroking her aching forehead. The next day Marcelline urged Grace to write Ruth, who was lonesome for the family, wanting desperately to visit the children. Marcelline could not invite her over because the Doctor acted "so insane on the subject."[8]

In the middle of it all, listening and remembering, was Ernest. Years later he would blame his mother for destroying his father and the happy home life he knew as a boy. Some would say that he hated his mother. In 1982, one of his own sons recalled that he was never allowed to visit Grandmother Grace because, Ernest told him, she was androgynous.[9] Allowing for Hemingway's penchant for hyperbole, the judicious reader will remember that love and hate are sometimes indistinguishable. All of Grace Hemingway's children were deeply influenced by her exuberance which led her unerringly to center stage. The more her husband retreated from the world, the more she filled the vacuum. Whether singing, painting or campaigning for local issues, Grace was always a public performer during those years when the feminist movement was redefining the roles of woman. Later as Hemingway reworked parts of his fictive life, he blamed his mother for what had happened to his father. By then the Doctor was dead, a suicide. Rather than admit to himself that his father's "nervous" problems might have been a mental disorder, Hemingway found it far more convenient to accuse his mother. Mental problems were frightening and might be hereditary. "Once they've had you certified as nutty," one of his characters would later say, "no one ever has any confidence in you again."[10]

Marcelline was barely home a week with the Doctor when she used her job in the South Church parish house as an excuse to move into a rented room. The day Clarence Hemingway was packing to join Grace at the lake, Marcelline wrote her mother:

> the temperamental clash that goes on in our house would absolutely ruin my disposition. . . . You and I know how perfect last summer was—How happy *all* of us were—and now we are not [happy] at home. The girls, Urs and Sunny, realize it, and we are very unhappy. I am sure it will be better when you get here. Dad does not *mean* to be irritable and exacting, and he does not even think that he is other than normal in every way, but the facts are that he is not normal at all, in his disposition or attitude toward us or our friends. I know he is tired and has been under a great strain, but. . . it is hard to adjust one's point of view to his outlook on life.[11]

In 1919, Ernest could not have ignored what was obvious to his sisters: their father had mental problems that had gradually over the previous sixteen years become more pronounced and more serious.

When Ernest was four, the Doctor took a week's Thanksgiving vacation to New Orleans, a self-prescribed cure for his depression. He went alone but wrote almost daily notes to the family. Two months later he said that the New Orleans trip had been his salvation.[12] In 1908, Clarence took a month off from his fall practice to attend a postgraduate course in obstetrics at the New York Lying-In Hospital. Only Grace and the family knew that he spent the last two weeks of the trip in New Orleans, once more alone. Grace counseled him; "the way to rest is *not* to read Oak Leaves and get into the old train of thoughts but to give your mind a vacation."[13] She was also concerned that no one in Oak Park know that he was going to New Orleans. "Do you want me to let the local press know about this vacation?" she asked. "Don't you think it perhaps wiser to let them keep the first idea in their minds that you are taking 'post-grad' work in New York?. . . Try to forget all about us while you are on board ship and rest the worry place in your brain. Just make a business of eating and sleeping and forgetting."[14] Later Ernest would say that his father had been caught in a trap only partially of his own making. What he did not want to discuss was the possibility that the trap was biological.

Dr. Hemingway's bouts with depression were, to a certain extent, triggered by financial stress: in 1903–04 and again in 1907–09, economic recessions may have been responsible. Between 1917 and 1919, he again exhibited signs of erratic behavior and depression; this time the stress of the war, the flu epidemic and the wounding of Ernest combined to produce his "nervous" condition. Simultaneously, Grace, who had always earned a considerable income from voice lessons, began to lose pupils to the more advanced musical academies then developing in Oak Park. With the Doctor probably making only four thousand dollars a year from his practice, the Hemingway annual income was seriously eroded.

Like any husband with a large family, Clarence Hemingway frequently worried about money: unnecessary household expenses; Grace's cottage; the college education of his children. In 1909, he left a letter to his wife and children listing almost $50,000 of life insurance spread out among eleven different companies and organizations as diverse as the Loyal Americans of Springfield ($1000), the Order of Columbian Knights ($5000), United States Life Endowment ($5000), and Equitable Life Assurance Society ($10,000). In the text of the letter, he gave Grace explicit advice to follow in the case of his death; "Understand—the Accident Policy is for Accidental Death or *blood poisoning,* and the Health Policy. . . is not a *life insurance. . . .* All others are for *death benefits. . .* don't let your grief or sentiment come in between your good dead husband [and] the future provision of and for the necessities, and education of the darling children and your own self—Grace my darling." With his meticulous list, he left explicit instructions for collecting on the policies: tell one story; write it out; tell all the companies the same story. "And don't tell all you know about your own affairs to every one. . . should there be any doubt at all as to the cause of death. . . make an autopsy and if a Coroner's Inquest is called have Dr. [unreadable] or Dr. Hocktorn [?] present in my interests for you. . . if *Accident* is Blood Poisoning you can realize on the Aetna Policy"[15]

In 1917, before undergoing surgery to correct a hernia, Dr. Hemingway left a similar list of insurance policies and instructions. In 1928, Dr. A. F. Benson, Coroner's physician, testified that on 6 December, Clarence Hemingway put a bullet into his "right temple 3 centimeters above the external auditory meatus and 3 cm. in front of the ear. The bullet pierced the brain looping under the skin, after shattering the bone of the skull in the left temple 5 cm. above and 7 cm. posterior to the external auditory meatus. There were powder burns at the point of entrance of the bullet. Blood was oozing out of the bullet wound."[16] Six Oak Park men on the Coroner's Jury ruled the death a suicide.

Viewed retrospectively, Clarence Hemingway's letter of 1909 reads, per- haps, more ominously than it was intended. There can be no doubt, however, that his "nervous" condition drew progressively more serious after 1904. His com- pulsive behavior increased steadily. When separated from Grace by their vaca- tions, he wrote a letter each day, and each day expected one from Grace in the mail. When he missed writing, he apologized, explaining in detail the reasons. The dark brooding over his own death, if not his possible suicide, is there in the 1909 letter. Clarence Hemingway's mind was not well. His wife had known it for some time. For the children, the recognition took longer.

In 1928 the family attributed his suicide to financial worries, the most socially acceptable explanation in Oak Park where men of good breeding took their own lives for only two reasons: financial problems and insanity. None of the family wanted to suggest insanity, and Clarence's brother George had reason to suppress information on the Doctor's financial condition. Grace Hemingway, too prostrate with grief she said to appear at the Coroner's Inquest, sent her thirteen- year-old son Leicester to give the bare facts of the suicide. Uncle George testified that his brother had diabetes and a bad heart—a "hopeless case." His mental condition, George said, had been sound and his financial affairs were "in good condition." Uncle George apparently wanted the jury to see the suicide as a mercy killing. What George did not say was that Clarence had mortgaged his debt-free house to invest in Florida land that George was touting. He did not say that the Florida land market had bottomed out; the Doctor was holding lots that were not appreciating.

Clarence Hemingway died at age fifty-seven, suffering from angina and diabetes. The diabetes was treatable with the newly synthesized insulin. A man could live a long time before dying from angina. His Oak Park house was worth more than his debts; his children were mostly grown and three of them were so financially secure that they could have helped in an emergency. He had his license to practice medicine in Florida where he planned to retire. When he closed the bedroom door, sat down on his marriage bed and put the steel barrel to his temple, it was not only the diabetes and the debts that squeezed the trigger. He fell back into a bed that had been a long time making, a bed so wide and deep that it took three of his own children to fill it completely.

Insomnia, erratic blood pressure, blinding headaches, and severe depression were the genetic heritage of Ernest Hemingway, his sisters and brother. They carried it as a legacy from both sides of the family. At forty-nine, Uncle Leicester Hall's insomnia, which bothered him over twenty years, became chronic. Grace, herself, suffered from mild insomnia, "nerves" and recurrent, blinding headaches that sometimes lasted five days. Her eyes, weakened she claimed by scarlet fever, were in fact genetically weak. Bright light hurt them. Clarence's brother Alfred was also an insomniac, who suffered from "bad nerves" and low blood pressure.

The genetic union of Hall and Hemingway produced serious problems unto the second generation. Almost all of their children had eye problems, requiring glasses. Ernest, who refused to wear the glasses until after his marriage, had myopic eyes, mildly light sensitive. Both Marcelline's and Leicester's eyes were markedly weak. Marcelline, Ernest and Ursula all suffered periodically from blinding headaches. Ernest's several severe concussions made worse a situation already serious. After being wounded in Italy, Ernest's insomnia grew worse, but Marcelline and Ursula suffered from the same complaint. Marcelline had low blood pressure; Ernest, high blood pressure. Marcelline and Ernest both suffered from diabetes, and both went through periods of severe depression. Eventually three of the Hemingway children took their own lives; Ernest in 1961; Ursula in 1966; Leicester in 1982. Though Marcelline's death in 1963 was reported to be from natural causes, Leicester suspected suicide. Neither Marcelline, Ernest, Ursula nor Leicester lived as long as three of their four grandparents. At least one of Marcelline's children suffered from insomnia, hysteria and depression. In high school, the child suffered a partial loss of memory and a nervous breakdown, attributed finally to a low thyroid condition, but the depression recurred even after thyroid treatment.[17]

When Ernest Hemingway put the muzzle of his double-barreled shotgun to his forehead the morning of a much later July, he suffered from all of his father's ills: erratic high blood pressure, insomnia, hypertension, mild diabetes, paranoia, and severe depression. Like his father, he kept meticulous lists. Like his father, he saved every totem that touched his hand. Like his father, he wrote letters with fanatic intensity. While courting Hadley Richardson, he wrote to her every day, sometimes twice a day, for almost a year. When he did not receive his daily reply, he was despondent. Like his father, he worried about money when he had no worries. Like his father, he frequently behaved erratically with rapid mood shifts and sometimes vicious responses. Under stress, real or imagined, the idea of suicide recurred insidiously. Like his father, he was caught in a biological trap not entirely of his own making. The bloodline of Clarence Hemingway and Grace Hall has left us several books that will last past all memory of Oak Park's fine families, but the cost was high.

1. See Carlos Baker, *Ernest Hemingway: A Life Story* (New York: Scribner's, 1969), pp. 1–17. The Doctor's giving up the Agassiz Club, dropping out of local events, and staying home in the summers comes from family letters and the newspaper *Oak Leaves*.

2. Ruth Arnold to Grace Hall Hemingway, 1909, Humanities Research Center, University of Texas; all materials from University of Texas are quoted with permission from the Humanities Research Center. Background on Ruth Arnold selected from various Oak Park directories and from the local newspaper *Oak Leaves*.

3. Ruth Arnold to Grace Hall Hemingway, 4 August 1919, Humanities Research Center, University of Texas.

4. Grace Hall Hemingway to Clarence Hemingway, n.d. (noted by CEH "ans to Aug. 2 letter fr CEH"), Humanities Research Center, University of Texas.

5. Marcelline Hemingway to Grace Hall Hemingway, 26 August 1919, Humanities Research Center, University of Texas.

6. Marcelline Hemingway to Grace Hall Hemingway, 30 August 1919, Humanities Research Center, University of Texas.

7. Ruth Arnold to Grace Hall Hemingway, 30 August 1919, Humanities Research Center, University of Texas.

8. Marcelline Hemingway to Grace Hall Hemingway, 31 August 1919, Humanities Research Center, University of Texas.

9. Patrick Hemingway at the Hemingway Conference, Northeastern University, May 1982.

10. "A Way You'll Never Be," *The Short Stories of Ernest Hemingway* (New York: Scribner's, 1953), p. 407.

11. Marcelline Hemingway to Grace Hall Hemingway, 16 September 1919, Humanities Research Center, University of Texas.

12. Clarence Hemingway to Grace Hall Hemingway, 10 January 1904, Humanities Research Center, University of Texas.

13. Grace Hall Hemingway to Clarence Hemingway, 18 October 1908, Humanities Research Center, University of Texas.

14. Grace Hall Hemingway to Clarence Hemingway, 17 October 1908, Humanities Research Center, University of Texas.

15. Clarence Hemingway to Family, 26 October 1909, Humanities Research Center, University of Texas.

16. Coroner's Inquest, held 7 December 1928, Oak Park, Illinois.

17. This abbreviated medical history was compiled from the several published biographical sources available, but the most significant parts were found in the Hemingway family collection at the University of Texas.

GRACE UNDER PRESSURE:
HEMINGWAY AND THE SUMMER OF 1920

MAX WESTBROOK

GRACE HEMINGWAY has been portrayed as a frustrated opera singer and failed mother. Supposedly she unmanned her husband and, in the summer of 1920, tricked him into supporting her cruel decision to evict Ernest from the family home.[1]

A reading of the Hemingway family letters suggests that this characterization is inaccurate and unfair.[2] A corrective essay on behalf of Mrs. Hemingway might seem, at first, a gratuitous and dubious courtesy. Surviving friends and relatives do not need second hand judgments; and, normally, family disputes should be left to family privacy. Five members of the Hemingway family, however, have written books which include their versions of one dispute or another; and Ernest himself, though insistent on his right to privacy, frequently indulged in public or unguarded criticism of his parents.[3]

More important is the fact that our understanding of Hemingway's parents influences and often controls our interpretations of stories featuring Dr. and Mrs. Henry Adams. The Adams-Hemingway association is so established, so automatic, that it is almost impossible to read the words *the doctor's wife* and not see in our imagination Grace Hemingway as Destroyer, rather than Grace as she actually was or Mrs. Adams, the literary character. Indeed, according to the approach commonly identified as psychological or Freudian, Hemingway's fiction should be interpreted in the context of family quarrels and on the assumption that Grace was a destructive person.[4] The thesis of this approach is that Ernest Hemingway never matured as a person or as an artist, his growth being stunted by adolescent resentment of his mother's tyranny. The result, so the argument goes, is a fiction limited to heroes who are either macho or emasculated and to heroines

Reprinted with permission from *Ernest Hemingway: The Writer in Context,* ed. James Nagel (Madison: University of Wisconsin Press, 1984), pp. 77–106.

who are either predators or mere sex objects. Hemingway was immature and dehumanized, and thus his fiction is immature and dehumanized.

The Hemingway family letters do not suggest that Grace has been totally misrepresented by the Freudian critics or by Hemingway's biographers. Rather, the evidence, which is mixed, has been selected and presented with a bias for Ernest and against his mother. What is needed is a judicious characterization of Grace Hemingway, not the replacement of one extreme with another. In brief, we read Hemingway's fictive mothers with glasses made by a flawed prescription. The lenses need adjusting.

Grace Hemingway was a strong and dogmatic person. The children did get on her nerves at times, and she did prefer the fine arts to domestic chores. But she tried to understand and to support her husband and her children and be a loving and devoted mother. The housework she is accused of neglecting was done by domestic help paid with money she earned by giving singing lessons. To a considerable extent, Grace was a liberated woman born too soon, and the much-loved Dr. Clarence was the family's best nominee for the role of cloying Victorian "mother." The family's problems, that is, were complex. There were no villains and no angels, just some unusually talented and energetic human beings, all of them fallible, all of them admirable. And if the eventual disillusionment was more painful than with most families, the cause, in part, was that the good times had been, for at least a dozen years, both extraordinarily fine and doomed.

The tensions and paradoxes characteristic of literature were present, and the Freudian critics are right in saying that Ernest kept on writing, more or less, about his family, It is also true that, even late in life, he made unkind remarks about his parents, especially his mother.[5] Perhaps such indiscretions can be attributed to alcohol, perhaps not. Certainly the extent to which he achieved a sympathetic understanding of Grace and Clarence is subject to debate. My contention is that Hemingway *as artist* grew beyond the advertised hang-up with his parents and achieved a vision that is mature, realistic, varied, often bitter, and yet affirmative.[6] Hemingway's use of Grace as the model for Mrs. Adams does not constitute a license for biographical criticism. The mother in "The Doctor and the Doctor's Wife" is fundamentally different from Grace Hemingway, and the mother in "Soldier's Home" is quite different from both Mrs. Hemingway and Mrs. Adams.

Grace and fictive versions of Grace have been merged because what we know about her has come primarily from two biased reporters, her sons. Whether innocent or guilty, Ernest was profoundly hurt when his parents "kicked" him out, the climax of conflicts which had begun earlier and which were soon to be heightened when Dr. and Mrs. Hemingway rejected his early publications. Under such circumstances, Ernest could not be a judicious and reliable source. Leicester, whose selected presentation of the family letters has been the major available source for others, charmingly confesses to hero worship of his big brother.[7] Granted the difference in age and the magnetic personality of the accomplished and successful Ernest, who could blame him? Grace's side in the family quarrels has been presented by her oldest daughter, Marcelline; but Marcelline was not present at Windemere in the climactic summer of 1920. She and Ernest were estranged, and her brief defense of Mrs. Hemingway—though fair and accurate so far as I know—has carried no weight.[8]

What happened in the summer of 1920, according to the story told by Ernest and Leicester, is that Clarence was innocently busy with his medical practice in Chicago while Ernest was vacationing with the family at Windemere and working to develop his writing skills. Grace supposedly became angry with Ernest because of an irreconcilable difference in temperament, because she did not believe that writing was work, and because Ernest had bravely opposed her self-indulgence in building a separate cabin for herself with money that should have been used to send the younger daughters to college. After winning Clarence's support with false information against Ernest, Grace is then said to have distorted a midnight picnic into a crime justifying Ernest's expulsion forever from the family home.

Ironically, there is enough information in Leicester's book to refute this standard version of what happened. The two most important pieces of previously available but consistently ignored information are that Clarence was at Windemere long enough to make his own decision—without depending on reports from Grace—and that he wrote two "kick out" letters *before* Grace finally spoke up in a way that could not be ignored.

The calendar of events needs to be established. On July 1, 1920, Clarence wrote Grace from Chicago about his plans to come up to the cabin.[9] After a two-week vacation at Windemere, Clarence returned to Chicago and promptly—on July 18—wrote to Grace at Windemere: "I have written Ernest. . . . I have advised him to go with Ted down Traverse City way and work at good wages and at least cut down his living expenses."[10] Writing to Grace on July 22, Clarence referred again to his first letter of dismissal to Ernest: "I have written to him that I wanted him to get busy and be more self supporting and respectful and leave the Bay and go to work down Traverse City way." In that same letter of July 22, we learn that Clarence has written a second "kick-out" letter to Ernest: "I will write to him and enclose herewith for you to read and hand to him."[11]

On July 25, Clarence wrote to Grace saying he had "received" her "big envelope letter with the letter of Thursday evening, after Ernest's birthday supper."[12] Leicester took this to mean that Grace prepared "a ceremonial dinner. . . while getting ready to slip the guest of honor a letter asking him to kindly leave the family premises."[13] The evidence, however, from passages Leicester chose for quotation, is that Grace did not provide a birthday feast topped off with an ill-timed letter of dismissal. Clarence's two remarks—"You surely gave him and his friends a good time"[14] and—"the wonderful 21st supper you wrote about"[15]—do not suggest an ugly scene. Clarence's July 25 letter, furthermore, reaffirms his understanding of what was going on: "I hope he went back to the Bay with Bill and that you read and have mailed him the letter I wrote to him to stay away from Windemere until he was again invited."[16] Thus it is clear that Clarence considered his letters to be decisions requiring Ernest to leave and that he expected Ernest to be gone by the time his second and confirming letter of dismissal had arrived. The conclusion must be that Clarence took the lead or was at least a full partner in the decision.

Grace's testimony, completely omitted by Leicester, also indicates that her actions followed Clarence's. On July 27, Grace wrote to Clarence: "I called Ernest and Beumice into the livingroom & told them to pack up all their things and leave this morning, that I did not wish to see them again this summer."[17] A copy of Grace's letter of dismissal begins with a formal notation: "Copy of letter handed to E.M.H. Tues., July 27th 1920."[18] The ink is different from that used in making the copy, suggesting that the notation was made after the letter had been copied; but the handwriting is clearly Grace's, and a variant appears on the envelope: "Copy of letter handed to Ernest Miller Hemingway July 27th 1920 at Windemere."[19]

On July 28, Clarence wrote Grace that he had "received a very definite letter of denial from Ernest."[20] Ernest, that is, was responding to a decision made by Clarence and not to the letter Grace handed her son on the twenty-seventh. This reading of the sequence is confirmed by a July 30 letter from Clarence to Grace—"Ernest's last letter to me after reading the one I sent you to hand him, does not require an answer"[21]—and by a July 28 letter from Grace to Clarence: "Your letter I handed to Ernest on Monday Morning [July 26]."[22]

What is supposed to have happened is that Grace conceived and initiated the whole affair, unjustly and on her own, deceiving the innocent Clarence, who was practicing medicine in Chicago and thus ignorant of the true story. What actually happened is that Clarence spent the first two weeks of July at Windemere, then returned to Chicago and promptly wrote Ernest two letters telling him to leave and go to work. Grace handed Ernest her letter of dismissal the day after Ernest received Clarence's second letter of dismissal.

The lightly dismissed midnight picnic also needs reconsideration. On the morning of the twenty-sixth, Grace handed Ernest his father's second letter of dismissal. "After reading it," Grace writes, "he chopped a few pieces of wood, enough for 2 days, about, then he tried to fix the pier, and *did* after a fashion though it is very wobbly."[23] On July 27, Grace wrote to Clarence explaining what happened next:

> Of course Ernest called me every name he could think of, and said everything vile about me; but I kept my tongue and did not get hysterical. The immediate cause was the pounding on my front door of Miss Loomis & Mrs. Loomis at 3 o'clock this morning with a lamp in hand—wanted to know of their 13 year old girls—Elizabeth Loomis and her little friend and what those men wanted with them. I made them come in while I investigated for I felt sure our children were all asleep. They had gone to bed quite ostentatiously—I ran up in my nightgown. . . and found Ernest & Beummie's, Ursula's & Sunny's beds empty and unslept in.
>
> Mrs. Loomis was in a towering rage, and said she would pack up & take her whole family back to Oak Park, unless we could do something to get rid of those grown men loafing around. . . .
>
> Oh! but he is a cruel son. I got supper for him when he came home at 9 o'clock, last night; and sat down with him, for I had had none, and he insulted me every minute; said "all I read was moron literature," that Dr. Frank Crane who writes such glorious helpful articles in the *American* was the "Moron's Maeterlinck" and asked me if I read the *Atlantic Monthly* just so some one would see me doing it.
>
> I did not explain to you that the escapade last night was a plan of the Loomis boys and girls to have midnight eats, and fire, up the lake, not wicked; except in the deceit practiced, and the general lawlessness that Ernest instills into all young boys and girls.
>
> He is distinctly a menace to youth.
>
> I think our girls have had a very good lesson but its most killed their mother.[24]

The feelings of someone named Mrs. Loomis may seem unimportant when reading Ernest Hemingway in the 1980s, but she awoke to find her thirteen-year-old daughter missing, along with her daughter's thirteen-year-old playmate, for whom she was responsible. It was 3:00 a.m., and they were in a sparsely populated country of lake and wilderness. Mrs. Loomis and Mrs. Hemingway could not chuckle and go back to bed. They could not say, "It's all right. Give him time, and he'll write *The Sun Also Rises*." Their rage, to any responsible parent, is understandable.

From the viewpoint of Ernest and the midnight revelers, the episode was innocent, and Grace recognizes this in telling Clarence that the outing was "not wicked." What has been omitted from previous accounts, however, is, first,

Grace's version and, second, the fact that three things happened on the same day. On Monday morning, July 26, Ernest received the second letter of dismissal from his father. That same evening, at a nine o'clock supper, he insulted his mother gratuitously; and, at some unknown time during that day, he agreed to accompany a party of youngsters who wanted to slip out of bed after midnight and go for a picnic. Even if we sympathize with Ernest and not with his mother, the timing does not suggest that Grace Hemingway was the villain. One could even argue that in responding to his father's dismissal by insulting his mother and leading a midnight escapade Ernest was insisting on his own eviction.

Clearly, the midnight picnic was not an isolated event which Grace, because of self-serving headaches, expanded into a pseudocrisis. She had been under considerable pressure for a very long time, and her efforts to act positively—rather than submit to pain—were often met with resistance. Her separate cabin, said to be another example of her selfishness, is also a different story when told from her viewpoint.[25]

The story, as told by Grace, begins with the draft of a letter to Clarence. There is no first page, no date, and the draft begins in midsentence. The year would be 1919, possibly in May:

> . . . until the agony in my spinal nerves forced me to lie down and then up again and at it, day in and day out. Too exhausted to swim or go anywhere when the opportunity offered. These have been my summers for many years until the very sight of Windemere brings the tears to my eyes and a sob to my throat.
>
> This year, hope, that springs eternal in the human breast, bade me rejoice, for I said to my husband, when he was not in a contentious mood, "Would it not be lovely to have a little 'haven of refuge' on our hill, a little shack where we could sleep, and be alone, for a while or have just the little children with us"—and he said "go ahead, look into it and see what can be done."[26]

Grace then describes herself "happily" drawing up plans, only to find that the cost, "almost $2,000," was too high. Working with a different builder, Grace then revised the plans to get the cost down to "approximately $1,100" and later to a proposed ceiling of $1,000.

Grace was an artist trying to take care of six children. She wanted the cabin as relief from pressures, paid for it with money she had earned, and handled the details herself in order to spare her husband. Drafts of letters to Mr. Morford, the builder, make this clear. "Now as Dr. has many things to take care of," Grace writes, "I want to say to you that I am assuming the entire Expense of this building with my own Earnings."[27] In another draft, Grace draws a neat sketch of the cabin for Mr. Morford and asks, "Would this be less expensive and more artistic?"[28] Another stresses her willingness to change the materials to keep the expenses down. On May 15, 1919, Grace drafted a letter to Mr. Morford which suggests that she has been driven to appealing outside the family for sympathy:

> Now, with these changes I wonder whether you could keep it within our limit of $1,000? I want so much to have this little house that I cannot bear to give it up for the present, though everybody is saying "What a foolish time to think of building."
>
> What do you think about it?[29]

Mr. Morford must have approved, or at least Grace was pleased with his work, but Clarence was adamantly opposed. On May 26, 1919, Clarence drafted a letter to the builder. The draft is unfinished and may or may not have been completed and mailed, but Clarence's thinking is clear:

> I have learned my dear wife Grace Hall-Hemingway is expecting to build a cottage on top of a hill known as "Red Top Mountain" on Lot 1., Section 10. Bay Township across the lake from our Windemere Bacon side of Walloon Lake. This [I] want you to know, that she assumes herself without my advice and agrees to pay for herself with her own money. She holds the title to the land. I own no land in my name. All was placed in her name. I am unable to understand the necessity.[30]

On the same day, Clarence wrote to Grace stating his opposition. He called her plan impractical, made it clear that she would have to pay all expenses from her own money, and added that he would write Mr. Morford and deny any responsibility for paying. This is rather strange, since Clarence had given his initial approval and since Grace had made it clear from the start that she would pay for the cabin with her own money. Clarence acts as if he is being badgered and tricked, implying that he must take steps to keep Grace from obligating him financially and against his expressed wishes.

Nonetheless, Grace responded as if she had to have Clarence's approval to spend her own money, drafting a long, carefully marshalled series of arguments. The draft, undated, is partially in outline form. "I have studied all your objections," she writes, "and will classify them under three heads." The first is "Those referring to the investment." Grace then quotes and answers each of her husband's objections. "Improvement does not appeal to average purchaser therefore could not sell," for example, is answered with the assertion that she wants "to live in it," not sell it. The second category, "those referring to the site," is concerned with argument and counter-argument about prevailing wind directions, drinking water, wash water, wood supply, refuse disposal, soil conditions, and accessibility. The third category, "Those referring to me and my needs," is the longest, turning finally from the outline format into the following poignant statement:

> It has been my purpose for 14 years ever since I purchased the farm in the face of strong opposition *and much abusive language* to build a little cottage on this very hill. It appealed to me so that I bought the farm to carry out this plan. That it has been steadily thwarted up to the present time not only piled up disappointment— as each year against my advice & desires the farm was leased to thieving tenants who stole from the place wood and crops, fruit and the very seed sent to them to plant. When finally they left having robbed the place to their utmost I renewed my pleas to build even the farm house which would be a stepping stone to my long looked forward to little nest on the hill top and which would appeal to even a farmer's sense of values in property. This was thwarted. I have gone faithfully 21 summers to the same place. Windemere which was very pleasant and adequate for 8 or 9 years but after my father's death & two subsequent attacks of typhoid fever which undermined [the last two words are inserted, fragmented] to say nothing of other causes the place became hateful to me, so much so that I had a nervous break down summer after summer when ever I was forced to spend a summer there, shut in by the hills & lake, no view, no where to go, acting the part of the family drudge, standing at sink & cook stove.[31]

So Grace felt that she had been appointed the family drudge, though she was accused of neglecting the duties of a housewife. Ernest, for his part, thought he was doing too much work for the family, while his parents thought he was doing too little. Who could adjudicate such disputes? One thing we can learn from the family letters is that the breakup did not start in 1920 or in 1919. However implacable Grace seemed to Ernest, she was and had been for a long time an individualist who was nonetheless devoted to traditional values. Returning from a visit to her brother Leicester, Grace received on January 4, 1904, a letter concerning some unde-scribed quarrel. Leicester asks forgiveness for his "brutal plainness in criticizing" Grace, asserts that he spoke out of love, and warns his sister that they "have both been handicapped by a careless bringing up." It is obvious that Grace has been found guilty of some breach of etiquette, for Leicester assures her that "true refine-ment of manners are absolutely essential." She must not "handicap" her "children by neglecting their training along these lines."[32]

As we learn from Marcelline, there were many other breaches of decorum by Grace, plus a lifelong habit of variations from the norm. She shocked the neighbor-hood by riding a bicycle, showed off to her children by kicking up to a lamp over her head and turning it off with her toes, took saw and hammer and made furniture for

Grace Cottage, published original songs, wrote verse, gave lectures on classical literature, learned how to paint and made money doing it, and late in life took seriously to a Christian version of spiritualism. Above all, she was a genuinely talented singer with a phenomenal memory for music.[33] Comparisons with Ernest are inescapable, though his variations from the norm were more shocking, his walking on broken glass, for example. Ernest held spiritualism in contempt, but he carried good luck charms and respected the power of both good and bad omens. His memory, like his mother's, was said to be remarkable.[34] Grace's problems, in a general sense, were comparable to her son's problems. Both wanted to create and thus needed solitude, both wanted a home and family yet found domestic and family responsibilities an interference, and both tried to compromise between the two. As with F. Scott Fitzgerald and others, Hemingway quarreled with his mother, at least in part, because she practiced what he considered a contemptible version of values embarrassingly close to his own. The contrast between Pilar reading Robert Jordan's palm and a Christian seance is instructive. Pilar sees death. Grace saw Christian beatitudes confirmed.[35]

Clarence's problems also had a long birthing and also need to be understood as those of an individualist who was nonetheless dedicated to traditional values and thus inclined to dichotomize reality. Clarence was an unusually good person, a dedicated and innovated physician, and a man who suffered, early on, from serious problems, It was his habit to write daily, when he and Grace were parted, and to write in a tone that was often martyred, cloying, perhaps obsessive. As early as 1904, he apologizes for missing a day. This was to become a major characteristic of Clarence's letters, the apology being followed by the explanation that he failed because he performed some other duty for some other person.

On October 18, 1908, Grace wrote to Clarence at the New York Lying-In Hospital, where he had gone to study obstetrics. She encourages him not to read *Oak Leaves* and "get into the old train of thought" but to rest and relax.[36] In a letter dated October 17, concerning Clarence's plans to vacation before coming home, Grace asks, "Do you want me to let the local press know about this vacation? Don't you think it perhaps wiser to let them keep the 1st idea in their minds that you are taking 'post grad' work in N.Y.?"[37] Grace does not say what the "old train of thought" is or why it might be invoked by a reading of the Oak Park newspaper; and the quotation marks around the words *post grad* may have been intended to indicate merely an abbreviation. It is clear, however, that Grace thought her husband's problems so serious that his vacation cure should be kept secret.

The letters of both Clarence and Grace, in fact, are characterized by a troubled determination to do what is right and by references to serious problems within. On September 5, 1914, Grace wrote Clarence from Nantucket about her own vacation cure: "I am in hopes of coming home rested and benefited, so I can be of help and not a hindrance to each of you."[38] On May 5, 1917, Clarence makes a comparable statement. Writing to Grace from Oak Park, he states that he will have a hernia operation on the seventh, expects "without any fear or sentiment" that he will do fine, and concludes, "I shall hope to return to my home duties the twenty second of May a better and stronger father and more able to carry on my life responsibilities."[39] Both shared their son's stoicism but unfortunately expressed it in a rhetoric opposite to the uncomplaining manner that Jake Barnes begins to learn and Thomas Hudson has mastered.[40] Grace responded to Clarence's letter about his operation, for example, by saying that even though broken herself she still has the bravery to think of her husband, that she is more concerned with his not feeling guilty than with her own suffering: "Don't think for a moment that your going to the hospital for a necessary operation has made me ill. I have been breaking down steadily since a year ago."[41]

Such protestations of concern for others may have, of course, their own integrity. Dr. and Mrs. Hemingway, I think, were two fine human beings. Still, the repeated claim of a devotion to duty when combined with confessions of intense suffering is a rhetorical trap, an invitation to self-pity, and may explain why Ernest became so contemptuous of people who agonized in public.[42] One striking example—a letter from Clarence to Grace, dated August 12, 1917—is further evidence that the family breakup had a long beginning and cannot be blamed on Grace alone. Ernest, Clarence writes,

> is just as headstrong and abusive and threatening as ever, I am sure if he can *work & board* at Dilmuths & pay his board it would be *good* for him. I am about to my limit with the *Six* alone. I try to make them happy and the more I do for them, the more they take advantage of me. No word whatever from Uncle Leicester. Erniest [*sic*] had not written him up to yesterday. He is so pessimistic, says it wouldn't do any good. Brother Tyler told him, he could get Ernest a job on the *Kansas City Star,* & Ernest could live at his house until he was well started. . . .
>
> Would appreciate very much if you would put your mind on Some of these problems and offer suggestions. . . . I made all very happy making three extra fine *blue berry pies* between 10:30 a.m. [and] 11:15 a.m.—Just like Mother used to *eat.* "[43]

Thus protestations of love and duty are undercut with bitterness, the word *eat* being underlined to make certain Grace does not miss the dig.

During the first two months of the summer of 1920, the tone of Clarence's letters to Grace and the children became even more plaintive long-suffering possessive. Featuring repeated assertions of his eagerness to do everything he can to make his family happy and including an astounding attention to details, the letters are replete with martyred protestations of his devotion and their negligence. He is working late hours, the weather is cruelly hot, but he will do all he is physically able to do for his family. When he does not hear from Windemere, he writes to ask if something is wrong. When a letter from Grace does not mention Carol and Leicester, Clarence writes to ask if they are sick. There is even something poignant, under the circumstances, about the fact that Clarence numbers his daily letters, as if he wanted Grace to see the count, the quantitative record of his devotion to family duty.

Clarence's "mothering" tone is especially clear in a letter of June 27. There has been a terrible train wreck and a difficult delivery in which the baby died, but Clarence is writing to "dear Gracie and all at Windemere" even though his arms are "nearly numb from the extra strain last night" and he can "hardly hold the place on the typewriter." This is not to appeal for sympathy, he explains, but merely to apologize for any "mistakes" he might make. Then, proving his devotion under any circumstances, Clarence mentions a church bulletin, enclosed, which he is certain will give them pleasure. Finally, he is also sending them a copy of today's *Oak Leaves*.[44]

Clarence's letter of June 28 is quoted extensively in *My Brother, Ernest Hemingway*, but Leicester omits the close: "We must believe that all things work together for good for those who love the Lord. Pray for me my darlings, as I need your help to keep you all having the good vacation."[45] This is, I think, the keynote of Clarence's letters: he is working to the point of exhaustion; the weather is extraordinarily hot in Chicago; he is happy that his family is having such a wonderful vacation up on the cool lake; he is delighted to take care of any minor detail that might give them the slightest pleasure; and, though longing to be on the lake with his family, he is happy to be able to work hard and suffer so much to provide so well for his family.

Frequently, Clarence's description of his own dedication is contrasted with the negligence of others. Marcelline's trunk arrives, on June 29, and "Daddy was here to attend to it, so again she is in luck. No word from her." Clarence then states it overtly: "I am planning all the time for you darlings, as unselfishly as I can, so there will be something to go on with next Fall and Winter."[46] On July 1, just before leaving for his own vacation at Windemere, Clarence makes a characteristic apology: "I was so overworked from early to late yesterday that I did not get time to qrite [sic] you."[47] After returning to Chicago, Clarence wrote on July 16 that he was "so glad to be here to help in many ways."[48]

Courteously omitted by Leicester are his father's letters indicating that the summer's "insurrection" included the Hemingway daughters. On September 1,

1920, with Grace continuing her vacation, Clarence wrote her about the impending return to Chicago of their daughters:

> I will have their rooms all clean and spick and span, and they are to keep them so, or in some way suffer the penalties of "Insurrection." There will be no "Sob-stuff" from me. They will get into the game and do right or they will wish they had. Tell them to do right and there will be no trouble whatever. I am to help them get an education, if they will accept it. If not they will have to go to "Work" and pay their own freight. See? I am sorry for you my darling. It is too bad that the daughters who have had so many privileges should pester you so by their great lack of appreciation of their mother's love. Keep up Courage, that is my pass word, one day at a time, always try and do our best.[49]

Once the girls returned to Chicago, Clarence may have pushed with excessive rigor. On September 13, he wrote to Grace:

> Marcelline does not see why I should be so anxious about the girls, and they are as you know some rebellious at times. I am firm and gentle and it would surprise you to see Sunny see it as I do while Ursula is going *off*! She cools off after a whoile [*sic*], but I can see in her Ernest's teachings.
> No need to worry.[50]

Just two days later, Clarence seems to have changed his mind:

> Get thoroughly rested and at peace with the world before you return. I want so much for you to regain the love and affection of all your daughters, and it will only be possible when all are rested and in reasonable frames of mind. I am doing the unselfish thing to stay here to protect and guide the girls and so far have succeeded and see no reason why they should not continue to improve all the time.[51]

The implication is that the girls have criticized their mother for her role in the quarrels at Windemere and that Clarence, at least to some extent, has been persuaded.[52]

Leicester's presentation of this September 15 letter has left us with a quite different impression. First, Leicester introduces his selected quotation with a sentence implying that Clarence's trust in Grace was collapsing before the evidence of her perfidy: "Another letter came from Ernest later and Father wavered even more in his belief that all had been as represented to him." Second, Leicester selects a single sentence on the subject of the Hemingway daughters, one suggesting that all is well: "The girls are all doing very well in school." Third, having set the context, Leicester then quotes a passage that could be taken only as damaging to Grace: "If you falsely accused him [Ernest], be sure to beg his pardon, even if he had made many mistakes. For false accusations grow more sore all the time and separate dear friends and relatives."[53]

And thus have we come to believe that Grace falsely accused Ernest to gain the support of an innocent Clarence in her plans to evict her son from the family home. It is far more likely that Clarence, who was much braver in correspondence than in direct confrontation, was wavering because of his own lack of strength. His September 18 letter to Ernest, certainly, is revisionist history, a distortion of complex events he had witnessed and a flat denial of the decision he had made himself: "In as much as there were a few misunderstandings between you and your mother this summer I am sure if you will make this effort [that is, close up Windemere for the winter], you may right the matters and I will continue to pray that you will love one another as you should."[54] As Clarence had to have known, the family problems were not merely "a few misunderstandings," were not simply a matter of the relations between Grace and Ernest, and would not be repaired by Ernest's willingness to do a simple chore for the family. Ernest had to have known, too; and it may well be that some of his harsh feelings toward his mother were caused by the fact that the father he loved but could not respect was unmanned not by Grace but by himself.[55] Grace, it is clear from the family letters, worked hard to bolster her husband, but she was guilty of having the strength that Clarence lacked.

Perhaps the climax of the Hemingways' "dangerous summer" is a letter from Clarence to Grace dated October 2, 1920, and written apparently from Windemere, where Clarence had gone to secure the cabin (Ernest must have rejected his father's simplistic proposal for a solution).[56] The spelling and punctuation are probably an indication of Clarence's emotional state:

> My darling I love you,—
>   Herewith check for One Thousand Dollars, in Case of some onforseen accident I should not return, also Keys,—Are Vault Box #686—Therein Liberty Bonds & Emergency funds.—Ford Keys & Spark Coils in little basket & gas turned off with Stilson wrench/.—I hope to be home by Oct 11. 1920
>
> Much love—
Clarence[57]

Without belaboring the implications of a possible suicide, we can assert that what seems to have happened in the summer of 1920—a son's adolescent rebellion against a Victorian and tyrannical mother—was but the manifest expression of far more complex problems. Essentially, Clarence and Grace were paradoxical combinations of determination and insecurity. Both were talented, energetic, loving, moral, and independent; yet both suffered from within and suffered severely. Life was full of wonders, but the center seemed in constant jeopardy. Challenges were to be met head on and duties performed without fail, but the capacity to do so needed constant reinforcement.

We cannot know the exact intentions behind Ernest's dismissal of his complicated parents, one with reluctance, the other with bitterness. When he called his mother "a bitch,"[58] was he telling the truth as he saw it, indulging in dramatics, simply defending himself, rewriting the past? A letter in the John F. Kennedy Library raises another possibility. On December 22, 1920, Ernest wrote to Grace saying he was obeying her wishes, behaving well, and working hard.[59] The letter is chatty and affectionate, making one think the eviction of 1920 may have been less damaging than the parents' rejection of Ernest's early publications.[60] Perhaps all of these conjectures have their element of accuracy. What can be said with confidence is that Ernest purged himself of his parents' Victorian taboos and then wrote about a world in which the good and honest life is jeopardized by the possibility that values may be illusions, by betrayal and weakness and sentimentality from within, and by indifferent powers and circumstances and authorities from without.

It is well known that Ernest adopted his father's love of fishing and hunting and good foods and shared his father's remarkable capacity for attending to details. In the Hemingway family letters, we find that the words Ernest used in testing fidelity within the family—*loyalty, betrayal*—are the same words used by his parents. The money analogy used by Grace in her "kick-out" letter has seemed absurd, but, as critics have shown, Ernest wrote effectively and carefully about the relation between money and ethical duty.[61] In generously hosting guests and insisting on taking care of every detail—at Key West, for example—Ernest repeated his parents' performance at Windemere, his good-humored graciousness turning, at times without warning, to resentment. With hindsight, we can see that there was something threatening the good times at Windemere: Grace's desperately needing an escape cottage, Clarence's shocking letter of October 2, implying possible suicide, Ernest's responding to his father's second letter of dismissal by bawling out his mother and lending his adult approval to the midnight picnic. And there is something threatening the good times of Jake's little family at Pamplona, the peacefulness of Frederic and Catherine in Switzerland, and—in a different sense—Thomas Hudson's sense of fulfillment at the beginning of *Islands in the Stream.*[62]

Living in what seemed to them an either/or world (we do it right, or else it is all wrong), Clarence and Grace fell into a rhetoric of absolutes. Their talented son's rhetoric to describe a realistic and far more complex version of right and wrong became, virtually, a new dialect of the English language. Basic to Hemingway's fiction, perhaps a rhetorical version of his iceberg theory, is the unsaid, the unvocalized lower layer. In its simplest form, one character sees realities another character does not see and—because of youth, a bad will, or illusions that have become internalized—need not be told.

"The Doctor and the Doctor's Wife," for example, is a story about what Dr. Adams discovers within himself and cannot possibly explain to his wife or to Nick or, indeed, scarcely accommodate within his own consciousness. In reading the story, we have slighted the unsaid and focused on Mrs. Adams as the Devouring Mother because we assume that Ernest was accurate in his comments on Grace and that Mrs. Adams is a portrait of Mrs. Hemingway.[63]

Certainly the model for Mrs. Adams is Grace Hemingway; but as Hemingway said himself, fictional characters based on actual people are *re*-created in the author's imagination and take on their own integrity.[64] Grace avoided bright lights because she had suffered from scarlet fever as a child, had been blind for a time, and, upon suddenly regaining her sight, found thereafter that bright lights were excruciatingly painful.[65] With Mrs. Adams, hiding from sunlight is obviously a comment on her character. She prefers her closeted world of eternal and total goodness. Her husband's suggestion that Boulton may have acted with a bad will is dismissed immediately and without need for evidence. Grace, by contrast, was fully aware of evil, could recognize it, and—as shown when she gave the game wardens a good dressing down for aggressive rudeness and for abuse of their badges—could be stout-hearted in standing up to it.[66] Mrs. Adams does not, as so often claimed, dominate her males.[67] She asks the Doctor what he is going to do next, he tells her, and there is no evidence suggesting he needs her approval. Nick's supposed defiance of his mother is actually a very casual putting off of an indefinite request: "*If you see Nick, dear, will you tell him his mother wants to see him?*"[68] And the screen door the Doctor is usually said to slam because of his humble apology is a trap for critics. The Doctor does not slam the door. "The screen door slammed behind him" (p. 102) means it slammed of its own accord, the spring snapping it shut because the Doctor's mind is elsewhere. His minimal apology, his not arguing with his wife about Boulton's intentions, the separate bedrooms, and, especially, his not telling her what he is really thinking are all signs of their relationship: the Doctor protects his wife from reality because she is constitutionally unable to face reality. Surrounded by defenses, Mrs. Adams is so totally committed to illusions that enlightening her is not even mentioned as a possibility.

Mrs. Adams thus adds one more turn of the screw to the story, for if the Doctor's idea about Boulton's intentions is immediately dismissed, how could he possibly share with her the much more shocking discovery he has made about himself? The story, then, is about the unsaid. Frustrated by Boulton's cool insolence, Dr. Adams breaks out, from some unacknowledged lower layer, and makes a tough-guy assertion: "If you call me Doc once again, I'll knock your eye teeth down your throat" (p. 101). The act itself, knocking a man's teeth down his throat, is violent enough. The specific detail, "eye teeth," is an appropriate threat for tough guys capable of selecting with precision the physical parts to be damaged. When the battle-wise Boulton says, "Oh, no, you won't, Doc" (p. 101), he speaks as one who knows his man. Of course Dr. Adams will not do any such thing. He is not that kind of person. He is not even the kind of person who voices such boasts. Physical cowardice and humiliation are subliminal tones in the story. They contribute to density, realism. But the story beneath the visible events is that the moral, controlled, and determinedly responsible good Doctor finds a part of himself he is shocked to find.

Thus the drama of "The Doctor and the Doctor's Wife" lies in discoveries that cannot be voiced or shared. If Mrs. Adams cannot believe that Boulton would intentionally start a fuss to get out of work, how could she possibly believe that her civilized husband has found himself capable of wanting to knock Boulton's eye teeth down his throat? Dr. Adams's distance from his own inner self is played off the distance—the separate rooms, the Christian Scientist married to a medical doctor—between the husband and wife. The Doctor is unable to handle something deep within, and the unopened medical journals—something else unhandled—are thus an irritating aside.

Following a paratactical contrast of her religious tracts with his shotgun, Hemingway creates an even more unnerving act of discovery by describing an apparently irrelevant action. Frustrated with Boulton, his wife, and with himself, Dr. Adams sits "on his bed now, cleaning a shotgun. He pushed the magazine full of the heavy yellow shells and pumped them out again. They were scattered on the bed" (p. 102). Talking to his wife, alone and unseen, he wipes "his gun carefully with a rag. He pushed the shells back in against the spring of the magazine. He sat with the gun on his knees. He was very fond of it" (p. 102).

Why does Dr. Adams load the shotgun, unload it, and load it again? Obviously, he would like to do a good deal more to Boulton than simply hit him. He is not going to shoot anyone, of course, any more than he is going to become an efficient brawler. He is merely toying with the dark desire he had discovered, and, ironically, it is Mrs. Adams who accidentally ends the game:

> "No. I can't really believe that any one would do a thing of that sort intentionally."
> The doctor stood up and put the shotgun in the corner behind the dresser.
> (p. 102)

The word "intentionally" is immediately followed by the action of putting the gun aside. Of course he cannot do it. Why play games with impossible intentions? But the dark desire is nonetheless real, and the gun is apparently set aside—contrary to the practice of good hunters—still loaded.

Dr. Adams has come to a place he does not want to be, and the chain of events began with his own choice, his *choosing* to believe that logs adrift on his beach would not be retrieved by their owners, his probably racist or class-conscious resentment of Boulton's lack of respect. He does not know what to do, where to go. The dock is a place he had to walk away from, aching with fury and frustration. The conversation with his unrealistic wife is certainly no relief. So he thinks of going for a walk, finds Nick wanting to go "where there's black squir-rels," and says, "All right. . . . Let's go there" (p. 103).

"Soldier's Home" also illustrates the need for critics to see that Hemingway's literary mothers should not be equated with characterizations of Grace, biased and unbiased. When Hemingway found the germ for a story in his family life, the artist would take over and—as with actual people made into liter-ary characters—rewrite the actual into something created and quite different from the original.[69] Mrs. Krebs is a stereotypical mother of her time and place. She is quite different from the Grace Hemingway who sang opera and painted pictures, who struggled throughout her life to assert her own individual self apart from the role assigned by society.

"Soldier's Home" is in part the story of a young man who wants to reject the life his parents have chosen for him. Thus it describes a situation that Mrs. Hemingway, Mrs. Krebs, and millions of other similar and dissimilar parents have found themselves in. What sets it apart from other tellings of this archetypal story is signaled by its most famous exchange:

> "Don't you love your mother, dear boy?"
> "No," Krebs said. (p. 152)

The pathetic and innocent-sounding "Don't you love your mother" is a sentimen-tal tyranny, a mother's demand for the loyalty oath. It is a rhetorical trap common to life and to literature, and it is a characteristic strategy in Hemingway's art, most notably in *A Farewell to Arms* when the battle police ask retreating officers why they have betrayed their country.[70]

The verbal mechanism of the trap is the blurring together of two quite differ-ent subjects. With Mrs. Krebs, *don't you want to settle down and live the life we want you to live* is blurred with *don't you love your mother*. Krebs, for his part, has been to war and found that—*contra* Nick Adams—he liked it and now wants to talk about it, though society assumes he will have been horrified by combat and unwilling to discuss it. Krebs will try to love his mother, or at least avoid hurting her, but he knows he cannot become a Charlie Simmons and marry the girl next door and clerk in a store.

In urging her son to settle down, Mrs. Krebs is playing Joe McCarthy on behalf of community values. She pretends that obeying mother is the same as loving mother, and yet Hemingway draws her portrait without viciousness. Mrs. Krebs is herself a victim of the indoctrination she is now trying to pass on to her son. Krebs's "No" is a defense against the rhetorical trap, a rejection of love which claims obedience as the price of continued love. Mrs. Krebs speaks as a representative of community values, and Krebs answers her accordingly. But in cheapening himself to make a clichéd apology and in going through the motions of prayer when he cannot pray honestly, Krebs is caught in the trap after all, at least for the moment. He is desperate not to hurt his mother, though he does, and she is incapable of hearing the truth. Like Dr. Adams and so many others, Krebs will have to live with his secret burden, the unsaid, the lower layer he has discovered but cannot explain, certainly not to his mother.

"Soldier's Home" is not the story of Windemere, but the scene in which Mrs. Krebs forces her son to kneel is—like Hemingway's eviction—the immediate and not the sufficient cause of a fundamental displacement. What lay behind Hemingway's break with his family was not simply the events of July 1920. There was the whole story of Clarence and Grace, sisters and neighbors and friends, of religious and community values in conflict with a developing young artist who loved much of what he learned from his parents but who kept discovering realities his parents could only call blasphemous. And what lies behind Krebs's leaving home is not merely a supposedly dominating mother. There is the whole story of college in Kansas, of veterans who say what society wants them to say, of pretty girls in fashionable clothes who are products of their time and place, and of parents who lead narrow lives and want their son to do the same.

Nonetheless, Krebs at the end of the story and Hemingway in 1920 do not leave home to seek a life of isolation; and when we give excessive weight to Leicester's interpretation of what happened during a single period of two weeks, ignoring the broad ranging experiences and stories he also recorded, then we are unfair not only to Grace but also to Ernest. Like Harry in "The Snows of Kilimanjaro," Ernest could, when hurt or angry, blame everything on a convenient woman, even while knowing what Harry Morgan learns, too late, about individual responsibility. In a sense, Ernest Hemingway left home in 1920 and spent the rest of his life trying to rewrite Windemere. He wanted to create in art and in life a home and family devoted to the good values; yet home and family seemed to require or to birth those very illusions and indoctrinations he held in contempt.

1. See, for example, Constance Montgomery, *Hemingway in Michigan* (New York: Fleet, 1966), pp. 172–82; and Carlos Baker, *Ernest Hemingway: A Life Story* (New York: Scribner's, 1969), pp. 71–73.

2. The Hemingway family letters, housed in the Humanities Research Center, University of Texas, Austin, Texas, are contained in twenty-eight Hollinger boxes, the total number to be reduced by a half-dozen or so when current rearrangement is completed. The collection consists mostly of letters within the family—not letters by or to Ernest—but includes stray report cards, business notes, songs and lectures by Grace, and various memorabilia. There is a minimal index consisting of approximately six hundred cards, some with single entries, but usually with brief, multiple listings. The entry on one index card, for example, is "158 letters from Clarence to Grace (1900–1928)." The entry on another card is "31 letters from Clarence to Grace and children at Windemere (1902–1924)." There are letters dated from the 1870s to the 1960s. I am grateful to Leicester Hemingway for his generous permission to quote from the Hemingway family letters. I have silently corrected minor errors, with exceptions noted, but have retained informalities characteristic of correspondence ("&" for "and") and relevant to meaning (capital letters for emphasis).

3. See Baker, *Life Story,* pp. 344, 452, 465, 487, 496–97. The five books are Leicester Hemingway, *My Brother, Ernest Hemingway* (Cleveland: World, 1961); Marcelline Hemingway Sanford, *At the Hemingways: A Family Portrait* (Boston: Little, Brown, 1961); Madelaine Hemingway Miller, *Ernie: Hemingway's Sister "Sunny" Remembers* (New York: Crown, 1975); Mary Welsh Hemingway, *How It Was* (New York: Knopf, 1976); and Gregory H. Hemingway, *Papa: A Personal Memoir* (Boston: Houghton Mifflin, 1976). Also, Hadley gave full cooperation to Alice Hunt Sokoloff's *Hadley: The First Mrs. Hemingway* (New York: Dodd, Mead, 1973).

4. See Richard Drinnon, "In the American Heartland: Hemingway and Death," *Psychoanalytical Review,* 52 (1965), 5–31; David Gordon, "The Son and the Father: Patterns of Response to Conflict in Hemingway's Fiction," *Literature and Psychology,* 16 (1966), 122–38; and Richard B. Hovey, *Hemingway: The Inward Terrain* (Seattle: University of Washington Press, 1968), pp. 36, 212–13.

5. Baker, *Life Story,* p. 474.

6. See my "The Stewardship of Ernest Hemingway," *Texas Quarterly,* 9 (Winter 1966), 89–101.

7. Leicester Hemingway, *My Brother, Ernest Hemingway,* pp. 13–15. Since the first permission for an outsider to study the family letters was granted in 1971, Leicester's selections from and treatment of the letters represented the only version available. Scholars, having to depend on Leicester's presentation of the letters and on remarks by Ernest, have been understandably biased against Grace.

8. An example of Marcelline's lack of influence is Scott Donaldson's *By Force of Will: The Life and Art of Ernest Hemingway* (New York: Viking, 1977), p. 291. Donaldson, in his generally excellent study of Hemingway, cites Marcelline's book as the source for statements about Grace as the negligent mother but ignores Marcelline's testimony that Grace gave singing lessons and earned money with which she hired domestics to do the chores customarily assigned to the wife-mother. Issues not yet fully resolved, however, include the family finances. Marcelline says Grace contributed to the family (*At the Hemingways,* pp. 204–05); Baker says Grace's negligence made domestics a necessity and caused "a steady drain on the family income" (*Life Story,* p. 8). Is Marcelline correct in saying that Grace was ill in 1920, unable to contribute the usual to the family income, and that this is why Clarence could afford only two weeks at Windemere rather than the full summer? It is hoped that the current research of Michael Reynolds will resolve these and other questions.

9. There would be no letters within the family, of course, while the family was together; but Leicester confirms the two-week vacation indicated by the dates of Clarence's letters (*My Brother, Ernest Hemingway,* p. 64).

10. Clarence Hemingway to Grace Hemingway, 18 July 1920, Hemingway Family Letters, Humanities Research Center, University of Texas, Austin, Texas. Hereafter cited as Family Letters.

11. Clarence Hemingway to Grace, 22 July 1920, Family Letters.

12. Clarence Hemingway to Grace, 25 July 1920, Family Letters. Ernest's birthday in 1920 fell on a Wednesday; Clarence made a slip.

13. Leicester Hemingway, *My Brother, Ernest Hemingway,* p. 69.

14. Clarence Hemingway to Grace, 25 July 1920, Family Letters.

15. Clarence Hemingway to Grace, 26 July 1920, Family Letters.

16. Clarence Hemingway to Grace, 25 July 1920, Family Letters. "Bill" is Bill Smith.

17. Grace Hemingway to Clarence, 27 July 1920, Family Letters. "Beumice," or "Beummie," is Theodore Brumback; see Baker, *Life Story,* pp. 70–74.

18. Grace Hemingway, Copy of Letter to Ernest, 27 July 1920, Family Letters.

19. Grace Hemingway, Envelope of Letter to Ernest, 27 July 1920, Family Letters.

20. Clarence Hemingway to Grace and children, 28 July 1920, Family Letters.

21. Clarence Hemingway to Grace, 30 July 1920, Family Letters.

22. Grace Hemingway to Clarence, 28 July 1920, Family Letters.

23. Grace Hemingway to Clarence, 28 July 1920, Family Letters.

24. Grace Hemingway to Clarence, 27 July 1920, Family Letters. Maurice Maeterlinck's *The Blue Bird: A Fairy Play,* a work of sentimental optimism, was popular in America in the early twentieth century. Printed by Dodd, Mead, in 1907, it was reprinted in 1909, 1911, and 1919. By "the *American,*" Grace means the *American Magazine.* Dr. Frank Crane was a preacher who left the pulpit for the larger audience available in print. Ernest, in his literary judgment if not in his treatment of his mother, was certainly right. Dr. Crane's superficial optimism in support of Christian capitalism does qualify him as the "moron's Maeterlinck." The fact that Dr. Crane also wrote a small book in which one sermon is entitled "Irony and Pity" and another refers to "The colonel's lady and Julia O'Grady" is surely a trap for the over-eager scholar (Dr. Frank Crane, *Four Minute Essays,* 6 [New York: William H. Wise, 1919], pp. 5–8, 131); but the fact that his parents liked superficial and commercialized versions of good values was important in Ernest's frustrated attempts to maintain relationships.

25. Baker cites Ernest's remark to Hadley that he might have gone to Princeton if his mother had not spent the money to build Grace Cottage (*Life Story,* p. 78). Montgomery is one of many to repeat the story that Ernest earned his mother's hatred by opposing her plan to spend "two or three thousand dollars to build a new cottage for herself," money that should have been used to send the younger girls to college (*Hemingway in Michigan,* p. 177). As with the eviction of 1920, the standard version of what happened is wrong in part because of a lack of information, in part because of bias. The facts concerning Grace Cottage have not been previously available, but the fact that Ernest did not want to go to college has long been known and has carried no weight in scholarly evaluation of the disputes between Grace and Ernest.

26. Grace Hemingway to Clarence, n.d., Family Letters.

27. Grace Hemingway to Ed Morford, n.d., Family Letters.

28. Grace Hemingway to Ed Morford, n.d., Family Letters.

29. Grace Hemingway to Ed Morford, 15 May 1919, Family Letters.

30. Clarence Hemingway to Ed Morford, 26 May 1919, Family Letters.

31. Grace Hemingway to Clarence, n.d., Family Letters.

32. Leicester Hemingway to Grace, 4 January 1904, Family Letters.

33. Sanford, *At the Hemingways,* pp. 49–67, 235–41.

34. Baker, *Life Story,* pp. 433–34; Donaldson, *By Force of Will,* p. 256; Sanford, *At the Hemingways,* p. 55.

35. Hemingway's lack of flexibility is perhaps the most puzzling part of his relations with his parents. Grace's Dr. Frank Crane wrote with incredible superficiality about the power of happy thoughts and the evil of negative thoughts, and Hemingway wrote with honesty and success—in "The Snows of Kilimanjaro," for example—about a realistic version of affirmative thinking and the destructive nature of despair; but the dogmatism he so resented in his parents is an objectionable characteristic found—according to numerous critics and friends—in his fiction and in his own personality. Perhaps, as we see in *A Farewell to Arms* and *For Whom the Bell Tolls,* Hemingway's rewriting of his parents' dogmatic devotion to virtues consists in his rejection of partisan politics, his devotion to freedom and abhorrence of all tyranny.

36. Grace Hemingway to Clarence, 18 October 1908, Family Letters.

37. Grace Hemingway to Clarence, 17 October 1908, Family Letters.

38. Grace Hemingway to Clarence, 5 September 1914, Family Letters.

39. Clarence Hemingway to Grace, 5 May 1917, Family Letters.

40. For a first-rate exploration of stoicism in Hemingway, see Thomas Barker, "The Stoic Ideal in Hemingway's Fiction," Diss. University of Texas (Austin), 1980.

41. Grace Hemingway to Clarence, 10 August 1917, Family Letters.

42. See Donaldson, *By Force of Will*, pp. 211–15.

43. Clarence Hemingway to Grace, 12 August 1917, Family Letters.

44. Clarence Hemingway to Grace and children, 27 June 1920, Family Letters.

45. Clarence Hemingway to Grace, Ursula, and Sunny, 28 June 1920, Family Letters.

46. Clarence Hemingway to Grace and children, 29 June 1920, Family Letters.

47. Clarence Hemingway to Grace, 1 July 1920, Family Letters.

48. Clarence Hemingway to Grace and children, 16 July 1920, Family Letters.

49. Clarence Hemingway to Grace, 1 September 1920, Family Letters.

50. Clarence Hemingway to Grace and Leicester, 13 September 1920, Family Letters.

51. Clarence Hemingway to Grace and Leicester, 15 September 1920, Family Letters.

52. Letters not quoted here make it clear that while differences and problems—as with all families—continued to occur, the Hemingway daughters loved their mother and enjoyed good relations with her, the summer of 1920 being, for them, a minor rough spot in the process of growing up.

53. Leicester Hemingway, *My Brother, Ernest Hemingway*, p. 68.

54. Clarence Hemingway to Ernest, 18 September 1920, Hemingway Collection, John F. Kennedy Library, Boston.

55. On Hemingway's inability to respect his father, see Donaldson, *By Force of Will*, p. 296.

56. There is no envelope for Clarence's letter of 2 October, but several letters make it clear that Clarence did return to Windemere to secure the cabin; for example, Clarence Hemingway to Grace, 6 October 1920, Family Letters.

57. Clarence Hemingway to Grace, 2 October 1920, Family Letters.

58. Lloyd R. Arnold, *High on the Wild with Hemingway* (Caldwell: Caxton, 1969), p. 79.

59. Ernest Hemingway to Grace, 22 December 1920, Hemingway Collection, John F. Kennedy Library.

60. Other family letters in the John F. Kennedy Library suggest that Clarence and Grace did appreciate their son's writing, at least his journalism; but the evidence would have to be more extensive to be convincing. There was, in any case, a finality about Ernest's reaction to his parents' rejection of *In Our Time*. Since writing literature that would offend Clarence and Grace was to be his life, what hope was there for a relationship?

61. See Delbert E. Wylder, *Hemingway's Heroes* (Albuquerque: University of New Mexico Press, 1969), pp. 40–49.

62. Wirt Williams convincingly describes Hemingway's artful combination of security and the ominous in the opening of *Islands in the Stream*; see his *The Tragic Art of Ernest Hemingway* (Baton Rouge: Louisiana State University Press, 1981), pp. 202–04.

63. See Carlos Baker, "A Search for the Man As He Really Was," *New York Times Book Review*, 25 July 1964, pp. 4–5, 14. Citing a letter from Clarence to Ernest about the authenticity of the story (p. 14), Baker demonstrates the close relationship between an actual event and the fictional account of that event, including the fact that the youthful Ernest was, in actuality, a witness. It is easy to see why critics have been led to believe that Nick is therefore present and that the story is about the unmanning of Clarence by Grace. Two excellent corrective essays which summarize the standard view and then offer much-improved readings are Joseph M. Flora, "A Closer Look at the Young Nick Adams and His Father," *Studies in Short Fiction,* 14 (Winter 1977), 75–78; and Richard Fulkerson, "The Biographical Fallacy and 'The Doctor and the Doctor's Wife,' " *Studies in Short Fiction,* 16 (Winter 1979), 61–65. Stephen D. Fox also avoids the biographical trap and quite rightly emphasizes the importance of Dr. Adams's *assuming* that the stray logs are driftwood and the importance of gentility in contrast with Boulton's outcast status. See his "Hemingway's 'The Doctor and the Doctor's Wife,' " *Arizona Quarterly,* 29 (Spring 1973), 19–25.

64. Hemingway made a sound distinction between describing (repeating) actual experience and making (creating) out of experience and other sources. He also said that a good writer could "make something through. . . invention that is not a representation but a whole new thing truer than anything true and alive. . . ." See George Plimpton, "An Interview with Ernest Hemingway," in *Ernest Hemingway: Five Decades of Criticism,* ed. Linda Wagner (East Lansing: Michigan State University Press, 1974), pp. 36, 38.

65. Sanford, *At the Hemingways,* pp. 50–51.

66. Leicester Hemingway, *My Brother, Ernest Hemingway,* pp. 35–37.

67. See, for example, Joseph DeFalco, *The Hero in Hemingway's Short Stories* (Pittsburgh: University of Pittsburgh Press, 1963), pp. 33–40.

68. Ernest Hemingway, *The Short Stories of Ernest Hemingway* (New York: Scribner's, 1954), p. 102 (italics added). Further quotations from "The Doctor and the Doctor's Wife" and from "Soldier's Home" are from this edition and are cited parenthetically.

69. For an excellent demonstration of how Hemingway moved beyond actual experience to invention, to art, see Robert W. Lewis, Jr., "Hemingway in Italy: Making It Up," *Journal of Modern Literature,* 9 (1981–82), 209–36.

70. For an illuminating exposition of Hemingway's abhorrence of tyranny, see Donaldson, *By Force of Will,* pp. 93–124. For Hemingway's revealing comments on Senator Joseph McCarthy, see Ernest Hemingway, *By-Line: Ernest Hemingway,* ed. William White (New York: Scribner's, 1967), p. 450.

DOS AND HEM: A LITERARY FRIENDSHIP

SCOTT DONALDSON

DANTE ALIGHIERI WAS A GREAT WRITER but "one of the worst jerks that ever lived," Ernest Hemingway observed in a 1949 letter to John Dos Passos. "This may be a lesson to us all," he added, and in fact his own behavior provided a case in point.[1] An intensely competitive man, Hemingway was given to breaking off friendships, violently, with anyone who'd ever done him a favor. Among those dismissed in this way were Sherwood Anderson, Gertrude Stein, F. Scott Fitzgerald, and Dos Passos himself. In the case of Dos Passos and Hemingway, however, other complicating factors—including politics, certainly, and sex, possibly— contributed to the end of their long and extremely close friendship.

I

These two men who were to become famous writers probably met briefly in Italy during 1918, when both were World War I ambulance drivers.[2] They became close friends six years later, in the summer of 1924, in Paris. Like almost everyone who met him in those days, Dos Passos was attracted by Hemingway's vitality and intelligence. One of the first things that struck Dos was Ernest's talent "for unmasking political pretensions. . . ." Another was his knack for involving others in his own enthusiasms, including horse racing and bullfights. Dos Passos was swept along to the fiesta in Pamplona in July 1924, when he found a full week of bullfights more than he'd bargained for but was impressed by Hemingway's determination to find out everything he possibly could about

Reprinted with permission from *The Centennial Review*, 29, No. 2 (Spring 1985), 163–85. This essay was prepared in connection with the NEH-funded Dos Passos project administered by Rappahannock Community College, Warsaw, Virginia, and coordinated by Suzanne Semsch and Marty Taylor.

41

bullfighting and its practitioners. These traits—the debunking instinct and the drive to become expert on every subject he touched—were later to sour their friendship. At the beginning, though, they spent long hours dining and drinking, discussing the complications of the craft of writing and reading aloud from a book they were both engrossed in, the Old Testament.[3]

From the start they made an odd couple (or foursome, if one includes Hadley Hemingway and Crystal Ross, Dos's occasional companion). Tall, aesthetic, and somewhat awkward, Dos was shy by nature and polite by training, while Hem was handsome, athletic and aggressively direct (perhaps as a reaction to his own shyness). Moreover, as the author of five books, including his widely-praised war novel *Three Soldiers*, Dos Passos had already made a name in the literary world where Hemingway, three years his junior, remained a neophyte. He had recently quit his job as foreign correspondent to devote himself to serious writing, but by mid-1924 had published only a few stories and poems.

This was a situation Dos Passos, among others, set out to remedy. Like Fitzgerald and Ford Madox Ford, Donald Ogden Stewart and Louis Bromfield, he admired Hemingway's early stories and felt sure they ought to be published in book form. While in New York in the winter of 1925, Dos told Horace Liveright as much and was instrumental in persuading Boni and Liveright to bring out *In Our Time*. "I never knew it was you trying to get the book over. . . ," Ernest wrote him in April. "You're a good guy, Dos, and I wish to hell you were here. Christ knows I appreciate you and Sherwood [Anderson] jamming it through." The rest of the letter commented in irreverent tones about the cuts his publishers had asked for and about the alleged drinking prowess of their mutual friend, the humorist Don Stewart. Don was "claiming to be a drinker now," Hem wrote Dos Passos. "Remember how he vomited all over Pamplona? Drinker? Shit."[4]

Cursing and tough talk formed a regular motif in their correspondence, which survives in some 60 letters from Dos to Hem and about half as many the other way around. As often as not Hemingway's letters proposed a reunion in Key West or Montana, Cuba or Spain. He liked Dos's company, their common bond as writers aside, and said so to others.[5] But the writing bond was there, too, and for a time Dos functioned as adviser to and commentator on his friend's work. In November 1925, for example, he tried to persuade Hemingway not to publish *The Torrents of Spring*, his bitingly satirical attack on Sherwood Anderson. Anderson had, after all, helped Ernest's career, and it seemed wrong to pillory him in return. "I thought I'd talked him out of [it]," Dos recalled in his memoir, *The Best Times*. "I suppose it wasn't any of my goddam business, but friends were friends in those days." Or so it seemed. Dos would probably have been surprised to know that Hemingway told Liveright Dos was "enthusiastic" about *Torrents*.

In the winter of 1926 he joined the Hemingways and Sara and Gerald Murphy at Schruns in the Austrian Vorarlberg for a week of skiing. It marked "the last unalloyed good time" he had with Ernest and Hadley, whose marriage was about to dissolve to enable Ernest to marry Pauline Pfeiffer.[6] He was surely surprised and hurt, decades later, to read what Hemingway wrote about that time in Schruns in *A Moveable Feast*.

There was little trace of personal animosity in Dos's unfavorable review of *The Sun Also Rises* for *The New Masses*. Indeed, he sent Hemingway a carbon of his December 1926 review before it appeared, along with an extremely uncomfortable letter. "Say Hem I've just read The sun also rises that the New Masses sent me over to review," he began, and "I've written a damn priggish mealy mouthed review of it that makes me sick. The book makes me sick anyway, besides making me very anxious to see you, and homesick for good drinks and woodcock [?] and Pamplona and bullfights and all that sort of thing, God damn it and them. I never felt so rotten about anything—book I mean. You write so damn well and the book's so damn readable and I'd like to get cockeyed on fine à l'eau in your company."

The way he felt about Hemingway's novel was undoubtedly influenced by the dark mood that had descended over Dos. He felt bad about Hem's breakup with Hadley, though he thought Pauline "an awfully nice girl. Why dont you get to be a Mormon?" he proposed. On a more sweeping level he was upset about conditions everywhere. "They're going to kill Sacco and Vanzetti and I saw Harry Will's last fight and everything is inexpressibly shitty." In this mood nothing he read seemed all right. "The Sun Also Rises is just about as bad as streets of night [his own 1923 novel], only its more entertaining and better written." Don Stewart's last book was lousy too. "Honestly its pretty god damn discouraging for the American Renaissance." None of them could write and they all ought to take up some other hobby, like batiking.[7]

The review itself objected that the epigraph from *Ecclesiastes,* about the generations passing and the earth abiding forever, built up hopes which were not fulfilled. "Instead of these things of deep importance you find yourself reading about the tangled love affairs and bellyaches of a gloomy young literatizing Jew, and an English lady of title who's a good sport" and so on. The book was awfully well-written, but it read more like "a cock and bull story about a lot of summer tourists getting drunk and making fools of themselves at a picturesque Iberian folk-festival" than an "epic of the sun also rising on a lost generation." In short, it did not seem to deal with anything important, anything serious. This was precisely the kind of criticism the *New Masses,* as an organ of the radical left, wanted. Art should be designed to serve the cause, to illustrate the need for revolution or at least reform, the Communists felt, and Dos for the time agreed. He could not persuade Hemingway to feel as he did about the impending execution of the Italian anarchists Sacco and Vanzetti, but he did feel enough of a kinship with him, politically as well as artistically, to propose, the following June, that Hem send some stories to the *New Masses*.[8]

Hemingway didn't do that, but neither did he let the review sever their friendship. "No, I think it was fine about his not liking the book and wanting it to be better," Hemingway rather defensively wrote his editor Maxwell Perkins, "but a poor criticism that Pamplona in the book wasn't as good as Pamplona in real life. . . ." He hadn't written *Sun* for people who'd *been* to the fiesta, he added, obviously missing the point of the review.[9] Soon thereafter he lectured Dos Passos directly on his writing. Dos was having some trouble finishing the play, *Airways, Inc.*, which he was writing for the left-wing New Playwrights theatre. "What the hell do you write a play for if it doesn't go or if you've got enough jack?" Hemingway wrote him. "Lay off and don't try and do a damn thing and let the juice come back. You've done too bloody much writing and you are stale as hell on it. For christ sake you've published six books that I know about and I don't know how many behind my back." Besides, he insisted, "publication is the fucking damn evil. I shdn't ever have published the stories in In Our Time. Nor written Torrents except for us guys to read at the time and then put it away. Sh'd never have published Sun etc."[10]

Dos Passos disagreed. "Honestly—Hem—," he wrote back, "I think that publication is the honestest and easiest method of getting rid of bum writing—Unpublished stuff just festers and you get to be like a horse that's pistol shy or whatever they call it when they are wonderful horses but can never start a race. In Our Time was a goddamn good thing to publish. So was The Sun Also. Its better to publish than burn as St. Paul said."[11] Among the interesting things about this exchange, in addition to the analogy both writers adopt between writing and sexual intercourse, is that Dos Passos did not relent and tell Hem it was all right to publish *Torrents*. Meanwhile, Hemingway was trying to assume the position of mentor and to transform Dos Passos's prolific publishing record into a handicap rather than an advantage.

In the spring of 1928 Dos made the first of many trips to visit Ernest and Pauline in Key West. He had gone there once before, in the early 1920s, and had been charmed by this sleepy city at the furthest reach of the keys. Hemingway liked it just as well or better, for there he could indulge his lifelong passion for fishing in ideal surroundings. He settled in fast, Dos recalled. "He knew all the barkeeps in the little bars. He was cozy with the Spaniards who ran the restaurants. He'd made friends with the family that owned the hardware store where they sold fishing tackle, and he was a conch with the conchs who handled the commercial fishing boats."[12] Still he needed someone to talk to and laugh with and drink with besides the conchs and barkeeps. Dos helped supply that need, and over the next few years their friendship solidified. For his part Dos could hardly help liking the man who introduced him to Katharine Smith.

Katy and Ernest had known each other for more than twenty years, since the time they'd spent summer vacations on Walloon lake in northern Michigan. Her younger brother Bill had once been Hemingway's closest friend. Ernest had also lived in a kind of cooperative apartment in Chicago run by her older brother Y. K. (Kenley), until the arrangement ended in a bitter quarrel. As for Katy and Hemingway, Dos Passos maintained that she treated him "affectionately-condescendingly as a girl does her younger brother."[13] According to "Summer People," a story Hemingway chose not to publish during his lifetime, there was more to it than that. In the story Nick (also known as Wemedge) seduces Kate (also known as Butstein). In life Hemingway did call Katy Butstein and she called him Wemedge, nicknames from the northern Michigan days, but that hardly proves that they'd been lovers. What is certain is that in Hemingway's imagination they were. Katy was nearly eight years his senior, but that was no bar to intimacy. Hadley Richardson, the first woman Ernest married, was eight years older too. She was also a friend of Katy's, as was Pauline Pfeiffer. Katy introduced Ernest to Hadley. She also told Edmund Wilson's daughter that she and Ernest had been engaged for a brief time.[14] In any event they went back a long way, those two, and Ernest felt strongly enough about her to warn his fiancée Hadley in the summer of 1921 that one of the things he intended to keep to himself as a married man was his relationship with Katy Smith, a remark which inspired her to suggest delaying the wedding a few months.[15] There was no delay, however, and once married Hemingway continued to correspond with Kate. In February 1922, for instance, he wrote her a rhapsodic letter about the joys of living in Paris and traveling to Switzerland for the winter sports and the country-side, especially "when you're with somebody you're lovers with" like Hadley. Why didn't Katy come on over? "It's so damned beautiful, Butstein, and we have so much fun." Why didn't Bill, who had sided with Y. K. in the quarrel, come along or at least write? Anyway she could write. "Please write a man. Aint I your best friend? Or aint I? Who's fonder of you than I am anyway?"[16]

Katy did respond, they kept in touch, and it was not surprising that she should have been visiting the Hemingways in May 1928 when Dos Passos came down to Key West to rest before his trip to Russia. Dos was somewhat wary of love—his own romances had led to engagements but not to the altar—but he was immediately smitten with Katy. Fishing on the Gulf Stream with Ernest and

Pauline, Waldo Peirce the painter, and Charles and Lorine Thompson, all fine companions, from the first moment Dos "Couldn't think of anything but [Katy's] green eyes."[17] To his delight he soon found her witty as well as attractive. She was also a talented writer who sold pieces to the women's magazines and later co-authored a guidebook to Cape Cod and a novel. She came, as Hemingway acknowledged, from a "brilliant family."[18] Kate was thirty-six and Dos thirty-two when they met: old enough to know what they wanted. The following winter they met again in Key West, and in September 1929 "Old Dos married Kate Smith," Hemingway wrote Fitzgerald. "She's a damned nice girl."[19] It was by all accounts an extremely successful marriage. They laughed at the same things. They loved to travel. They were devoted to maintaining friendships. In the first years of their marriage, they saw a great deal of their friends Ernest and Pauline.

In December 1929 Dos took his bride off to Europe. They saw the Hemingways and Fitzgeralds in Paris, then went to Switzerland to spend a glorious Christmas with Ernest and Pauline, Sara and Gerald Murphy, Pauline's sister Jinny, and Dorothy Parker. When Dos and Katy returned from Europe in April 1930, they made a point of stopping at Key West, where they may have seen Ernest, drunk on absinthe, hurling knives at Pauline's new piano.[20] In October of that year, Dos traveled to Montana to join Ernest on an elk hunt, after which Hemingway broke his arm in an auto accident. Actually, Dos was not greatly interested in either fishing or hunting. He admired Hemingway's sense of topography, which made him a marvelous hunter, and the strength and stick-to-itiveness which made him an accomplished deep sea fisherman, but his own preference was for hiking and swimming. He went along on Hemingway's expeditions—three-day fishing trips off Key West in February 1931 and again in February 1932 for example—mostly for the companionship. At this time Dos and Hem had become about as close as friends ever do.

II

During that period too each consistently sought to support the other's work. In his review of *A Farewell to Arms* (1929), Dos called it "the best written book that has seen the light in America for many a long day," composed in a style that was "terse and economical, in which every sentence and each phrase bears its maximum load of meaning, sense impressions, emotion." It was a triumph of craftmanship, "a magnificent novel. . . ."[21] Dos was not quite so enthusiastic about *Death in the Afternoon* (1932), which he read in typescript two years later. The book was "absolutely the best thing" on bullfighting, he wrote his friend, but he had reservations "about the parts where old Hem straps on the long white whiskers and gives the boys the lowdown" about writing and politics, life and love. The volume was "so hellishly good" and the language "so magnificiently used" that it would be a shame to "leave in any unnecessary tripe." Authors should be judged by the quality of the stuff they cut out.[22]

That was good advice, Ernest responded, and he made some cuts accordingly. Meanwhile, he praised the volumes of *U.S.A.*, Dos's masterful trilogy, as they were published. *1919* (1932) was splendid, he wrote Dos in March 1932, four times as good as *The 42nd Parallel* (1930)—"and that was damned good." But he took the occasion to caution Dos Passos against resorting to propaganda in the third volume of the trilogy (which was published as *The Big Money* in 1936). As the fair-haired boy of the Communists, Dos was under pressure to produce the appropriate political and economic sentiments. But Hemingway insisted, "For Christ sake don't try to do good. Keep on showing it as it is. If you can show it as it really is you will do good. If you try to do good you'll not do any good nor will you show it." Dos Passos could write "the best of any of the bastards writing now," and that was what he should continue to do.[23] Feeling somewhat sheepish after delivering this harangue, Hemingway advised Dos Passos to "poop on any literary advice" in his next letter. Dos needed it less than anyone. Then he joshed about starting their own revolution by seceding the South Western Island Republic (Key West) from the Union and taking it over in a coup d'etat:

> On the first night we massacre the catholics and the jews. The second the protestants who have been lulled into a false sense of security by the events of the first evening. The third night we butcher the free thinkers, atheists, communists and members of the lighthouse service. The fourth day we fish the gulf and capture another ship to feed our faithful jigs. That evening we knock off a few counter revolutionaries and if things aren't going well we burn the town. The fifth and sixth days are free and members of the party can amuse themselves as they like. On the Seventh day we elect Butstein the Goddess of Reason and order MacLeish to write an Epic Poem about the Movement. Late that evening we shoot Macleish as his poem has turned out Lousy and send for Even Shipman. You can see how it will be. Just one gay hilarious round with everyone busy and happy. At the end of twelve days we raise wages to beat hell and massacre the poles.

"Damn swell epistle," Dos wrote back, "and Katy and I laughed like fools over it."[24]

But politics was a subject neither man could long make fun of during the climatic 1930s. Hemingway's often-articulated position was that politics and art didn't mix. "I do not follow the fashions in politics, letters, religion, etc.," he insisted in a July 1932 letter. "If the boys swing to the left in literature you may make a small bet the next swing will be to the right and some of the same yellow bastards will swing both ways." But, he added, Dos Passos was different. He "doesn't swing. He's always been the same."[25] Hemingway was righter than he knew.

What was happening during the early and middle 1930s was that he himself was drifting leftward, largely as a consequence of his hatred for fascism, while Dos Passos—having completed his dissection of monopoly capitalism in *U.S.A.*—was becoming increasingly disillusioned by what he saw of communist movements in Europe and the United States. Actually the two held very similar views. Both were primarily interested in the welfare and the autonomy of the individual, and opposed to governments which restricted personal freedom. In Dos Passos's case, the offending institutions consisted not only of governments but of big business, during the twenties and thirties, and big labor, during the forties and fifties. The enemies changed, but his devotion to the cause of the individual remained solid as a rock. The basic similarity of their beliefs did not keep them from disputes, however, particularly as Hemingway continued his practice of issuing pronouncements and making judgments on every possible subject.

Privately Dos and Katy took to calling Hemingway the Old Master "because nobody could stop him from laying down the law, or sometimes the Mahatma on account of his having appeared in a rowboat with a towel wrapped around his head." They still had good times together, but Hemingway needed "some best pal and severe critic" to arrest his oracular tendencies, Katy wrote in the spring of 1935, "to tear off those long white whiskers he is wearing."[26] The situation was complicated by the fact that from 1932 on Dos Passos almost always owed Hemingway money. Dos never made much money on his books, even on *U.S.A.* during his lifetime, and was frequently strapped for funds. Hemingway, whose books sold well and who was married to a rich woman in Pauline, responded with generosity. In March 1932 he covered a $200 check of Dos Passos that had bounced and advised him not to send another. "Would like to have a 200 seed stake in the god-damned fine way you are writing." He even advanced money without being asked. "I enclose 100 in case you can use it," he wrote Dos a year later. "If you need more let me know. I don't mean need. I mean if you cannot get it conveniently from our natural enemies." When Dos Passos suffered an attack of rheumatic fever in April 1933, Hemingway sent him $1,000. The money had come from Pauline's uncle Gus, to finance a trip to Africa, he told Dos, and then went on in rough camaraderie:

> There's plenty to go to Africa still and even come back from Africa. I couldn't make a trip to Coney Island let alone Africa with you, you ignorant

Portuguese having some lousy disease that swells the hands and saps the brain. So cash this before I change it into pennies and pelt you publicly as a hypochondriac. . . Hope to christ I haven't been intrusive. But I was spooked about you.

Dos repaid the money when and as he could; he returned $300 in October 1934, for example, but part of the debt stayed outstanding.[27]

His judgmental streak grew out of his desire for expertise, which also led eventually to the break-up of their friendship in a dispute over the Spanish Civil War. Dos Passos understood Spain and the Spanish very well; he'd lived there as a young man, getting to know the people, studying the language, the culture, and the political structure. This circumstance did not keep Hemingway, whose interest in Spain derived from his interest in bullfighting, from holding forth on the subject for Dos's benefit. As early as June 1931, while in Madrid doing research for *Death in the Afternoon*, Hem—who said he'd been "following politics closely" and had seen "a few funny things"—issued a number of pronouncements on the current situation: "Andalucia is coming to boil. . . ." "Navarra has gone for el Christo Rey in the biggest possible way. . . ." "Catalonia is waiting to do business." "Madrid loves the Republic—which, as soon as anyone takes power—. . . they shift from left to right faster even than in France."[28]

Expert or not, when a Hollywood producer suggested to Hemingway that he write a film about Spain early in 1933, he turned immediately to Dos Passos. Come on down to Cuba, he wrote Dos, and then the four of them could go to Spain together and hire a car and make notes on the movie. "You would do better on your damned perpetual education of Henry J. Passos to go to Spain this summer than anywhere," he added. Rheumatic fever put a crimp in those plans, but by late May Dos was ready to travel. "Damn Tootin we'll be in Spain, dead or alive," he wrote, but they foregathered there only briefly in mid-August. Over lunches with Claude Bowers, the American ambassador, they chatted amiably, but that—Dos recalled—was "the last time Hem and I were able to talk about things Spanish without losing our tempers."[29] Hemingway was probably annoyed that Dos and Katy had spent so much time en route visiting the Murphys on the Riviera. "Marx the whimpering bourgeois living on the bounty of Engels," he confided in a note to himself, "is exactly as valid as Dos Passos living on a yacht in the Mediterranean while he attacks the capitalist system."[30] It was uncharitable of Hemingway to accuse his friend of hypocrisy; it was worse when he later accused him of selling out.

During 1934 and 1935, the Dos Passoses spent much of the winter and spring in Key West, since a tropical climate was recommended for his illness. They saw the Hemingways regularly, and outwardly, at least, remained good friends. In December 1934 Dos vigorously defended Ernest against attacks by leftwing critics. "Say about Hemingway," Dos wrote Malcolm Cowley, "he has his hunting license in the fact that nobody living can handle the damn language like he can. I don't think it's entirely because he's a good friend of mine that I'm beginning to get thoroughly sick of every little ink shitter who can get his stuff in a pink magazine shying bricks at him."[31] By 1936, however, the ties between had weakened: Dos declined invitations to join Hemingway in Cuba in the spring, in Wyoming in the fall. The collapse of their friendship was imminent.

III

In the fall of 1936, Hem and Dos exchanged letters about the worsening conditions in Spain. It seemed to Dos Passos that a Fascist takeover was inevitable, and that a Fascist Spain would lead to a Fascist France. Hemingway was more optimistic. He hated not being in Spain, but intended to go over as soon as he finished *To Have and Have Not*. The war would last for a long time, he thought, and the Fascists couldn't hold Madrid even if they took it.[32] Early in 1937, both of them did go to Spain in order to make a film depicting the anguish of the war. Hemingway, who had also lined up a reportorial assignment with the North American Newspaper Alliance, went over first (with his mistress, Martha Gellhorn) and established himself as the premier American correspondent. Because of his fame, the Republican generals and propagandists went out of their way to flatter Hemingway, and he came to think of himself as an insider. When Dos arrived in April, they immediately clashed about the focus of the film: Hem wanted battle scenes, Dos thought it should concentrate on the suffering of the people.[33] But the final split came in connection with José Robles, Dos's friend from his early days in Spain. Robles had left his teaching post at Johns Hopkins to fight with the Loyalists, but was arrested late in 1936 and eventually executed as a Fascist spy. Dos did not know this when he arrived in April 1937, and was determined to do what he could for his friend. When he learned of Robles's death, Dos was completely undone. Robles must have been killed, he concluded, because he disapproved of the Communists' ulterior motives in Spain. But Hemingway, who'd been told by the head of the department of justice that Robles was guilty, casually assured Dos that his friend was "worthless." If the Loyalists had shot Robles, he insisted, he must have deserved it.[34] Disillusioned about the conduct of the war and what he regarded as appropriation of the Spanish Republican cause by Russian Communists, Dos Passos stayed in Spain only a few weeks. Which side was he on anyway? Hemingway demanded when he saw Dos and Katy at the train station in Paris. If he wrote what he thought about Spain now,

he warned Dos Passos, the reviewers in New York would kill him. All three understood at once that Ernest had insulted Dos's integrity, and Katy would not stand for
it. "Why, Ernest," she countered, "I never heard of anything so despicably oppor-
tunistic in my life!" Then they got on the boat train, Hemingway wheeled about,
and the friendship was over.[35]

Some last words were yet to be uttered, though, and Hemingway said most
of them in his March 1938 letter to Dos. He'd just finished reading Dos's article
in the February *Red Book*, he started, and thought Dos ought to get his facts
straight. "You give the impression that it is a communist run war and you name a
Russian General you met." In fact the article by Dos Passos presents a sympathetic picture of the International Brigade in Spain, with the exception of "the
Russian staff officer who goes by the name of General Walter," can speak only
pidgin Spanish, and is followed deferentially by "his little bantam-cock of an
aide-de-camp," a young man "with popping black eyes and sleek black hair, in an
over-tailored green uniform." There is no overt comment about a "communist-
run war."[36] But General Walter, Hemingway insisted, was not a Russian but a Pole
(what he did not say, or did not know, was that Walter had been trained in Russia). "I'm sorry, Dos, but you didn't meet any Russian generals," he added.
Hemingway's letter, which became more bitter as it went along, was clearly the
work of a man so convinced by the rightness of his views as to consider any
deviation a form of betrayal. The only reason he could see for Dos's "attacking,
for money, the side" he was "always supposed to be on" was "an unsuppressable
desire to tell the truth," he wrote. But Dos hadn't been in Spain long enough to
find out the truth. Dos might feel like attacking him now, but that wouldn't help
him. "When people start in being crooked about money," Hemingway went on,
"they usually end up being crooked about everything." If Dos ever made any
money and wanted to pay him back "(not the Uncle Gus money when you were
ill. I mean others, just small ones, afterwards)," he had plenty of uses for it.
"Now I won't send the letter," he went on, "because of. . . old friends." Then he
did send it, with a vitriolic conclusion:

> So long, Dos, Hope you're always happy. Imagine you always will be.
> Must be a dandy life. Used to be happy myself. Will be again. Good old
> friends. . . . Got them that will knife you in the back for a dime. Regular price
> two for a quarter. Two for a quarter, hell. Honest Jack Passos'll knife you three
> times in the back for fifteen cents and sing Giovanezza free. Thanks pal. Gee
> that feel's good. Any more old friends? Take him away, Doc he's all cut. Tell
> the editor's secretary to make Mr. Passos out a check for $250. Thank you Mr.
> Passos that was very very neat. Come around any time. There's always work
> here for anyone who thinks as you do.[37]

There was another brief meeting later that year, in the Murphys' New York apartment. Dos and Hem went out on the balcony to talk, and when they returned, Dos said to Gerald, "You think for a long time you have a friend, and then you haven't."[38] Obviously he was hurt, and so was Katy. "Oh Wemedge," she wrote him in September 1938, "how did we all get where we are, starting from Walloon?" and in November she wired Ernest in New York: DEARY COME TO PROVINCE-TOWN HAVE STOOD TEST OF TIME DARK RED HEART BROKEN IF DONT SEE YOU NOW—BUTSTEIN.[39] Hemingway stayed put, and in correspondence blamed her for what he regarded as Dos Passos's moral and literary decay. When she died in an auto accident in 1946, it was horrible, he wrote Cowley, that she'd been killed after Dos had sacrificed his honor for her.[40] One of the reasons writers' quarrels become so hostile is that they know so well how to make words sting. Hemingway and Dos Passos alike used their work to attack each other and justify themselves. As early as *To Have and Have Not* (1937), Hemingway drew so many of Dos's lineaments into his derogatory portrait of the fellow-traveling novelist Richard Gordon that *Esquire* editor Arnold Gingrich thought he was risking libel. But that was his last assault on Dos, in print, for many years, and there were even inklings of a reconciliation during the 1940s. Dos never lost a friend willingly, and Hem acknowledged to MacLeish in 1943, after apologizing for his "great 37–38 epoch" of intolerance, that he missed "Dos like hell," at least the way he used to be.[41] In the winter of 1949 Dos stopped off for a few hours to visit Hemingway and his wife Mary in Havanna. That summer he offered to pay off his debt by supplying Hemingway with French royalties. He'd "sure as hell like to have those francs," Ernest replied in the course of congratulating Dos on his marriage to Elizabeth Holdridge, and issued what was at best a lukewarm invitation: "All good luck, kid, and if your wife would like to see the Finca this is the place to see it."[42] There was a rather friendlier exchange of correspondence after Pauline's death in 1951. "I was very fond of her," Dos wrote. "Lord it seems longer than half a lifetime ago, when I first met the dark-haired Pfeiffer girls with you in Paris." She was fond of Dos too, Hem replied in October, and then he launched into reminiscence of the fine times in Pamplona and the Vorarlberg, Key West and Paris. He was awfully glad to have Dos's address, he said, and supplied his phone number in Cuba. "Take care of yourself and die as little as possible," he concluded.[43]

IV

A few months later Hemingway read *Chosen Country*, and any possibility of a reconciliation vanished. Like most of Dos Passos's work, this 1951 novel contained a strong undercurrent of social and political history: his purpose as a writer was to provide a chronicle of his times. Yet *Chosen Country* is also a highly autobiographical book, with a hero, Jay Pignatelli, modeled on Dos himself, and a heroine, Julie Harrington, fashioned on Katy. In a sense the novel represents a paean to Katy, tracing her origins back to northern Michigan and to her acquaintance with a youth named George Elbert Warner. Georgie Warner is obviously a portrait of Hemingway. He appears first as a kind of rude Huck Finn, dirty and unkempt but a passionate hunter and fisherman. His father, like Hemingway's, is a doctor, but Doc Warner is a mean man, respected by no one in the community. From the start, Georgie/Ernest is obviously smitten by Lulie/Katy, but finds peculiar ways of showing it. With the other boys of the summer crowd, he confronts Lulie and the visiting Jay Pignatelli with a shotgun. The "tribe" is angry, he announces: it "doesn't allow its women to consort with foreigners." Later, when Georgie actually proposes, Lulie has to turn him down; she has given her heart to Pignatelli. "I couldn't marry you both now could I?" she says.

It is clear by then, however, that she wouldn't have wanted to marry Georgie in any event, for she finds him progressively more unattractive on each appearance. In his boyhood Lulie had thought him loutish but a "sweet lout." Subsequently she is upset by the "slight cast" in one of his eyes and the "jiggle of the pupils," put off by "the old sullen injured look on his face and that curl she had never liked to his lips," troubled by his sad brown "dog's eyes," and annoyed by "the bristling, conceited look" of his mustache. Finally Georgie—now a reporter—proves himself unworthy of her by writing a sensational newspaper account of the "love nest maintained by her brother and his wife—Zeke and Mugsie in the novel, Y. K. and Doodles in life. The implication was clear: he'd sold out his friends to the press.[44]

When Hemingway read the novel, he was enraged. To Charles A. Fenton, who had written him proposing a critical biographical study, he tried to set the record straight:

> Dos has heard lots of stories about Michigan at our house and with Katey. In 1951 he brings out a novel called Chosen Country. A big part of it is about Michigan and I am one of the more loathsome characters in it. He takes badly remembered anecdotes heard at our table when he was a guest and fouls them up a little more. He takes the incident when Bill's brother Y. K. [and] his wife. . . got involved in some sort of a killing out at a place called Palos Park south of Chicago. Some woman who was in love with Y. K. shot a gardener by mistake I believe. . . Dos makes the loathsome character who is supposed to be me in the book then betray Kate, Y. K. et al by publishing a photograph and writing a feature story in some Chicago newspaper accusing them of weird sex

cult rites. . . . The true gen is, of course, that I was in Europe and knew
nothing about the case except what I read in the paper.[45]

In a letter to Edmund Wilson, Hemingway denigrated Dos as a writer and a
person. Reading *Chosen Country* had made him sick, Ernest said. "My only
hope for him as a writer was that it was a re-write of something dear Katy had
written for a Woman's Magazine. . . . Have you ever seen the possession of
money corrupt a man as it has Dos?" He had trained a pack of fierce animals to
attack one-eyed Portuguese bastards on sight, he wrote Bill Smith.[46] (Dos Passos
had lost an eye in the accident that killed Katy, he came of Portuguese stock on
his father's side, and as a good friend Hemingway was one of those privileged to
know that he'd been born out of wedlock). In letters like these, in conversations
such as those reported in A. E. Hotchner's *Papa Hemingway,* and in his memoir
of Paris called *A Moveable Feast,* Hemingway retaliated brutally. He was a bad
man to get into a nastiness contest with.

At the time Dos did not know he was under seige. He heard nothing from
Hemingway directly about *Chosen Country*, no one saw fit to pass on Ernest's
epistolary diatribes, and *A Moveable Feast* was not published until 1964. In 1953,
then, Dos consented to serve on a committee "to award a gold medal" to
Hemingway. When word reached him that his old friend was ill, in April 1961, he
sent a short cheering note. And when Ernest died in July of that year, "I didn't
realize how fond I'd been of the old Monster of Mt. Kisco," he wrote Sara
Murphy that summer, until he heard of his passing.[47]

From beyond the grave, though, Hem lobbed a few more grenades at Dos.
The fiercest burst came in *A Moveable Feast,* where Dos Passos (though
unnamed) appears as a "pilot fish" who leads the predatory rich to destroy
Ernest and Hadley's idyllic marriage. Mere paraphrase cannot compete with
Hemingway's actual language.

> The rich have a sort of pilot fish who goes ahead of them, sometimes a
> little deaf, sometimes a little blind, but always smelling affable and hesitant
> ahead of them. . . . He is always going somewhere. . . and he is never around
> for long. He enters and leaves politics or the theater in the same way he enters
> and leaves countries and people's lives. . . . Nothing ever catches him and it is
> only those who trust him who are caught and killed. He has the irreplaceable
> early training of the bastard and a latent and long denied love of money. He
> ends up rich himself, having moved one dollar's width to the right with every
> dollar that he made.[48]

Here again was the standard accusation that Dos had trimmed his politics to suit
his increasing wealth. Even on the surface this was untrue: Dos Passos did not

become a rich man, and Hemingway knew it. And here again was the reference to Dos's bastardy, which was true enough, but with the word twisted into its most damning sense.

Two years later, in *The Best Times,* Dos Passos emphasized in his sketch of Hemingway what an excellent companion he'd been before he turned arrogant and vain. There were limits to his tolerance, though, and these must have been exceeded when he discovered in Hotchner's biography (1966) that Hemingway had accused him of cowardice during the trip to Madrid in 1937. He could no longer forgive Ernest. Vacationing on Walloon Lake in 1968, Dos conspicuously rose and left a church service when a memorial to Hemingway was read. And in *Century's Ebb,* the novel he was working on when he died, he took a measure of revenge by depicting George Elbert Warner as a foolhardy foreign correspondent whose bravado, during the Spanish war, had caused the death of a good many Loyalist soldiers.[49]

V

Yet if Dos Passos sniped at Hemingway, he did so relatively gently, as in *The Best Times,* or in the guise of fiction, as in *Chosen Country* and *Century's Ebb,* and always, only under extreme provocation. He was a man who valued friendships, and went out of his way to avoid confrontations that might damage them. Hemingway, on the other hand, seemed invariably driven to cut any ties that threatened to become binding, whether they were ties of love—he had four wives, and broke off with the first three—or of friendship.

The difference between them emerges clearly in comparing their relationships with F. Scott Fitzgerald. Dos met the Fitzgeralds in New York in 1922, and later saw them in Paris and Baltimore on numerous occasions. Though he immediately sensed that something was wrong with Zelda, Dos became and remained Scott's friend. Hemingway and Fitzgerald met in Paris in the spring of 1925. For the next few years, they were the closest of friends, but then—as Hemingway's eminence eclipsed that of Fitzgerald—a chill descended. After the late twenties, when Scott's life and work and fortunes went into a state of decline, largely from drink, Ernest had almost nothing good to say about him. Dos Passos, on the other hand, consistently gave him the benefit of the doubt. In the winter of 1931, for example, Dos Passos ran into Scott in New York. Fitzgerald, who'd come back to the States for his father's funeral, seemed "to have much less nonsense about him than other times"; he was "fundamentally a pretty solid proposition," Dos wrote Edmund Wilson.[50]

Hemingway was less charitable. "Writing a fine book about Scott Fitzgerald oddly enough," he told Dos in April 1932. ". . . Am going to have a camera eye looking up a horse's ass and newsreels of you singing in chinese and give a drink of hot kirsch to every customer." Fitzgerald was "some topic," Dos acknowledged. Everyone on the west coast was shaking his head about Scott, but then, he characteristically added, "they shake their heads about everybody out there." The next year, when Dos came down with rheumatic fever in Baltimore, Scott visited him every few days. "Scott's in pretty good shape," he wrote Hemingway, "aging up damn well—hell of a lot less flighty than he used to be. He's certainly had no picnic these last years."[51]

When Fitzgerald published his three "Crack-Up" articles in *Esquire,* early in 1936, both Hemingway and Dos Passos were appalled. Hem simply wrote Scott off as a friend and artist. "My god did you read Scott's account of his crackup written under influence of Wm. Seabrook," he wrote Dos and Katy after reading the first "Crack-Up" piece. ". . . Had been writing to Scott trying to cheer him up but no cheer up. See the reason now. He's officially cracked up. . . . Max [Perkins] says he has real liver trouble."[52] Then he reflected in print—in "The Snows of Kilimanjaro"—on how "poor Scott Fitzgerald" had been "wrecked" by his worship of the rich. Dos Passos wrote Fitzgerald directly and urged him to get back to work. "We're living in one of the damnedest tragic moments in history—if you want to go to pieces I think it's absolutely o.k. but I think you ought to write a first rate novel about it (and you probably will) instead of spilling it in little pieces. . . anyway, in pieces or not, I wish I could get an hour's talk with you now and then, Scott. . . ."[53] It was such a letter as one friend might send to another when both of them happened to be writers, and one of them needed bucking up.

More than almost anyone of his time, Dos Passos made and maintained literary friendships—with Sherwood Anderson, Malcolm Cowley, E. E. Cummings, Fitzgerald, Robert Hillyer, Archibald MacLeish, and Edmund Wilson, for example. He seems to have been almost totally unaffected by that sense of rivalry that so often undermines such friendships, and welcomed the extraordinary popular success of Hemingway. "Do you realize you're the king of the fiction racket?" he wrote Ernest in the fall of 1929, just after *A Farewell to Arms* emerged. Two different publishers had asked him in hushed tones if he knew Mr. Hemingway, and what could be done to lure him away from Scribner's. "Keep away from New York and let 'em make you offers," Dos suggested, with no indication whatever of envy.[54] His attitude was that it was good for the profession when any good writer made money or got recognition.

Only rarely did Hemingway achieve a similar measure of artistic objectivity. Almost never did he maintain a lasting friendship with another writer. The usual pattern was one of initial camaraderie, followed by a bitter competitive fissure that did not admit of healing. In the Hemingway papers at the Kennedy library, Linda Wagner found this tribute to Dos Passos.

> He alone of American writers has been able to show to Europeans the America they really find when they come here. Even in translation his vitality, his observation, his broad culture, his honesty and his passion persist. . . .
>
> He has all the honesty that is the lone virtue of our dull writers;. . . and he combines with it the vigor and invention of the true creative writer. . . .
>
> What he writes is damned interesting.[55]

The passage is undated. It would be nice to think that Hem put aside his differences with Dos and wrote it *after* their 1938 quarrel in and about Spain, but on the evidence that seems unlikely. As Hortense Calisher once observed, "authors should not be met."[56] And some of them should be met less than others.

---

1. Ernest Hemingway to John Dos Passos, 17 September 1949, *Selected Letters 1917–1961,* ed. Carlos Baker (New York: Scribner's, 1981), pp. 676–77.

2. Townsend Ludington, *John Dos Passos: A Twentieth Century Odyssey* (New York: Dutton, 1980), p. 159.

3. John Dos Passos, *The Best Times* (New York: New American Library, 1966), pp. 140–42, 154–56; *The Fourteenth Chronicle: Letters and Diaries of John Dos Passos,* ed. Townsend Ludington (Boston: Gambit, 1973), pp. 337–38.

4. Ernest Hemingway to John Dos Passos, 22 April 1925, *Selected,* pp. 157–58.

5. Ernest Hemingway to Howell Jenkins, 9 November 1924, and Ernest Hemingway to William B. Smith, Jr., 6 December 1924, *Selected,* pp. 131, 137.

6. John Dos Passos, *Best Times,* p. 158; Ernest Hemingway to Horace Liveright, 19 January 1926, *Selected,* p. 191.

7. John Dos Passos to Ernest Hemingway, 10 November 1926, Kennedy Library; with the letter Dos Passos sent a carbon copy of his review which is sarcastically annotated in the margins by (I believe) Dos Passos himself. The comment at the top of the page reads: "I've sworn off writing reviews, after this. God this is a rotten review."

8. John Dos Passos, "A Lost Generation" (review of *The Sun Also Rises*), *New Masses,* 2 (December 1926), 26 (in the October 1926 number of *New Masses,* Ernest Walsh had savaged Hemingway's *The Torrents of Spring*); John Dos Passos to Ernest Hemingway, 9 June 1927, Kennedy Library.

9. Ernest Hemingway to Maxwell Perkins, 21 December 1926, *Selected,* p. 239.

10. Ernest Hemingway to John Dos Passos, 16 February 1927, Alderman Library, University of Virginia.

11. John Dos Passos to Ernest Hemingway, 27 March 1927, *Fourteenth,* p. 368.

12. John Dos Passos, "Old Hem Was a Sport," *Sports Illustrated,* 20 (29 June 1964), 60.

13. John Dos Passos, *Best Times,* p. 200.

14. Ludington, *Odyssey,* p. 265.

15. Scott Donaldson, *By Force of Will: The Life and Art of Ernest Hemingway* (New York: Viking, 1977), pp. 20, 145–46; the research of Michael S. Reynolds for his forthcoming book on Hemingway's early years makes it clear that before Ernest and Hadley's engagement could be announced, he had to break off with Katy.

16. Ernest Hemingway to Katharine Smith, 16 February 1922, Alderman Library, University of Virginia.

17. John Dos Passos, *Best Times,* pp. 199–200.

18. Ernest Hemingway, MS. 700, Kennedy Library.

19. Ernest Hemingway to F. Scott Fitzgerald, 13 September 1929, *Selected,* p. 307.

20. Ludington, *Odyssey,* p. 288.

21. John Dos Passos, "Books," *New Masses,* 5 (1 December 1929), 16, in *Ernest Hemingway: The Critical Reception,* ed. Robert O. Stephens (New York: Burt Franklin, 1977), pp. 95–97. The review goes at length into the virtues of craftmanship (as, presumably, opposed to the monotonous piecework required by capitalism).

22. John Dos Passos to Ernest Hemingway, February 1932, *Fourteenth,* pp. 402–03.

23. Ernest Hemingway to John Dos Passos, 26 March 1932, *Selected,* p. 354.

24. Ernest Hemingway to John Dos Passos, 12 April 1932, *Selected,* p. 357; John Dos Passos to Ernest Hemingway, (?) May 1932, *Fourteenth,* p. 407.

25. Ernest Hemingway to Paul Romaine, 6 July 1932, *Selected,* p. 363.

26. John Dos Passos, *Best Times,* p. 211; Katharine Dos Passos to Gerald and Sara Murphy, 3 December 1934, *Fourteenth,* p. 421.

27. Among the letters in which loans are discussed are Ernest Hemingway to John Dos Passos, March 1932, *Selected,* p. 355; Ernest Hemingway to John Dos Passos, c. March 1933, Kennedy Library: "You certainly fooled the banks by not having any money in them"; John Dos Passos to Ernest Hemingway, 24 April 1933, *Fourteenth,* p. 425; Ernest Hemingway to John Dos Passos, c. 15 May 1933, *Selected,* p. 389; Ernest Hemingway to John Dos Passos, 1 October 1934, Alderman Library, University of Virginia: thanks Dos for return of $300 loan, first money he's loaned for three years that's come back; John Dos Passos to Ernest Hemingway, 9 January 1937, *Fourteenth,* p. 503: unable "to pay. . . back any dough."

28. Ernest Hemingway to John Dos Passos, 26 June 1931, *Selected,* p. 341.

29. Ludington, *Odyssey,* pp. 315, 319; John Dos Passos to Ernest Hemingway, *Fourteenth,* p. 431.

30. Ludington, *Odyssey,* p. 333.

31. John Dos Passos to Malcolm Cowley, 1 December 1934, *Fourteenth,* p. 456.

32. Ernest Hemingway to John Dos Passos, 22 September 1936, Alderman Library, University of Virginia; John Dos Passos to Ernest Hemingway, October 1936, *Fourteenth,* p. 492.

33. *Fourteenth,* p. 495.

34. Ludington, *Odyssey,* pp. 366, 370–71.

35. Ludington, *Odyssey,* p. 374.

36. John Dos Passos, "Interlude in Spain," *Red Book,* 70 (February 1938), 53, 64, 66.

37. Ernest Hemingway to John Dos Passos, c. 26 March 1938, *Selected,* pp. 463–65: "Giovanezza" was a song associated with Italian fascism; Ludington, *Odyssey,* p. 390.

38. *Fourteenth,* p. 498.

39. Katharine Dos Passos to Ernest Hemingway, September 1938 and 10 November 1938, Kennedy Library.

40. Ludington, *Odyssey,* p. 433.

41. Carlos Baker to John Dos Passos, 5 April 1966, Alderman Library. Baker's letter summarizes and quotes from three Hemingway letters to MacLeish: 4 April 1942, *Selected,* p. 544, and 30 June 1943 and 26 December 1943, unpublished.

42. Ernest Hemingway to John Dos Passos, 17 September 1949, *Selected,* p. 676.

43. John Dos Passos to Ernest Hemingway, 23 October 1951, *Fourteenth,* p. 597; Ernest Hemingway to John Dos Passos, 30 October 1951, Kennedy Library.

44. John Dos Passos, *Chosen Country* (Boston: Houghton Mifflin, 1951): see especially the chapters entitled "New World Wind Northwest," "Lady of the Lake," and "A Girl Employed in Office Work."

45. Ernest Hemingway to Charles A. Fenton, 29 July 1952, *Selected,* pp. 775–76.

46. Ernest Hemingway to Edmund Wilson, 8 November 1952, *Selected,* p. 793; Carlos Baker, *Ernest Hemingway: A Life Story* (New York: Scribner's, 1969), p. 495.

47. John Dos Passos to Van Wyck Brooks, 14 November 1953, *Fourteenth,* p. 604; John Dos Passos to Ernest Hemingway, 28 April 1961, Kennedy Library; John Dos Passos to Sara Murphy, August 1961, *Fourteenth,* p. 623.

48. Ernest Hemingway, *A Moveable Feast* (New York: Scribner's, 1964), pp. 207–08.

49. Ludington, *Odyssey,* pp. 372, 499.

50. John Dos Passos to Edmund Wilson, 15 July 1931, *Fourteenth,* pp. 398–99.

51. Ernest Hemingway to John Dos Passos, c. 12 April 1932, *Selected,* p. 356; John Dos Passos to Ernest Hemingway, (?) May 1932 and 10 May 1933, *Fourteenth,* pp. 408, 429.

52. Ernest Hemingway to John Dos Passos and Katharine Dos Passos, 13 January 1936, *Selected,* p. 433. Seabrook had written a book on the evils of alcoholism.

53. John Dos Passos to F. Scott Fitzgerald, September 1936, *Fourteenth,* p. 488.

54. John Dos Passos to Ernest Hemingway, 24 October 1929, Kennedy Library.

55. Quoted in Linda W. Wagner, *Dos Passos: Artist as American* (Austin: University of Texas Press, 1979), unpaginated front matter.

56. Hortense Calisher to Scott Donaldson, 21 January 1970.

II: The Work, Early Stories and Novels

TOUGH EARTH

PAUL ROSENFELD

HEMINGWAY'S SHORT STORIES belong with cubist painting, *Le Sacre du printemps*, and other recent work bringing a feeling of positive forces through primitive modern idiom. The use of the direct, crude, rudimentary forms of the simple and primitive classes and their situations, of the stuffs, textures and rhythms of the mechanical and industrial worlds, has enabled this new American storyteller, as it enabled the group to which he comes a fresh recruit, to achieve peculiarly sharp, decided, grimly affirmative expressions; and with these acute depictions and half-impersonal beats to satisfy a spirit running through the age. Hemingway's spoken prose is characteristically iron with a lyricism, aliveness and energy tremendously held in check. With the trip-hammer thud of *Le Sacre* his rhythms go. Emphatic, short, declarative sentences follow staunchly upon the other, never precipitously or congestedly or mechanically, and never relenting. The stubby verbal forms are speeded in instances up to the brute, rapid, joyous jab of blunt period upon period. Hemingway's vocabulary is largely monosyllabic, and mechanical and concrete. Mixed with the common words, raw and pithy terms picked from the vernaculars of boys, jockeys, hunters, policemen, soldiers, and obscurely related to primitive impulse and primitive sex, further increase the rigidity of effect. There is something of Sherwood Anderson, of his fine bare effects and values coined from simplest words, in Hemingway's clear medium. There is Gertrude Stein equally obvious: her massive volumes, slow power, steady reiterations, and her intuition of the life of headless bodies. The American literary generations are learning to build upon each other. This newcomer's prose departs from the kindred literary mediums as a youngling from forebears. Wanting some of the warmth of Anderson and some of the pathos of

Reprinted with permission from *The New Republic*, November 1925, pp. 22–23.

Gertrude Stein, Hemingway's style nonetheless in its very experimental stage shows the outline of a new, tough, severe and satisfying beauty related equally to the world of machinery and the austerity of the red man.

It comes on the general errand of the group, the realization of a picture of the elements of life caught in barest, intensest opposition. In the world of Hemingway's stories, characters and principles are boxers crouched and proposing fists. Stocky rudimentary passions wrestle for a throw. The sport of the two youths snowshoeing in high Alps is brusquely, casually interrupted by consciousness of pregnancy and the responsibility seeking out the man. A lad sees his sensitive father beset by the active brutality of men and the passive brutality of women. Inside the hotel room in the rain male and female face each other for a swift passage of their eternal warfare. The sheer unfeeling barbarity of life, and the elementary humor and tenderness lying close upon it, is a favorite theme. The amazing pages previously assembled in a booklet by the Three Mountains Press in Paris, sandwiched between the longer stories in the Liveright volume and connecting these with the doings of an epoch, bring dangerously close in instantaneous pictures of the War, of the bull-ring and the police-world, the excitement of combat, the cold ferocity of the mob, the insensibility of soldiering, the relief of nerves in alcoholic stupor, the naked, the mean, the comic brute in the human frame. Against these principles, set invariably in crude, simple, passionate opposition, the author plays the more constructive elements. We feel the absorption and fine helpfulness of the handicapped doctor performing a Caesarean operation with a jackknife and releasing a child; the tender, subtle feeling for woman's life found among certain of the ordinary people of Europe; the enjoyment of the body in the physical play of life; the seriousness in the young man making him accept responsibility and automatically limit his narcissistic impulse to freedom. And both these forces and the uglier ones are given sharp physiognomies by the dramatic counterpoint; and what certain of them owe Sherwood Anderson is made good by the personal intensification of the passionate opposition between them.

There is little analysis in this narrative art. We are given chiefly, at times with marvelous freshness and crispness, what the eye sees and the ear hears. The conflicting principles are boldly established without psychologizings. Yet Hemingway's acceptation of the aesthetic responsibility of getting his material into action in instances remains near gesturing. His units are not brought into actual opposition in all his pieces. Or, formally introduced, they remain at inadequate degrees of tension, while a youthfully insolent sense of the stereotype in life blinds the author. "Soldier's Home" is one of Hemingway's forms half left in the limbo of the stencil. The happy relief to this and other incompleted pieces is furnished by stories like "Cat in the Rain," "Indian Camp," and "My Old Man."

In these, plastic elements accurately felt are opposed point against point, and a whole brought into view. It is a whole this newcomer has to show. It is one from which the many beauties of his book are fetched. He shares his epoch's feeling of a harsh impersonal force in the universe, permanent, not to be changed, taking both destruction and construction up into itself and set in motion by their dialectic. With the blood and pain, he makes us know the toughness of the earth, able to meet desire, nourish life, and waken in man the power to meet the brutalities of existence. This bald feeling is the condition of an adjustment to life begun in men before the War, but demanded even more intensely of them by its ghastlier train, and natural at all times to the products of primitive America. Through it men are reconciled to perpetual struggle, and while holding themselves tight work in relation to something in the universe. This adjustment is not the sole possible one. It is not necessarily the one of next year or of the year to follow, for any. But it had and still has its reality; and the rhythms, and tempi which communicate it share in its permanence.

THE STRUCTURE OF *IN OUR TIME*

ROBERT M. SLABEY

THE READER OF ERNEST HEMINGWAY'S *In Our Time* is left with the impression that this book is more than a random selection of short stories. For the 1930 Scribner's edition Hemingway added an ironic "Introduction by the Author" ("On the Quai at Smyrna") to fifteen "chapters" or miniatures, many of them reworkings of his journalism, a similar number of stories, and "L'Envoi."[1] While numerous readers—F. Scott Fitzgerald and Allen Tate among them—have praised *In Our Time*, certain critics have commented on its nature. Edmund Wilson described it as "an odd and original book. It had the appearance of a miscellany of stories and fragments; but actually the parts hung together and produced a definite effect."[2] Ray B. West called *In Our Time* "a collection of curiously related stories," and D. H. Lawrence thought that it resembled "a fragmentary novel."[3] E. M. Halliday believed that there was no particular sequence to the "chapters," the intention being to give an impression of disorder, with the stories extending the theme of chaotic irony.[4] George Hemphill, who has given closest attention to the structure, felt that the book was anomalous in form; its unifying principle was Hemingway's thematic obsession with the cruelty of life.[5] Several other critics have observed this unity of subject matter. Philip Young, however, found a personal and chronological order in the miniatures based largely on Hemingway's own experiences."[6] But the vignettes, when assigned approximate dates and locations, reveal an inconsistent chronology:

> Introduction—1922, Asia Minor
> I—1918, France
> II—1922, Asia Minor
> III and IV—1918, Belgium

Reprinted with permission from *South Dakota Review* (August 1965), pp. 38–52.

V—1922, Greece
VI and VII—1918, Italy
VIII—1917, Kansas City
IX to XIV—1922–1924, Spain
XV—1918, Kansas City
"L'Envoi"—1923, Greece."[7]

In addition, some of the chapters (III, IV, V) are based on neither Hemingway's direct experiences nor his observations.

The structural arrangement of *In Our Time* (both chapters and stories) is not chronological but ideological. "On the Quai at Smyrna" introduces the principal theme of the book—death—with a picture of death, cruelty, violence, and the failure of traditional values to vitalize experience. There are two major sequences within the fifteen chapters: I-VII picture scenes of war (World War I and the Greco-Turkish War) while IX-XIV are concerned with the bullfight. Two vignettes of crime in America (VIII and XV) punctuate the larger sequences and extend the picture of violence and sudden death. Charles A. Fenton has, quite correctly, called the interview with the Greek King in "L'Envoi" the ultimate irony in the book's picture of contemporary experience: "The leader of an ancient nation, whose people had recently fought and lost a painful, costly war, out of which had come the catastrophic Thracian refugee processions, was discovered to be an amiable, inept facsimile of an English gentleman." One of the major techniques of this book is a pervasive irony, initiated by the titular allusion to a phrase in the Book of Common Prayer: "Give peace in our time, O Lord." There is an irony of phrase, of situation, and of structure.

The various settings and nationalities utilized in Chapters I to VII universalize the theme. The characters emphasize the plight of modern man: Brittons, Americans, Greeks, Italians. In "On the Quai at Smyrna" the narrator, a British naval officer, is deeply affected by the refugees' screaming at night, by the women's refusal to give up their dead babies, and by the Greeks' abandoned baggage animals, their forelegs broken: "It was all a pleasant business. My word yes a most pleasant business." Hemingway thought that he had really learned about war and about horror from watching the battles in Asia Minor.[8] Greek refugees, on the road out of Adrianople, also appear in Chapter II. In I the persons involved are American enlisted men in France, while III and IV picture British officers. The execution of the Greek cabinet ministers is reported in V; the former members of the war cabinet, held responsible for the debacle in Asia Minor, were shot near Athens on November 28, 1922.

The symbolic center of the whole book occurs in VI. Here a soldier named Nick Adams is wounded in the spine. With his friend Rinaldi he plans to desert, making "a separate peace." The following sketch (VII) seems related to Nick's wound, but its action precedes the wounding. In time this chapter would not follow VI, unless, as is quite possible, it records Nick's second wound. The autobiographical location, near Fossalta, makes the identification of its nameless protagonist as Nick plausible since it was near Fossalta that Hemingway was wounded on July 8, 1918. The utter failure of traditional religious and ethical values in VII marks the conclusion of the war cycle. The shooting of two thieves by Kansas City policemen (VIII) records the stupidity, sadism, and incipient fascism of the police, but, more importantly, the sketch shows that violence and sudden death—the absurdities of war—are present in an American city.

Up to VIII there has been a growing awareness of the hostility and violence of the world. However no code capable of vitalizing experience has appeared. There has been a breakdown not only of tradition but also of manhood and individuality. The major function of the remaining vignettes is to discover and articulate a code of manhood. In the bullfighter's discipline and courage Hemingway found a way to live and a way to die. In war, in crime, in the bullfight—in life itself—there are violence, disaster, chaos, and sudden death. But only in the bullfight is there pictured a man successfully coping with the world's dilemma. The matador's life-and-death struggle provided Hemingway with the image he needed to shape violence into art (even though the bullfight is not a natural struggle but an artificial and ceremonial confrontation). In his formal conduct, the bullfighter epitomized the spiritual substance of religious values. The bullfight became for Hemingway a profound aesthetic and spiritual experience. Definitively examined in *Death in the Afternoon* (1932), it could become also a source of release for rebellious and destructive impulses. The perfect bullfight is one in which death (in the form of a brave bull) is conquered artistically and valiantly. The matador, and vicariously the spectators, makes a gesture of defiance at man's ultimate fate and achieves a temporary victory over it. In this way a perfect bullfight provided a norm around which Hemingway developed the idea of the morally undefeated. The great *torero* Maera, whose death is recorded in XIV, became the prototype for Manuel Garcia in "The Undefeated," one of Hemingway's pivotal stories.[9]

There is, moreover, a definite pattern in the bullfight sketches. The point-of-view in IX is that of an American tourist uninitiated into the mystique. In X it is someone casually acquainted with bullfighting, while XI and XII are narrated by an *aficionado*. In contrast with the incompetent *torero* in XI and the drunken bullfighter in XIII, the great Villalta appears in XII, and XIV narrates the death of Maera. This supreme image of taking ultimate risks and facing death with courage is ironically followed in XV with the execution of frightened and cowardly criminals (an American parallel of the execution of the Greek cabinet in V). Hemingway has nothing but contempt for those who die without valor or bravery. The sketch of the congenial but inept Greek monarch in "L'Envoi" forms an ironic epitaph. As Fenton suggested, the king of a great nation is shown to be less a leader than a short-order cook in Chicago. There is an additional irony in the king's desire to visit America when one recalls the many American soldiers who fought in Europe. The basic thematic movement of the chapters of *In Our Time,* therefore, is two-fold: the loss of values (I-VIII) and the search for a code (IX-XIV), concluded with an ironic postscript-picture of decadence and impotence.

In broad outline, with occasional counterpoint, the fifteen stories trace chronological events in the life of one man, Nick Adams. The list below indicates a four-part pattern:

    A. Nick Adams: The Young Man
        I. "Indian Camp"
        II. "The Doctor and the Doctor's Wife"
        III. "The End of Something"
        IV. "The Three-Day Blow"
        V. "The Battler"

    B. The Effects of War
        VI. "A Very Short Story"
        VII. "Soldier's Home"*[10]
        VIII. "The Revolutionist"*

    C. The Failure of Marriage
        IX. "Mr. and Mrs. Elliot"*
        X. "Cat in the Rain"*
        XI. "Out of Season"
        XII. "Cross-Country Snow"*

    D. Sports: The Search for a Code
        XIII. "My Old Man"*
        XIV. "Big Two-Hearted River I"
        XV. "Big Two-Hearted River II"

The first five Adamic stories are closely sequential. Their prefatory chapters are vignettes of war; both stories and chapters reach an initial climax with the wounding of Nick in VI, the event which concludes his youth.

For Nick Adams, the events of boyhood are initiations into the painful and disruptive circumstances of life in our time. Theodore Bardacke feels that *In Our Time* "reads almost like an autobiographical novel of maturation and deals with the gradual loss of illusions as man grows out of childhood into the reality of war, violence and tragedy."[11] In "Indian Camp" Nick, an impressionable young boy, observes pain, birth, and death. He is present when his doctor-father performs an unanaesthetized Caesarean with a jackknife and when the woman's husband, unable to bear the tension, commits suicide. Nick's ambivalent relationship with his parents is pictured in the next story. The contrasting calm of "The Doctor and the Doctor's Wife" is only superficial. There is no surface violence, but there is inner tension between Dr. Adams and Dick Boulton, between Nick's parents, and between Nick and his mother. Nick chooses his dishonest and kindly father, who is fond of hunting and fishing, over his cold, pious, nagging mother. In "The End of Something" the adolescent Nick breaks up his romance with Marjorie, rejecting love and domesticity for the camaraderie of men without women, which is celebrated with his friend Bill in "The Three-Day Blow." Again Nick confronts two motivating forces (embodied here in Marjorie and Bill) which provide the psychological tension. Nick has left home and is on the road in "The Battler." After being knocked off a freight by a brakeman, he encounters the strange, possibly sinister menage of the demented ex-fighter Ad Francis and the gentle Negro Bugs. In spite of his unpleasant, perplexing, and sometimes violent experiences, Nick's basic innocence seems invincible. His maturation is not only painful; it is painfully slow.

Nick's war wound (described in VI), the culmination of his education into maturity and the last in a series of psychic wounds, makes him forcefully aware of his precarious position in an irrational and hostile world. The effects of war are presented in the second sequence of stories. "A Very Short Story," "Soldier's Home," and "The Revolutionist" focus on romance, home and parents, and politics respectively. "Soldier's Home" gives the fullest direct picture of the repercussions of war. The returned veteran, Harold Krebs, disillusioned by war, becomes disenchanted with civilian life. Above all he desires to be free of responsibilities, complexities, and involvement. Krebs resembles Nick and faces an analogous home situation. Malcolm Cowley explained the feelings of such members of the "lost generation":

> [The lost generation] was lost because it tried to live in exile. It was lost because it accepted no older guides to conduct and because it had formed a false picture of society and the writer's place in it. The generation belonged to a period of transition from values already fixed to values that had to be created. . . [Its members] were seceding from the old and yet could adhere to nothing new; they groped their way toward another scheme of life, as yet undefined. . . .[12]

The marital troubles of Mr. and Mrs. Elliot and of the couple in "Cat in the Rain" parallel the breakup of Nick's marriage. Because he is "sick" and prefers the life of a sportsman, Nick's marriage fails. The other marriages fail because of sterility; parental desires remain unfulfilled. Egotism and an incapacity for love are also important causes of marital distress. The "cat" epitomizes the pathos of misdirected maternal instincts. The Elliots' final solution is a travesty of marriage, and the big tortoise-shell cat is an absurd child-surrogate. In "Out of Season" it is not only the fishing and the weather that are unseasonal: it is the conjugal relationship as well. The chilly mood of this story recalls the tense atmosphere of "The End of Something." In "Cross-Country Snow" Nick, temporarily separated from his pregnant wife, would prefer skiing with George to the resumption of his familial responsibilities.

"My Old Man" offers several examples of honest and dishonest behavior: little Joe's affection for his jockey-father recalls Nick's attitude toward his father, who also was "swell" but weak and dishonest. Nick is, at this time, about to become a father himself. The five non-Nick stories universalize the theme at the same time that their events parallel Nick's experiences. There is an overlapping of thematic material in the last three sequences. All of the marriage group, as well as "The Revolutionist" and "My Old Man," involve expatriates. And "Cross-Country Snow," like the concluding series, deals with sports (skiing, like fishing in "Big Two-Hearted River," has therapeutic values).

The Nicksaga is for the time[13] concluded in the twin story "Big Two-Hearted River," one of Hemingway's best works and a thoroughly integrated symbolic construct. Up to this point Nick has been seen in multiple relationships—most of them disruptive—relationships with his parents, with friends, with his wife, with society; now he is seen in relationship with nature and with himself. The mature Nick, with his many wounds, returns to the Michigan woods for the same reason Thoreau retired to Walden Pond—"to live deliberately, to front only the essential facts of life." Nick makes camp alone and fishes in solitude. Melvin Backman rightly observed that in this story Nick wants to rub out his immediate past and begin clean again. In relationship to "Big Two-Hearted River" the previous stories and chapters have the effect of painful memories of which Nick must rid himself to exorcise their evil spell.[14] The grim interchapters (XIV and XV) which preface the two parts of the story epitomize the memories which Nick tries to repress.

Nick has already passed through the valley of the Shadow (represented by the burned-out town of Seney) in his journey, the dark night of the soul. Nick "felt he had left everything behind, the need for thinking, the need to write, other needs. It was all back of him." Nick's heavy pack represents the burden of the human condition which he has learned to bear. Since the only refuge left is Self, Nick returns to the scene of his boyhood adventures. He has left the wasteland behind. He has come to fish in the deep, fast-moving river. And fishing is more than recreation or relaxation; it is a search for something permanent. (The fish is an ancient symbol of faith and water a symbol of regeneration). Nick has a proper respect and reverence for the creatures of Nature. His struggle with the big trout, conducted with skill and according to the rules of fair play, is followed by a feeling of serenity. The "good place" where he makes camp is the one place in a disruptive universe that he can keep "clean" and "well-lighted."[15] This is a psychological place, a "region" of ultimate value. Nick, an initiate into a chaotic and irrational world, has had an existential encounter with nothingness. The maintenance of the clean, well-lighted place represents a conquest both of nature and of nothingness. Nick, formerly unable to sleep without a light and still tense, has come to terms with darkness.

The ideational pattern of *In Our Time,* completed in this story, is centered around a metaphysical quest, finding a way to exist. The fundamental issue is a moral one—"How to be"—living and dying well. Nick Adams has the same feeling Frederic Henry will have for "how it ought to be" and the same purpose Jake Barnes will have "to know. . . how to live it." Nick must find a way to live with the physical and psychic scars he has received. But each of these heroes must face the facts of life and death alone and work out for himself the code which prepares man for the ultimate ends of existence. The code requires that one be self-reliant, adhere to the "rules" and play the "game" skillfully. The capital sin is cowardice; the greatest fear is of fear itself. The code provides an image of what a man can achieve, of how he can be defeated, but only on his own terms. In learning the code, a posture of manhood is replaced by humanity; manhood is not a pose but becomes a fact. Those not living by the code—the "herd"—are easily identified by their lack of discipline, fortitude, and honor; they are "outsiders" unacquainted with the tragic nature of existence.

Another related pattern in *In Our Time* is now apparent—a pattern of movement, flight, and desertion, a pattern clearly introduced in "On the Quai at Smyrna." In "The Doctor and the Doctor's Wife" Nick rejects his mother; in "The End of Something" he leaves Marjorie; shortly thereafter he leaves home. In Chapter VI he deserts the army and resigns from society. And Nick is only one of many expatriates in the book. "A Very Short Story," the only "love story," is a record of betrayals: Nick deserts Luz, Luz forsakes Nick, and a Chicago girl betrays Nick. Krebs, whose isolation is extensively analyzed, finds out that he has no "home." Both Nick and Krebs retreat from responsibility and involvement. This pattern is reversed in the later story "Cross-Country Snow," the action of which precedes Nick's imminent return to wife and country. This story repeats the choice of "The Doctor and the Doctor's Wife," except that here the mature Nick reluctantly heeds the female summons. In "Big Two-Hearted River" the return "home" is accomplished symbolically and ceremonially.

At the end of his "Indian Camp" experience Nick naively thought that he would "never die." He had just witnessed a painful birth and a bloody death. The Indian committed suicide because he could not bear pain (mostly his wife's pain). Nick's subconscious equation of pain and unpleasantness with women is the beginning of an increasing misogyny. There is in *In Our Time* the implication that a deep, enduring relationship between men and women is impossible. While male solidarity is celebrated in several stories, its sordid aspect is encountered in "The Battler." (It should be recalled that Ad Francis' career had been ruined by a woman.) The collapse and breakup of marriage is possibly symptomatic of a larger dissolution of human institutions and of traditional human values. Interpreted universally, many of the immature Nick's rejections and denials are of the burdensome sufferings of humanity, the common legacy of Adam.

Although "My Old Man," one of Hemingway's earliest works which is reminiscent of Sherwood Anderson, in the use of racing as an occasion of a boy's maturation, is probably the least characteristic story in the book, it does have a thematic function. If love and marriage do not always take precedence over male companionship, fatherhood does (as Nick is forced to realize in "Cross-Country Snow"). "My Old Man" ends with the death of Joe's father, the death of the horse, and the death of Joe's diminishing illusions. In *Death in the Afternoon* Hemingway defended his almost obsessive interest in death: ". . . all stories, if continued far enough, end in death, and he is no true-story teller who would keep that from you." One critic described the special quality of Hemingway's prose as a vision of things as they might be seen by a man on the day he knew he would die. As a result of his initiation into different kinds of violence and pain, Nick Adams learns that the great enemy of life is not war, not society, not women, but death. In battle Nick has seen the grim face of death: he found out that death and defeat are inevitable, And in the discipline and the courage of the bullfighter he could find a vision of how to face death like a man.

Although one distinction between chapters and stories, other than length and development, is that the former are general pictures and the latter specific ones, the chapters are occasionally illumed by brief flashes of individual human experience. In both chapters and stories there are parallels between present and past, maturity and youth, war and peace, death and life, bravery and cowardice. The relationship between the two is similar to that of a motion picture which has newsreel clips inserted at strategic moments within its dramatic action, for either realistic background or ironic contrast. In a letter to Edmund Wilson Hemingway commented on his arrangement of stories and chapters:

that is the way they were meant to go—to give the picture of the whole between examining it in detail. Like looking with your eyes at something, say a passing coastline, and then looking at it with 15X binoculars. Or rather, maybe, looking at it and then going and living in it—and then coming out and looking at it again.[16]

John Steinbeck utilized a similar cinematic technique in *The Grapes of Wrath* where the story of the Joad family is accompanied by inter-chapters reporting the general plight of the "Okies." Both Hemingway and Steinbeck, of course, had the model of *Moby-Dick* with its famous cetalogical chapters.

In *In Our Time* there are several incidental connections between adjacent or closely placed vignettes and stories. In both "On the Quai at Smyrna" and Chapter II there are women in labor: in the first story Dr. Adams performs an emergency Caesarean. The heavy drinking of American soldiers in I is repeated with the conviviality of Nick and Bill in "The Three-Day Blow" and with the obsequious Peduzzi in "Out of Season." The autumn storm of "The Three-Day Blow" has its parallel in the rain storm of V which follows it. Two possessive mothers, Mrs. Adams and Mrs. Krebs, share the same naive piety. Nick is wounded in VI and has a brief hospital-romance in the adjacent "A Very Short Story." At the end of "Soldier's Home" Krebs decides to go to Kansas City, the locale of VIII. And in this vignette two Hungarians (mistaken for Italians) are shot; in "The Revolutionist" the protagonist leaves Budapest for Italy. The basic relationship of the material reveals that in both peacetime America and wartime Europe, pain and brutality are omnipresent. Man is always enveloped in suffering which is beyond his control. The sheer animal force of the bull which the matador must face is an appropriate image of man pitted against the overwhelming odds of the "brutality" in life and the inevitability of death.

Along with a developing interpretation of man's place in the universe, the body of Hemingway's fiction is characterized by a rather narrowly defined range of experience. This homogeneity was initially established in *In Our Time,* his first examination of a central problem of his generation. Minor incidents from this book are re-used later: the crippled mules of Chapter I, for instance, reappear in "The Snows of Kilimanjaro" and in *Death in the Afternoon.* Details of the Greek retreat at Smyrna were transmuted into the description of the Caporetto retreat in *A Farewell to Arms.* Human types are recurrent: soldiers, writers, sportsmen, young men, unhappily married couples. The "wounding" chapter pictures a central event of the entire canon and, with the first half of "A Very Short Story," provides a prototype for *A Farewell to Arms.* Mr. and Mrs. Elliot belong with the sterile and vacuous Bohemians in *The Sun Also Rises*; and Nick and George in "Cross Country Snow" parallel Jake and Bill in the same novel.

The mountain "freedom" of this story and the ominous rain of "Cat in the Rain" foreshadow symbolic motifs in *A Farewell to Arms*. And in "Big Two-Hearted River" Nick avoids the deep water where fishing would be "tragic," exactly the region where Santiago had his tragic adventure in *The Old Man and the Sea*.

In Our Time, then, is more than a fresco of the "way it was"; the book possesses a highly subtle unity of structure, coherence of meaning, and development of theme. Though not a novel, it does merit a designation somewhere between collections of interrelated stories (Joyce's *Dubliners*, Edmund Wilson's *Memoirs of Hecate Country*, Eudora Welty's *The Golden Apples*, Mary McCarthy's *The Company She Keeps*, Louis Auchincloss' *Powers of Attorney*, to mention but a few) and novels which incorporate independent short stories (Sarah Orne Jewett's *The Country of the Pointed Firs*, Sherwood Anderson's *Winesburg, Ohio*, Faulkner's *The Unvanquished* and *Go Down, Moses*, and Steinbeck's *The Pastures of Heaven, Tortilla Flat*, and *Cannery Row*). Frank O'Connor has remarked that "A good book of stories like a good book of poems is a thing in itself, the summing up of a writer's experience at a given time" and it should be treated as a unit.[17]

There are a few obvious resemblances between *In Our Time* and *U.S.A.* (especially *1919*), but Dos Passos' trilogy is more panoramic, episodic, and experimental in structure and style. *In Our Time* more closely resembles *The Gallery*, John Horne Burns' important novel of World War II (published in 1947).[18] *The Gallery* shares with Hemingway and Dos Passos a realistic study of existential anguish, spiritual bankruptcy, and the fragmentalization of lives, a strong feeling of disillusionment and despair, and a synecdochic picture of the riddle of war and the meaning of life. Burns records the impressions of one first-person observer in eight "Promenades" which are framed by an "Entrance" and an "Exit" and interspersed with nine "stories" (Burns labels them "Portraits"), each story focusing on different characters who at some time pass through the Galleria Umberto Primo in Naples, the novel's focal setting.

Numerous story-collections possess an inevitable unity in the revelation of the mind and mood of their creators. But a psychological or structural progression (in idea, attitude, place, or time) appears much less frequently. In *In Our Time* the ordering of chapters and stories does have significance and creates a feeling of unity and coherence. The arrangement of materials is clearly, from all available evidence, not by date of composition or, with previously published work, that of publication.[19] In placing chapters and stories Hemingway reveals an acquaintance with such literary and musical devices as repetition and counterpoints. No major shifts would improve the effect achieved by the present arrangements of parts. The structure is neither chaotic nor arbitrary but closely related to the emergent theme. Hemingway's careful artistry, antedating the structural perfections of *The Sun Also Rises* and *A Farewell to Arms*, supports his statement, in *Death in the Afternoon*, that "Prose is architecture, not interior decoration." *In Our Time* is obviously not the result of instinctive creativity but of thoughtful planning. In preparing this book Hemingway acquired "discipline" as a writer, practicing the art of arrangement as well as the arts of economy and revision. Structure, along with the simple, evocative style and the objective, dramatic method, was produced by conscious craft.

1. This volume is otherwise a re-issue of the Boni and Liveright edition (New York, 1925). The "lower-case" Paris version (1924) contained the fifteen vignettes, along with "L'Envoi" and two of the briefer stories, "A Very Short Story" and "The Revolutionist."

2. Edmund Wilson, "Hemingway: Gauge of Morale," *The Wound and the Bow* (New York, 1947), p. 214.

3. Ray B. West, *The Art of Fiction* (New York, 1949), p. 622. D. H. Lawrence, *A Review of* In Our Time, rpt. in *The Portable D. H. Lawrence*, ed. Diana Trilling (New York, 1947), p. 644.

4. E. M. Halliday, "Hemingway's *In Our Time*," *The Explicator*, 7, No. 35 (1943).

5. George Hemphill, "Hemingway and James," *Ernest Hemingway: The Man and His Work*, ed. John K. M. McCaffery (New York, 1950), pp. 329–39.

6. Philip Young, "Hemingway's *In Our Time*," *The Explicator*, 10, No. 43 (1952).

7. The numbering of chapters throughout this article is that of the 1925 (and subsequent) editions of *In Our Time*. The original 1924 sequence differed from the expanded version in only two instances: "IX" was given second position, and "A Very Short Story" and "The Revolutionist" were placed between "VIII" and "X." James M. Harrison, using internal evidence, identified the speaker or point-of-view character in each vignette ("Hemingway's *In Our Time*," *The Explicator*, 18, No. 51 [1960]). For pertinent facts of Hemingway's biography see Charles A. Fenton, *The Apprenticeship of Ernest Hemingway* (New York, 1954), especially Chapter XI. Fenton claimed that the only chronology of the sketches was the chronology in which they were written. Hemingway's later story-collections are conventional in form (or formlessness)—*Men Without Women* (1927) and *Winner Take Nothing* (1933)—though their respective titles indicate a degree of thematic unity. *To Have and Have Not* (1937) is Hemingway's novel which is most experimental in structure and least successful.

8. Malcolm Cowley, "A Portrait of Mister Papa," *Hemingway*, ed. McCaffery, pp. 34–56.

9. See Keneth Kinnamon's perceptive analysis, "Hemingway, the *Corrida*, and Spain," *Texas Studies in Language and Literature*, 1 (Spring 1959), 44–61.

10. The asterisk indicates that Nick is not the protagonist of the story. The preceding roman numeral is that of the "chapter."

11. Theodore Bardacke, "Hemingway's Women," *Hemingway*, ed. McCaffery, p. 344.

12. Malcolm Cowley's *Exile's Return* (New York, 1951), p. 9.

13. The biography of Nick Adams is supplemented in later stories: "Ten Indians" (1927) (Michigan youth); "The Killers" (1927) and "The Light of the World" (1933) (Wanderjahre); "A Way You'll Never Be" (1933), "Now I Lay Me" (1927), and "In Another Country" (1927) (war wounds); "An Alpine Idyll" (1927) (expatriation); "A Day's Wait" (1933) and "Fathers and Sons" (1933) (fatherhood). In his movie-scenario *Adventures of a Young Man* (1962) Hemingway's friend, A. E. Hotchner, also utilized material from the non-Nick stories "Soldier's Home" and "A Pursuit Race" and attempted to suggest more Adams-Hemingway parallels than there are in the fiction.

14. Melvin Backman, "Hemingway: The Matador and the Crucified," *Modern Fiction Studies*, I (1955), 2–11. Joseph De Falco discusses Hemingway's use of the theme of initiation in *The Hero in*

Hemingway's Short Stories (Pittsburgh, 1963). George Hemphill's general outline of the thematic structure is apt (cf. note 5 above). He found the first half of *In Our Time* concerned with an "enveloping situation," the awareness of the conditions of heroism, the second half concerned with insiders and outsiders, those aware of the "enveloping situation" and those unaware of moral uncertainty and the need for heroic discipline. He designated Chapter V (the execution of the Greek Cabinet) the thematic center which reveals that life, as well as war, is cruel (one of the ministers has typhoid fever).

15. Cf. Hemingway's pivotal story "A Clean Well-Lighted Place." Nick's "good place" has other equivalents in the priest's mountain-home at Abruzzi (*A Farewell to Arms*) and Burguete where Jake and Bill fish (*The Sun Also Rises*).

16. The letter (dated 18 October 1924) is quoted by Edmund Wilson in "Emergence of Ernest Hemingway," *Hemingway and His Critics,* ed. Carlos Baker (New York, 1961), p. 60.

17. Frank O'Connor, *The Lonely Voice: A Study of the Short Story* (Cleveland, 1963), p. 113.

18. *The Gallery*, in turn, is reminiscent of Dos Passos' portrait of an American inferno, *Manhattan Transfer.* After the present article was completed I discovered that Michel Mohrt had already noted the similarity of structure between *The Gallery* and *In Our Time: Le Nouveau Roman American* (Paris, 1955), p. 144.

19. Nine of the stories had been previously published ("Indian Camp," "The Doctor and the Doctor's Wife," "Soldier's Home," "Mr. and Mrs. Elliot," and the last five stories); early versions of some of the chapters had been published in newspapers. For facts of publication see Carlos Baker's checklist in *Hemingway: The Writer as Artist,* 2nd edition (Princeton, 1956), pp. 331–40, and Fenton, *Apprenticeship, passim.* To my knowledge there is no evidence that any other than Hemingway had a hand in planning *In Our Time.*

WHAT'S FUNNY IN *THE SUN ALSO RISES*

JAMES HINKLE

> "Hemingway, why do you always come here drunk?"
> "I don't know, Miss Stein, unless it's to see you."
> (quoted in John Atkins, The Art of Ernest Hemingway)
>
> "Uh, it was a joke then."
> "Yes. To laugh at." (The Sun Also Rises, p. 18)

READERS HAVE COME UP WITH MANY REASONS for admiring *The Sun Also Rises* but no one, so far as I know, has made much of the jokes in the novel. The free-associating banter of Bill Gorton, the fractured English of Count Mippipopolous, occasional sardonic comments by the narrator, Jake Barnes, have of course been noted. But jokes in *The Sun Also Rises*? What jokes? Most readers seem to find the book no funnier than did Harold Loeb, prototype of *The Sun Also Rises*'s humorless Robert Cohn: "I do not remember that Hem was much of a spoofer as a young man. Perhaps he developed a taste for it as age overtook him."[1] The prototype of Bill Gorton, Donald Ogden Stewart, a professional humorist himself, said flatly that "written humor was not his [Hemingway's] dish."[2]

Yet I propose to point to about sixty submerged jokes in *The Sun Also Rises*— if by "jokes" I can be understood to mean all of the various kinds of plays on words whose effect is incongruous or funny once they are recognized. Few of them will make anyone roll in the aisle, but they have their moments. My aim is not to defend Hemingway's sense of humor or to sort his jokes into categories. My aim is simply to identify his jokes—to demonstrate by example that there are many more of them in *The Sun Also Rises* than we have realized. Playing with the multiple meanings inherent in words is a pervasive feature of Hemingway's writing.

Reprinted with permission from *The Hemingway Review*, 4, No. 2 (Spring 1985), 31–41.

Most readers have approached Hemingway with serious expectations, and these expectations have determined pretty much and limited what they have found. But Hemingway always claimed to be at least a part-time humorist. He is consistently unsympathetic to those who looked down on him when he himself "committed levity":

> [L]ots of criticism is written by characters who are very academic and think it is a sign you are worthless if you make jokes or kid or even clown.[3]
>
> The bastards don't want you to joke because it disturbs their categories.[4]
>
> "Joke people and you make enemies. That's what I always say." (*The Sun Also Rises*, p. 58)

Anyone who has read through Hemingway's letters must have been struck by his persistent reliance on humor. Even when he is most serious he often develops his argument in an ironic or flippant or mocking tone. We know from his letters that he thought the first draft of *The Sun Also Rises* was funny. *The Torrents of Spring*, clearly intended as a funny performance, he wrote between finishing the *The Sun Also Rises* first draft and before starting the revision. And in an inscribed copy of the printed *The Sun Also Rises* Hemingway called the novel a "little treatise on promiscuity including a Few Jokes."[5]

I want to present my sixty *The Sun Also Rises* jokes roughly in order of their difficulty, moving from relatively obvious examples to more subtle or ingenious or likely-to-be-overlooked ones. Begin with a simple pun whose effect is mild humor:

> Everything is on such a clear financial basis in France. . . If you want people to like you you have only to spend a little money. I spent a little money and the waiter liked me. He appreciated my valuable qualities. (p. 233)

But that is not a typical *The Sun Also Rises* pun, because it calls attention to itself. Most of Hemingway's puns are less insistent:

> Brett was radiant. . . The sun was out and the day was bright. (p. 207)

That should be a clear example. Here is another:

> for six months I never slept with the electric light off. That was another bright idea. (p. 148)

Sometimes a pun is introduced and then played with:

> The publishers had praised his [Cohn's] novel pretty highly and it rather went to his head. (p. 8)

Where else except up would high praise go? This is followed on the next page by adding "steep" to the pun on "high":

> playing for higher stakes than he could afford in some rather steep bridge
> games. (p. 9)

Another example:

> In the dark I could not see his face very well.
> "Well," I said, "see you in the morning." (p. 195)

That is a variation of:

> There is no reason why because it is dark you should look at things differently
> from when it is light. The hell there isn't! (p. 148)

The narrator, Jake Barnes, is not the only one in the book who is alive to
puns. On the evening Bill Gorton arrives in Paris Jake asks him:

> "What'll we do to-night?"
> "Doesn't make any difference. Only let's not get daunted. Suppose they
> got any hard-boiled eggs here?" (p. 73)

"Hard-boiled" eggs to guard against becoming daunted. The meaning of "hard-
boiled" we already know from Jake:

> It is awfully easy to be hard-boiled about everything in the daytime, but at night
> it is another thing. (p. 34)

Sometimes the pun depends on the reader knowing at least something of a
foreign language. After Cohn and Jake have their first near-fight:

> we walked up to the Café de la Paix and had coffee. (p. 40)

At least one *The Sun Also Rises* pun is based on a catch phrase of the day.
When Jake leaves Cohn at the end of the first chapter he says:

> "I'll see you to-morrow at the courts." (p. 7)

He means the tennis courts, but his sentence is a play on "See you in court."

Sometimes *The Sun Also Rises*'s words make a statement that is literally true
in more ways than the presumably intended one. While the effect of these second
meanings is usually funny, that is not always the case. Consider the scene when
Jake learns from Brett that it was Robert Cohn she had gone to San Sebastian
with:

> "Who did you think I went down to San Sebastian with?"
> "Congratulations," I said . . .
> We walked along and turned a corner. (p. 83)

Their relationship at that moment did indeed turn a corner. Jake can't keep back his bitterness after Brett explains that she rather thought the experience would be good for Cohn:

> "You might take up social service."
> "Don't be nasty." (p. 84)

Shortly after Jake has helped set up Brett with Romero, Cohn comes looking for her:

> "Where's Brett?" he asked.
> "I don't know."
> "She was with you."
> "She must have gone to bed." (p. 190)

Yes, that is exactly where she is—in bed, with Romero.

When Brett and Jake approach the Café Select after reaching a romantic impasse in a Paris cab:

> On the Boulevard Raspail, with the lights of Montparnasse in sight, Brett said:
> "Would you mind very much if I asked you to do something?"
>   "Don't be silly."
>   "Kiss me just once more before we get there."
>   When the taxi stopped I got out and paid. (pp. 27–28)

That last is quite a line. Literally it means that Jake gives the taxi driver five or ten francs. But it also means that Jake has an emotional price to pay for his hour in the cab close to Brett. He leaves the Select shortly afterward, walks to his apartment alone, thinks of his wound and of Brett, and then cries himself to sleep.

Mike sees that Brett has a new hat:

> "Where did you get that hat?"
> "Chap bought it for me. Don't you like it?" (p. 79)

Doesn't he like what? The hat or the idea that a man bought it for her? The first is probably what Brett intended but the second has more meaning for the novel.

Brett makes a remark to Romero that the reader can (and probably should) take in more than one way:

> "The bulls are my best friends. . . "
> "You kill your friends?" she asked.
> "Always," he said in English, and laughed. "So they don't kill me." He looked at her across the table.
> "You know English well." (p. 186)

There are three meanings in Brett's last comment: first, she could be simply complimenting Romero on his ability to speak English; second, she could be saying that his sure manner, his way of looking at her, show that he knows very well how to make himself attractive to a English lady; third, and more ominous she could be saying that he knows English people very well if he realizes that English friends could kill him. This last meaning is supported by several other passages: Mike says it was his friends, false friends, that did him in. Montoya says about Romero: "Any foreigner can flatter him. They start this Grand Hotel business, and in one year they're through" (p. 172). Jake has already told us that "any foreigner was an Englishman" (p. 31), and Brett says in Madrid after she had sent Romero away, "I'd have lived with him if I hadn't seen it was bad for him" (p. 243), and she hopes it is true when she says "I don't think I hurt him any" (p. 241).

Religion is put in its place by one brief comment:

> That afternoon was the big religious procession. San Fermim was translated from one church to another. . .
> "Isn't that the procession?" Mike asked.
> "Nada," some one said. "It's nothing." (pp. 155, 158)

Jake goes to confession several times in Pamplona. Brett would like to go with him but Jake tells her:

> not only was it impossible but it was not as interesting as it sounded, and, besides, it would be in a language she did not know. (p. 151)

Jake's minor joke here is that his confession would not be likely to interest Brett because he does not have any sexual items to report. A more significant meaning concerns the language Brett would not understand. Confessions in a Spanish church would be in Spanish. But in the following sentence we learn that Brett has her fortune told at a gypsy camp, and that too would be in Spanish, and there is no mention then of her not being able to understand what was said. Nor does she have any trouble understanding and being understood by Romero, or the other Spanish men who use her as an image to dance around or to sing to in their hard Spanish voices. The point seems to be that it is the language of the church that Brett doesn't know and it makes no difference whether one takes that to be Spanish or Latin. As she says herself, "I'm damn bad for a religious atmosphere. I've the wrong type of face" (p. 208).

At the end of the book Brett suggests that the satisfaction resulting from decent behavior might substitute for the consolation of religion. Jake is not so sure, so he gently proposes a pain-killer more in line with her temperament:

> "You know it makes one feel rather good deciding not to be a bitch. . .
> It's sort of what we have instead of God."

"Some people have God," I said. "Quite a lot."
"He never worked very well with me."
"Should we have another Martini?" (p. 245)

Mike obviously has reached the same conclusion concerning Brett:

"These bull fights are hell on one." Brett said. "I'm limp as a rag."
"Oh, you'll get a drink," Mike said. (p. 169)

The most frequent kind of joke in *The Sun Also Rises* is the peculiarly literal one that results when someone (the narrator or one of the other characters) understands (or pretends to understand) a word in a different sense (usually a more literal one) than might reasonably have been expected. This pattern is easier illustrated than described. "The Snows of Kilimanjaro" has a pure example:

"I don't see why that had to happen to your leg. What have we done to have that happen to us?"
"I suppose what I did was to forget to put iodine on it when I first scratched it. Then I didn't pay any attention to it because I never infect. Then, later, when it got bad, it was probably using that weak carbolic solution when the other antiseptics ran out that paralyzed the minute blood vessels and started the gangrene." He looked at her, "What else?"
"I don't mean that." (SS, p. 55)

Frank O'Connor tells a story of an evening when he was James Joyce's guest:

[I] touched the frame of a picture on the wall.
"What's this?"
"Cork."
"Yes, I see it's Cork. I was born there. But what's the frame?"
"Cork."
Some time later, in conversation with Yeats, [I] told him about the picture and its frame. Yeats sat up straight.
"That is mania. That is insanity."[6]

Mania it may be, but it is also funny.

Words deliberately taken as words are the basis of much of the humor in *The Sun Also Rises*. The simplest form of this basic joke in *The Sun Also Rises* can be seen when Jake tries to get by difficult moments with Brett by responding literally to her words rather than to their intended meaning:

"Don't look like that, darling."
"How do you want me to look?" (p. 56)

"What did you say that for?"
"I don't know. What would you like me to say?" (p. 83)

>"Darling, don't let's talk a lot of rot."
>"All right. Talk about anything you like." (p. 181)

>"I was in school in Paris, then. Think of that."
>"Anything you want me to think about it?" (p. 244)

Sometimes the literal joke is buried in a seemingly innocent remark. After Cohn knocks Jake out, Jake reluctantly goes to Cohn's room and finds Cohn feeling sorry for himself:

>"Now everything's gone. Everything."
>"Well," I said, "so long. I've got to go." (pp. 194–95)

and:

>"You were the only friend I had. . . ."
>"Well," I said, "so long." (p. 194)

One time Cohn drops by Jake's Paris office and wants to talk. When it becomes apparent Cohn isn't going to leave, Jake invites him downstairs for a drink:

>"Aren't you working?"
>"No," I said. (p. 11)

Literally that is a accurate response. Jake isn't working; he is at the moment talking with Cohn. But he wants to work and is maneuvering to get rid of Cohn so he can get back to work.

"Hell" is the subject of several instances of unexpected literalness. In one, Jake has just told Cohn that Brett is a drunk and is going to marry Mike Campbell:

>"I don't believe it.". . .
>"You asked me what I knew about Brett Ashley."
>"I didn't ask you to insult her."
>"Oh, go to hell."
>He stood up from the table his face white, and stood where white and angry behind the little plates of hors d'oeuvres.
>"Sit down," I said. "Don't be a fool."
>"You've got to take that back."
>"Oh, cut out the prep-school stuff."
>"Take it back."
>"Sure. Anything. I never heard of Brett Ashley. How's that?"
>"No. Not that. About me going to hell."
>"Oh, don't go to hell," I said. "Stick around. We're just starting lunch."
>(p. 39)

Jake suggests the crowded condition of hell when he is talking with Cohn about going to South America:

> "Well, why don't you start off?"
> "Frances."
> "Well," I said, "take her with you."
> "She wouldn't like it. That isn't the sort of thing she likes. She likes a lot of people around."
> "Tell her to go to hell." (pp. 37–38)

An interesting use of hell occurs after Jake has helped set up Brett with Romero and then Cohn comes looking for her:

> "Tell me where Brett is."
> "I'll not tell you a damn thing."
> "You know where she is."
> "If I did I wouldn't tell you."
> "Oh, go to hell, Cohn," Mike called from the table. "Brett's gone off with the bull-fighter chap. They're on their honeymoon."
> "You shut up."
> "Oh go to hell!" Mike said languidly.
> "Is that where she is?" Cohn turned to me.
> "Go to hell!"
> "She was with you. Is that where she is?"
> "Go to hell!" (p. 190)

It is hard to say whether Cohn's "Is that where she is?" refers primarily to "honeymoon" or "hell"—if the two are not indeed the same thing, for when Jake gets to Madrid to rescue Brett from her "honeymoon" she reports: "I've had such a hell of a time" (p. 241), and earlier she had said about being in love: "I think it's hell on earth" (p. 27).

Sometimes someone (usually Jake) deliberately and perversely misunderstands what is said to him:

> "Would you like to go to South America, Jake?"
> "No."
> "Why not?"
> "I don't know. . . . You can see all the South Americans you want in Paris anyway."
> "They're not the real South Americans."
> "They look awfully real to me." (p. 9)

Sometimes Jake deliberately misunderstands but doesn't expect his off-center response to be picked up. Romero is asking about Mike:

> "What does the drunken one do?"
> "Nothing."
> "Is that why he drinks?"
> "No. He's waiting to marry this lady." (p. 176)

Sometimes someone misunderstands unintentionally:

> "You never come here any more, Monsieur Barnes," Madame Lecomte said.
> "Too many compatriots."
> "Come at lunch-time. It's not crowded then." (p. 76)

Jake's objection, of course, is not to the number of customers at the restaurant but to the fact that most of them are American tourists.

Sometimes the twisting of meaning is intended by the speaker to be recognized as a joke. Mike tries it:

> "How did you go bankrupt?" Bill asked.
> "Two ways," Mike said. "Gradually and then suddenly." (p. 136)

and Brett:

> "Here come the gentry," Bill said.
> They were crossing the street. . . .
> "Hello, gents!" said Bill. (p. 165)

and Bill:

> "Well " I said, "the saloon must go."
> "You're right there, old classmate," Bill said. "The saloon must go and I will take it with me." (p. 123)

and Jake:

> I found Bill up in his room. He was shaving. . . .
> "How did you happen to know this fellow, anyway?"
> "Don't rub it in."
> Bill looked around, half-shaved, and then went on talking into the mirror while he lathered his face. (p. 101)

It would be easy to read right over that passage without realizing that Jake has made a small joke with "Don't rub it in" and that Bill, by interrupting his lathering and turning around, acknowledges that he understands it.

Sometimes the joke is in a seemingly innocent throwaway line that goes along with a conversation :

> "I can't stand it any more."
> He lay there on the bed. (p. 195)
> "All my life I've wanted to go on a trip like that." Cohn said. He sat down. . . "But I can't get started." (p. 10)

> "Don't just sit there. . . Don't sit there looking like a bloody funeral." . . .
> "Shut up," Cohn said. He stood up. (pp. 141–42)

> "I'm just low, and when I'm low I talk like a fool."
> I sat up, leaned over, found my shoes beside the bed and put them on. I stood up. (p. 56)

This last example tells us quite a bit about Jake. Only to a person with an enormous regard for words would it ever occur to think of standing up as a remedy for feeling low.

Sometimes words trigger a bizarre train of thought. A waiter asks:

> "Shrimps?"
> "Is Cohn gone?" Brett asked. (p. 206)

Sometimes an expression is acted out:

> "Ask her if she's got any jam," Bill said. "Be ironical with her."
> "Have you got any jam?"
> "That's not ironical". . .
> The girl brought in a glass dish of raspberry jam. . .
> "Poor," said Bill. "Very poor. You can't do it." (p. 114)

Bill and the waitress in different ways give Jake the raspberry.

Brett comes to Jake's room and wakes him up at half-past four in the morning. Jake makes drinks and listens while Brett talks on about her evening with Count Mippipopolous: "Offered me ten thousand dollars to go to Biarritz with him. . . Told him I knew too many people in Biarritz." Brett laughs but Jake doesn't.

> "I say, you are slow on the up-take," she said. I had only sipped my brandy and soda. I took a long drink.
> "That's better. Very funny." (p. 33)

Jake's taking a long drink is not simply a clever response to Brett's saying he is "slow on the uptake." It is also his way of indicating he had understood when Brett on the previous page by taking a drink had acted out one meaning for "one of us":

> "The count? Oh, rather. He's quite one of us."
> "Is he a count?"
> "Here's how.". . . She sipped at her glass. (p. 32)

Occasionally a passage needs to be read aloud for us to realize what is funny. Brett first appears in the book at a bal musette with a group of flamboyant male homosexuals. We recognize them by how they talk when they see Georgette:

> "I do declare. There is an actual harlot. I'm going to dance with her, Lett. You watch me.
> The tall dark one, called Lett, said: "Don't you be rash."
> The wavy blond one answered: "Don't you worry, dear." And with them was Brett. (p. 20)

Hemingway and Jake do not care for homosexuals. Jake was away. When he returns to the bal Mrs. Braddocks brings up a young man and introduces him as Robert Prentiss. If we continue reading aloud we discover that Prentiss too must have been part of Brett's entourage:

He was from New York by way of Chicago, and was a rising new novelist. He had some sort of an English accent. I asked him to have a drink.
> "Thanks so much," he said. "I've just had one."
> "Have another."
> "Thanks, I will then.". . . "You're from Kansas City, they tell me," he said.
> "Yes."
> "Do you find Paris amusing?"
> "Yes."
> "Really?". . .
> "For God's sake," I said, "yes. Don't you?"
> "Oh, how charmingly you get angry," he said. "I wish I had that faculty."
> (p. 21)

When Jake hears that last speech, he gets up and walks away again. Mrs. Braddocks follows:

> "Don't be cross with Robert," she said. "He's still only a child, you know."
> "I wasn't cross," I said. "I just thought perhaps I was going to throw up."
> (p. 21).

Robert Cohn wants to be a writer, but listen to his first words in the book:

> "For God's sake, why did you say that about that girl in Strasbourg for?"
> (p. 6)

Can anyone who can say a sentence like that ever become a decent writer?

Sometimes in order to see what is funny the reader has to do more than read aloud: he has to follow up on implied instructions. Consider this passage taken from Jake's and Bill's first morning at Burguete:

> As I went down-stairs I heard Bill singing, "Irony and Pity. When you're feeling. . . Oh, Give them Irony and Give them Pity. Oh, give them Irony. When they're feeling. . . Just a little irony. Just a little pity. . ." He kept on singing until he came down-stairs. The tune was: "The Bells are Ringing for Me and My Gal." (p. 114)

There is nothing funny here when we simply read the words, although we do quickly figure out what the rhyme word for "pity" is—the word that caused Maxwell Perkins to insist on three spaced periods.[7] But see what happens if we try to sing Bill's words to the tune of "For Me and My Gal." We discover there is no way Bill's words can be made to fit that tune. This tells us that Bill must be splendidly rhythm-deaf, and this leads us to understand funny meanings for several other passages—when the Spaniard beats time on Bill's back while trying to teach him a song and Jake comments that Bill "wasn't getting it," and what it must have sounded like when Bill plays the piano to keep warm at the inn at Burguete. As the old advertising slogan put it: "They laughed when I sat down at the piano, but then I started to play. . . "

Some of Hemingway's jokes are like syllogisms with the middle term unstated and which the reader must use his ingenuity to supply. Jake takes the train at Irun and "after forty minutes and eight tunnels I was at San Sebastian." Surely "forty" and "eight" are meant to suggest the wartime 40 and 8 military transport cars (40 hommes/8 chevaux) and represent Jake's comment on the primitive Spanish rail accommodations of the 1920s. This has to be Hemingway's purpose in the passage, for the manuscript of *The Sun Also Rises* shows "forty minutes and six tunnels" and Hemingway later changed it to 40 and 8.[8]

One of Hemingway's funniest and most obscure jokes is in Bill's comment about Robert Cohn's telegram to Burguete:

> The telegram was in Spanish: "Vengo Jueves Cohn."
> I handed it to Bill.
> "What does the word Cohn mean?" he asked. (p. 127)

Bill is just learning Spanish. Among the first phrases one picks up in any language (after "yes," "no," "where is," and "how much") is "I come." So Bill presumably has gotten far enough in Spanish to understand "Vengo." But "Jueves" (Spanish for "Thursday") he apparently hasn't learned yet and the appearance of the word gives him no help. "Jueves" is J-U-E-V-E-S. What does that look like or suggest to a America who doesn't know Spanish? Jew. And thus Bill's comment: Why add Cohn? His point is that the message already says "I come, Jew." What other Jews does Cohn think we might be expecting?—This joke is no doubt objectionable in the 1980s but in the 1920s it was one of the ways the game was played.

We recognize Mike's less than rigorous thinking when he says:

> "I gave Brett what for, you know. I add if she would go about with Jews and bullfighters and such people, she must expect trouble." (p. 203)

Jews and bullfighters and such people? What kind of category is that? I suppose he means people who are not "one of us," but it would be hard to imagine a more vague way of defining that group.

When Jake takes the prostitute Georgette to join his literary friends for coffee after dinner, he introduces her as his "fiancée, Mademoiselle Georgette Leblanc." This is Jake's attempt at a mild joke. The girl is obviously a prostitute, his friends know he has no fiancée, and Georgette Leblanc was the name of a well-known real person—the ex-mistress of Maeterlinck, an actress, singer, and past-middle-aged eccentric who regularly bicycled around Paris in a flowing medieval robe of gold-flowered velvet. The men at the table go along with Jake's joke and all stand up. But Mrs. Braddocks, "a Canadian [with] all their easy social graces" (Hemingway didn't think much of Canada and Canadians), understands nothing of what is happening. She takes Jake's introduction seriously and talks "cordially" with Georgette. When it finally gets through to her that Jake's introduction is not entirely accurate, she calls down the table to her husband to report what she considers an amusing discrepancy: "Did you hear that, Henry? Mr. Barnes introduced his fiancée as Mademoiselle Leblanc, and her name is actually Hobin." At which point Braddocks makes his joke—for the benefit of the others at the table. Proud of his innocent wife and secure in knowing she will not see anything amiss in his saying he knows a prostitute, he says: "Of course, darling. Mademoiselle Hobin. I've known her for a very long time" (p. 18).

Brett's jokes are usually more worldly. Count Mippipopolous drives to the far side of Paris to bring back a basket of champagne for Brett and Jake:

> "I think you'll find that's very good wine," he add. "I know we don't get much of a chance to judge good wine in the States now, but I got this from a friend of mine that's in the business."
> "Oh, you always have some one in the trade," Brett said.
> "This fellow raises the grapes. He's got thousands of acres of them."
> "What's his name?" asked Brett. "Veuve Cliquot?"

"No," said the count. "Mumms. He's a baron." (pp. 56–57)

There are two jokes here—one intended by Brett and a second possible only for Jake and Hemingway. Brett knows the count is interested in women, since he had already offered her ten thousand dollars to go with him to Biarritz or Cannes or Monte Carlo. So when he says he has a friend in the champagne business Brett adds up what she knows and makes her joke: "What's his name? Veuve Cli-quot?" Her guess has a kind of oblique logic, since "Veuve Clicquot" is the name of one of France's four great champagnes. Her point is that "Veuve Clic-quot" *means* something in French that seems to her to fit the situation—"the widow Clicquot." In fact Veuve Clicquot champagne is called in British slang "the merry widow." Thus, if the count says he knows a champagne grower, Brett is suggesting it would probably be the merry widow. Hemingway's joke is that Brett simply picked the wrong brand. The count actually *does* know one of the great French champagne producers—Baron Mumm.

Earlier in the book Brett makes a joke that Hemingway specifically identi-fies as joke, but readers seem not to have bothered to try to make sense of it. Jake and Brett are sitting in a taxi at night, moodily discussing how Jake's wound has made impossible what might have been a satisfying relationship. Brett says:

"When I think of the hell I've put chaps through. I'm paying for it all now."
"Don't talk like a fool," I said. "Besides, what happened to me is sup-posed to be funny. I never think about it."
"Oh, no. I'll lay you don't."
"Well, let's shut up about it."
"I laughed about it too, myself, once. A friend of my brother's came home that way from Mons. It seemed like a hell of a joke. Chaps never know anything, do they?" (pp. 26–27)

What seemed like a hell of a joke? Answer: Not just to be wounded in the groin but to be wounded in the groin at Mons. Mons was, of course, a major battlefield of World War I, but "mons" is also the "mons veneris" which, as anyone who has had a high school course in sex education knows, is the polite term for a woman's pubic mound. For a man to have an encounter at "mons" and come away with damaged sexual apparatus does indeed act out the ancient female threat of "vagina dentata"—vagina with teeth. As Brett says, "It seemed like a hell of a joke."

Mike shouts drunkenly to Jake: "Tell him [Romero] Brett is dying to know how he can get into those pants." "Pipe down," someone says. Yes, pipe down. If Joyce in *Ulysses* can make a joke out of "U-P up," Hemingway in *The Sun Also*

Rises can explain to anyone who doesn't already know that bullfighters fit into their tight pants "pipe down" (p. 176).

Near the beginning of the book Jake watches a red and green stop-and-go traffic signal. At the end he sees a traffic policeman raise his baton, forcing the cab Jake is riding in with Brett to a sudden halt. Between these two scenes we find a number of references to people waving things—the drummer waving his drumsticks, Bill waving a chicken drumstick, Marshal Ney waving his sword, "the inventor of the semaphore engaged in doing same." All seem to prepare us for the policeman's raised baton of the final page. It would be hard to imagine a more explicit symbolic acting out of a reminder of the reason Jake cannot satisfy Brett.

I am not the first, of course, to have noticed the sexual overtones of the policeman's raised baton, but I am not aware that anyone has spelled out how the details of the scene work. The baton is a twelve-inch white club. When not being used—when it is at rest—it dangles from the policeman's waist. The policeman is a "mounted" policeman. "Mounted" is itself a sexual word. Presumably here it means that he is riding a horse—[9] thus in the saddle, an easy rider—and this takes us back to Bill's "puts a man on her horse" which is in turn based on "puts lead in your pencil." The policeman is wearing khaki. That suggests a military uniform and is a reminder of the reason Jake cannot now go ahead. But khaki (rhymes with "tacky") is a relatively recent and specifically American pronunciation. In the 1920s in Europe it was "cock-ee" which has an unavoidable sexual suggestion. Add to this that a few minutes earlier Jake had trouble entering Brett's hotel because he could not make "the elevator" work,[10] and then he was told that the personages of her establishment were "rigidly selected." The policeman's raised baton forces Jake to confront the fact that he will never qualify for admission to Brett, since "making the elevator work" and a selection process involving "rigid" represent for him impossible requirements.

Jake's jokes (and thus Hemingway's in *The Sun Also Rises*) are all in the ironic mode—variations on Bill's "Give them Irony and Give them Pity." Surely, taken together, and at the very least, the jokes represent one possible and reasonably effective defensive stance for someone who has been wounded in a rotten way on a joke front—which, less literally, seems to have been the situation of almost all young men and women of feeling after World War I.

1. Bertram D. Sarason, *Hemingway and the Sun Set* (Washington, D.C.: NCR, 1972), p. 115.

2. Donald Ogden Stewart, "Recollections of Fitzgerald and Hemingway," *Fitzgerald/Hemingway Annual, 1971*, p. 184.

3. Carlos Baker, *Ernest Hemingway: Selected Letters, 1917–1961* (New York: Scribner's, 1981), p. 767.

4. Letter from Hemingway to Arnold Gingrich, 3 April 1933, in the substantial private Hemingway collection of Maurice Neville, Santa Barbara, California. Quoted with the kind permission of Mr. Neville.

5. Matthew J. Bruccoli and C. E. Fraser Clark, Jr., *Hemingway at Auction 1930–1973* (Detroit: Bruccoli-Clark, 1973), p. 42.

6. L. A. G. Strong, *The Sacred River: An Approach to James Joyce* (New York: Pellegrini and Cudahay, 1951), pp. 144–45.

7. At no time—not in manuscript nor in typescript—had Hemingway written "shitty." He used long dashes instead. Perkins insisted the dashes could not stand, but why he thought the three spaced periods he substituted would be less offensive is hard to understand.

8. In 1950 I took the train from Irun to San Sebastian to see how many tunnels there were then. Six or eight or even twenty could be an accurate count, depending on what one wants to consider a tunnel. The roadbed ran through cliffs along the shore and there were many semi-tunnels of twenty-or-so feet which could or could not be counted. The present train route from Irun to San Sebastian is farther inland and has almost no tunnels.

9. Both the French and Spanish translations of *The Sun Also Rises* take "mounted" to mean mounted on a horse. Because that meaning may be right and because it fits the argument of my paragraph, I go along with it here. Really, however, I suspect "mounted" means standing on a raised platform in the center of the intersection. That would have been a better position from which to direct traffic and it corresponds to 1950s Madrid practice and to 1920s photos of at least Paris traffic policemen.

10. Jake tells us he was wounded while flying on the Italian front. The "elevator" was the name for the control on World War I planes that made them climb and kept them from plunging. Perhaps the reason Jake is forever unavailable to Brett is that also on an earlier day in 1917 or 1918 he could not make the elevator work.

"AN IMAGE TO DANCE AROUND":
BRETT AND HER LOVERS
IN *THE SUN ALSO RISES*

SAM S. BASKETT

IN AN EARLY RECOGNITION OF HEMINGWAY'S "literary" and "historical" accomplishment, John Peale Bishop observed in an essay taking its title from Emily Dickinson's "The Missing All." "It is the mark of the true novelist that in searching the meaning of his unsought experience, he comes on the moral history of his time."[1] Hemingway studies over the years have further secured this recognition, particularly for *The Sun Also Rises.* Given what has become the critical consensus that this first novel somehow expresses the way it was in Hemingway's early time, there has been surprising disagreement about just what is revealed by the distinctly different experiences of Jake Barnes, Pedro Romero, Robert Cohn and Bill Gorton, each of whom has received consideration as the moral center of a work that has also often been read as having no moral center. These contradictory readings have not been easy to reconcile, supported as they largely are by seemingly convincing evidence. Yet the counterpointed experiences of the novel's principal characters do resolve into a clearly discernible moral pattern if they are brought into sharp "literary" and "historical" focus, a pattern that in part constructs the time's moral history as well as embodies it.

This is to say that the several lovers of Lady Brett Ashley fix upon her as an uncertain image of great value: to paraphrase the Lady herself, she is sort of what they have instead of God. To their image of her they make such overtures as the time and their individual capacities permit, overtures recalling the question Frost's oven bird "frames in all but words / . . . what to make of a diminished thing": for the value each affixed to Brett is a function of his value of himself and the life he is able to live. From these combined self-definitions emerges the "meaning" of the

Reprinted with permission from *The Centennial Review*, 22 (Winter 1978), 45–69.

novel, the significance of which is most fully realized in the context of the patterns of a number of other authentic American "fictions" of the early twentieth century.

Most radically, the pattern of the twentieth century has been sought by Henry Adams. Adams had been delighted to discover that Lucretius "In perhaps the finest [lines] in all Latin literature. . . [had] invoked Venus exactly as Dante invoked the Virgin"—as one who governed the nature of things.[2]

Turning to the twentieth century, however, he found that Woman as Force had been replaced by the dynamo. In the consummate poem which now seems to epitomize the emerging "modern" era, T. S. Eliot's Prufrock describes a circumstance of chaos counterpointed by his desire for a center of meaning symbolized by the attracting power of woman. Thus, a central autobiography and a central poem of the time Hemingway inherited present a compelling version of the same image which dominates *The Sun Also Rises*. That image is also dominant in the novel which impressed Hemingway as an "absolutely first rate work"[3] in May, 1925, two months before he began his own novel. In *The Great Gatsby*, he found a situation similar to the one he would employ, that of a woman idealized far beyond her "perishable"[4] features controlling the world of her "high-bouncing lover" of the epigraph. In her depletion, Lady Brett Ashley, of course, is more akin to Daisy Fay, as she is finally realized, than either to Adams's or Eliot's "one." How well both seemed to illustrate the extremity of the new age is apparent in Joseph Wood Krutch's *The Modern Temper*, published in 1929. The chapter "Love—or the Life and Death of a Value" describes a generation attributing to love "some of the functions of the God they had lost," although inexorably rationalism and physiology were stripping it of its "mystical penumbra."[5] Krutch thus points to a major transformation in the treatment of Woman by Fitzgerald and Hemingway as opposed to that of Adams and Eliot. For both the historian and the poet, at least in *The Education* and "Prufrock," are primarily concerned with Woman as symbolic of highest value, even if that symbol now seemed superseded or inaccessible. The two novelists, however, in a "time of troubles," were not only concerned with what R. P. Blackmur termed "a kind of irregular and spasmodic, but vitalized metaphysics," but also with "a broad and irregular psychology."[6] Daisy is elevated to the role of goddess in Gatsby's romping mind, but she continues to exist, and ultimately *only* exists on a human psychological plane. In the presentation of several "visions" of Lady Brett Ashley, however, Hemingway was to hold in more ambiguous, if precarious, balance the perishable and transcendent, as a complex parade of lovers offer her their varied services in keeping with such value as love retains in their scheme of things.

Brett's complicated characterization is enigmatically voiced in both French and English by Jake's concierge: "that lady, that lady there is some one. An eccentric, perhaps, but quelqu'une, quelqu'une."[7] Assuredly, Brett is "some one," in more than one language. As a type of the new woman of the 1920's, she radiates independence, intelligence and beauty. She sees through "rot," sharing with Jake a more profound appreciation of the "modern temper" than that of the other characters. Her appearance reflects the new idea of beauty, her short hair "brushed back like a boy's"—indeed, Jake claims proudly, "she started all that." In a striking image that suggests both her femininity and her impersonality, she is described as being "built with curves like the hull of a racing yacht, and you missed none of it with that wool jersey" (p. 22). Apparently her own woman, in only a few weeks she engages sexually with at least two men in addition to her fiancé. Under the gaiety of Mike's quip that their hotel is a brothel is the serious theme of Brett's debasement of sex. Half asleep, Jake can confuse her voice with that of Georgette, the *poule* he takes to dinner.

Yet in her feminine attractiveness, debased or otherwise, Brett remains essentially unfathomable, somehow apart, as Jake states expressly. She has a way of looking "that made you wonder whether she really saw out of her own eyes. They would look on and on after every one else's eyes in the world would have stopped looking." This is surely extraordinary seeing, both in relation to Brett and in relation to Jake as he sees Brett seeing. Jake immediately adds the ordinary, human dimension, however, appearing to recognize that the powers he attributes to her are illusory: "She looked as though there were nothing on earth she would not look at like that, and really she was afraid of so many things" (p. 26). But Brett, even when she is most "afraid," at least until the final scenes, is principally a contained figure to whom her suitors react, rather than a human being whose motives are susceptible to psychological analysis. Brett's "mystical penumbra" is greatly intensified by a number of suggestions that she is more than "just personal," even to Jake, "my own true love. . . [my only] friend in the world" (pp. 55, 58). In a passage of over one hundred words excised from the manuscript, Jake makes this dimension of their "own true love" even more explicit in an aside to his reader, disclaiming any psychological understanding of Brett or of his unbelievable passion for this person who determines his world. Perhaps Hemingway felt that enough evidence of Brett's strangeness remained in the novel, for there are many motifs suggesting her uniqueness, even apart from her magnification by her different lovers. For example, ironically enough, her promiscuity, which seems almost maternal, never casually salacious. She rejects the count's offer of high-priced prostitution, even though she finds him entertaining and she always needs money; she is "looking after" (p. 203) Mike; she goes with Cohn because she thought it would "be good for him" (p. 83); she sends Romero away not to be "one of these bitches that ruins children. . . . It's sort of what we have instead of God" (pp. 243–45); and, as Chaman Nahal has convincingly argued, on one occasion, in a passage exquisitely handled by Hemingway, she affords Jake some sort of sexual gratification so that he will "feel better" (p. 55).[8] In some of these instances she acts for reasons not fully specifiable, at least as the data is given in the novel, but surely her motives go beyond simple self-gratification on any level, motives somehow related to the symbolic beauty of one who "started all that."

In another persistent motif, Brett seems to seek absolution for her actions through her compulsion to bathe, a persistence that expresses a desire for purification transcending cleanliness. But Brett's extraordinary dualities are most directly suggested in Pamplona, where on one occasion she walks through the crowd, "her head up, as though the fiesta were being staged in her honor" (p. 206). Earlier, on the afternoon of "the big religious Procession" when "San Fermin was *translated* from one church to another,"[9] Brett is stopped inside the church because she is hatless. Clearly she is the wrong image for the church, too much a disheveled Venus to be allowed in the presence of the Virgin. Even appropriately attired, "I'm damned bad for a religious atmosphere. . . . I've got the wrong type of face" (p. 208). Outside, however, in the street that runs

> from the chapel into town. . . lined on both sides with people keeping their place. . . for the return of the procession. . . dancers formed a circle around Brett and started to dance. . . . They took Bill and me by the arms and put us in the circle. Bill started to dance, too. They were all chanting. Brett wanted to dance but they did not want her to. *They wanted her as an image to dance around*." (p. 155, italics added)

The interpretation is Jake's, of course, but Brett's actions here, as throughout much of the novel, indicate that, try as she will to be merely a dancer, she possesses an aspect, however "wrong," that causes her to be an image "translated" from one sort of "church" to another—the otherwise empty space between the "chapel" and "town" around which a number of people dance in the absence of the return of "the big religious procession."

Six men in *The Sun Also Rises* offer Brett such love as they have: Bill Gorton, Count Mippipopolous, Mike Campbell, Pedro Romero, Robert Cohn and Jake Barnes. The first three listed are without illusions, governed as they are not by an ideal but by the nature of things in naturalistic versions of the formula Adams had learned from Lucretius and Dante. To them, there is no supreme value and Brett, far from incarnating such an ideal, is a sexually tantalizing woman whom each in his own way wants to possess. It is easy to overlook the fact that at first Bill is much taken by her. Appreciative of the "Beautiful lady. . . .

Going to kidnap us" before he has even met her, he responds to her spirited, openly flirtatious manner with a wittily veiled allusion to fornication[10] and a promise to join her later. In only a few minutes, he has decided she is "Quite a girl" (pp. 74–76), but on learning of her engagement to Mike he backs away, and there are no more charged exchanges, even rarely any conversation, between them. His immediate and total withdrawal expresses both his attitude toward Brett and his general approach to life. It is revealing that his friend Edna wishes that Bill had been present when Cohn fights Jake and Mike. "I'd like to have seen Bill knocked down, too. I've always wanted to see Bill knocked down. He's so big" (p. 191). Through the ironic code he tries to teach Jake, Bill remains "big" by limiting his risks, with Brett or anyone else. Having casually noticed the "Beautiful lady," he as casually dismisses her from his concern, despite an encouragement that would have fulfilled Cohn's greatest dreams, when he realizes love for her would not be an uncomplicated "exchange of values" (p. 72). And so he continues loveless, a quality apparent even in his relation with Jake, the person he is "fonder of. . . than anybody on earth." Ultimately, they don't really speak the same language. "You don't understand irony" (pp. 114, 116), he jeers at Jake jokingly, whereas Bill, entertaining, charming friend though he may be, lives through irony.

The count explains to Jake and Brett the "secret" of his enjoyment of life: "You must get to know the values." Having established his scheme in terms of what he can buy, he buys—champagne from his friend Baron Mumms, gourmet meals, a "houseful" of antiquities, eighteen-eleven brandy, ladies with "class." Later, praying to "make a lot of money" (p. 97), Jake is reminded of the count. When Brett amusedly queries whether love has any place in his values,—a question in itself emphasizing her role in the novel—he responds that he is always in love. "That, too, has got a place in my values." Brett retorts, "You're dead," for she well understands that place: ten thousand dollars if she will go to Biarritz with him. To the count—who never "joke[s] people. Joke people and you make enemies" (pp. 58–62)—love is obviously a serious business; it is either purchasable or not. With his love, as with his wine, the count does not intend "to mix emotions up" lest he will "lose the taste." Despite his impressive wounds, the count is hardly the hero much critical commentary has made of him.

Like Bill and the count, Mike sets a high value on his fiancée's sexual attractiveness: she, to him, is "a lovely piece." His emotions, of course, are involved to an extent precluded by Bill's irony and the count's accountant practicality, but they arise from his need for a mutual dependence, rather than any commitment to ideal worth. As Mike writes to Jake, "I know her so well and try to look after her but it's not so easy" (p. 126). Nor is it easy for Brett to look after Mike, in his view the original basis of their relation: "she loves looking after people. That's how we came to go off together. She was looking after me" (p. 203). At the end, although she cannot bring herself to marry him, she plans to go back to Mike, and they doubtless will live in a brothel of sorts, alcohol and good-natured carelessness Mike's only defense against their mutual inadequacies in "looking after" each other.

Bill, the count and Mike remain unchanged by their "love" for Brett. Cohn, on the other hand, is vulnerable to passion and transformed by it. Boyishly cheerful, "he had been moulded by the two women who had trained him." His present "lady"—so designated four times in one page by Jake—had taken him in hand: "Cohn never had a chance of not being taken in hand. And he was sure he loved her" (p. 5). "[L]ed. . . quite a life" (p. 7) by this demanding mistress, he is also the servant of a romantic imagination, stimulated by his reading of "splendid imaginary amorous adventures. . . in an intensely romantic land"—as a guidebook to what life holds in Jake's appraisal, "about as safe as it would be. . . to enter Wall Street direct from a French convent, equipped with a complete set of the more practical Alger books" (p. 9). In this unique figure facetiously suggesting an "exchange" of financial and religious values, Jake dramatically presents Cohn's danger, and his own as I will consider presently. It is a danger arising from utter commitment to a supreme value, all the more dangerous because so immaturely conceived,[11] as opposed to the relative safety of the other "lovers" just discussed who contemplate a more or less "[s]imple exchange of values" (p. 72) for the fulfillment of their different ideas of satisfaction.

Cohn is thus by temperament recklessly ready for "amorous adventures" of greater intensity than that afforded by his liaison with Frances, who, even though she is unaware of Brett, describes what Cohn is looking for.

> I know the real reason Robert won't marry me. . . . It's just come to me. They've sent it to me in a vision in the Cafe Select. Isn't it mystic? Some day they'll put a tablet up. Like at Lourdes. . . . Why, you see, Robert's always wanted to have a mistress. . . . And if he marries me. . . that would be the end of all the romance. (p. 51)

The "mystic" vision, recalling Adams's allusion to the power of belief in a divine mistress revealed at Lourdes, is not Frances's, of course, but Cohn's; for from the first, he looks at Brett as Moses looked "at the promised land" (p. 22), a vision superseding his desire for romantic life in South America. He is ready to fight the next day when Jake calls her less than perfect. Cohn finds in her a certain indescribable "quality": "I shouldn't wonder if I were in love with her" (p. 38). Even in such a detail as his tennis game he is changed by his love. Formerly he had "loved to win"; now he doesn't care when "People beat him who had never had a chance with him" (p. 45). Faced with her profanation of what he regards as a sacramental union, he calls her Circe, but never denies her power over him, following her around "like a poor bloody steer" (p. 142), in Mike's drunken analogy. Cohn does not think of himself as a steer, however, and he ultimately does "battle for his lady love" (p. 178) until he is routed from the ambiguous world represented by Brett.

Concerned as he is with being a writer, Jake confesses in Chapter VI, to a difficulty in showing Cohn clearly, giving as the reason, "I never heard him make one remark that would, in any way, detach him from other people" until he fell in love with Brett. Again, "If he were in a crowd nothing he said stood out" (p. 45). Yet manifestly Cohn does stand out for Jake—he begins his novel with him, is concerned to show him clearly and comes to be "blind, unforgivingly jealous of what had happened to him" (p. 99). One explanation, beyond jealousy, for Jake's blindness toward Cohn is that in him he may well see himself, both in his hopeless love and in the attitudes that make him vulnerable to such a love. Cohn has often been compared to Gatsby in his "romantic readiness," but in this respect neither is Jake totally unlike Fitzgerald's hero. The yacht image by which Jake first describes Brett suggests not only her feminine attractiveness, but a realm of inaccessible beauty, much as Dan Cody's yacht seen "over the most insidious flat on Lake Superior" represents to Gatsby "all the beauty and glamour in the world" (pp. 98, 101), the vision he was later to translate into Daisy's "white face." Jake's romantic readiness is in evidence throughout much of the novel. For example, he shares Cohn's interest in the "innocent occupation" of reading "romantic" books. Even if he does not take *The Purple Land* as "literally" as Cohn does, its "splendid imaginary amorous adventures" are his assessment; moreover, any possible irony in this description is undercut by his enjoyment of a similarly "sinister" book at Burguete, "a wonderful story" about a woman and "her true love" who waited twenty-four years for her husband's body to be recovered from a glacier. This protracted postponement of consummation mirrors Jake's spellbound attendance on his "own true love," revealing as it does that whether he fully realizes it or not he is in effect taking such a work as "a guide-book to what life holds" for him.

Of course, he does realize, particularly at night, that such "waiting" is unsatisfactory. "What do you do nights, Jake?" asks his fellow correspondent. What he does is to take a *"poule"* to dinner, having "forgotten how dull it could be" (p. 16). This is not the first time, the point is clear, that, waiting for Brett, he has made such a futile gesture to quicken his life. "You're getting damned romantic" (p. 23), Brett quips insensitively. More characteristically, Jake cries about what he cannot have. "It is awfully easy to be hard-boiled about everything in the daytime, but at night it is another thing" (p. 34). Decidedly, he is not "hard-boiled" with Brett. The two most obvious instances in which he seems to allow Brett to wrench the course of his life into her service are his taking her to Romero and his unquestioning obedience to her call at the end. But throughout the book, and over a considerably longer period than Cohn, he slavishly makes himself fully available to Brett, as she requires his services.[12] Although in his "hard-boiled" moments Jake recognizes Brett "only wanted what she could not have" (p. 31), when they are first alone in the Paris taxi, he is unable to resist offering himself abjectly to her. He kisses her, professes not to understand when she draws back, begs her to love him and questions hopelessly, "Isn't there anything we can do about it?" then answering, "And there's not a damn thing we could do." He rouses himself, "We'd better stay away from each other," and almost immediately, "It's good to see each other" (pp. 26–27). After the episode in Jake's bedroom previously noted, he entreats Brett to live with him, saying he could bear her being unfaithful, unaware she has promised to go to San Sebastian with Cohn. Jake persists:

> "Can't we go together?"
> "No. That would be a hell of an idea after we'd just talked it out."
> "We never agreed."
> "Oh, you know as well as I do. Don't be obstinate, darling."
> "Oh, sure," I said. "I know you're right. I'm just low, and when I'm low I
> talk like a fool." (p. 56)

In this infatuated state dancing to the tune of "You can't two time—," Jake summarizes his predicament: "I had the feeling of a nightmare of it all being something repeated, something I had been through and that now I must go through again" (p. 64). Although Brett is the most frustrating aspect of his life, he cannot do without her whenever she will suffer his attendance.

Irrevocably committed to his unavailing love, Jake is forced to see his attitude in perspectives provided by the calculating appraisal of the count, the lusty dependency of Mike, the romantic worship of Cohn, the passing interest of Bill. However, none of these "lovers" is able to function as his "tutor"—to employ Earl Rovit's general term[13]—with the possible exception of Bill Gorton. The count, Mike and Cohn provide in their various ways clearly negative examples: ultimately, Jake is unable to take any of the three seriously as living a satisfactory life. Bill's stance is more problematical, especially since he is so convinced of its efficacy and since he so insistently concerns himself with what might be called "The Education of Jacob Barnes." When he arrives in Paris at the beginning of

Book II, he immediately senses his friend's depression, and, without knowing the cause, light-heartedly undertakes a cure, continuing intermittently until he learns the dimensions of Jake's malaise at Burguete. Claiming to be on an extended spree, actually Bill is in complete control, and his barbed alcoholic prolixity turns out to be brilliantly pointed in their first scene together. As a writer, he first tells Jake a "travel story," moralizing "Injustice everywhere," a clear antidote to the self pity he must have discerned in him. He then takes another tack, this time as a "nature writer." Walking down the Boulevard, they come first to a statue of two men whom Bill identifies as inventors of pharmacy, and then to a "taxidermist." Bibulously inspired, he is up to the connection, urging Jake to buy "Just one stuffed dog" as a cure of sorts. "Certainly brighten up your flat. . . . Mean everything in the world to you. . . . Simple exchange of values. You give them money. They give you a stuffed dog." Jake pretends to believe that Bill is drunk, but when Brett joins them and flirtatiously remarks, "You've a nice friend," he responds wryly, "He's all right. . . . He's a taxidermist," signalling his awareness that Bill has been trying to stuff him, to fill up his hollowness and "brighten up. . . [his] flat" (pp. 71–75).

In this and ensuing conversations, Bill lays down a barrage of imperatives, functioning, as Morton L. Ross has noted, "very much as does the preacher in Ecclesiastes," his "sermon" consisting principally of "commandments" which he announces as "universal guides to action"[14] but it should be kept in mind he is only addressing Jake. Many of his instructions have often been read as facetious chatter, but even what seems mere badinage is charged with thematic significance. Whatever the degree of flippancy, his advice may be collected under four major precepts which are the basis of his life, the life he is urging on his best friend: Utilize a little; Never be Daunted; Show Irony and Pity; Do not Question. The reason for his instruction is obvious. For clearly Jake is not fully utilizing; he is often daunted; instead of showing irony and pity when he's "feeling" he is only "hard-boiled" in the daytime and self-pitying at night; and he continues to be "pretty religious."

Explicitly, Jake neither accepts nor rejects Bill's "commandments." In the Paris street scene, as noted, he evasively accuses Bill of being a hundred and forty-four drinks ahead of him. He is more relaxed at the Burguete inn, away from Paris and Brett, literally warming up to Bill's friendly advice, as echoes of Ecclesiastes, heretofore unnoticed, make clear.[15] The feeling of warmth is quickly dispelled the next morning, however. Jake gets up early to dig fishing worms for both of them. Returning, he encounters a renewed ironic onslaught. "What were you doing? Burying your money?. . . You go out and dig some more worms and I'll be right down. . . . Work for the good of all!. . . Show irony and pity." Bill thus jibes that Jake is still not properly utilizing: the skilled fisherman uses flies; the knowledgeable buyer does not bury his money.[16] Jake, unable to claim Bill is intoxicated in this instance, is reduced to retorting, "Oh, go to hell!'" and leaving the room thumbing his nose as Bill launches into his irony and pity song of "feeling" to the tune of "The Bells are Ringing for Me and My Gal." At break-fast, however, under Bill's urging, he attempts to "Say something pitiful": "Robert Cohn." Bill approves and extends his instruction. "That's better. Now why is Cohn pitiful? Be ironic," but Jake has had enough. "Aw, hell!. . . It's too early in the morning" (pp. 113–14). At lunch Bill returns to his exhortation, giving his mock sermon,

> "Utilize a little, brother. . . . Let us not pry into the holy mysteries. . . with simian fingers. Let us accept on faith and simply say—I want you to join with me in saying—What shall we say, brother?. . . Let us kneel and say: 'Don't eat that, Lady—that's Mencken.' "

Jake attempts to "join" Bill repeating part of the lesson, "Utilize a little," in reference to a bottle of wine, although he ignores the other ironic reference to communion: "Don't eat that, Lady," and as Bill continues his anti-questioning preachment with the inspired conceit that Bryan, Mencken and he "all went to Holy Cross together"—sacrilegious hilarity coupling simple fundamentalism, strident, skepticism, traditional Catholicism and mocking irony—Jake is reduced again to accusing Bill of being "cock-eyed." His tutor, however, pushes on with sober understanding to Jake's two overwhelming questions: Brett and "what it was all about" (p. 148). For the first time Bill asks Jake directly, "Were you ever in love with [Brett]?" and then, immediately, in an apparent *non sequitur*, "[A]re you really a Catholic?" (pp. 122–24).

The two questions are closely related to Jake's condition, of course. The love he passionately desires to realize with Brett and the divine love of those who "have God. . . [quite a lot]" (p. 245) are both unavailable to Jake.[17] In this inti-mate scene he admits the dual source of his most fundamental "feeling," but despite this intimacy his answers are reserved. He admits to being in love with Brett, "Only I'd a hell of a lot rather not talk about it"; and he is "[t]echnically" a Catholic, although he disclaims any knowledge of what that equivocation signi-fies. Jake's brusqueness seals off Bill's probing, and he shifts from jabbing irony to sympathetic support, even to the extent of carrying the despised fishing worms.

How much of Bill's tutelage Jake finds acceptable is only gradually appar-ent. And two central episodes indicate that he must learn more profoundly from other sources: the fight with Cohn and the last day of bull fighting. In the Cohn encounter Jake pays the price of not following Bill's precepts, becoming in the latter's telling phrase, "Old Jake, the human punching-bag" (p. 199). His love for Brett has now led him to act as a "pimp" and then to try to fight Cohn. Quickly knocked unconscious, he is revived with "a carafe of water on my head" to find "everything looked new and changed. I had never seen the trees before. . . . It was all different." In this awakening, he is a way he has not been before; he still cares, but he is now more irreversibly aware of the unreality of his dream of Brett and all she represents to him. The experience is intensified by his recollection of the effects of another head "wound," of having been "kicked in the head" in a youthful football game and returning to full cognizance carrying his suitcase through his home town, only "it was all new. They were raking lawns and burning leaves. . . . It was all strange" (pp. 191–93).[18] Now in this similarly transformed world he has a feeling of carrying a "phantom suitcase," the luggage of his new awareness he must carry for the rest of his life, the burden of full consciousness that Bill is determined to avoid.

Stunned as he has been by Cohn, Jake must descend still further from his romantic expectations. After reluctantly shaking hands with his kindred adversary, he wants "a deep, hot bath to lie back in. . . a hot bath in deep water" but, significantly, "the water would not run" (pp. 191–93). More or less in a state of shock, still unable to cope with his feelings, he goes to bed. The next day, waking with "a headache," he must cope with even more: the articulation of his new awareness in the art form of the bull fight. Jake had loyally defended Bill's understanding of bull fighting to Montoya, who had merely repeated "but he is not aficionado like you" (p. 131). Montoya is astute in perceiving that Bill is an interested spectator rather than a passionate enthusiast. There are no knowledgeable exchanges between Bill and Jake at the fights as there had been in the "country" around Burguete; in fact, a number of comments reveal his limited appreciation. And during the afternoon of Romero's triumph, described in a passage of over nine pages, Bill's only recorded response is the scarcely insightful, "There he goes" (p. 219), as Romero kills his first bull. Jake's appreciation of bull fighting as tragedy is on an entirely different plane, one prepared for by his observation on the second day of the fights. "Romero's bull-fighting gave real *emotion*," not "a fake *emotional feeling*, while the bull-fighter was really safe" (p. 168). Through this vocabulary, bull fighting is linked to Bill's song of "Irony and Pity," "When you're *feeling*. . . . When they're *feeling*" (p. 114, all italics added). The last day of the festival this motif is continued and charged with greater emphasis by the appearance of *sensation* three times on the same page, the only occurrences of the word as opposed to over forty instances of some form of *feeling*. With this underscoring, the concept of tragedy is specifically introduced.

Belmonte, in his best days, worked always in the terrain of the bull. . . . This
way he gave the *sensation* of coming *tragedy*. People went to the corrida to see
Belmonte, to be given *tragic sensations*, and perhaps to see the death of
Belmonte. . . the element that was necessary to give the *sensation of
tragedy*. . . . (pp. 213–14, italics added)

Jake goes to the bull fights to see great matadors work "in the terrain of the
bull" and thus to be given the traditional "tragic sensations" of pity and fear.
What he must be struck by, however, is the pointed contrast with the way he had
been living his life, in self pitying, futile aspiration, rather than "all the way up"
(p. 10) as he had once characterized the life of the bull fighter to Cohn. "Everybody behaves badly," he tells Brett. "Given the proper chance, I'd be as big an
ass as Cohn" (p. 181), and the "phantom suitcase" he now carries is part of his
new recognition of himself in this light, in expecting from Brett, and from life,
what he is not going to get. Romero, however, does not "behave badly" in or out
of the ring, and as a bull fighter, through his "greatness" he enables his audience,
including Jake, to experience the "sensations" of tragedy. Romero, in keeping
with his name either as "pilgrim" or "pilot fish," provides Jake with a momentary vision of the stance he would like to be able to assume, not in the bull ring
but in his entire life. In this sense Romero, in another dimension than Bill, serves
as Jake's tutor.[19]

But what of Romero outside the ring? There remains to consider him as
Brett's lover. After saying that Romero had the "greatness," Jake adds, "he loved
bull-fighting and I think he loved the bulls, and I think he loved Brett" (p. 216).
Certainly he responds to Brett's encouragement, even though he has earlier been
informed that Mike is doing "[n]othing. . . waiting to marry this lady" (p. 176).
In contrast to Bill, he is undeterred by this information. And he performs for her
in the bull ring, maneuvering the action in front of her, presenting her with the
ear he is awarded for his triumph. But he is distinctly not a knight like Cohn,
"ready to do battle for his lady love." His performance as a matador, as well as
his fight with Cohn, is first of all for himself and only incidentally for Brett. He
even has a bit of condescending humor as he presents the ear to her. " 'Don't get
bloody,' Romero said, and grinned" (p. 221). He defines himself not primarily as
Brett's lover as do Cohn and Jake, but as a bull fighter, with no commitment of
any sort between himself and his vocation. Jake makes the distinction: "He loved
bull-fighting. . . and I think he loved Brett."

In what way does he love her? After "a final look to ask if it were understood" (p. 187), he proceeds sexually in accordance with that understanding. His
initial tentativeness arises both from his natural disbelief that this woman from

what must seem another world is available, and also from his youth. He is repeatedly designated a "lad," "boy," "kid," or "child" by Montoya, Jake and Brett.
Montoya is particularly concerned with his immaturity outside the ring. " 'Any
foreigner' can flatter [a boy like that]" (p. 172). Learning that this nineteen-year-
old primitive wanted to marry the thirty-four-year-old sophisticate, Jake summons enough humor to say, "Maybe he thought it would make him Lord Ashley."
After Brett sends him away, she feels good at not ruining "children." And
Romero, surely dimly understanding that he is out of his element, does go—back
to his true love, bull fighting. He would have married her, Brett tells Jake, "to
make it sure I could never go away from him," after she had grown her hair out
and "gotten more womanly, of course." Romero, in his boyish self-confidence,
wants Brett for his woman. He has only "been" with two before, Brett says, and
until this experience "never cared about anything but bull-fighting" (pp.
242–45). But he only wants to marry Brett if she will fit *his* naïve image of a
wife, the wife of a matador committed to his vocation. We do not fully know
Romero's story, of course, but there is nothing in what we do know to suggest that
Brett determines his world in the way she does that of Cohn and Jake: she is not
his goddess. It is as impossible to consider his momentary expression of youthful
male ardor for a sexually exciting woman as committed love as it is to understand
how he has been read as fully heroic.

This is not to deny that he passes his first test of true "greatness" in the bull
ring on the last day of the festival. But, as Cohn responded to Jake's rather rigid
aphorism that only bull fighters live life all the way up, "That's an abnormal life"
(p. 10). What, to consider an example given dramatic focus in the novel, are we to
make of Belmonte, a significant figure in Jake's education who has received little
attention?[20] Not one of Brett's lovers, he is Jake's unwitting tutor—an example of
heroism, loving nothing, "going through his pain." Once, one of the greatest
matadors, he can no longer live in his vocation "all the way up," providing an
answer to Romero's youthful confidence, "I'm never going to die" (p. 186). In his
prime strong and fully accepting of danger, he is now old and sick, avoiding risks
by picking bulls for their "safety." "[N]ot sure that there were any great
moments," "He no longer had his greatest moments in the bull-ring." Where
then, the phrasing seems to ask, does he have "his greatest moments"? Jake has
just observed him in such a moment. Belmonte, having failed in the eyes of the
crowd with his second bull, smiled contemptuously

> when he was called something particularly insulting, and always the pain that
> any movement produced grew stronger and stronger, until finally his yellow
> face was parchment color. . . he passed through into the callejon and leaned on

the barrera below us, his head on his arms not seeing, not hearing anything, only going through his pain. When he looked up, finally, he asked for a drink of water. He swallowed a little. . . took his cape, and went back into the ring. (pp. 214–15)

Observing such greatness as Belmonte can now achieve in the tragic human circumstance figured forth on the "parchment color" of death with which he, and Romero, as well as Belmonte are all ultimately faced, Jake is surely "given tragic sensations." Jake's identification with Belmonte is emphasized not only by the phrasing, "going through his pain," which recalls his earlier description of having been through a nightmare "that now I must go through again," but also by the fact that there is no indication that his perception of Belmonte's agony is shared or even perceived by anyone else—Bill, Brett or the crowd.

After the bull fights are over, it is not surprising that Jake, feeling "like hell," under Bill's ministrations gets "drunker than I ever remembered having been." Bill wants him thus to get over his "damn depression" (p. 223), that is to follow the advice he has been giving—to go through less pain. Jake has cause for his deepest depression. Brett has gone off with Romero, reinforcing the finality of his earlier "nightmare" that his dream has become. Also, in the same afternoon he has been "given" two different sets of "tragic sensations." He has experienced the classic tragic emotions evoked by Romero's public artistry transmuting the dangers of life to a higher form. But he has also identified with the private agony of Belmonte "looking at nothing," his "great moments" in the past. Jake recognizes that there are unlikely to be any "great moments" for him, that his life is to be in considerable part his going through a pain that will never be completely alleviated by pleasure, God, love or by any other opiate, reality or value. This recognition of himself and his world has not exhilarated him, but it has transformed him, even more dramatically than Robert Cohn's blows. At such a "boundary situation"[21] he is no longer "blind." He now looks "strange" to himself in the mirror and his "world was not wheeling anymore. It was very clear and bright, and inclined to blur at the edges" (p. 224). Strengthened by this tragic perception of his life as he must live it, not the "abnormal" life of Romero, but the "normal" life of Belmonte, he is now able to rejoin Bill soberly, eat some proffered soup and start living his life as best he can, at the end of his line.

Jake has not thus facilely achieved tragic dimensions, but the issue of tragedy as opposed to therapy has been raised in the novel. Hemingway, of course, explicitly raised it himself, in two different letters shortly after publication. "It's funny to write a book that seems as tragic as that and have them take it for a jazz superficial story," and three days later, the book was not "a hollow or bitter

satire, but a damn tragedy with the earth abiding forever as the hero."[22] These
remarks, together with the several references to tragedy in *The Sun Also Rises*—
even without anticipating the discussion of bull fighting as tragedy in *Death in the
Afternoon*—call attention to the movement of the novel, and the life of its narrator, in the direction of the tragic vision. At the beginning, Jake, in Rovit's terminology, is the tyro, but by the end he has learned much from three tutors, Bill,
Romero, and Belmonte; from the negative examples of Cohn, Mike and the
count; as well as from the head blows of Cohn, Brett's lover most like himself.
The extent of his development, and its limitation, is apparent in the final scenes.

In Book III, which opens just after Jake's "world was not wheeling any
more," it is "all over." Specifically, it is the fiesta that is finished, but more
widely, it is the entire sequence of events that has wrought a change in Jake and
his world, most particularly, his love of Brett. He says goodby to Bill in France,
and Jake goes back to Spain, "recover[ing] an hour": they are in different countries and times. Jake proceeds steadily and quietly through the routine of his days
in San Sebastian, seeming to gather strength from swimming in the "green and
dark" water, from vistas of a "green mountainside" and "a green hill with a
castle." Very explicitly, after Jake has filled out his "police bulletin" and is
swimming in the sea, there is imagery of depth, anticipating the elevation of the
Madrid scenes.

> Then I tried several *dives. I dove deep* once, swimming *down* to the *bottom.* I
> swam with my eyes open and it was green and *dark.* The raft [with two lovers
> on it] made a *dark shadow.* I came out of the water beside the raft, pulled up,
> *dove* once more, holding it for length, and then swam ashore." (pp. 234–35,
> italics added)

Both his state of mind and the natural scenery suggest something of the mood of
the episode at Burguete, but there is a difference. In San Sebastian, he sustains
himself, unsupported by Bill's noisy camaraderie, and he seems more in control
of his universe.[23]

This serenity is put to test when Brett summons him to Madrid. At first, he
seems in danger of reverting to the self-pitying attitude of Paris:

> That seemed to handle it. That was it. Send a girl off with one man. Introduce
> her to another to go off with him. Now go and bring her back. And sign the
> wire with love. That was it all right. (p. 239)

Here again is the familiar tone of helpless, desperate commitment. Jake seems
ready to resume his dance around Brett's image, transfixed in a desire that can
neither be denied nor satisfied—in effect endowing Brett with a "mystical

penumbra" and making his worship of her serve for his "big religious possession." Jake is different, however, as a careful reading makes clear. Brett is now
reduced to "a girl" in difficulty, and "love" is a "sign." For better and worse,
Jake is no longer dancing around Brett's image in quite the same measures.
Immediately after sending the telegram "I went in to lunch," not only an indication of his new equanimity, but an illustration of his determination to "utilize" as
best he can, to be further shown in the climactic scenes in Madrid. These passages are carefully prepared for by Jake's journey to the "end of the line" through
symbolic scenery intensified by the concentration of a number of images of elevation as well as by reverberations in the words here italicized, of portions of Section V of *The Waste Land*. He sees Madrid "come up over the *plain*, a compact
white sky-line on the top of a little *cliff* away across the sun-hardened country. . .
we climbed up through the *gardens*, by the *empty palace* and the unfinished
church on the edge of the *cliff*, and on up until we were in the high, hot modern
town." Unable to work the "elevator," he walks up to the second floor of the
Hotel Montana—*"Mountain"*—to be admitted by a maid with a *"sullen face"* (pp.
239–40). The "arid plain" is now behind Jake, and he is ready to set his lands in
order by shoring up his ruins with such fragments as he has. He proceeds to
exemplify in his actions and attitudes several of the commandments of his "nice
friend," the "taxidermist." He takes Brett to Botin's, "one of the best restaurants
in the world," where, as the name translates, he collects his "bounty" or "spoils
of war" in a sumptuous meal. "I like to drink wine," he tells Brett, "I like to do a
lot of things" (pp. 245–46). Just how much he enjoys "utilizing a little" remains
uncertain, but in sharp contrast to his behavior in Paris, he is "undaunted" in
Brett's presence.

More significantly, as he "feels"—some form of the verb occurs seven times
in two pages—he stabilizes his world with irony and pity. His tenderness toward
Brett is continually apparent, as he supports her firmly while asking nothing.
"Tell me about it. . . . You were probably damn good for him. . . . You ought to
feel set up. . . . Dear Brett" (pp. 241–43). And, as noted, he can even be ironical
about Romero's motives for wanting to marry Brett. All of his remarks to Brett,
as well as all of his actions, show attitudes designed to palliate the pain each is
going through. In Paris, Jake had been the weaker of the two, but in Madrid,
following some of Bill's instructions, he is much stronger. And so in the magnifi-
cently evocative last lines of the novel, he can sum up the growth he has achieved
in his response to Brett's shallow *cri de coeur*, "we could have had such a
damned good time together," with "Yes. . . . Isn't it pretty to think so?" (p. 247).
Yet there is more to his response than irony and pity, for as he had signed his wire
"with love," so this response also bears the mark of love. Jake now sees his love

more clearly for what it is—even his comforting response is punctuated as a question. But in seeing his love in its diminishment, he still holds on to it, not desperately but with perspicacity. "Feeling" however diminished is preferable to calculated "simple exchange." Jake is now able to act for the first time as a Hemingway hero, having made his play, to back it up.[24]

Bill had been concerned, of course, to get Jake not to make this play, the play for the love of Brett, the play for ultimate rather than simple "exchange." Aware that Jake could never have had a "damned good time" with Brett—with her his destiny would always be most likely that of the "human punching-bag"— Bill also believes that Jake's search for answers will be equally fruitless. In short, as a substitute for frustrated faith, human and divine, in whatever formula of precarious consubstantiation, he has recommended taxidermy and self-protection. Tutored as he has been by all of his experience of a world that is neither his own nor himself, and true to his own feelings, Jake, however, must make a more complicated play, a search for love as a value that transcends both utility and fantasy, even as Brett's mystery disperses under his more penetrating gaze.

By the final scenes in Madrid, Jake is able to hold himself steady in the paradox of wanting everything and having nothing except himself—Emily Dickinson's paradox of "The Missing All"—both states expressed in his absurd, magnificent passion for Brett, and captured in his final words. He is not yet a tragic hero pushing resolutely toward a victory of spirit against the inevitable defeat of circumstance, but he is at his own "boundary situation." If he is not, like Santiago, "beyond all the people in the world," he is farther out than he has been before. Much closer in time and situation to Nick Adams in "Big Two-Hearted River," who "wanted to be a great writer," he is not yet ready to fish "In the swamp [where]. . . the fishing would be tragic. In the swamp fishing was a tragic adventure. Nick did not want it." Neither does Jake seem to "want it" as he holds himself tautly against the pressures of his life in the final scenes of the novel.

But Jake obviously does "want it." His experiences do not end in Madrid, in the taxi with Brett. They end with his seeking out the meaning of his impossible/possible love for Brett through the writing of *The Sun Also Rises*, even as Nick Carraway's "lost words" are recaptured in the telling of Gatsby's story. Recognizing that he may indeed have to live without the love of God, or any sufficient image thereof, the predicament cited as characteristic of the "modern temper" by Krutch, he still refuses to deny the attracting power of both. "[T]o find, / Not to impose. . . / It is possible, possible, possible. It must be possible," Stevens was to write in *Notes Toward a Supreme Fiction*, and Jake from this position sets out to order his "poem of the mind." The overtones of Stevens are far from gratuitous: Stevens himself recognized the affinity in a 1942 letter stating that although Hemingway was not usually regarded as a poet, he considered him "the most significant living poet as far as the subject of EXTRAORDINARY ACTUALITY is concerned."[25] In the process of writing the "poem" of his life, Jake composes, in effect, his "love song"—the uniqueness distinguishing his human syllable from that of Brett's other lovers whom he knows in se 'et kinship. Faced with playing things as they are, he finally neither asserts in fo .ish desperation as Cohn, nor abdicates his full human responsibility as do the other lovers in their separate ways. Rather as the artist he set out to "create in honesty"[26] a world in which he can live as a moral being. Bill had taunted him at Burguete with not knowing irony and pity, "And you claim you want to be a writer, too. You're only a newspaper man. An expatriated newspaper man." Bill is a writer, and a successful one; but he limits himself to "travel stories" and "nature-writ[ing]." Tragedy is beyond his reach. Jake, however, will not accept such limitations. Unlike Bill, and Cohn, another writer of limited vision, he really is ultimately concerned with "an abnormal life," one lived "all the way up." *The Sun Also Rises* is a record of how he attempts to learn to live that life. Seeing all around him, as well as inside himself, evidences of the death of value, Jake chooses, even in recognition of that extinction, to create his own "All"—*The Sun Also Rises*—and in the act of so doing comes on a "moral history" that at once follows the pattern of the age but also deepens and enriches its tragic colors.

1. "The Missing All," *Virginia Quarterly Review*, 13 (Winter 1937), 118. Cited in Carlos Baker, *Hemingway: The Writer as Artist* (Princeton: Princeton University Press, 1972), p. 75.

2. *The Education of Henry Adams* (New York: The Modern Library, 1931), p. 384.

3. Carlos Baker, *Ernest Hemingway: A Life Story* (New York: Charles Scribner's Sons, 1969), p. 146.

4. F. Scott Fitzgerald, *The Great Gatsby* (New York: Charles Scribner's Sons, Student's Edition, 1953), *passim*, but especially pp. 111–12.

5. *The Modern Temper* (New York: Harcourt Brace and World, Inc., 1929), pp. 73, 78.

6. R. P. Blackmur, *Anni Mirabiles: 1921–1925* (Washington, D.C.: The Library of Congress, 1956), p. 26.

7. *The Sun Also Rises* (New York: Charles Scribner's Sons, The Scribner Library Edition, 1954), p. 53. Subsequent citations in text.

8. *The Narrative Pattern in Ernest Hemingway's Fiction* (Rutherford, N.J.: Fairleigh Dickinson University Press, 1971), pp. 42–45.

9. In the only other use of the word in the novel, four pages later, when Brett wants a bath, Bill Gorton offers, in diction so awkward as to demand attention, "Let's *translate* Brett to the Hotel" (p. 159, italics added).

10. The language refers to Eliot's epigraph to "Portrait of a Lady" taken from *The Jew of Malta*: "Thou has committed / Fornication: but that was in another country, / And besides, the wench is dead."

11. William Bysshe Stein has discussed Hemingway's treatment in his short stories of the "illusion of redemptive passion [which] identifies the arrested adolescence of the American adult" in "Love and Lust in Hemingway's Short Stories," *Texas Studies in Language and Literature*, 3 (Summer 1961), p. 239.

12. It is a possibility previously unremarked that the reasons he has withdrawn $600 from his account since the first of the month—twice Cohn's monthly allowance from his mother, a fact rather nastily set down by Jake—is that he is providing Brett with considerable sums. It is surely significant that as meticulously as he keeps his accounts, even noting a two-franc tip, he does not itemize this large expenditure. Interesting in this connection is the fact that about the time he had finished the first draft of *The Sun Also Rises*, Lady Duff Twysden asked to borrow 3,000 francs from Hemingway. Baker, *Ernest Hemingway: A Life Story*, pp. 155–57.

13. *Ernest Hemingway* (New York: Twayne Publishers, 1963), pp. 53–57.

14. "Bill Gorton, the Preacher of *The Sun Also Rises*," *Modern Fiction Studies*, 18 (Winter 1972–73), 520.

15. As they enter the town there are eight separate references to the cold. At the inn they drink hot rum punch against the cold; and the evening concludes "After supper we went upstairs and smoked and read in bed to keep warm. Once in the night I woke and heard the wind blowing. It felt good to be warm and in bed" (pp. 108–11). In the relevant verses of Ecclesiastes, "Two are better than one; because they have a good reward for their labour. For if they fall, the one will lift up his fellow: but woe to him that is alone when he falleth for he hath not another to help him up. Again if two lie together, then they have heat; but how can one be warm alone?" Ecclesiastes 4:9–11.

16. In addition to the four commandments I have listed, Ross includes "Work the good of all." Yet in the "fishing worm" context this is heavily ironic, and, furthermore, there is no evidence that either Bill or Jake is ever concerned with the common good.

17. Stein has noted how Hemingway is concerned in his short stories with the "degradation of the Passion by sexual passion." Again, "in dramatizing the absurdities of modern love—the nostalgia for passion—[Hemingway] succeeds in defending the principles of his crypto-Catholicism" (pp. 236, 239).

18. Both experiences of this new, strange world are described in terms evoking Gatsby's new world after he realizes no call is coming from Daisy. "He must have looked up at an unfamiliar sky through frightening leaves and shivered as he found how raw the sunlight was upon the scarcely created grass. A new world, material without being real. . . that ashen fantastic figure. . . the amorphous trees. . ." (p. 162). Mark Spilka, whose remarks are usually illuminating and always provocative, does not see this passage as indicative of Jake's awakening. "Barnes seems to have regressed here to his youthful football days. . . . Cohn has also regressed to his abject college days: they are both emotional adolescents, about the same age as the nineteen-year-old Romero ," "The Death of Love in *The Sun Also Rises*," *Twelve Original Essays on Great American Novels*, ed. Charles Shapiro (Detroit: Wayne State University Press, 1959), p. 251. I am, of course, arguing that it is precisely at this point that Jake is advancing beyond Cohn and Romero.

19. Noting the translation of Romero's name, Bruce L. Grenberg goes on to state that Romero provides Jake with an ideal. But, as he properly notes, "His heroism *per se* cannot be translated directly into the modern world Jake occupies." "The Design of Heroism in *The Sun Also Rises*," *Fitzgerald/Hemingway Annual, 1971*, pp. 283–84.

20. Most commentators have ignored Belmonte. Rovit, whose reading of Hemingway generally and *The Sun Also Rises* particularly, is most persuasive and stimulating in almost every instance, unaccountably dismisses Belmonte. Belmonte is a "tutor" and "code-hero" (p. 955) and yet "One of the few extraneous scenes in *The Sun Also Rises*. . . concerns itself with the appearance of Juan Belmonte in the Pamplona bull ring" (p. 32). On the contrary, I read his introduction as absolutely crucial to Jake's tragic development.

21. In noting the use of this term by Kierkegaard, Jaspers and Tillich among others, Richard B. Sewall writes, "The tragic vision impels the man of action to fight against his destiny. . . the artist in his fictions toward. . . 'boundary situations,' man at the limits of his sovereignty. . . . The hero faces as if no man had ever faced it before the existential question or Job's question "What is man?" *The Vision of Tragedy* (New Haven: Yale University Press, 1959), pp. 5, 151.

22. Baker, *Hemingway: The Writer as Artist*, pp. 79–81.

23. The contrast between the two similar times is shown in at least two incidents. At Burguete, he had remained dry, fishing from the dam with worms. He had used flies and "was wet from the waist down." Now he swims feeling that he "could never sink." Earlier, he and Bill had stumbled into a bit of sexual double entendre involving pedals, joysticks, and bicycles that both immediately back away from as too painful for Jake. At San Sebastian he maintains an "ironical" equanimity when similar references come up in the conversation with the bicycle riders and their girls.

24. Again, I am indebted to Rovit's discussion, in this instance of Colonel Cantwell's definition of a "tough boy," pp. 59–60.

25. *Letters of Wallace Stevens*, ed. Holly Stevens (New York: Knopf, 1966), pp. 411–12.

26. Blackmur, p. 8.

HEMINGWAY'S BEGINNINGS AND ENDINGS

BERNARD OLDSEY

THE MANUSCRIPTS IN THE HEMINGWAY COLLECTION have two remarkable and almost contradictory characteristics. One is the free-flowing and finished quality of the prose that makes up most of the interior passages of the stories and novels. There are some emendations and reworkings of these passages, and in some instances the changes do provide insight into the author's method and meaning; but the remarkable thing is that there are so few of these, relatively speaking, and that the interior prose runs on so smoothly and ineluctably for such long stretches at a time.

The other striking feature of the manuscripts—and one that is much more rewarding critically—manifests itself in the numerous drafts and emendations of beginnings and endings done for both the short stories and the novels. These do not, of course, signal strange or unusual difficulties peculiar to Hemingway. Anybody who has ever written anything will understand why this is so: as George Eliot once confided in correspondence, "Beginnings are always troublesome" and "conclusions are the weak point of most authors." What is unusual, and critically gratifying, is that Hemingway left behind such an abundance of evidence showing how a writer overcomes these difficulties.

From this evidence emerges a pattern of writing and rewriting, vision and revision, that transforms raw material into finished art. The manuscripts show that Hemingway was not only a great natural writer, possessed of verve and linguistic flow, but also a fine editor of his own fiction. His sense of what was right, what would work, was uncanny. The papers reveal that he made very few, if any, incorrect decisions about how to begin or end a narrative. In this respect,

Reprinted with permission from *College Literature* special Hemingway issue, published in book form as *Ernest Hemingway: The Papers of a Writer*, ed. Bernard Oldsey (New York: Garland Publishing Co., 1981), pp. 37–62.

113

Ezra Pound's irreverent summation of Hemingway's talent is not inappropriate: "The son of a bitch's *instincts* are right!"

Even in those rare instances where the record indicates that outside advice was offered, Hemingway chose wisely which advice to accept and which to reject. He did, as we now know, accept F. Scott Fitzgerald's advice on how to begin *The Sun Also Rises*. At various stages of development it began with Brett Ashley, Jake Barnes, with Nino de Palma; but then because of Fitzgerald's advice, Hemingway cut deeply into the early drafts and started with Robert Cohn, thereby ridding the book of much useless stuff. As treated by Philip Young and Charles Mann, this instance became, quite rightly, a rather famous case of modern literary influence.[1] But later, with the Hemingway papers more readily and fully available, it was discovered that the influence-ledger was in need of some balancing. As indicated in a recent study (*Hemingway's Hidden Craft*, 1979), Hemingway rejected a number of Fitzgerald's suggestions about the composition of *A Farewell to Arms*, including one about how to conclude the novel; and subsequently, Fitzgerald fashioned the ending of his own *Tender Is the Night* on the basis of something that he learned from Hemingway, something that came out of the "troubles with the very end of *A Farewell to Arms*."[2]

Hemingway's Hidden Craft discusses these troubles—examining and codifying forty-one concluding attempts for the novel, including clusters of variants like "The Nada Ending," "The Fitzgerald Ending," "The Religious Ending," "The Live-Baby Ending," "The Morning-After Ending," "The Funeral Ending," "The Original *Scribner's Magazine* Ending," as well as five versions of "*The* Ending," as published. These revisions depict the story behind the story, detailing how Hemingway finally arrived at the flat, nihilistic, numbing conclusion that the novel now has.[3]

This study also discusses what is probably the original beginning of *A Farewell to Arms* (Item 240 in the papers). Consisting of two chapters, the early manuscript starts at a point roughly equivalent to Chapter XIII (the first chapter of Book Two) of the novel as published. In one of the few instances to be found in the papers, Hemingway here reversed his usual method of arriving at a true beginning by cutting: here he added twelve chapters of vital plot and character introduction to the original beginning—in which the already wounded protagonist (named Emmett Hancock) is being carried to a room in a hospital in Milan. One important result of this recasting is that the novel now opens with its celebrated lyrical overture instead of a secondary action in *medias res*.[4]

The opening and closing variants of *A Farewell to Arms* may well be among the most dramatic and revealing changes to be found in the Hemingway manuscripts; but they have been fully discussed elsewhere, and they are by no means unique in their ability to reflect Hemingway's editorial perception and narrative craftsmanship. So it is the intent of this present analysis to concentrate on the manuscripts of three other works—three representative short stories that underwent radical beginning and/or ending changes and were thus transformed into remarkably different works from those originally intended. Examining these stories should demonstrate the kind of critical information that resides within the boxed manuscripts. An Aladdin's rub may summon forth nothing more than testimony that reinforces previous readings and opinions of these works; or it may, in producing a clearer picture of Hemingway at work, clarify technical and thematic aspects of his fiction that cannot be perceived by reading it only in final form.

I. "Indian Camp"

One of the manuscripts chosen for examination here is Item 493, the earliest extant version of "Indian Camp." This is, of course, a key work in the Hemingway canon: the first of the Nick Adams stories, both in publication and in the chronology of this cycle, it is also a typical *tranche de vie*, done as Hemingway most often did these pieces, from a third-person-singular point of view, with touches of omniscient adjustment. Furthermore, most of this manuscript has been made public, and it contains an example of a particular kind of auctorial epiphany that characterizes much of Hemingway's work.

The story as published (in *Transatlantic Review*, April 1924, under the indicative heading of "Work in Progress") opens with the line "At the lake shore there was another row boat drawn up."[5] In manuscript, this line does not appear until p. 9. The previous eight pages, published with slight changes as "Three Shots" in *The Nick Adams Stories* (1972), constitute a small flashback, recounting the events of the previous evening: Nick has accompanied his father and his Uncle George (Uncle *Joe* in the first, rejected paragraph of the manuscript) on a camping-fishing trip; and what he remembers is that on the evening before, left behind in camp while his father and uncle go off to fish by jacklight, he behaved in a cowardly manner. (Later, in writing "The Short Happy Life of Francis Macomber," Hemingway would use much the same method of beginning, with a flashback to an act of cowardice. And as we shall see, he had to make as drastic a change to get Macomber's story properly started as he did in this instance with Nick's.)

According to Julian Smith, excision of the first eight pages from "Indian Camp" was nothing more than "the kind of editorial cut many authors make without greatly altering the effect or meaning of a story,"[6] But in making this statement Smith proves to be the critical victim of not knowing; and his article on

"Hemingway and the Thing Left Out," which is basically a good one, stands as an example of previous commentary that needs revision in light of the manuscripts. The article appeared in 1971, before "Three Shots" was published; and Smith made his comment without firsthand knowledge of the manuscript, solely on the basis of a summary account provided by Carlos Baker.[7]

Actually, the initial eight pages of the manuscript shed considerable light on the central motivation and effect of "Indian Camp." Philip Young, who did have access to this material before writing " 'Big World Out There': the Nick Adams Stories," quite rightly emphasizes the change in thematic tack the story underwent.[8] In the first section of the manuscript the author had concentrated on Nick's fear of death, his realization that his own "silver cord" would be cut. The story as published retains no mention of this motivational background; instead, it moves on to a truer, more valid, kind of perception: the realization that a young boy might feel "quite sure that he would never die." As Young concludes, "children don't really believe in their own demise. Death is obviously something that happens to other people."[9]

Young's perceptive comment indicates how knowing a manuscript can help elucidate the work as published. But the matter is psychologically and artistically more complicated than he concludes. Does the ending of the story present us with the thoughts of a child, or with those of a child becoming a man? It should be observed that the first eight pages of this manuscript do much to establish Nick Adams—even at this tender age, when his father still calls him "Nickie"—as the essential Hemingway hero, who cannot sleep nights, has fears that he may cease to be, and badly needs some kind of therapeutic device, or activity, to help him through his nocturnal anxiety. In a flashback within a flashback, Nick recalls another time when he was beset by cowardly fear: this is a night at home when "he sat out in the hall under the night light trying to read Robinson Crusoe to keep his mind off the fact that someday the silver chord [sic] must break."[10] He recognizes that this is the same kind of fear that made him poke his rifle outside the tent and fire three times, recalling his father and uncle by prearranged signal in case of emergency.

The silver-cord motif tied the entire manuscript together before Hemingway made his cut. The idea enters by way of a hymn that Nick knows from church, and in his mind it connotes death. Of course, quite literally it denotes the umbilical cord and thus the beginning of life. And in both senses it was quite fitting within the terms of the story, with the birth of the Indian child and the death of the Indian father—who severs his own lifeline by slitting his throat.

When Hemingway excised the first eight pages of the manuscript, the narrative lost its informing image, but the after-effect of this particular "thing left out"

can still be sensed in the beautifully worked out conclusion of the story. And here
too the manuscript is fascinatingly informative. After the life and death events of
the night, Nick and his father return to their camp in a row boat. Dr. Adams
answers his son's questions about the pains of birth and the pains of dying. What
was to have been the last paragraph runs like this:

> They were seated in the boat, Nick in the stern his father rowing. The sun
> was coming up over the hills. A bass jumped making a circle in the water. Nick
> trailed his hand in the water. It felt warm in the sharp shell of the morning.[11]

In other words, Hemingway was tempted to end the story with this pretty line of
imagery depicting the welcome arrival of day. Right after it he placed the journalist's mark of "30." The two inches of manuscript between the initial "30" and
the next one, which marks the end of the story as we know it, represents a
quantum leap in artistic insight. For here Hemingway added that irresistibly
shrugging one-sentence paragraph which gives the story so much of its concluding power: "In the early morning on the lake sitting in the stern of the boat with
his father rowing he felt quite sure he would never die."[12]

How are we to read this remarkable final sentence, with its pulsing and
carefully modifying prepositional phrases? Is it to be read only as an ironic indication of childish egocentrism? Another manuscript example—this from Stephen
Crane's papers—may help provide an answer. For at one time Crane was tempted
to conclude *The Red Badge of Courage* on a similar note of youthful self-
centeredness: in an early version of the novel, he represented his protagonist,
Henry Fleming, as having "been to touch the great death" and finding that "after
all, it was but the great death *and was for others."*[13] But eventually Crane removed
those four final incriminating words, and in doing so allowed his young Union
soldier to stand as something more than a case of arrested literary development,
and the butt of the author's irony.

Hemingway did somewhat the same thing in Nick Adam's case, except that
he added words in his final instance instead of removing them. And here again
the papers indicate how artistically right Hemingway could be at a deep intuitive
level. As he first set the concluding sentence of "Indian Camp" down on paper, it
was simple, flat, and unexceptional: all it said was, "In the early morning on the
lake he felt quite sure he would never die." But with the touch of a twenty-five-
year-old genius, Hemingway piled on those phrases that move the sentence, cir-
cumscribe its meaning, and mitigate whatever irony it may contain.

What he finally leaves the reader with is a genre painting of transcendental
potential. There in the row boat on the lake sitting safely in the stern of the boat is
a youthful Nick Adams who has not quite severed the psychic umbilical cord

stretching between him and his father, the master of life and death questions. His father sits before him in the boat, and all's right with the world, as a fish jumps and makes a perfect circle in the water. And yet looked at from another view, isn't the boy Nick already father of all those fictional men of Hemingway's later making? All those who have to sleep with the light on, who have to think of women they have known, streams they have fished, in order to achieve some kind of solace at night? Those who have to learn how to use the abiding beauty of the earth as something of a stay against neurotic fear and trembling?

On a day like this, within "the sharp shell of the morning," any man or child might believe that he could live forever. It may be an egocentric thought, but it is also therapeutic, and Nick Adams, age approximately fourteen, has as much right to it as all the primitive, and not so primitive, theologians and transcendentalists who have purveyed it since time immemorial. With certain elements of glory in sight, this boy about to become a man may entertain intimations of immortality as well as any grown-up Wordsworth. And if any irony attaches, it applies to both the boy and the poet.

II. "Big Two-Hearted River"

Though they are important, even vital, the changes Hemingway made in "Indian Camp" look rather minor when compared to the major surgery he performed on another Nick Adams story called "Big Two-Hearted River," which was published a year later, in *This Quarter* (May 1925), and was used as the culminating story of *In Our Time* (also 1925). Thirty-four years later—in an unpublished introductory piece entitled "The Art of the Short Story"— Hemingway disclosed many of his theories about the writing of fiction. Some sections of this typescript are ga-ga and silly, but others are penetrating and wise, representing a series of criteria the author had worked out for himself. One of the most revealing of these statements deals with the efficacy of omission, with particular reference to "Big Two-Hearted River":

> A few things I have found to be true. If you leave out important things or events that you know about, the story is strengthened. If you leave out or skip something because you do not know it, the story will be worthless. The test of any story is how very good the stuff is that you, not your editors, omit. A story in this book called Big Two-Hearted River is about a boy coming home beat to the wide from a war. Beat to the wide was an earlier and possibly more severe form of beat, since those who had it were unable to comment on this condition and could not suffer that it be mentioned in their presence. So the war, all

mention of the war, anything about the war, is omitted. The river was the Fox river, by Seney, Michigan, not the Big Two-Hearted. The change of name was made purposely, not from ignorance nor carelessness but because Big Two-Hearted River is poetry, and because there were many Indians in the story, just as the war was in the story, and none of the Indians nor the war appeared. As you see, it is very simple and easy to explain.[14]

Of course, it is not "very simple and easy to explain"; nor are the distant war and vanishing Indians the only things the author omitted from the story. By the time he wrote "The Art of the Short Story" (dated June 1959), Hemingway may have forgotten the difficulties he had had with the composition of "Big Two-Hearted River." But several manuscripts (Items 274, 275, and 279) show that he eventually changed much more than the name of the river. They indicate, in fact, that he had at least two chances to ruin the work—once before it even got properly under way, and once when it started to run out of control at the end. In both instances, the story went through a process that entailed omission of extraneous matter and a reconceptualization of the narrative structure.

The story as published begins, "The train went on up the track out of sight, around one of the hills of burnt timber." Nick Adams has just hopped off the train at the site of what had been a town. Now everything is in ruins—including all "thirteen saloons that had lined the one street of Seney," as well as the "burned-over stretch of hillside, where he expected to find the scattered houses of the town." After this quick survey of peacetime devastation, Nick immediately (in the second paragraph) sets off down the railroad track to the river he intends to fish.

Startlingly enough, the earliest manuscript fragment of the story (Item 279) begins in this way: "*They* got off the train at Seney. There was no station."[15] The reader is amazed to discover that this work—which so depends for its effect upon a solitary figure set within a physical and mental wilderness—was initially conceived with three characters in it: Nick, Jack, and Al. Continued in this fashion, this piece might well have developed into one of Hemingway's typical boon-companion scenarios (like that in "Cross-Country Snow" and in the fishing section of *The Sun Also Rises*) where men escape the consequences of civilization by fishing or skiing together in a wilderness setting. Actually, some of this scenario carried over into a later typescript version of the story (Item 275), as Nick recalls all the times he had fished with male companions, like "Bill Smith, Odgar, the Ghee, all the old gang." But now these times are over with—he realizes—because in accepting the responsibilities of marrying (*Hadley* in one version, *Helen* in another) he had admitted there was —something more important than fishing."[16]

Another feature of the fragment (Item 279) that immediately strikes the reader is the viewpoint from which it is told. Hemingway struck through the first word of this version, changing the pronoun "We" to "They." In the first instance, he would have been stuck with a first-person point of view; in the second, he committed himself to an omniscient approach—for the duration of the fragment, which runs for only three pages.

What Nick, Jack, and Al do within these three pages is something that Hemingway eventually left out. Gathering together their gear from the railroad tracks, they proceed to inspect the burnt-out town, particularly the ruins of the Mansion House Hotel. As they poke around in the basement debris, they find four gun barrels, "pitted and twisted by the heat"; and in the magazine of one gun, they discover how the "cartridges had melted" and "formed a bulge of lead and copper." The fragment stops at this point. Hemingway obviously pushed it aside as a false start and began all over again, retaining little from the fragment except the general setting and the principal character. Had he retained some of the descriptive detail, he might have reinforced an idea that some commentators have, with critical hindsight, caught a glimmer of—namely, that the initial scene of burnt pine lands and ravaged town is the peace-time equivalent of war-time devastation.[17] But since the author knew about the war and the twisted guns, knew that the foundation of the hotel was "lime stone chipped and split by fire," he could, in terms of his own theory, leave that information out of the story and strengthen it. And when, as Mark Twain might put it, he found that having Jack and Al around would prove embarrassing, he simply buried them in the basement pit of the Mansion House. For to have provided Nick with what Hemingway later called "the comforting stench of human companionship" would have ruined the entire effect of this story, which of all his works is most dependent upon a single sensibility, an almost perfectly controlled "center of intelligence," confronting itself in the wilderness.[18]

The solution Hemingway found to the problem of beginning "Big Two-Hearted River" was vital but relatively simple. Reaching a proper conclusion called for a more involved process of revision. The concluding section of the story starts about four pages from the end, where Nick just misses catching the biggest trout he "ever heard of." His struggle with the fish threatens his emotional stability: he feels "a little sick, as though it would have been better to sit down." Somewhat later he sits on a log with his feet dangling over the water. While eating some sandwiches and then smoking a cigarette, he is perfectly at ease, until he notices how the river narrows and enters a swamp. Troubled by the thought that "the fishing would be tragic" in the swamp, he decides not "to go down the stream any further today." Instead, he busies himself, killing the two trout he has caught, and cleaning them in the stream. This done, he climbs the bank of the river and walks toward the high ground and his camp. Taking a final look back toward the river, he tells himself, in the very last sentence of the story, that there will be "plenty of days coming when he could fish the swamp."

Much has been written about the suppressed tension and lingering after-effect of this work, produced in great part by its tautly understated conclusion. Scott Fitzgerald, although he could not quite understand it, thought this one of the most hauntingly beautiful pieces of prose in the English language. Malcolm Cowley was one of the first to discover how the story gained meaning when placed in context with other works, particularly "Now I Lay Me," "A Way You'll Never Be," "In Another Country," and "Chapter VI" of *In Our Time*. But Fitzgerald, Cowley, and other admirers of the story would have been disappointed in their readings had Hemingway kept to his original conclusion.[19] He did, as a matter of fact, stay with it to the extent of advancing it, with minor changes, to what was for him often the publishing stage—namely, typescript.

In both handwritten and typescript form (Items 274 and 275 respectively), the concluding section begins at a point somewhat before that in the published story where Nick hooks the giant trout.[20] It consists mainly of a rambling interior monologue that catalogues those persons, places, and events which have made a strong impression on Hemingway-cum-Nick Adams: Bill Smith, Bill Bird, Hadley Richardson (Helen), Belmonte, Maera, Gertrude Stein, Ezra Pound, James Joyce, Paul Cézanne. . . ; Petoskey, Horton's Creek, the Black River, Paris, Madrid, Valencia. . . .[21] In discursive fashion, Nick mulls over such matters as fishing, marriage, bull fighting, writing, and painting.

Although Hemingway was to use this method later in "The Snows of Kilimanjaro" and some of the basic material in *A Moveable Feast*, he wisely deleted all of the interior monologue from "Big Two-Hearted River." He submerged the ideas it raised as thoroughly as he had those about the war and Indians. Had they been retained, the story would have emerged as a truncated *Künstlerroman*, a portrait of the artist as a young fisherman—presenting us with a rather self-conscious Nick Adams (the friend of Ezra Pound, Gertrude Stein, and the matador Maera), who is aware of hundreds of tricks in writing invented by James Joyce, and who is himself represented, in dizzying mirror fashion, as the author of "My Old Man" and "Indian Camp." Fortunately, this tricky piece of self-portraiture was, along with everything else in the monologue, excised from the story.

This wholesale act of omission contains several critical implications. Philip Young sees in it a kind of symbolic farewell to youth, to northern Michigan, to marital responsibilities—all of which had to give way to the responsibilities of art. But it is important to note that Hemingway also dropped all considerations of art from the story, except as he may have put them to use in its making. In doing so, he was able to maintain the vital line of his narrative, holding to an existence level of hiking, camping, fishing, eating. Only twice does the published story vary from this basic line of action and thought. The first variance comes near the end of Part I, with the introduction of the "coffee according to Hopkins" episode. And in this instance, when Nick realizes that his mind is "starting to work," he is relieved to discover that he can "choke it," that he can, in other words, suppress any mental activity beyond that needed for existence.

The auctorial suppression revealed by the manuscripts emphasizes the critical fact that "Big Two-Hearted River" is preeminently a story of suppression. Nick Adams is a shadow figure of the author in "choking off" all thoughts about war, art, and civilization as such. Except for the already noted lapse in the Hopkins episode, he holds himself to the simplest of thought processes until the very end of the story, when a concept of tragedy wells up. The singular success of the story is due to the manner in which very primitive matters are accorded very civilized treatment, in terms of emotive restraint and purity of prose. The kind of tension, or balance, Hemingway here achieves accounts for the success of many of his works, most notably perhaps *The Old Man and the Sea*, another account of a solitary fisher. But "Big Two-Hearted River" is subtler, more severely controlled, than any of the other works. Each of its segments consists of a singularly objectified picture that contains, nonetheless, a potentially emotive center. One vital picture follows the other until at the very end some undefined aspect of the human condition hovers in the air, moving well beyond the physical stopping place. In this fictive atmosphere, it is possible to catch some glimmer of a Sisyphean distinction between existence and essence.

To achieve this haunting effect, Hemingway had to do much more than simply eliminate the interior monologue section that threatened to ruin the entire work. He had to re-sight his objective and reconstruct the final scenes. Peculiarly enough, the manuscripts reflect the kind of auctorial enlightenment he went through to attain his end. To see how this happened, it is necessary to examine three particular elements of the conclusion which he prepared in the earliest of the manuscripts (Item 274).

Actually, Hemingway brought this handwritten version of the work to a close twice (see pp. 98 and 99 of Item 274), with a small stutter-step variation thrown in for good measure. Instead of the life-taking incident that informs the conclusion of the published story (the killing of the two trout), Item 274 ends initially on a note of life-preservation similar to that in William Faulkner's "The Bear," where Isaac McCaslin refrains from killing Big Ben. In like manner, Nick Adams decides to set free the giant trout which (in this version of the story) he succeeds in catching, with the declaration that the fish was, after all, "too big to eat."

As though he were not satisfied with this humane gesture, Hemingway added another by tacking on one more page to Item 274. Here, as Nick makes his way back to camp, he finds a stricken rabbit lying "flat out on the trail"—

> There were three ticks on the rabbits head. Two behind one ear and one behind the other. They were gray like the rabbits ear skin, tight with blood, as big as grapes. Nick pulled them off, their heads tiny and hard with moving feet. . . Nick picked up the rabbit, limp, with button eyes, and put it under a sweet fern beside the trail. Its heart was beating as he laid it down. He went on up the trail. *He was holding something in his head.* (p. 99, italics added)

This last page marks a clear advance over the preceding one, where the author had placed first a "30" and two sentences later the words "The End." At these points, Nick simply gets his fishing line caught on a branch and he, like the story, is "stopped" ("30"); and then, after freeing his line, he sets off for camp "his rod out before him" ("The End").

Like a double-exposed photograph, these incidents reflect the predicament of both the author and his character. What Nick and Ernest succeed in freeing is more than a fishing line, for what they eventually hold in their minds is a solution to a problem in artistic representation. Just before and during the fish-freeing and rabbit-saving incidents, Nick has been thinking about Paul Cézanne and certain of his works, including one that depicts "soldiers undressing to swim," and another that shows "the house through the trees." He believes that Cézanne got away from using tricks in his work, that he succeeded in breaking painting down to its essentials, and then proceeded from there. This is why Nick wants "to write the way Cézanne painted."[22] And when he perceives how the French painter would do "this stretch of river," he is filled with a sudden sense of urgency. He wants "to get back to camp and get to work"—presumably on something like the very story in which these matters are being presented. Here again the mirror effect is dizzying, as—

> Nick, seeing how Cézanne would do the stretch of country, stood up. The water was *cold and actual*. He waded across the stream, *moving in the picture*. It was good. He kneeled down in the gravel at the edge of the stream and reached down into the trout sack. The old boy was alive. . . . He slid the trout into the shallow water and watched him move off through the shallows. . . .[23]

This is an intricate passage, mingling actuality with imagination. Nick the author is sketching a picture, and Nick the character is "moving in the picture" as well as the "cold and actual" water, while Hemingway is trying somehow to frame it all off with a proper ending. Of course the irony is that, if Nick (and thus

Hemingway) wants to write the way Cézanne painted, he will have to forgo exactly the kind of *trompe l'oeil* trickery employed in the passage quoted above. He will have to get rid of the non-essential interior monologue, including the self-defeating discussion of Joyce's trickery versus Cézanne's integrity. Indeed, he will have to go back to what he had been doing quite simply and naturally earlier in the story—breaking everything down into sharp basic pictures of existence.

This was how Hemingway ultimately solved the problem of ending "Big Two-Hearted River" effectively. Sometime after seeing the original conclusion clearly represented in typescript, he presumably found something more artistically efficacious "in his head" than Nick Adams had. In any event, the published conclusion depends upon a final series of essential "pictures"—man sitting on a log, man eating sandwich, man smoking, man killing two trout, man cleaning trout in cold water, man wading across stream, man climbing an embankment, man walking up path toward camp, and then, most significantly, man taking a last backward glance at where the river narrows and enters the dark swamp. Writing of this kind gains power from its ancient glyphic, pictographic source; it is capable of merging a primitive outer landscape with a sensitive, modern inner one. Done with fine Hemingwaysque detail (down to the milt shucked from the trout), it embodies clarity and mystery at the same time, like Cézanne's painting of the "House of the Hanged Man," which contains no overt sign of either a man or a hanging.

If all this can be characterized as the solution according to Cézanne, it might with some justification also be called a solution according to Henry David Thoreau—that countryman of Hemingway's who, in *Walden* and *A Week on the Concord and Merrimack Rivers,* proves to be his closest rival in the literary depiction of the solitary life in the American woods. Although Hemingway's remarks about Thoreau in *Green Hills of Africa* indicate no direct line of influence, the two men wrote to the beat of related drummers. It was, after all, Thoreau who preceded Hemingway with exhortations to "simplify, simplify," to reduce all things to their "lowest common denominator," and to "Say what you have to say, not what you ought." It was also Thoreau who went before in driving life into a woodland corner, there to examine it closely and objectively in order to discover whether it was "mean" or had sublimity. Hemingway would certainly have agreed with these pragmatic attitudes and methods, as well as Thoreau's metaphoric extension of them in such a statement as "Time is but the stream I go a-fishing in."[24] Moreover, as the manuscripts of "Big Two-Hearted River" attest, Hemingway was also aware that the artist can control the flow of that stream in his work, and can arrange himself (or a fictional double) just so within the stream, fishing for eternity.

III. "The Short Happy Life"

"The Short Happy Life of Francis Macomber" came out of the same cluster of experiences that produced *Green Hills of Africa* (1935) and "The Snows of Kilimanjaro" (1936). Published initially, and somewhat incongruously, in a woman's magazine (*Cosmopolitan*, Sept. 1936), "The Short Happy Life" was used as the lead story in *The Fifth Column and the First Forty-Nine Stories* in 1938—placed there by an author who listed it first among his favorites in the short preface he did for this collection. The story has remained a favorite among anthologists also, with the result that it has been read and discussed by thousands of college students, and has received perhaps as much critical attention as any of Hemingway's short narratives.[25] Some of the most important critical questions it has raised deal with such technical matters as the structure of the work and its shifting point of view. But within the last decade and a half, a period coinciding with the rise of the Feminist Movement, most of the questions have concerned such social and moral matters as Robert Wilson's reliability as code hero, Francis Macomber's conversion from cowardice to courage, and Margot Macomber's motives in her various actions, including the killing of her husband.[26] In certain respects, this critical debate has resembled the line of inquiry followed in a court case, with charge and counter-charge, prosecution and defense, resulting in some rather willful and even perverse readings of the story.

If used properly (with due respect for the concept of the intentional fallacy, and with a clear understanding that sub-texts are not to be equated with *the* text), certain papers in the Hemingway Collection should help answer some of these critical questions, both social and technical, that have been exacerbated and clouded by partisan furor. The pertinent papers are Item 689, a four-page handwritten beginning of the story; Item 690, a five-page handwritten variation of the previous beginning; Item 692, a one-page handwritten list of sixteen possible titles for the story; and Item 251, a twelve-page typescript entitled "The Art of the Short Story," mentioned previously in connection with "Big Two-Hearted River."

Item 689, the initial beginning, opens with the line "Of course by the third day the old man was gone about her." In narrative tone and method, this fragment represents a peculiar return to those days when a neophyte Hemingway was emulating Sherwood Anderson, particularly in "My Old Man." The first-person narrator of the fragment is an underling who stands in considerable awe of the unnamed white hunter: "I work for him driving cars," he tells us, "so I keep pretty good track of his eyes," and, "he can still spook me with his eyes. . . I can't look at them when he's angry."[27] Through this secondary figure, who is doomed to literary limbo after the second manuscript, we have an opportunity to watch Hemingway's initial attempts to adjust his view and sketch in the necessary elements of his sex triangle. "The husband," we learn, "was one of these Yale old bones men who are so pleasant and such a good fellow and such a fine sportsman that you don't know what it's all about for a long time." The "O. M.," or old man, is "a strange bird," according to the narrator: "You would have to have seen him young to know what it's all about because since cars came in he's got himself covered in a perfect disguise made out of his own body that's put on a belly there and thickened up here and filled his face out so you can't see what it's about."[28]

The wife, named *Dorothy* Macomber in these early versions (her husband is named *Denny*), seemed to be the most difficult of the three major characters to sketch in. It was almost as though there were too much to say about her; and although both manuscripts begin by emphasizing her, supplying a considerable amount of partially conflicting commentary, Hemingway crossed most of this material out, cutting to "the old man" and the way in which he is taken with her beauty. In Item 689, the narrator speaks of her in this manner:

> She was dark and smooth and cool and very expensive looking. . . . They're the goddamndest women on earth, really. They only have them in two countries, ours and yours. I suppose they're lovely looking and damned nice if you don't care. . . . And they hunt alone, in pairs, and in packs too. . . . She was a fine sample of how good the best of them can look. . . . But they never stop hunting.[29]

In Item 690, a less jumbled and disconnected version, the huntress aspect of the lady is all but eradicated, and her expensive good looks played up:

> She looked like all those pictures of the women who endorse things in the shiny paper magazines. You know, smooth and cool and very expensive. The kind you can't imagine being mussed or excited or breathing hard or up too early in the morning. . . what we call the backgammon bitches but she was no bitch particularly. No. And the funny thing was she didn't play backgammon either.[30]

Although this entire opening paragraph was eventually crossed out, it contained a further concession about Mrs. Macomber in a line that said, "She was a nice enough woman."[31]

The variance in these two early depictions of Margot, *née* Dorothy Macomber indicate trouble in bringing her into proper narrative focus. Twenty years after the fact, in doing "The Art of the Short Story," Hemingway was much surer about the kind of woman he intended to portray. This unpublished typescript provides us with background information about all three of the major figures in "The Short Happy Life," but most tellingly about the character of Mrs. Macomber:

> This is a simple story in a way, *because the woman, who I knew very well in*

real life but then invented out of, to make the woman for this story, is a bitch for
the full course and doesn't change. You'll probably never meet the type because
you haven't got the money. I haven't either but I get around. Now this woman
doesn't change. She has been better, but she will never be better anymore. *I
invented her complete with handles* from the worst bitch I knew (then). . . .

There is more of the same, on the woman, and then on the two men, all of it
definite in the mind of the author:

The woman called Margot Macomber is no good to anybody now except for trouble. . . . The man is a nice jerk. *I knew him very well in real life, so invent him too
from everything I know.* So he is just how he really was, *only he is invented.* The
White Hunter is my best friend and he does not care what I write as long as it is
readable, so I don't invent him at all. I just disguise him for family and business
reasons, and to keep him out of trouble with the Game Department.[32]

The reader is, of course, free to accept or reject these hindsight assurances by
the author about the nature of his characters. What is more important is that
Hemingway, here and elsewhere in this typescript, recognizes the fact that the
story makes demands upon the author and shapes his characters, through the invention referred to repeatedly in the italicized phrases above. Until the story shapes up,
the characters are still matters of gestation. The manuscript beginnings show this is
true not only of the Macombers but also the white hunter—even though
Hemingway would later, in characteristically offhand manner, declare that this
character was simply his "best friend" disguised "for family and business reasons,
and to keep him out of trouble." Yet the "beautiful red-faced Mr. Wilson" who
shares his cot with Mrs. Macomber in the finished story is a long imaginative leap
away from the fleshy old man with the threatening eyes who is described by the
narrator of the two fragments. This early prototype may be more closely aligned
with the "Pop" figure of *Green Hills of Africa,* who is based on the real-life Philip
Percival. In any event, this old man is "gone about her by the third day," and he
"always falls in love with them or thinks he does." Obviously, then, the story
demanded a considerably different white hunter, in both attitude and appearance.

If anything, the prototype Francis (Denny) Macomber had to undergo an
even more severe adjustment. In the first fragment (Item 689) he is simply presented as a rich Ivy-league type, the necessary appendage of the beautiful wife
who is so attractive to the white hunter. All that happens in this instance is that
the three of them, described by the self-effacing narrator, engage in conversation
around the camp fire:

Now the wife, Dorothy Macomber, was a lovely looking woman and
Macomber was a good looking young fellow and they looked nice sitting there

by the fire light in the evening with the O. M., all leaning back in the canvas chairs, she with a gimlet and the two men with whiskeys and sodas and it getting dark and the boys working around their fires.

The only action added to this Abercrombie and Fitch scene is the overhead flight of some flamingoes making a "whicha-whicha-whicha" sound in their "flight-ing." The old man explains that they are on their way to a nearby lake, where they may be seen "in the daytime." The fragment breaks off just after Mrs. Macomber responds to this information, saying, "It's wonderful. . . . Aren't you glad we came, Denny?"

These flamingoes fly off and are never heard of again. The second manu-script makes no mention of them, nor does it use this campfire scene. It estab-lishes the camp and then moves off to hunting territory. There, through a series of actions, it fills out the character of Macomber considerably. In fact, this version focuses fully on him, presenting him as an intriguing, perhaps even dominating figure, and above all an extraordinarily good shot. As the narrator relates mat-ters:

> . . . the old man took them out to Mutu-umbu to see if they could learn to shoot a little first. We camped there in the big trees and took them up the valley the next morning. This fellow Macomber, the husband, was a good shot. He made a nice shot on a wildebeeste. Then he made a hell of a good shot on quite a good Grant.

When the old man wants to see more of his clients' shooting ability, the party drives off to where there is a herd of "Tommys" (Thomson's East Africa gazelle), and Macomber is set up for a very difficult piece of hunting:

> So Macomber gets out and sits down and we drive away about four hundred yards and the Tommys move off too. What he has now is a hell of a shot, the wind is blowing a big breeze and the light has started to get that heat haze. It was a long shot and a bad one to make. I wouldn't have tried it. But we saw him sitting there, comfortable looking, well back on his heels, using the sling to steady himself in the wind and saw the rifle spit and whack the Tommy was down and the rest of them bounding off. . . . We drove over and he came walking up.

The manuscript here becomes repetitively insistent about Macomber's abil-ity. The old man questions him about what windage adjustment he had made and the spot he had aimed for; after examining the dead animal he declares, "Well, you *can* shoot. . . That was a damned fine shot," and a bit later repeats, "You can shoot." But Macomber's reaction to this accolade from the master is noteworthy. As the narrator observes, "Macomber didn't seem very pleased and he didn't seem very happy."

Two paragraphs later the fragment stops. In the first of these it is established that Mrs. Macomber is an unexceptional shot: "The woman could shoot just like any woman," the chauvinist narrator declares—"She could hit them fine and miss them just as well and didn't know why she did either." Again, however, he returns to the husband, stating, ". . . this fellow Macomber was a rifle shot. But there was something funny about him." The something funny is emphasized in the last paragraph, which describes the party sitting around in camp drinking: the old man and Dorothy Macomber begin to "feel good," but as the very last lines inform us, "Macomber was serious as hell and wanted to talk about shock, and penetration and all the rest of it."

What kind of story would "The Short Happy Life," with this or some other title, have turned into had Hemingway continued with this manuscript beginning? Would it have ended with Mrs. Macomber killing her husband, or with her husband, that strangely intense and expert shot, killing her or the white hunter, or both? Was Hemingway preparing for a zany duel between white hunter and husband, to be brought on by the wife's sexual transgression? Unless other papers are discovered, we will never know. Perhaps the author was already preparing to contrast Macomber's ability to shoot with his inability to act courageously in hunting dangerous game. And perhaps the ending of the story as we know it is foreshadowed in the line about Mrs. Macomber's ability with a gun—"She could hit them fine and miss them just as well and didn't know why she did either."

We do know Hemingway solved the narrative problems implicit in the two manuscript beginnings. The first thing he did was to get rid of the awkward first-person narrator. In doing so, he shifted to an omniscient point of view, but with a special built-in hall of mirrors feature that allowed him to round out, and at the same time deepen, the major characters. "The Short Happy Life," along with "The Snows of Kilimanjaro," stands as one of Hemingway's most technically intricate and subtle works, mainly because of the various angles of vision and perception it provides. Although the story operates on a point-counterpoint principle, we perceive fear, cowardice, humiliation, the need to learn, and finally the exhilaration of courage mainly through the sensibilities of Francis Macomber. The values of rich clients, the vicious games that they play, the American battle of the sexes, the management of hunting activities, the sexual attractiveness of Margot Macomber, the need for some kind of code of personal and professional behavior, and the reactions of Margot after the shooting of her husband—all of these things are made known to us from Robert Wilson's angle of perception.

Most of the story, in fact, is told from these alternating male points of view. Only a few times does Hemingway resort to other viewpoints. Twice he makes important use of Margot as viewer and assessor, once near the beginning of the story and once toward the end. In both instances we see the two men through her eyes:

> She looked at both these men as though she had never seen them before. One, Wilson. . . , she knew she had never truly seen before. He was about middle height with sandy hair, a stubby mustache, a very red face and extremely cold blue eyes with faint white wrinkles at the corners that grooved merrily when he smiled. He smiled at her now and she looked away from his face at the way his shoulders sloped in the loose tunic he wore with the four big cartridges held in loops. . . .

This is a fairly frank appraisal of masculine, perhaps even priapic, attractiveness, reminding the reader of Liz Coates' appraisal of Jim Gilmore in "Up In Michigan." Here Francis Macomber suffers by contrast, for though he is a handsome young man (of thirty-five), he has "just shown himself, very publicly, to be a coward." In the second instance, however, Margot sees the two men in a different relationship, as comrades in arms:

> From the far corner of the [car] seat Margot Macomber looked at the two of them. There was no change in Wilson. She saw Wilson as she had seen him the day before when she had first realized what his great talent was. But she saw the change in Francis now.

It may be true that Hemingway was psychically incapable of seeing more of any story from a female point of view: none of his works show the hermaphroditic sensibilities that produced Emma Bovary, Anna Karenina, and the insatiable Molly Bloom. But there are two good reasons for holding mainly to the male angles of vision in "The Short Happy Life": the first of these is technical, and the second, as we shall see, is thematic.

Technically, the plot demands that the reader not know for certain what goes through Margot Macomber's mind when she shoots her husband. To have placed emphasis on her thought processes throughout the narrative and then to have avoided her thoughts and feelings at the crucial point, would have severely damaged the artistic integrity of the story. As it was, Hemingway had to work very carefully at this vital juncture in his narrative, resorting to auctorial reportage, and stating that "Mrs. Macomber, in the car, *had shot at the buffalo as it seemed about to gore Macomber*, and had hit her husband about two inches up and a little to one side of the base of his skull." The italicized section of the passage (italics added) is quoted in part by Warren Beck in his article entitled "The Shorter Happy Life of Mrs. Macomber." He offers the words "shot at the buffalo" as proof of the lady's innocence, stating that although Hemingway was "a highly implicative artist," he was not "notably given to double talk."[33] Had he had access to "The Art of the Short Story," Beck might have been less sure about his statement, for in that piece Hemingway concludes his remarks about "The Short Happy Life" in a contradictory manner:

That about handles that story. Any questions? No, I don't know whether she shot him on purpose any more than you do. I could find out if I asked myself because I invented it and I could go right on inventing. But you have to know where to stop. That is what makes a short story. Makes it short at least. The only hint I could give you is that it is my belief that the incidence of husbands shot accidentally by wives who are bitches and really work at it is very low. Should we continue?

In between the wise-guy comments, we catch sight of the integrity that separates the artist from the man. It is the artist in Hemingway that says, "I don't know whether she shot him on purpose any more than you do." And it is the artist who must give Mrs. Macomber her due, allowing for psychological ambiguity, and keeping the fictional case moot—in between involuntary manslaughter and second-degree murder (perpetrated with a 6.5 *Mannlicher*, which Mark Spilka has noted means "manly" in German and suggests man-licker, or -defeater, in English).[34]

As we can see from observation of the wavering manuscript beginnings, with their indefinite stereotype figures, Hemingway finally constructed his characters as the plot demanded. Each of the three major figures is flawed in personality. Macomber has been a spoiled young rich man, a cowardly cuckold, and an amoral materialist who knows something about motor cars and "court games" but very little about men and women. Mrs. Macomber is represented as being equally amoral and materialistic—a woman who has used her beauty as a social and economic stay, and her sexual transgressions, both past and present, as an assertive club. Robert Wilson is a hunting guide who is himself guided by the tawdry standards of his pre-jet-set clients in all things except hunting, and who bends the rules of his profession as he sees fit. It should be noted, however, that Wilson does try to live up to his own personal code, even if he is not "a bloody plaster saint." Moreover, he possesses what for Hemingway and the old Stoic philosophers is the *sine qua non* of all human virtues—courage.

In Wilson's understanding of male courage we find the thematic, and thus structural, reason for Hemingway's holding mainly to the contrapuntal viewpoints of the two men in this story. Wilson, we learn, has "seen men come of age before and it always moved him." It moves him to view Macomber's transformation in this perceptive and sympathetic fashion:

Beggar had probably been afraid all his life. Don't know what started it. But over now. Hadn't had time to be afraid of the [buffalo]. That and being angry too. Motor car too. Motor cars made it familiar. . . . More of a change than any loss of virginity. Fear gone like an operation. Something else grew in its place. Main thing a man had. . . .[35]

This passage emphasizes the fact that, thematically, "The Short Happy Life" is above all a compressed *Bildungsroman*, or more precisely, *Erziehungsroman*, which might very well have been labelled "The Education of Francis Macomber."

Structurally, the story depends upon a sometimes obscured catechism of direct and indirect questions and answers. In fact, the beginning of the story that Hemingway finally devised centers on the seemingly unimportant question of what one should drink at lunch on an African safari. It begins in the middle of things, with Macomber, already the odd man out, asking, "Will you have lime juice or lemon squash? Robert Wilson and Margot Macomber brush aside the implicit suggestion of a soft drink, declaring the necessity of something alcoholic under the circumstances. Macomber capitulates in his response: "I suppose it's the thing to do. . . . Tell him to make it three gimlets."[36]

Just a partial list of these questions shows how they run the gamut from the most trivial customs to the most vital aspects of morality, ethics, and law:

> How much should the "beaters" be tipped after a hunt?
> Should one wear one's hat at noon, "even under the canvas"?
> May a Swahili servant stare at a hunting client, even a cowardly one?
> Is it permissible to punish such a servant by whipping him?
> Should a white hunter tell tales about a client?
> Should the client ask that information about him be suppressed?
> How should the hunter behave afterward in the company of a client who makes
>   such a request?
> How should the client react after he realizes how cowardly he has been?
> Should a wife shoot at a charging buffalo when there is a good chance she will
>   kill her husband in the process?

There are many more such questions imbedded in the story—about whether it is legal to hunt from moving vehicles, and, of course, what must be done after wounding a lion. Some of these pertain directly to Margot Macomber, like that asked by Robert Wilson: *"How should a woman act when she discovers her husband is a bloody coward?"* And, indeed, the ending of the story—built on the moot point of whether she shot her husband purposely or accidentally—asks how a wife should behave after she has shot her husband.

As the story is constructed, however, Robert Wilson functions as the catechist and Francis Macomber as the principal catechumen. The main lesson to be learned is not how to hunt lions or buffalo, but how to face up to life. And in terms of the way in which Hemingway built this story, finishing off a wounded lion or standing up to a charging buffalo is no more important than learning how to face up to one's wife.

Along with its companion piece, "The Snows of Kilimanjaro," this story of Mr. and Mrs. Macomber helps expand the series of short narratives Hemingway had already done about the battle of the sexes—including "The Doctor and the Doctor's Wife," "Mr. and Mrs. Elliot," "Cat in the Rain," "Out of Season," "Cross-Country Snow," "Hills Like White Elephants," "A Canary for One," "The Sea Change," and "Homage to Switzerland." Anyone who has read these works closely knows that Hemingway represented male and female characters with varying degrees of sympathy. In some, the female character is fine and understanding, while the male is insensitive and cloddish (as in "Cat in the Rain" and "Hills Like White Elephants"); in others, the female is insensitive and cruel, while the male is weak and maltreated (as in "The Doctor and the Doctor's Wife" and "Mr. and Mrs. Elliot").

What Hemingway had to do in "The Short Happy Life" was to fuse the matter of matrimonial struggle with the hunt and the temporary emergence of a self-respecting man. His task is made apparent by a note he wrote to himself on a sheet of paper (Item 692), on which he also listed sixteen possible titles for this story. The note simply says:

> To look up
> Man
> Marriage
> Fear
> Courage.

The titles reinforce the note. Most of them refer directly or indirectly to marriage; others intertwine marriage and hunting; and the remainder (like "The New Man" and the title eventually selected, with one important modification) point toward Macomber's transformation:

> A Marriage Has Been Arranged
> The Coming Man
> The New Man
> The Short Life of Francis Macomber [sic]
> The End of the Marriage
> Marriage Is a Dangerous Game
> The More Dangerous Game
> A Marriage Has Been Terminated
> The Ruling Classes
> Brief Mastery
> The Master Passion
> The Cult of Violence

The Struggle for Power [in margin]
_____
Marriage is a Bond
Through Darkest Marriage [back of photocopy][37]
_____

Hemingway was as careful and precise in the selection of titles as he was in the actual writing and revision of his works. At times he used working titles during the early stages of composition (*The World's Room* and *Nights and Forever* were so used for *A Farewell to Arms*), but most often it was Hemingway's practice to make up lists of potential titles during the revision stage of composition, or, as he informed George Plimpton, after a work was actually finished.[38] With "The Short Happy Life" it would appear that he followed his usual practice. There were no working titles attached to the early manuscripts; and the thematic inclusiveness of the sixteen titles in Item 692 indicates that the author had the story well in mind, either finished or nearly so, by the time he made up the list.

In this instance, the titles are somewhat different from others devised by Hemingway, who tended toward literary allusion and resonance, or the indication of climatic, topographic, or geographic features (as with *For Whom the Bell Tolls*, "Cross-Country Snow," "Hills Like White Elephants," and "The Snows of Kilimanjaro," which combines two of these features). Only one of the titles listed above makes even indirect reference to a geographic element, with the reworking of the common phrase "through darkest Africa" into "Through Darkest Marriage." And only one has literary reference. With "The More Dangerous Game" Hemingway was referring to a cheap thriller of his day, Richard Connell's "The Most Dangerous Game," published in 1924. This, too, is a hunting story, but with an implausible plot, unbelievable characters (two big-game hunters who try to kill each other), and what Hemingway would call a "wow ending."

It was Hemingway the self-editor who rejected "The More Dangerous Game," with its oblique reference to Connell's soggy story, and with its harsh suggestion that women are more dangerous than wounded lions or buffalo. It was Hemingway the artist who selected "The Short Life of Francis Macomber" and added the vital attributive adjective "Happy" to it, applying the revised title as thematic indicator and capstone. Years later, in "The Art of the Short Story," Hemingway the man would express considerable satisfaction with both his titular selection and narrative accomplishment. "Now there is another story called The Short Happy Life of Francis Macomber," he begins in that offhand manner he affects throughout most of this piece: "Jack, I get a bang even yet from just writing the titles. That's why you write, no matter what they tell you."

And that, as the papers indicate, is why you *rewrite* also, fusing the talents of the writer and the self-editor to produce literary works that we can all get a "bang" out of. The manuscripts examined here show that Hemingway was capable of cold editorial excision—in cutting away the first half of "Indian Camp," and in removing the bulge of reminiscence and artistic commentary that threatened the vital flow of "Big Two-Hearted River." He had the ability to reject stock situations and stereotyped characters, to begin again, and again if necessary, to discover where he was really headed with a story like "The Short Happy Life." Through such examples we learn much about Hemingway's process of composition—how he omitted unnecessary information; how he discovered better points of view and deeper points of interest; and how, in some instances, he shed personal prejudices or attitudes to produce works of universal appeal.

Of course, the papers do not tell us everything. We have no manuscript, for example, that tells how Hemingway reworked the plot of "The Short Happy Life"—by employing a central flashback to Macomber's act of cowardice, so that he was able to construct an inductive mystery, beginning with the "lemon squash" and "gimlets" dialogue, which nicely sets the tone for the entire catechism of questions and answers that follows. Nor do we have a variant manuscript that tells when, or *why,* Hemingway decided to inject into the story that tour de force segment in which he perceives things from the viewpoint of the hunted lion.[39]

Besides the lessons briefly reviewed here, however, there are many others to be learned from Hemingway's handling of beginnings and endings as reflected in the manuscripts. It is the job of criticism to determine, in each instance, what is known and what is unknown, and perhaps unknowable, since much of creation remains hidden from the eye, sometimes even the eye of the creator. Beyond this, all the critic can do, even with privileged peeks behind the curtain, is to prepare a set of clumsy and partial blueprints that may, despite their inadequacies, reveal the problems and beauties of the finished structures, and provide all readers with a better basis of analysis and appreciation than they might otherwise have.

1. See Philip Young and Charles W. Mann, "Fitzgerald's *Sun Also Rises:* Notes and Comment," *Fitzgerald/Hemingway Annual, 1970,* pp. 1–9.

2. Bernard Oldsey, *Hemingway's Hidden Craft: The Writing of* A Farewell to Arms (University Park: Pennsylvania State University Press, 1979), pp. 74–75.

3. Ibid., pp. 71–91, 100–10.

4. Ibid., pp. 57–68.

5. All of the publication information about Hemingway's works used in this study is taken from Audre Hanneman's *Ernest Hemingway: A Comprehensive Bibliography* (Princeton: Princeton University Press, 1967); see p. 8 in this instance.

6. Julian Smith, "Hemingway and the Thing Left Out," rpt. in *Ernest Hemingway: Five Decades of Criticism,* ed. Linda W. Wagner (East Lansing: Michigan State University Press, 1974), p. 189.

7. Ibid., p. 199.

8. " 'Big World Out There': The Nick Adams Stories," in *The Short Stories of Ernest Hemingway: Critical Essays*, ed. Jackson J. Benson (Durham, N.C.: Duke University Press, 1975), p. 32. In this essay, written originally to act as an introduction to *The Nick Adams Stories*, Young led the way in making manuscript information count for something in the critical reconsideration of Hemingway stories.

9. Ibid.

10. See Item 493 in the Hemingway Collection.

11. Item 493, italics added. In the line preceding the first end mark of "30," a mark which was then crossed out, Hemingway had written the word *shell*; afterward he wrote over the *s*, making it a *c*, and then placing a dot over the *e*, changed the word *shell* to *chill*.

12. In Item 493 the last sentence appears to have been added as an afterthought, and then built up with modifying phrases.

13. *Stephen Crane: An Omnibus*, ed. R. W. Stallman (New York: Knopf, 1952), p. 369.

14. Although the catalogue of the Hemingway Collection identifies this item (251) as having a full title in note form of "The Art of the Short Story and Nine Stories to Prove It," the only title given on the typescript itself is "The Art of the Short Story." Dated from La Consula, Churriana; Malaga, Spain—June, 1959, it appears to have been written as a preface for a forthcoming collection of Hemingway's stories, but which one is not clear.

[After hearing this article read, Mr. Charles Scribner, Jr. informed the author that "The Art of the Short Story" was prepared as an introduction for *The Snows of Kilimanjaro and Other Stories* (New York: Scribner's, 1961). "When we rejected it," Mr. Scribner said, "that was the sorest I can ever remember Hemingway being with me. He was really mad. But luckily Mary agreed with me that it wasn't suitable."]

15. Italics added.

16. Here, as in a number of his manuscripts, Hemingway reveals his tendency to begin stories with the names of actual persons (like *Scott Fitzgerald*, a name that lasted all the way into the first publication of "The Snows of Kilimanjaro," and *Ag*—for Agnes von Kurowsky, that did the same in "A Very Short Story").

17. Carlos Baker, following in the path of Malcolm Cowley's remarks in *The Portable Hemingway*, states this critical perçu succinctly and well: "In some special way, the destroyed town of Seney and the scorched earth around it carry the hint of war—the area of destruction Nick must pass through in order to reach the high rolling pine plain where the exorcism is to take place." See Baker's *Hemingway: The Writer as Artist*, 3rd ed. (Princeton: Princeton University Press, 1963), p. 127.

18. See Carl Ficken's close analysis of "Point of View in the Nick Adams Stories," as reprinted in *The Short Stories of Ernest Hemingway,* ed. Benson (op. cit.), pp. 106–07.

19. The standard traumatic-therapeutic reading is Philip Young's—in *Ernest Hemingway: A Reconsideration* (University Park: Pennsylvania State University Press, 1966), pp. 43–48. Needless to stress, there could have been no such reading had Hemingway held to his earlier line.

20. These are represented, with certain changes made, in the selection entitled "On Writing," in *The Nick Adams Stories* (New York: Scribner's, 1972).

21. There are some forty specific places and persons that enter into this monologue section. Theodore Dreiser and Sherwood Anderson are mentioned among the other writers, like Joyce, Pound, and Stein.

22. See Raymond S. Nelson, *Hemingway: Expressionist Artist* (Ames: Iowa State University Press, 1979). Nelson uses some of this material, taken from an account by Carlos Baker, but seems not to have availed himself of the pertinent Hemingway papers or the piece "On Writing" in *The Nick Adams Stories*.

23. See Item 274, pp. 96–97; italics added.

24. These lines from Thoreau are to be found in the widely used *Walden and Civil Disobedience*, ed. Sherman Paul (Boston: Houghton Mifflin, 1960), pp. 62, 223, 68, respectively. It is worth noting that during this period of composing his African works, Hemingway did have Thoreau on his mind. In an

early version of "The Snows of Kilimanjaro" he gave his protagonist the name of "Henry Walden."

25. With notes, articles, and commentaries in books, the critical bibliography on "The Short Happy Life" would run well over fifty items. Among the most important of these items are the following: Ronald S. Crane, "Ernest Hemingway: 'The Short Happy Life of Francis Macomber,' " in *The Idea of the Humanities and Other Essays Critical and Historical*, II (Chicago: University of Chicago Press, 1967), 315–26; James G. Watson, " 'A Sound Basis of Union': Structural and Thematic Balance in 'The Short Happy Life of Francis Macomber,' " *Fitzgerald/Hemingway Annual, 1974*, pp. 215–28; Warren Beck, "The Shorter Happy Life of Mrs. Macomber," *Modern Fiction Studies*, 21 (Autumn 1975), 363–76, with an afterword in which Beck discusses the original publication of his essay and the comments made on it by Mark Spilka; and Mark Spilka, "The Necessary Stylist: A New Critical Revision," *Modern Fiction Studies*, 6 (Winter 1960–61), 283–97, and "Warren Beck Revisited," *Modern Fiction Studies*, 22 (Summer 1976), 245–55.

26. In addition to the works by Beck and Spilka mentioned above, see Virgil Hutton, "The Short Happy Life of Macomber," rpt. in *The Short Stories of Ernest Hemingway: Critical Essays*, ed. Jackson J. Benson, op. cit., pp. 239–50; Robert B. Holland, "Macomber and the Critics," *Studies in Short Fiction*, 5 (Winter 1968), 171–78; John S. Hill, "Robert Wilson: Hemingway's Judge in Macomber," *University Review*, 35 (Winter 1968), 129–32; and Anne Greco, "Margot Macomber: 'Bitch Goddess' Exonerated," *Fitzgerald/Hemingway Annual, 1972*.

27. It is difficult to speculate about the age or the background of this narrator. Although his speech pattern is American, there is a hint later that he might be British.

28. This out-of-shape character who has become overly dependent upon motor vehicles, seems quite some imaginative distance away from Robert Wilson.

29. Here the narrator speaks of "two countries, ours and yours." Is he referring to the U.S. and Great Britain, or the U.S. and some other country? Nothing in the manuscript makes this clear. The phrase could be an ironic ploy, meaning *any* other country, and "yours."

30. Interjected lines and cross-outs make this passage from Item 690 and the previous one quoted from Item 689 somewhat difficult to represent; but as they are quoted here, these passages contain all but the most minor elements, and in as close to manuscript order as is editorially possible.

31. The narrator is less interested in Mrs. Macomber than is the O.M., but the narrator shows early signs of Hemingway's attempt to represent the female character of his story objectively.

32. Italics added. (Hemingway continued with his insistence on inventing character: "This information is what you call the background of a story. You throw it all away and invent from what you know.")

33. *Modern Fiction Studies*, 21 (Autumn 1975), 375.

34. "Warren Beck Revisited," *Modern Fiction Studies*, 22 (Summer 1976), 253.

35. Robert Wilson here shows a concern and an understanding that the Wilson haters do not seem to take into consideration. Virgil Hutton (see note 26 of this study) seems to be the most vindictive, almost critically perverse, of the anti-Wilson partisans. He reads everything in the story as an indication of how hateful a bully Wilson is, how hypocritical a guide and judge. In fact, he tries to show how Hemingway himself undercut Wilson through having him advance the Shakespearian line (about owing God "one life," etc.) in ignorance of its real meaning. Anyone who knows Hemingway's life and work knows he doted on this saying, using it as a clue to courage for men going off to war, in the anthology he edited during World War II, entitled *Men At War*.

36. In a manuscript scheduled for journal publication in spring 1982, Bert Bender (in "Margot Macomber's Gimlet") analyzes this opening scene and the symbolic meaning of this drink in an ingenious and meaningful way.

37. It is difficult to know whether this is one sheet, front and back, or just one page in photo-reproduction. [The author is grateful to Leger Brosnahan, who provided the following information after hearing this article read: "A forthcoming study of the carbon copy used in the setting of the collected edition of the story, shows that the story went untitled until the completion of the final typed copy. . . ."]

In addition, it should be noted that only one of the ten tentative titles listed by John M. Howell and Charles Lawler in *Proof*, 2 (1972), 217–18, appears in Item 692. Those represented by Howell and Lawler run as follows: Than a Dead Lion, The Manner of the Accident, Fear's End, The Short Happy

Life of Francis Macomber (with the "Happy" in place), The Tragic Safari, The Lion's Portion, Mr. and Mrs. Macomber, The Macombers, The Macomber Safari, and The Safari of Francis Macomber (with full allusion to the saint, martyrdom, as well as the birds and the beasts).

Also in *A Life Story* (p. 284), Baker states that Hemingway "completed a story, tentatively called 'The Happy Ending,' " still another designation.

38. See pp. 14–16 in *Hemingway's Hidden Craft*. Hemingway told Plimpton, in their *Paris Review* interview that he made "a list of titles after" finishing a story or book—"sometimes as many as a hundred." There is good evidence, however, that he often started the titling process during revision periods, and sometimes even earlier.

39. This may very well have been a narrative mistake, and one not typical of Hemingway, who elsewhere shows the ability to cut unnecessary stuff. In "The Art of the Short Story," Hemingway speaks defensively about inclusion of this material: "That's all there is to that story except maybe the lion when he is hit and I am thinking inside of him really, not faked. I can think inside of a lion, really. It's hard to believe and it is perfectly okay with me if you don't believe it. Perfectly." He then goes on to discuss some unnamed writer who used the same method of narrating from an animal point of view, "making only one mistake." He then adds, somewhat ruefully, "Making any mistake kills you. This mistake killed him and quite soon everything he wrote was a mistake." Obviously all this still weighed on Hemingway's mind, twenty years after the story was published.

Howell and Lawler (see note 37) make a good point about the function of the lion in respect to Macomber's change from the status of a cowardly, bolting "rabbit" to a dying but dignified lion. Without solving the problem of potential ambiguity and irony, they point to two of the tentative titles as being meaningful in this respect—"The Lion's Portion," as in the expression "the lion's share"; and "Than a Dead Lion," an allusion to Ecclesiastes (9:4) and the idea that "a living dog is better than a dead lion."

HEMINGWAY AND VANITY FAIR

C. HUGH HOLMAN

"IN HEMINGWAY, THE EMOTIONS that are not there are a silence underlying all sound, a lack which, once felt, constantly gives poignancy to the whole," John Peale Bishop has said. In Hemingway's first major novel, *The Sun Also Rises,* the poignancy of this "missing all" defines the unexpressed theme: the moral vacuum in which the expatriate veterans of the First World War were living. It is the intensity of this sense of loss—a loss of love, of health, of meaning, and most disastrously of all, of hope—that gives point and strength to the story of the emasculated Jake Barnes and the emotionally trapped Lady Brett Ashley.

As Hemingway himself has reminded us, "you'll lose it if you talk about it," and it is dangerous to conceptualize this unexpressed context in his novel. Yet, recognizing that danger, we may say that in one significant sense, what has been lost is the traditional religious view of life and man, a view that gives life meaning.

In this meaningless world Hemingway's characters move with frenetic energy, attempting with strident gaiety to impose upon their world, if not value, at least pleasure. And they drive themselves, with all their laughter, their drinking, their love-making, closer and closer to lonely, disintegrating despair.

The parallel between this story and that of the Fisher King and his impotence in Eliot's *The Waste Land* has often been pointed out. I believe that the novel also has parallels to the concept of Vanity Fair, and that those parallels illuminate certain aspects of Hemingway's view of his world.

The concept of Vanity Fair—a frantic, materialistic, gay but joyless search for pleasure in defiance of recognized values of life—is fairly wide-spread in the world's literature. Almost certainly it finds its origins in the book which Herman Melville called "the fine hammered steel of woe," *Ecclesiastes,* the Biblical book

Reprinted with permission from *Carolina Quarterly,* 8 (Summer 1956), 31–37.

whose author declares, "Vanity of vanities, saith the Preacher, vanity of vanities; all is vanity. What profit hath a man of all his labour which he taketh under the sun?"

In several obvious ways, *The Sun Also Rises* invites comparison with *Ecclesiastes*. Its title comes from the Biblical book; it bears an epigram from it, an epigram underscoring the transience of man and the enduring quality of the earth:

> One generation passeth away, and another generation cometh; but the earth abideth forever. . . . The sun also ariseth, and the sun goeth down, and hasteth to the place where he arose. . . . The wind goeth toward the south, and turneth about unto the north; it whirleth about continually, and the wind returneth again according to his circuits. . . . All the rivers run into the sea; yet the sea is not full; unto the place from whence the river come, thither they return again.

Hemingway wrote to his editor Maxwell Perkins that the point of the book was "that the earth abideth forever," that he had "a great deal of fondness and admiration for the earth, and not a hell of a lot for my generation," and that he cared "little about vanities."

Taking his pictures of the Boulevard Montparnasse and the fiesta at Pamplona as variations on Vanity Fair, as Carlos Baker has suggested that they may be taken, I shall attempt to set them against the pictures of Vanity Fair drawn by John Bunyan and by William Makepeace Thackeray.

In 1678 John Bunyan, a dissenting preacher lodged in Bedford Prison for preaching "the truth" in the post-Commonwealth world of the Stuart Restoration, looked from the prison cell of his sainthood upon a world where vanity had run mad—a materialistic, lecherous, drunken, giddy world of lost values and depraved conduct. And he imprisoned this vision of his world in parts of his allegory of Christian's pilgrimage from earth to Heaven, *Pilgrim's Progress*.

After Christian and Faithful emerge from the wilderness, they find themselves in an ancient town called Vanity, which has a fair of which Bunyan says:

> . . . at this fair are all such merchandise sold, as houses, lands, trades, places, honours, preferments, titles, countries, kingdoms, lusts, pleasures, delights of all sorts, as whores, bawds, wives, husbands, children, masters, servants, lives, blood, bodies, souls, silver, gold, pearls, precious stones, and what not.
>
> And, moreover, at this fair there is at all times to be seen jugglings, cheats, games, plays, fools, apes, knaves, and rogues. . . thefts, murders, adulteries, false swearers, and that of a blood-red colour.

Unmistakably here is an allegory in which the orthodox Protestant views of man and religion are brought to bear upon materialism and vanity. Man becomes a citizen of Bunyan's evil city only when he defies a clear religious tradition and is false to an accepted truth. Salvation from the inner corrosion of selfishness is to be found in Evangelist's words. There is a knowable God who overrules the worst efforts of "the Lord Carnal Delight, the Lord Luxurious, the Lord Desire of Vain Glory, my old Lord Lechery, Sir Having Greedy, and all the rest. . . the nobility [of] our noble prince Beelzebub." Faithful, who dies under scourging in the prison, "straightway was carried up through the clouds, with sound of trumpet, the nearest way to the celestial gate." And Bunyan tells us that "he that overrules all things having the power of their rage in his own hand, so wrought it about that Christian for that time escaped them and went his way; and as he went he sang."

In 1847 and 1848 William Makepeace Thackeray looked out upon a world of selfishness and unhappiness and bodied it forth in an extensive novel which he called *Vanity Fair*. His purposes, like Bunyan's, were moral. In a letter to his mother, on July 2, 1847, he wrote:

Of course you are quite right about Vanity Fair and Amelia being selfish. . . .
Don't you see how odious all the people are in the book (with the exception of
Dobbin)—behind whom all there lies a dark moral I hope. What I want is to
make a set of people living without God in the world (only that is a cant phrase)
greedy pompous mean perfectly self-satisfied for the most part. . .

But Thackeray is very much a citizen of Vanity Fair, and toward himself and his fellow vain ones he takes a tolerantly mocking air. In the prologue to the novel, he defines his attitude:

As the Manager of the Performance sits before the curtain on the boards, and
looks into the Fair, a feeling of profound melancholy comes over him in his
survey of the bustling place. There is a great quantity of eating and drinking,
making love and jilting, laughing and the contrary, smoking, cheating, fighting, dancing, and fiddling. . . . Yes, this Vanity Fair; not a moral place certainly; nor a merry one, though very noisy. . . the general impression is one
more melancholy than mirthful.

In the nineteenth chapter, in one of his hundreds of authorial interruptions, he says:

. . . the bustle, and triumph, and laughter, and gaiety which Vanity Fair
exhibits in public, do not always pursue the performer into private life. . . . O
brother wearers of motley! Are there not moments when one grows sick of
grinning and tumbling, and the jingling of cap and bells? This. . . is my amiable object—to walk with you through the Fair. . . come home. . . and be perfectly miserable in private.

And he brings his records of vanity, selfishness, and frenetic despair to a conclusion with this comment: "Ah! *Vanitas Vanitatum!* Which of us is happy in this world? Which of us has his desire? or, having it, is satisfied?"

Clearly the simple physical facts of Thackeray's Vanity Fair are similar to those of Bunyan's. The difference between the two writers is chiefly in the attitudes they take toward Vanity Fair. The Puritan preacher had called, like an Old Testament prophet, for the vain, materialistic world to repent; and he had been horrified by the evil which it did to others, as symbolized by Christian and Faithful. Thackeray's prophecies seem at least partially self-directed; the evil of which he seems most aware is one which Vanity Fair does to itself; and it is upon his "fellow wearers of the motley" that he lavishes his cynical sympathy. Bunyan had judged Vanity Fair by a pattern of absolute religious belief. Thackeray's judgment is relative and ethical, not absolute and religious. Although there are significant contiguous qualities abut them, Bunyan's standard of Godlessness is heavenly in its orientation and Thackeray's standard of selfishness is earthly in its orientation. Bunyan views the sins of a group who defy God; Thackeray looks at himself and his fellows as they futilely struggle to realize unsatisfiable dreams.

Thackeray's world of Vanity Fair is discouraging, despairing, hopeless, vain and empty in its materialistic values, hollow and frightening in its spiritual sterility. Yet it is not inescapable; its denizens are there because of moral failures of their own; and they may win their ways out by moral triumphs. Thus the ultimate measure of Thackeray's Vanity Fair is the traditional moral-ethical system of values, lost but still very real and capable of being refound. What these people must learn is humility. Writing to his mother, Thackeray had also said:

> Dobbin & poor Briggs are the only 2 people with real humility as yet. Amelia's is to come, when her scoundrel of a husband is well dead with a ball in his odious bowels; when she has had sufferings, a child, and a religion—But she has at present a quality above most people whizz: LOVE—by wh. she shall be saved. Save me, save me too O my God and Father, cleanse my heart and teach me my duty.

Ernest Hemingway, former volunteer ambulance driver on the Italian front, newspaper correspondent, writer, and American expatriate, in Spain and later in the capital of "all the sad young men," Paris, set down in 1925 a picture of one group of postwar people. He showed them at their standard pleasure-seeking activities in Paris, and then he moved them to a Spanish fiesta at Pamplona. He gave them plot unity by selecting a group that revolved around Lady Brett Ashley, whose first fiancé, the true love of her life, like Catherine Barkley's fiancé in *A Farewell to Arms*, has been killed in the war; whose second husband is evil and cruel; and whose lover, Jake Barnes, is an emasculated war casualty. She has become an alcoholic nymphomaniac. The action of the book is shaped by her affair with Robert Cohn, "not one of us," and its culminating aftermath, an affair with a fine young bullfighter, Pedro Romero.

The spiritual malaise of Thackeray's people has been intensified into a brooding disease, almost a death, of the spirit. Hemingway defines this illness in a brief passage which illustrates his incomparable ability to make the simplest physical facts mean two things and imply a whole realm of unexpressed meaning. Early in the novel, Jake has picked up a French prostitute:

> She touched me with one hand and I put her hand away.
> "Never mind."
> "What's the matter? You sick?"
> "Yes."
> "Everybody's sick. I'm sick, too."

In the opening sequences of the novel, Jake, Brett, and their crowd are in Paris participating in the endless spree. Everything is seen through Jake's eyes, and the imagery is blurred and hazy. Physical objects, usually sharp in Hemingway's writing, have an alcoholically uncertain quality. The streets are wet with rain and they shimmer unstably. The air is intense, filled with noise, almost palpably feverish. Brett, the symbol of insatiable emptiness, dominates everybody's thinking and feeling.

Then Jake and his friend Bill Gorton leave for Spain and the fiesta. Suddenly the air is clean and clear and cold. The mountains are sharply etched across the horizon. The men fish in waters almost incredibly clear. The frenzy and the heat and the disease seem far away. A physical measuring stick—the natural, cool, calm earth—has been imposed upon the Paris group. And the imagery has sharpened to the point where a bracing, healthy sharpness seems almost tangible on the pages.

Then Jake and Bill move on to Pamplona and the fiesta and are joined by Brett and her gang. Once more the drunken spree gets underway. Again the images grow frenzied and then muddled and at last become a desperate alcoholic haze. Here though a symbol of order is imposed. It is Pedro Romero, a young bullfighter of great promise. His disciplined life, his youthful health, his passion for his profession, the graceful control with which he moves—all serve as standards to measure the expatriates by. He is, seemingly, the closest thing possible for man to that natural, cool, calm earth of the middle section of the novel.

Then he becomes Brett's lover. Almost with despair his friends watch him begin a course which will sap from him the spiritual strength which makes him potentially great. Then Brett herself senses what he is and what she is and sends him away almost unharmed. Again the point is implied in a dialogue, this time between Brett and Jake:

> ". . . You know I feel rather damned good, Jake."
> "You should."
> "You know it makes one feel rather good deciding not to be a bitch."
> "Yes."
> "It's sort of what we have instead of God."
> "Some people have God," [Jake] said. "Quite a lot."
> "He never worked very well with me."
> "Should we have another Martini?"

Earlier Hemingway has carefully stated the essentially religious nature of Jake, who is like Frederic Henry in *A Farewell to Arms,* a young man who understood and longed for the peace of the Priest's "homeland," but who was condemned by his world never to go there. Brett, as Carlos Baker has pointed out, is in sharp contrast. She is never at home in a church and cannot pray even when she wants to. She is pure pagan. The day before the fiesta of San Fermin at Pamplona, Jake "went to church a couple of times, once with Brett. She said she wanted to hear [him] go to confession, but [he] told her that not only was it impossible, but it was not as interesting as it sounded, and, besides, it would be in a language she did not know."

But if Brett represents a people who do not know the language of religion (for almost certainly Hemingway intends the double meaning), it must be said, too, that Jake knows only the language and not the meaning. Like Frederic Henry, what he has is an understanding of what religion has meant to other people and a nostalgia for that certainty for himself, but he lives in a condition where it does not touch his problems at all, except in incidents like that just described, where it serves to define them.

Hemingway uses a natural order—the cool, sweet earth—and a strong, disciplined, and healthy person—Pedro Romero—in something like the same way that Bunyan used his religious absolutes and Thackeray used his ethical unselfishness. For each of the earlier writers, though in decreasing strength, there existed an external system of values by which man might be judged. For Hemingway, God has been replaced by the purely personal act—Brett's renunciation of Romero, a very primitive kind of personal morality, is what she has in place of God.

Thackeray's people, Hemingway's are all within Vanity Fair, and almost despairingly so. As Mike Campbell says, "This is all awfully amusing, but it's not too pleasant. It's not too pleasant for me." But Thackeray's people are there because of their own acts, and by suffering they can learn the way out. Hemingway's people are there because of suffering, and there is no exit from their Vanity Fair. His novel records how two people live with their world by recognizing its nature and imposing their own personal codes upon it, however helpless they may be in every other respect. Brett may not change herself in any way, but in renouncing her hold on Romero she does remain faithful to an inviolable personal being, however painful the faithfulness may be. Jake, that stoic who weeps alone at night over the lost Brett and himself, maintains his own controlled response. He, too, remains faithful to an inviolable personal self. The book ends on this note:

> "Oh, Jake," Brett said, "we could have had such a damned good time together."
> . . . The car slowed suddenly pressing Brett against me.
> "Yes," I said. "Isn't it pretty to think so?"

Hemingway's Vanity Fair is an Existential one. Men live in this hollow world, not because they defy God as the citizens of Bunyan's city of Vanity do, nor because they are willfully and cynically selfish as the citizens of Thackeray's Vanity Fair are, but because they are in a jungle where God is a word in a forgotten language and only in the self is value to be found. Their position is hardly tragic, but it is certainly pathetic. Theirs is the Existential dictum to give it personal meaning by facing its meaninglessness with dignity and poise. The classic virtue of humility has been replaced by self-assertion.

THE SOCIAL BASIS OF HEMINGWAY'S STYLE

LARZER ZIFF

MY REMARKS ABOUT THE EARLY STYLE of Ernest Hemingway apply, I believe, to all of his fiction through 1933 at least although I am basing them principally on one representative passage, the first two and one-half paragraphs of Chapter X of *The Sun Also Rises* (1926). Devoid of high incident, the passage is essentially descriptive, designed to link the dramatized occurrences of one day with those of the next. I claim that the passage is typical on the basis of my own sense of Hemingway's prose rather than as the result of statistical analysis. The only validation I can seek for my claim, therefore, must come from the assent of readers familiar with Hemingway's work.

> In the morning it was bright, and they were sprinkling the streets of the town, and we all had breakfast in a café. Bayonne is a nice town. It is like a very clean Spanish town and it is on a big river. Already, so early in the morning, it was very hot on the bridge across the river. We walked out on the bridge and then took a walk through the town.
>
> I was not at all sure Mike's rods would come from Scotland in time, so we hunted a tackle store and finally bought a rod for Bill up-stairs over a drygoods store. The man who sold the tackle was out, and we had to wait for him to come back. Finally he came in, and we bought a pretty good rod cheap, and two landing-nets.
>
> We went out into the street again and took a look at the cathedral. Cohn made some remark about it being a very good example of something or other, I forget what. It seemed like a nice cathedral, nice and dim, like Spanish churches. Then we went up past the old fort and out to the local Syndicat d'Initiative office, where the bus was supposed to start from. There they told us the bus service did not start until the 1st of July. We found out at the tourist

Reprinted with permission from *Poetics,* 7 (1978), 417–23 (North-Holland Publishing Company).

office what we ought to pay for a motor-car to Pamplona and hired one at a big garage just around the corner from the Municipal Theatre for four hundred francs. The car was to pick us up at the hotel in forty minutes, and we stopped at the café on the square where we had eaten breakfast, and had a beer. It was hot, but the town had a cool, fresh, early-morning smell and it was pleasant sitting in the café. A breeze started to blow, and you could feel that the air came from the sea. There were pigeons out in the square, and the houses were a yellow, sun-baked color, and I did not want to leave the café.

I would, initially, point out five features that are typical of Hemingway's style, a style that came to be known as *the* Hemingway style.

First, of sixteen sentences, only two are complex; the remainder are simple.

Second, the modifiers are relatively blank; that is they are far less focused or heightened than a large number of approximate words that could have been selected. Indeed, in editing the writing of a beginner, most advisors would suggest to him that he put greater precision into his modifiers: that he use "glaring" for example rather than Hemingway's "bright"; "splendid" rather than "nice"; "immaculate" rather than "very clean"; "burning" rather than "very hot," etc.

Third, the figures of speech are grudging rather than expansive, so niggardly as almost to be tautological. Bayonne is "like a very clean Spanish town." To be sure, it is actually a French town and presumably French towns are cleaner than Spanish towns. Still, in view of the fact that it is very close to the Spanish border, to liken Bayonne to a Spanish town is to offer a simile that takes only one, small, calculated step toward being a figure of speech. Similarly, the cathedral is "like Spanish churches."

Fourth, the scene is actualized through a relatively high use of proper nouns: Bayonne, Pamplona, Syndicat d'Initiative, Municipal Theatre. Their frequency is not so great in this particular passage as elsewhere in Hemingway—indeed, the earlier chapters of the novel were used as a guidebook to Paris by would-be Bohemians, so abundant were the proper nouns—but is still notable.

Fifth, indirect constructions are relatively frequent: "it was bright"; an indefinite "they were sprinkling"; "took a walk" rather than walked; "took a look" rather than looked.

The effect of these features is to communicate a feeling of receptivity rather than activity on the part of the narrator. What he experiences is essentially flowing in upon him rather than being enacted or willed by him. He seems, at first glance, numbed. His uncomplex, chronological presentation of events invites a similar undergoing on the reader's part, a submission to a seemingly unvalued succession of events rather than a participation in them in response to a narrative voice that reacts expressively and binds the separate syntactic units into a generalizable whole.

But the numbness is a surface numbness and the separateness of units is also only superficial. The last sentence quoted ends "and I did not want to leave the cafe." The narrator likes what has been happening to him, feels good, and thus signals the liking without talking about his feelings: "There were pigeons out in the square, and the houses were a yellow, sun-baked color, and I did not want to leave the café." Not because of the pigeons and the houses, nor *therefore* I did not want to leave the café, but two statements linked by 'and', followed by a third similarly linked although of a content that is not parallel with the content of the first two units of a compound sentence which invites a parallel completion. The failed rhetorical parallel is, needless to say, a completed emotional one. Hemingway thus contrives to have his cake and eat it too; contrives, that is, to keep an unemotional face presented to mundane experience and yet communicate sensitivity to it.

The last quoted sentence underlines Hemingway's achievement but is not, on reflection, the strongest contribution to it. Rather, the series of simple sentences which appear to have only a chronological relationship are actually bound together by a studied repetition of words rhythmically moved about to different positions in succeeding sentences. In the first paragraph, for example, "town" occurs in the middle of the first sentence but is highly stressed arriving, as it does, after a dactyllic run-up to it: "sprinkling the streets of the town." It occurs as predicate in the next sentence, in which "river" is introduced. In the following sentence "morning" is repeated from the first sentence to replace the temporarily dropped "town" and yet maintain the repetitive beat, and the "river" has "bridge." Then, in the final sentence, in which "walk" and "walked" both occur, "town" reoccurs linked with the river through the reoccurrence of "bridge," both repeated nouns the location of the repeated "walk."

We know from Richard Bridgman's fine book, *The Colloquial Style in America*, that the replacement of the coherence to be gained from compound constructions with that gained from the rhythmic repetition of key words and phrases is a dominant feature of American prose style as developed by Mark Twain, an artful rendering in writing of the feeling of speech although, of course, far from the mere transcription of speech. We know also that Hemingway admired Twain's work and said that all American literature begins with *Huckleberry Finn*.

To Twain's influence, then, we may attribute in some part Hemingway's fondness for understatement. But Twain's less severe turn away from the rhetorical, the complex, and the fulsome is a result of his distrust of abstract expression which he equated with hypocritical cant, believing it was used in his day with such mindless frequency that it was no longer available except to denote insincerity. He was not opposed to the expression of deep feeling but to the vocabulary and syntax of its expression that had come into use in a society he considered to be pompous and counterfeit in its emotional structure.

Hemingway shares a good deal with Twain but goes beyond him in this matter. His style stems not only from a distrust of a debased public language of feeling but from a disapproval of the sensibility that would want to express feeling directly in whatever language. In amplification of this contention I turn to what in my title I mean by "social basis."

The central figure in Hemingway's early story "Soldier's Home" (published in *In Our Time*, 1925), is Krebs, a soldier who returns from World War I to his Kansas town after the great wave of veterans have come back so that he is not a novel center of attraction as they were. More importantly, his attempt to render his experiences in conversation encounters an audience that has by now heard a good deal of such talk and has formed a definite set of expectations.

> His town had heard too many atrocity stories to be thrilled by actualities. Krebs found that to be listened to at all he had to lie, and after he had done this twice he, too, had a reaction against the war and against talking about it. A distaste for everything that had happened to him in the war set in because of the lies he had told. All of the times that had been able to make him feel cool and clear inside himself when he thought of them; the times so long back when he had done the one thing, the only thing for a man to do easily and naturally, when he might have done something else, now lost their cool, valuable quality and then were lost themselves.
>
> His lies were quite unimportant lies and consisted in attributing to himself things other men had seen, done or heard of, and stating as facts certain apocryphal incidents familiar to all soldiers. Even his lies were not sensational at the pool room. His acquaintances, who had heard detailed accounts of German women found chained to machine guns in the Argonne forest and who could not comprehend, or were barred by their patriotism from interest in, any German machine gunners who were not chained, were not thrilled by his stories.
>
> Krebs acquired the nausea in regard to experience that is the result of untruth or exaggeration, and when he occasionally met another man who had really been a soldier and they talked a few minutes in the dressing room at a dance he fell into the easy pose of the old soldier among other soldiers: that he had been badly, sickeningly frightened all the time. In this way he lost everything.

Krebs lies in order to gain the attention of an audience that is incapable of responding to anything other than the sensational even though it is far more drenched in the sensational than in the actual. This paradox has, of course, been a characteristic of the popular audience since the beginning of the modern period and continues to mark television programs today: the falsely heightened becomes addictive and the audience craves greater and greater heightening rather than the sanatory actual. The artist who indulges the audience in its habit does not so much sin against an abstract moral canon that prohibits falsehood—the lies are relatively harmless insofar as they misinform—as he destroys himself by destroying the part of his own character that received value from the experiences which he falsifies.

The dilemma which Krebs the oral anecdotist cannot overcome is that which Hemingway the writer set himself to overcome through the art of prose. How render profound experience so as, on one hand, not to betray it by the very expressing of it, or, on the other, not to deny it by assuming the knowing guise of an insider addressing a sophisticated coterie? Literary success may hinge on the solution, but literature is not what impels the question. Rather the question arises from the courageous self's struggle to be true to what it has undergone.

In an echo of the uncharacteristically full explanation in "Soldier's Home," the narrator at the close of *The Sun Also Rises* summarizes the matter tersely when he says, "You'll lose it if you talk about it." The mere act of articulation falsifies feeling in the receiver and destroys it in the speaker. "It," then, must be rendered through the development of a style that evokes feeling without mentioning it, that maintains a surface placidity which is, nevertheless, consistent with an inner sensitivity. How this is accomplished I have attempted to indicate in my discussion of the admittedly slight passage from *The Sun Also Rises*.

Beyond this is the fuller context of Hemingway's involvement in the First World War when he had done "the one thing" there was to do and was the beneficiary of its "cool, valuable quality." It must be seen as Hemingway saw it, through the subsequent verbal distortion of its meaning by statesmen, journalists, and popular writers whose rhetorical embellishments and generalized interpretations amounted for Hemingway to a betrayal of the dead and a psychic wounding of the survivors. The values inherent in the undoubted experiences were in danger of being lost to their possessors in exchange for a return to what Pound had called "old men's lies." In his response, Hemingway would turn in wrath from the presumptuousness of imposing upon human undergoing a synthetic scheme of proportion, an idealized and unreal pattern of emphases and subordination.

Accordingly the complex sentence with its central reliance on ordering experience into the independent and the subordinate evaporates in favor of serial, simple sentences asserting the integrity of each thing that happens. Things happen one by one, linked by whatever similarity may accumulate rather than by a causal scheme. Moreover, no one thing *at the moment it is occurring* can possibly be seen as subordinate to some other thing not then occurring; indeed comparison is scarcely possible. The pleasure of a cold beer on a hot day is, at that moment, absolute, not relative to the pleasure of a Mozart sonata nor even to the possibility of cooling off with a swim instead. Dying is a private suffering not a public action, patriotic or otherwise, felt in itself not in terms of all the others who die.

The blank modifier comes forth prominently because it does not push toward a forced coloring but invites filling in terms of its substantive-heavy context. Hemingway is especially fond, we know, of "nice" and "swell," modifiers which have been so overused in common speech that they have lost almost all focus and are as apt to be used in dismission, ironic disapproval, or absent-minded ejaculation as they are in approval. How they are to be taken, then, depends on context to a far greater, an almost total, degree than is usual with modifiers; that is, the modifier is modified by what it presumably modifies rather than the reverse, a pointed reminder of the "lying" quality it conventionally possesses and an efficient way of calling attention to the thing itself rather than to an interpretation of it.[1]

The uniqueness of what occurs as it occurs is reinforced by the heavy use of the proper noun, standing for the only one of its kind in the world, and the resulting impression is further reinforced by the simile that expands so stingily as ultimately to call attention to the incomparability of what it compares. In such a style the preference for passivity and indirectness in verbal constructions heightens the objective illusion that it is all there outside us happening and flowing in and affecting us cumulatively rather than being controlled and ordered by our will (let alone a divine plan) or being received through categories imposed by the mind.

In *The Sun Also Rises*, one central character, Robert Cohn, does not share the narrator's perception of the truth of integral experiences and the self-destruction inherent in receiving reality through the explanatory formulas prepared by the intellect. He lingers in the fuzzy verbal world of pre-war generalizing and serves as a gauge whereby we can measure how well we have emerged from such untrue living into a capacity to receive the actual. In the passage quoted, "Cohn made some remark about it being a very good example of something or other, I forget what." He came to the cathedral blinded by guidebook phrases about Baroque, Gothic, and Romanesque and failed to feel it but rather talked about it in words that had been formed before his experience of it. The narrator says of the cathedral, "It seemed a nice cathedral, nice and dim like Spanish churches." His dismissive "example of something or other" and his restrained "nice" repeated so as to emphasize "dim," together with the grudging simile, do not reveal him as a hard-boiled cynic but, rather, mark him as a man of feeling in a world in which expression poisons feeling. His are the remarks of an artist who is keeping faith with what his generation has undergone in contempt for the lying, elevated glosses that have been put upon it.

Later in the same chapter the narrator, his friend Bill, and Cohn ride in a car where

> there were trees along both sides of the road, and a stream and ripe fields of grain, and the road went on, very white and straight ahead, and then lifted to a little rise, and off on the left was a hill with an old castle, with buildings close around it, and a field of grain going right up to the walls and shifting in the wind. I was up in front with the driver and I turned around. Robert Cohn was asleep, but Bill looked and nodded his head.

Those who have learned to unlearn language's abuses have access to the power of the genuine. The generalizing Cohn sleeps, dead to specific experience, while its receivers share its value with a silent gesture.

In such ways, with such a style does Hemingway respond to the question he had set himself—how to talk about it without losing it. It is a style that works effectively only in conjunction with material that supports the view that public ideals are false and truth resides solely in unverbalized private experience. And it is a style that, once analyzed, is easily imitated. Imitations, however, fail to achieve the effects Hemingway achieved because they are merely stylistic, unrelated to the larger social view that gives the style its meaning in the early Hemingway.

Perhaps the most notorious unsuccessful imitator of the style is the later Hemingway who went on employing it relatively unchanged after his world view had changed. Recommitted to political ideals and confident, even arrogant, in his sense of a reading public, he had need of a changed style to mirror his new perceptions. The marvelous style that was created to fill the hollow left by the death of idealism and to hold the parts of the wounded self together in delicate conjunction lest the psyche fracture could not serve the altered outlook of its creator and the result was one of self-parody.

To trace the features of a literary style to their social basis is, I recognize, a risky enterprise. I believe, however, that Hemingway's style, important in the history of English prose, cannot be understood until stylistic analysis is grounded in such a context, and, I venture further to suggest, analyses of other literary styles also invite, indeed demand, connection with the social world that shaped their creation.

1. To his development of this attitude toward modifiers we may relate Hemingway's fondness for British upper-class or officer's-mess speech. The deliberate limitation of expressions of emotion in this speech to a handful of words—"I say," "quite," "smashing," etc.—in response to the view that to have a precise word for each feeling is to commit the social sin of revealing personal feeling, to be, that is, in bad taste, provides characters whose dialogue demands of the writer a sharp eye for contextual detail and a sharp ear for nuance since the words themselves mean little lexicographically. As an American, Hemingway, in the main, prudently restrained his use of such characters but his successes with them are notable; for example, Lady Brett.

SEMANTICS AND STYLE—WITH THE EXAMPLE OF QUINTESSENTIAL HEMINGWAY

RICHARD L. McLAIN

THERE ARE TWO GENERAL USES OF THE TERM "style" in current literary criticism: one derives from the discovery of patterns of words, sounds, and syntax (usually formal linguistic properties) in order to describe the characteristic language of a writer, period, or school; the second derives from the notion that the surface form of language, in some unspecified way, may contribute to, "imitate," reproduce, or re-enforce the semantic content of the utterance. The central issue over which these two concepts of style separate (or, as many will argue, become mutually exclusive) is the question of whether the surface patterns of sentences can have semantic value, or whether the patterns are simply that—patterns.[1] The literary arguments over the interaction of form and content are well known in formalist critical theory.[2] But recent developments in linguistic theory—specifically transformational grammars—have complicated the discussion by contending that the *form* of sentences (what grammarians call the "surface structure") and their *content* ("deep structure") are accidentally, albeit conventionally, connected through a chain of optional and obligatory transformations.[3] Assuming this dualism of form and meaning, linguistic critics of literature have laid out the following tasks for empirical stylistics: first, to reconstruct the network of formal operations which have resulted in given surface structures (that is, the optional transformations); second, to characterize the *patterns* of these transformations independently from the *meanings* of the utterances (that is, to interpret the transformational patterns not as meanings, but as indicators of an effect, an ambience, or a *Weltanschauung*). These tasks are seen by some as a way to release the

Reprinted with permission from *Language and Style*, 12, No. 2 (1979), 63, 71–76.

literary critic from the fetters of "impressionistic" labels imposed by traditional grammatical and rhetorical analyses of style.[4]

. . . .

The Semantics of Causation in Hemingway's Style

Hemingway stylistics provides an introduction to the potential for semantic-feature analysis for the stylistician. I choose Hemingway because the critical response to his prose style has been remarkably uniform. He is said to have a distinctive style; some even find it mannered. Also, an extraordinary number of both casual and explicit statements and characterizations have been made of Hemingway's style.[5] The arsenal of casual descriptions includes such adjectives as "simple," "journalistic," "incantatory," "repetitive," and "cinematographic."[6] However, explicit analyses have proven just how elusive these terms are, how difficult it is to justify such characterizations from the analyzable features of diction, syntax, or phonology.

Here, for instance, are two frequently discussed passages from Hemingway's short story "Big Two-Hearted River":

> I. The ground rose, wooded and sandy, to overlook the meadow, the stretch of river and the swamp. Nick dropped his pack and rod-case and looked for a level piece of ground. He was very hungry and he wanted to make his camp before he cooked. Between two jack pines, the ground was quite level. He took the ax out of the pack and chopped out two projecting roots. That leveled a piece of ground large enough to sleep on. He smoothed out the sandy soil with his hand and pulled all the sweet fern bushes by their roots. His hands smelled good from the sweet fern. He smoothed the uprooted earth. He did not want anything making lumps under the blankets. When he had the ground smooth, he spread his three blankets. One he folded double, next to the ground. The other two he spread on top.
>
> With the ax he slit off a bright slab of pine from one of the stumps and split it into pegs for the tent. He wanted them long and solid to hold in the ground. With the tent unpacked and spread on the ground, the pack, leaning against a jackpine, looked much smaller. Nick tied the rope that served the tent for a ridge-pole to the trunk of one of the pine trees and pulled the tent up off the ground with the other end of the rope and tied it to the other pine. The tent hung on the rope like a canvas blanket on a clothesline. Nick poked a pole he had cut up under the back peak of the canvas and then made it a tent by pegging out the sides. He pegged the sides out taut and drove the pegs deep, hitting them down into the ground with the flat of the ax until the rope loops were buried and the canvas was drum tight.

II.   There was a long tug. Nick struck and the rod came alive and dangerous, bent double, the line tightening, coming out of water, tightening, all in a
heavy, dangerous, steady pull. Nick felt the moment when the leader would
break if the strain increased and let the line go.

The reel ratcheted into a mechanical shriek as the line went out in a mash.
Too fast. Nick could not check it, the line rushing out, the reel note rising as
the line ran out.

With the core of the reel showing, his heart feeling stopped with the
excitement, leaning back against the current that mounted icily his thighs, Nick
thumbed the reel hard with his left hand. It was awkward getting his thumb
inside the fly reel frame.[7]

The two passages are taken from the two parts of Hemingway's story. The first
begins a section of the narrative where the protagonist, Nick Adams, sets up his
camp; the second comes halfway in Nick's encounter with the river.

In a richly compact and, I believe, representative reading of this story,
William Bysshe Stein states that the twofold division of the story is a crucial
strategem; the first part is a "ritual of preparation," the second part a "ritual of
initiation." Also, Stein says that the building of the camp in part one is analogous
to a "sacred rite of construction. . . ordained by custom and tradition," it is a
"ceremonial gesture," "sacramental."[8] Stein's discussion of the local qualities of
Hemingway's language in passage (I) harmonize with his reading of the total
force of the first part of the story: "Here [passage (I)] even the prose style is in
keeping with the aura of ritual. Precise, controlled, and prayerfully iterative, it
signals Nick's release from self-doubt, his attainment of a new spiritual balance."
In the context of the whole story the reader accedes to these statements; they are
perfectly acceptable interpretations of the passage. However, the difficulty is in
finding some way to connect the actual features of the language to our sense of its
style.

There is a quality to passage (I), in particular, that strikes one as mannered
or stylized. For the Hemingway reader there is a recognizable texture here; it is
quintessentially Hemingway. Other, similar passages occur in Hemingway's writings (particularly preparation-sequences of one sort or another), but none is quite
so unmistakably Hemingway. Moreover, critics do, uniformly, claim that this
story maintains a tighter bond between the configurations of Hemingway's sentences and the ritualistic effect of the whole. But in what features of the language
do we find it? If we look at passage (I) there is very little that our grammatical
terminology allows us to latch onto in order to make any bridge between form,
meaning, and style. Our descriptive terminology does not seem fine enough to
allow us to separate out the grains of the problem.

James Green, in "Symbolic Sentences in 'Big Two-Hearted River,' " has attempted to make connections between syntax and meaning in passage (I) by claiming that the sentences are "short" and "monotonous," that almost all are "simple sentences with the predominate subject-verb-object pattern," and that this inexorable rhythm is appropriate to Nick's state of mind (p. 310). Another critic, Curtis Hayes, has pointed out that a large portion of Hemingway's sentences are syntactically simple, "more so than might be expected among English-speaking novelists" ("A Study in Prose Styles," p. 293). Perhaps Hayes' statistical analysis bolsters Green's more casual account of the style. But, of course the preponderance of "simple" sentences (meaning fewer embedded complements and fewer conjoined structures to the main sentence) does not entail content that is "simple" (uncomplex, more easily accessible, or trivial). Asserting a one-to-one relationship between the syntactic description "simple sentence" and semantic simplicity engages the critic in the least interesting sort of claim for a connection between form and meaning. Besides, studies in syntax and psycholinguistics show that the grammarian's traditional terms for sentence structure—i.e., simple, compound, and complex—merely gloss over a reader's or hearer's highly intricate strategies for gaining access to the content of an utterance. Of far greater importance to these strategies than the number is the kind of embedded or compounded structures and the specific manner in which one sentence is embedded in, or compounded to, another.[9]

Perhaps the critic might construct a more reasonable hypothesis of imitative form by claiming that the form of sentences imitates not their own content but the form of other sentences. The Hemingway critic (and Stein's analysis of the passage at hand suggests this) might argue that the syntax or lexicon of Hemingway's paragraphs imitates the syntax of incantations or of initiate instructions which usually accompany ritual. As yet, however, no one has made such art argument for "imitative" style.

My own remarks on Hemingway's language ignore the possibility of imitation, focusing instead on pattern in the text itself. The semantic theory I have outlined above argues the recoverability of some aspects of logical and semantic form from syntactic form. If this is the case, we can explore constituent patterns at levels deeper than that of syntactic form. Thus, close examination of the first passage from Hemingway reveals the following information:

(a) In both passages he has chained together a number of activity-predicates, that is, predicates which take agents and which represent the structure *someone-(or thing)-does-something*. Twenty-eight of the 45 predicates in passage (I) are activities, as are 21 of the 25 predicates in the second passage.[10]

(b) The specific agents invoked for the various activities differ significantly between the two passages: in (I) Nick is the agent for 27 of the 28 activities while in (II) Nick is the agent for only six.

(c) In the first passage nearly all of the active predicate constructions (24 of 28) are causative: i.e., *drop pack, make camp, take ax out, chop out roots, level ground, smooth out soil, pull [out] bushes, smooth earth, make lumps, spread blankets, fold blankets, spread blankets, split off slab, split slab, tie-rope, pull tent up, tie rope, poke a pole up under the peak, cut pole, make canvas [into] a tent, peg out sides, peg sides out taut, drive pegs deep,* and *hit pegs down into the ground.*

(d) Of the remaining, non-causative, predicates in passage (I), seven make use of verbs which, like *open*, have both causative and non-causative uses in the language. These non-causative uses represent, in this passage, reports of resultant states brought about by actions named in the predicate. In other words, these state-predicates imply causation, causation produced by Nick's actions: *had the ground smooth, tent unpacked, tent spread, pack leans, tent hangs, loops were buried, canvas was tight.* Thus, altogether in passage (I) there are some 28 resultant states named or entailed, and 27 named or implied actions on the part of Nick. (One negative sentence not included in this accounting of causative states and actions is the sentence "He did not want anything making lumps." I have excluded it because it has neither an explicit nor an implicit agent.)

(e) Although causatives, as noted above, are ambiguous as to the agent's intention, or will, to bring about some result, Nick's intentions as regards the resultant states in the first passage are in the context of the predicate "wanted to make his camp." This does not settle the question of intention in the accompanying actions which will result in the completed camp, but it does imply some measure of *control.* The verb *want*, repeated several times in the passage, posits some vague intentions, a vague sense of Nick's own criteria for satisfactory conclusions—perhaps a semiconscious control of his actions.

On the other hand, in the second passage:

(f) Few of the actions in passage (II) are either causative or intentional. Of the 21 named actions only three entail a resultant state brought about by Nick's actions: *let the line go, leans back against the current,* and *gets his thumb inside the frame.*

(g) All of the causatives in the second passage are ambiguous as to Nick's intention or will. In particular, the lexical choices in two of these causative predicates seem to deliberately avoid causative predicates which would imply

Nick's intention to act—i.e, *let the line go* vs. *release the line,* and *get his thumb inside* vs. *put his thumb inside.*

In general, critics agree on the centrality of these passages in the two parts of this story, and formal semantic analysis of these passages brings out the same contrast between Nick's control and Nick's lack of control that most readers find to be the seminal contrast between parts one and two of the story. Moreover, Nick's control of events in passage (I) is consistent with the concept of ritual, as are other features of the predicate structure. Nick performs activities with entailed resultant states—the passage lists a string of activities and accomplishments. Here Nick is not just a conscious active being; his activities, no matter how trivial, have results. Each action leads to an individual accomplishment. Each offers an isolated satisfaction and, simultaneously, another step toward some larger accomplishment, satisfaction, or desire—in this case, a *made* camp. Although the narrative does not characterize Nick's actions as ritualistic, the semantic pattern has a great deal in common with the function and nature of ritual involvement: agency, prescribed activity, individual accomplished fixities, stages toward some vague satisfaction of an emotional state.

By the time we arrive at the action of the second passage, however, Nick has become disengaged from the action. He can no longer accomplish; he has neither agency nor control. The world in which Nick is engaged is itself active, but there is no obvious source of intention, no will. In this context there are no results and agency is out of Nick's hands: *there was a tug, rod comes alive, rod bends double, line tightens, line comes out of the water, line tightens, leader breaks, strain increases, reel ratchets, line goes out, line rushes out, reel note rises, line runs out, reel shows, heart stops, current mounts.* When Nick does act (e.g., lets the line go, gets his thumb inside the reel frame), the force of his will is semantically mitigated.

Immediately following the second passage Nick withdraws from further engagement with nature. He backs off from the river, from areas and activities over which he has no control and from which he can derive no satisfaction. In the final paragraphs of the story Nick returns to the pattern of action and result that had engaged him earlier:

> III.   He took out his knife, opened it and stuck it in the log. Then he pulled up the sack, reached into it and brought out one of the trout. Holding him near the tail, hard to hold, alive, in his hand, he whacked him against the log. The trout quivered, rigid. Nick laid him on the log in the shade and broke the neck of the other fish the same way. He laid them side by side on the log. They were fine trout.

Nick cleaned them, slitting them from the vent to the tip of the jaw. All the insides and the gills and tongue came out in one piece. They were both males; long gray-white strips of milt, smooth and clean. All the insides clean and compact, coming out all together. Nick tossed the offal ashore for the minks to find.

He washed the trout in the stream. When he held them back up in the water they looked like live fish. Their color was not gone yet. He washed his hands and dried them on the log. Then he laid the trout on the sack spread out on the log, rolled them up in it, tied the bundle and put it in the landing net. His knife was still standing, blade stuck in the log. He cleaned it on the wood and put it in his pocket.

Nick stood up on the log, holding his rod, the landing net hanging heavy, then stepped into the water and splashed ashore. He climbed the bank and cut up into the woods, toward the high ground. He was going back to camp. He looked back. The river just showed through the trees. There were plenty of days coming when he could fish the swamp. (pp. 231–32)

The language at the end of the story re-engages Nick; he renews himself with agency and accomplishment, with the ritual stages of action and result. This is brought about by Hemingway's renewal of the earlier semantic pattern, or style. Thus, in passages (I) and (III) the semantic patterns are fundamental to our perception of their style and meaning. More directly, we can say that style is meaning.

I am not proposing that Hemingway has any single style, or even that the style of the language I have chosen from "Big Two-Hearted River" is dominant in Hemingway. Such obvious semantic patterning may make up a very small proportion of his prose; however, the recognizable texture seems to me identifiable with the writer's whole ethos.

But the central claim of this paper is that linguistic models are on the verge of providing important inroads into the semantic form of language, and thus into recurrent, stylistic features that have been heretofore unapproachable. In the case of Hemingway, I have not made a comprehensive semantic or syntactic analysis—as I have said, the insights of an adequate linguistic description are still becoming. We need to know more about the scope and structure of semantic primitives, more about the role that appropriateness and context-sensitive conditions play on linguistic structures, and more about the linguistic and pragmatic nature of utterances beyond the scope of the sentence. Nevertheless, a linguistic model which by its very nature posits a single theory to account for semantic form and syntactic form must foreshorten the distance of the interpretive leap which is so necessary to a theory of style in literature.

1. For recent discussion of these issues see E. D. Hirsch, Jr., "Stylistics and Synonymity," *Critical Inquiry,* 1 (1975), 559–79; Roger Fowler, "Style and the Concept of Deep Structure," *Journal of Literary Semantics,* 1 (1972), 524; and Richard McLain, "The Problem of 'Style': Another Case in Fuzzy Grammar," *Language and Style,* 10 (1977), 52–65.

2. See, for example, A. C. Bradley's discussion of the "heresy of separable form" in his *Oxford Lectures on Poetry* (Bloomington: Indiana University Press, 1961), p. 12 ff.

3. Jerrold J. Katz and Paul M. Postal, *An Integrated Theory of Linguistic Descriptions* (Cambridge: MIT Press, 1964); Noam Chomsky, *Aspects of the Theory of Syntax* (Cambridge: MIT Press, 1965).

4. See, for example, Curtis W. Hayes, "A Study in Prose Styles: Edward Gibbon and Ernest Hemingway," *Texas Studies in Language and Literature,* 7 (1966), 371–86.

5. I do not mean to belittle casual characterizations of language in contrast to explicit (meaning justified by linguistic evidence) ones. On the contrary, casual descriptions are often more satisfactory in that they are not entangled in categories of linguistics. Nevertheless, it is the task of the linguistic critic to reach out for explanation, descriptive adequacy, *and*, hopefully, satisfaction.

6. A sampling from Sheldon Grebstein, *Hemingway's Craft* (Carbondale: Southern Illinois University Press, 1973); Curtis W. Hayes, "A Study in Prose Styles: Edward Gibbon and Ernest Hemingway"; Harry Levin, "Observations on the Style of Ernest Hemingway," *Contexts of Criticism* (Cambridge: Harvard University Press, 1948), pp. 140–67; James L. Green, "Symbolic Sentences in 'Big Two-Hearted River,' " *Modern Fiction Studies,* 14 (1968), 307–12; and John Graham, "Ernest Hemingway: The Meaning of Style," *Modern Fiction Studies,* 6 (1960), 298–313.

7. *The Short Stories of Ernest Hemingway* (New York: Charles Scribner's Sons, 1953), pp. 214–15, 226.

8. William Bysshe Stein, "Ritual in Hemingway's 'Big Two-Hearted River,' " *Texas Studies in Language and Literature,* 1 (1960), 556.

9. See Noam Chomsky, *Aspects,* pp. 10–15; and D. Terence Langendoen, "The Accessibility of Deep Structures" in *Readings in English Transformational Grammar,* ed. Roderick A. Jacobs and Peter S. Rosenbaum (Waltham, Mass.: Ginn & Co., 1970), pp. 99–104.

10. In my accounting of predicates I do not include pre-posed adjectives but only surface-predicate adjectives.

REVIEW OF *MEN WITHOUT WOMEN*

DOROTHY PARKER

ERNEST HEMINGWAY WROTE A NOVEL called *The Sun Also Rises*. Promptly upon its publication, Ernest Hemingway was discovered, the Stars and Stripes were reverentially raised over him, eight hundred and forty-seven book reviewers formed themselves into the word "welcome" and the band played "Hail to the Chief" in three concurrent keys. All of which, I should think, might have made Ernest Hemingway pretty reasonably sick.

For, a year or so before *The Sun Also Rises*, he had published *In Our Time*, a collection of short pieces. The book caused about as much stir in literary circles as an incompleted dogfight on upper Riverside Drive. True, there were a few that went about quick and stirred with admiration for this clean, exciting prose, but most of the reviewers dismissed the volume with a tolerant smile and the word "stark." It was Mr. Mencken who slapped it down with "sketches in the bold, bad manner of the Café du Dôme," and the smaller boys, in their manner, took similar pokes at it. Well, you see, Ernest Hemingway was a young American living on the left bank of the Seine in Paris, France; he had been seen at the Dôme and the Rotonde and the Select and the Closerie des Lilas. He knew Pound, Joyce and Gertrude Stein. There is something a little—well, a little *you-know*—in all of those things. You wouldn't catch Bruce Barton or Mary Roberts Rinehart doing them. No, sir.

And besides, *In Our Time* was a book of short stories. That's no way to start off. People don't like that; they feel cheated. Any bookseller will be glad to tell you, in his interesting argot, that "short stories don't go." People take up a book of short stories and say, "Oh, what's this? Just a lot of those short things?" and put it right down again. Only yesterday afternoon, at four o'clock sharp, I saw and

Reprinted with permission from *The New Yorker*, 29 October 1927, pp. 92–94.

163

heard a woman do that to Ernest Hemingway's new book, *Men Without Women*. She had been one of those most excited about his novel.

Literature, it appears, is here measured by a yard-stick. As soon as *The Sun Also Rises* came out, Ernest Hemingway was the white-haired boy. He was praised, adored, analyzed, best-sold, argued about, and banned in Boston; all the trimmings were accorded him. People got into feuds about whether or not his story was worth the telling. (You see this silver scar left by a bullet, right up here under my hair? I got that the night I said that any well-told story was worth the telling. An eighth of an inch nearer the temple, and I wouldn't be sitting here doing this sort of tripe.) They affirmed, and passionately, that the dissolute expatriates in this novel of "a lost generation" were not worth bothering about; and then they devoted most of their time to discussing them. There was a time, and it went on for weeks, when you could go nowhere without hearing of *The Sun Also Rises*. Some thought it without excuse; and some, they of the cool, tall foreheads, called it the greatest American novel, tossing *Huckleberry Finn* and *The Scarlet Letter* lightly out the window. They hated it or they revered it. I may say, with due respect to Mr. Hemingway, that I was never so sick of a book in my life.

Now *The Sun Also Rises* was as "starkly" written as Mr. Hemingway's short stories; it dealt with subjects as "unpleasant." Why it should have been taken to the slightly damp bosom of the public while the (as it seems to me) superb *In Our Time* should have been disregarded will always be a puzzle to me. As I see it I knew this conversation would get back to me sooner or later, preferable sooner— Mr. Hemingway's style, this prose stripped to its firm young bones, is far more effective, far more moving, in the short story than in the novel. He is, to me, the greatest living writer of short stories; he is, also to me, not the greatest living novelist.

After all the high screaming about *The Sun Also Rises*, I feared for Mr. Hemingway's next book. You know how it is—as soon as they all start acclaiming a writer, that writer is just about to slip downward. The littler critics circle like literary buzzards above only the sick lions.

So it is a warm gratification to find the new Hemingway book, *Men Without Women*, a truly magnificent work. It is composed of thirteen short stories, most of which have been published before. They are sad and terrible stories; the author's enormous appetite for life seems to have been somehow appeased. You find here little of that peaceful ecstasy that marked the camping trip in *The Sun Also Rises* and the lone fisherman's days in "Big Two-Hearted River" in *In Our Time*. The stories include "The Killers," which seems to me one of the four great American short stories. (All you have to do is drop the nearest hat, and I'll tell you what I think the others are. They are Wilbur Daniel Steele's "Blue Murder,"

Sherwood Anderson's "I'm a Fool," and Ring Lardner's "Some Like Them Cold," that story which seems to me as shrewd a picture of every woman at some time as is Chekhov's "The Darling." Now what do you like best?) The book also includes "Fifty Grand," "In Another Country," and the delicate and tragic "Hills Like White Elephants." I do not know where a greater collection of stories can be found.

Ford Madox Ford has said of this author, "Hemingway writes like an angel." I take issue (there is nothing better for that morning headache than taking a little issue). Hemingway writes like a human being. I think it is impossible for him to write of any event at which he has not been present; his is, then, a reportorial talent, just as Sinclair Lewis's is. But, or so I think, Lewis remains a reporter, and Hemingway stands a genius because Hemingway has an unerring sense of selection. He discards details with a magnificent lavishness; he keeps his words to their short path. His is, as any reader knows, a dangerous influence. The simple thing he does looks so easy to do. But look at the boys who try to do it.

ON HEMINGWAY

CLAUDE McKAY

ERNEST HEMINGWAY WAS THE MOST TALKED ABOUT of young American writers when I arrived in Paris. He was the white hope of the ultra-sophisticates. In the motley atmosphere of Montparnasse, there was no place for the cult of little hero worship. James Joyce was worshipped, but he had won out with a work that took men's eyes like a planet. But in Montparnasse generally writers and artists plunged daggers into one another. That atmosphere in its special way was like a good tonic, if you didn't take too much of it. Good for young creative artists who have a tendency to megalomania, and many of them do. And also it was an antidote for the older ones who have already arrived and are a little haughty, expecting too much homage from the young.

It was therefore exciting that Ernest Hemingway had won the regard and respect of the younger creative artists and even of the older. I remember Nina Hammett pointing him out to me at the Dôme and remarking ecstatically that Hemingway was a very handsome American and that he had a lovely son. But it was long after that before I met him for a moment through Max Eastman.

In Our Time, that thin rare book of miniature short stories, was published, and it was the literary event among the young expatriates. I cherish an unforgettable memory of it and of Montparnasse at that time. A cultivated and distinguished American, liberal of attitude and pocket to unpopular causes, was sitting at the Dôme, reading a copy of *In Our Time*. He invited me to his table and offered a drink. He read aloud Chapter III, and wondered whether there was a *double entendre* in that last sentence: "It rained all through the evacuation." I said I did not know and did not think it mattered, and I asked the *garçon* to bring me a double cognac. My friend and host said: "They are talking in a big way about

Reprinted with permission from *A Long Way From Home* (New York: Lee Furman, Inc. 1937), pp. 249–52.

167

this Hemingway, but I just can't get him. I like the young radical crowd and what they are aiming to do. But this thing here"—he pointed to *In Our Time*—"I don't like it. It is too brutal and bloody."

"But so is life," I ventured to say, and not too aggressively, because I was expecting my host to come across with a gift of money.

"The only thing I admire about this book is the cover," he said. "That sure is in our time all right. If you like it you can have it." My hand trembled to take it. The book was worth something between thirty and fifty francs, which was more than I could afford. I have it still. It became so valuable that I once consigned it for a loan. But I redeemed it and, excepting my typewriter, I hardly ever trouble to redeem the things I pawn.

Yet I would be lying, if I should say here that when I read *In Our Time* in 1924 I thought the author soon would be one of the famous American writers. I liked the style of the book, but I thought more of it as a literary rarity, and that the author would remain one of the best of the little coterie writers.

I must confess to a vast admiration for Ernest Hemingway the writer. Some of my critics thought that I was imitating him. But I also am a critic of myself. And I fail to find any relationship between my loose manner and subjective feeling in writing and Hemingway's objective and carefully stylized form. Any critic who considers it important enough to take the trouble can trace in my stuff a clearly consistent emotional-realist thread, from the time I published my book of dialect verse (*Songs of Jamaica*) in 1912 through the period of my verse and prose in *The Liberator*, until the publication of *Home to Harlem*.

But indeed yes I was excited by the meteor apparition of Ernest Hemingway. I cannot imagine any ambitious young writer of that time who was not fascinated in the beginning. In Paris and in the Midi, I met a few fellows of the extreme left school, and also a few of the moderate liberal school and even some of the ancient fossil school—and all mentioned Hemingway with admiration. Many of them felt that they could never go on writing as before after Hemingway.

The irritating pseudo-romantic style of writing about contemporary life—often employed by modernists and futurists, with their punctuation-and-phraseology tricks, as well as by the dead traditionalists—that style so admirably parodied in *Ulysses*; had reached its conventional climax in Michael Arlen's *The Green Hat*. When Hemingway wrote *The Sun Also Rises*, he shot a fist in the face of the false romantic-realists and said: "You can't fake about life like that."

Apparently Hemingway today is mainly admired by a hard-boiled and unsophisticated public whose mentality in a curious way is rather akin to that of the American who contemptuously gave away Hemingway's first book to me. I don't think that that is any of Hemingway's fault. And what excites and tickles me to disgust is the attitude of the precious coteries toward Hemingway. One is not certain whether they hate Hemingway because of his success or because of his rough handling of some precious idols. The elect of the coteries could not possibly object to the Hemingway style and material. For the Hemingway of *In Our Time* is the same Hemingway of *The Sun Also Rises, A Farewell to Arms,* and the masterpiece of *Death in the Afternoon.* The only difference I see is that whereas Hemingway is a little cryptic in the earlier work, he is clear, unequivocal and forthright in his full-sized books. *In Our Time* contains the frame, the background, and the substance of all of Hemingway's later work. The hardboilism— the booze, blood and brutality are all there. The key to *A Farewell to Arms* may be found in *In Our Time.* The critics whose sensibilities were so shocked over *Death in the Afternoon* will find its foundation in the six miniature classics of the bull ring in *In Our Time,* developed and enlarged with riper experience in the big book.

I find in Hemingway's works an artistic illumination of a certain quality of American civilization that is not to be found in any other distinguished American writer. And that quality is the hard-boiled contempt for and disgust with sissyness expressed among all classes of Americans. Now this quality is distinctly and definitely American—a conventionalized rough attitude which is altogether un-European. It stands out conspicuously, like the difference between American burlesque shows and European music-hall shows. Mr. Hemingway has taken this characteristic of American life from the streets, the barrooms, the ringsides and lifted it into the realm of real literature. In accomplishing this he did revolutionary work with four-letter Anglo-Saxon words. That to me is a superb achievement. I do not know what Mr. Hemingway's personal attitude may be to the material that he has used, and I care less. All I can say is that in literature he has most excellently quickened and enlarged my experience of social life.

CATHERINE BARKLEY AND RETROSPECTIVE NARRATION IN *A FAREWELL TO ARMS*

JAMES NAGEL

MUCH OF THE RECENT SCHOLARSHIP on *A Farewell to Arms*, especially criticism that deals with the portrait of Catherine Barkley, proceeds on the assumption that the novel is a "realistic" construct and that the author and the characters presented can be "judged" in an objective sense for their behaviour and personalities.[1] This assumption has led some critics to complain that Catherine is too idealistic, too selflessly loving and giving to be believed as a character. The logical extreme of this contention, represented by the views of Judith Fetterley, is that such "idealization is a basic strategy for disguising and marketing hatred," that "Frederic wants and needs Catherine's death," and that through her death he "avoids" having to face the responsibilities incumbent upon a husband and father. Her death reflects his desire to remain uncommitted and it gives him a marketable explanation for doing so."[2] These opinions, buttressed more by contemporary social and political views than by any viable reading of the novel, have nonetheless developed a currency in Hemingway scholarship that needs to be tempered by a fresh reading of the novel as a work of art, a novel told by a narrator with a definable point of view, at a certain time, and for a discoverable purpose. All of these matters affect and determine the content and tone of the story presented in the novel.

A Farewell to Arms is fundamentally *not* a realistic novel about World War I narrated by Ernest Hemingway; it is, rather, a retrospective narrative told by Frederic Henry a decade after the action has taken place for the purpose of coming to terms emotionally with the events. As is the case with all first-person retrospective novels, a popular form in American literature, the narrative has a

Given at the 1986 Italian Hemingway Conference, and published here for the first time with the consent of the author.

171

dual time scheme: the time of the action set against the time of the telling. The time of the action is easily dated in that it relates to actual historical events, the most important of which is the retreat from Caporetto in October of 1917. This is the retreat during which the Italian troops fall into disorder, the soldiers desert their posts, and the army shoots its own men as they attempt to cross the bridge over the Tagliamento river. Frederic Henry is stopped at the bridge and would surely have been executed had he not escaped by plunging into the river. At this point he has been in the army for two years, 1915–1917. After the Caporetto episode, he and Catherine escape into Switzerland in the autumn of 1917, make their way to Montreux for the winter, and then proceed to Lausanne in the spring of 1918, where, in April, Catherine hemorrhages and dies during childbirth.

When the novel is told is more difficult to establish, but most likely the time of the narration is roughly synonymous with the period of composition in 1928. As he wrote the novel, a decade removed from his own war experiences in Italy, Ernest Hemingway imagined a protagonist telling his story at the same temporal distance from the events he relates. Although the precise date of the narration cannot be established, the fact that Frederic Henry at one point says that Babe Ruth was a pitcher *then,* at the time of the action, implies that he is not one *now,* at the time of the telling. Babe Ruth did his last pitching in 1919 while playing for the Boston Red Sox. He joined the New York Yankees in 1920 and became known primarily as a hitter. But he would not have been sufficiently notable to qualify as a time referent until after the season of 1927, when he hit 60 home runs to set a major league record that was to last over three decades. By March of the following year, when Hemingway began *A Farewell to Arms,* Ruth would have been one of the most popular figures in America, and it would make sense to have Frederic refer to him.[3]

Apart from the Babe Ruth references there are numerous time indicators that establish that the telling is a long period after Catherine's death and that there is a continual disparity between the time of action and the time of telling. Frederic reflects at one point that the priest knew *then* some important things about the value of domestic life that he came to realize only *now* (p. 14). He says that he has forgotten some of the details of the events, as he naturally would over a period of years (p. 291). That the events recalled are at some temporal distance from the moment of narration is evident throughout Frederic's story. At one juncture he observes that Count Greffi was living to be 100 which, since he is 94 during the billiard game in Stresa, would be six years later than the time of action (pp. 142, 263). But more important than the precise moment of the telling is the awareness that many of the judgments expressed in the novel must be perceived as having derived not from insight contemporaneous with the action but from the older and painfully wiser perspective of Frederic Henry as narrator.

What an awareness of the dual time scheme of the novel reveals is that Catherine Barkley exists in the novel only in the memory of Frederic Henry, only in the reflections of a man who came to love her, who lost her, and who grieves and assesses his behaviour a decade after she has died. To expect him to present a fully realized portrait, an objective and realistic account of his lost love, is to be insensitive to the emotional context of the telling of the novel. What he renders is understandably less a realistic portrait than a "lyric evocation," the tragic but sweet image that lingers in the mind. Indeed, the pertinent standard for assessing the "realism" of the portrait of Catherine would be not whether she resembles actual persons in their complexity and imperfection but whether Frederic's memories of her seem plausible, whether they are the kinds of reflections a man would have about the woman he lost. As Sheldon Grebstein has said, "In the memory every attribute of the loved one becomes exalted and rendered more precious than in life."[4]

These evaluations from the time of the telling are often broad philosophical observations, summary judgments gleaned from the total impact of the experience, and only occasionally assessments of a single event. When Frederic reflects on the wisdom of the priest early in the novel, it is clear that his respect for the domestic values the priest espouses developed *after* he had lost Catherine and the child and not before, in the period in which his nightly visits to the Villa Rossa constituted a debasement of the values he would later endorse: "But I did not know that then, although I learned it later" (p. 14). His account of his first encounter with Catherine involves the idea of the loss of Catherine for Rinaldi, however superficial their relationship was; the nearly pathological grief of Catherine for the lover who was killed; and a corresponding bereavement for Frederic Henry at the time he tells the story. Catherine's comments about her fear of the rain and how she sees herself dead in it would not have had nearly the emotional resonance at the moment she said it as it does when Frederic remembers it.

Henry recalls at one point that with Catherine he felt alone against the world in his close union with her, and he reflects, clearly from a later viewpoint, "it has only happened to me like that once" (p. 258). That comment, along with the attendant observation that the world breaks everyone and the courageous it has to kill in order to break, seem most distinctly the painful conclusions of a lover who has lost everything and is trying to find some meaning or consolation in what has happened. This passage is related to the one at the end of the novel in which Frederic, having learned that the baby is dead, realizes that Catherine too will die and that "the first time they caught you off base they killed you" (p. 338). At times there is a correlation between the feelings of the action and the feelings of the telling, as when he remembers the time he got drunk before he went to see her at the hospital and she refused to see him; it was his first feeling of loss for her, but not his last (p. 43). Indeed, the very scenes that Frederic chooses to present in his story suggest a principle of selection from memory along several lines of thought: his duplicity as opposed to her selflessness and nobility; his growing commitment to her as he moves from the hope of sexual exploitation to genuine love; his progression from an intense involvement in a group to his present status, at the time of narration, of loneliness and isolation.

His early role-playing in their relationship, in many ways a standard lover's ploy, is unusual only in Catherine's extreme vulnerability, her lover having been killed. When Frederic first hears of Catherine it is from Rinaldi, who has been seeing her and who is himself engaged in a modest deception, attempting to impress on her that he is a "man of sufficient wealth" (p. 12). Frederic remembers that at the same time Rinaldi went to call on her, Frederic was having a conversation with the priest, who had advised him to go to the Abruzzi region on leave, which Frederic failed to do. As he tries to explain his motivation to the priest, he says:

> I tried to tell about the night and the difference between the night and the day and how the night was better unless the day was very clean and cold and I could not tell it; as I cannot tell it now. . . . He had not had it but he understood that I had really wanted to go to the Abruzzi but had not gone and we were still friends, with many tastes alike, but with the difference between us. He had always known what I did not know and what, when I learned it, I was always able to forget. But I did not know that then, although I learned it later. (p. 14)

Later in the novel, the priest and Frederic discuss the nature of love, moving from spiritual to carnal, and the priest's observations are instructive:

> "When you love you wish to do things for. You wish to sacrifice for. You wish to serve."
> "I don't love."
> "You will. I know you will. Then you will be happy." (p. 75)

Significantly, Frederic associates his earliest memories of Catherine with his betrayal of the domestic values of the priest, in the first instance, and with his denial of love in the second. Before the novel is over, however, he will come to endorse the positions his friend had earlier taken.

In his first meeting with Catherine, he learns that she was engaged to a young man for eight years who was killed the year before in the Somme. Now, in reflection, she regrets not having had sexual relations with him: "I could have given him that anyway. But I thought it would be bad for him" (p. 19). Frederic's comments during this conversation are guarded and calculated, as he senses immediately the nature of her condition and the ways in which it might work to his advantage. He is restrained and charming, and it is clear that Catherine is taken with him, as Rinaldi acknowledges:

"Miss Barkley prefers you to me. That is very clear. But the little Scotch one is very nice."
"Very," I said. I had not noticed her. "You like her?"
"No," said Rinaldi. (p. 21)

In the early stages of the courtship, Frederic is insincere and calculating, confident of her attraction to him and of his eventual conquest. Even when Catherine slaps him when he tries to kiss her on their next encounter, he feels assured: "I was angry and yet certain, seeing it all ahead like the moves in a chess game" (p. 26). He seems emotionally uninvolved even when she does kiss him a moment later:

"Oh, darling," she said. "You will be good to me, won't you?"
What the hell, I thought. I stroked her hair and patted her shoulder. She was crying. (p. 27)

When he returns to his room that evening, Rinaldi knows precisely what the situation is: "You have that pleasant air of a dog in heat," he says (p. 27). Through the telling of their memories of these encounters, Frederic reveals the cynicism of his early relationship with Catherine and develops an unflattering portrait of his motivation and character. The confessional edge of telling these painful memories must have a cathartic function for Frederic, for there can be little pleasure in recalling them.

That Frederic has dwelt on the nature of the early stages of his relationship with Catherine is also evident from the precision he brings to the relating of the events. Having thought it all through, he can even remember the number of days between meetings, even though it all happened many years earlier:

I was away for two days at the posts. When I got home it was too late and I did not see Miss Barkley until the next evening. (p. 29)

The formality of their interaction is echoed by Catherine: as she is Miss Barkley to him, he is Mr. Henry to her (p. 38), at least at the beginning of the scene. The significance of the formal titles is that this encounter in Chapter VI forms a transition in their relationship from formal to personal, from flirtatious interest to direct expressions of affection:

She looked at me, "And you do love me?"

"Yes."
"You did say you loved me, didn't you?"
"Yes," I lied. "I love you." I had not said it before. (p. 31)

In this scene the emphasis is on the growing intensity of emotion between them, with love on her side and seductive expectation on his. At the time of telling the values are confessional, as Frederic reveals the painful truth to himself and his readers: "I thought she was probably a little crazy. . . . I knew I did not love Catherine Barkley nor had any idea of loving her" (p. 31). Frederic recalls that he regarded their interaction to be like a "game, like bridge, in which you said things instead of playing cards." He also remembers that Catherine, on a deeper level, was very much aware of his duplicity, despite her surface delusions: "This is a rotten game we play, isn't it?" she says to him (p. 32). As they part for the evening Frederic walks home past the Villa Rossa, the brothel he had previously frequented, but he rejects the temptation and goes home. This gesture suggests that his sexual desires have transferred to Catherine, about whom he now has erotic fantasies (p. 39). It also reveals a degree of commitment to Catherine that he had not yet formulated in language.

These implications are strengthened in the next chapter when Frederic returns from the front. While there he thought often about her, about how he would go see her, and they would make love in the night. When he returns, however, he becomes caught up in the fraternalism of the mess hall, drinks too much in a contest with Bassi (p. 41), goes drunk to see Catherine, and is informed that she will not see him that night. His feelings are a revelation to him:

I went out the door and suddenly I felt lonely and empty. I had treated seeing Catherine very lightly, had gotten somewhat drunk and had nearly forgotten to come but when I could not see her there I was feeling lonely and hollow. (p. 43)

This is a poignant memory for Frederic to relate in 1928, when his feelings of loneliness and hollowness at the loss of Catherine would be inexorable and pervasive. This initial rejection was his first realization of his need for her and of the pain of her absence. The double function of the scene is that the pain of loss is a key issue in both of the time schemes of the novel. This passage is one of the best examples of the congruence of emotion on both temporal levels.

When Frederic finally does see her the next day, the encounter fulfills none of his fantasies, for he is on his way to the front and stops at the hospital for only a few moments. Both of them handle the incident of the night before with great delicacy. He accepts, strategically, the fiction of her illness: "I stopped to ask if you were better." He does not wish to force her to an accusation of his boorish behaviour of the night before, and she too wishes to pursue their relationship on

the best of levels: "I'm quite well," she said, "I think the heat knoc
yesterday" (p. 44). This is once again game playing, but it is a mutual acceptance
of falsity for a benevolent purpose, since they can proceed in the relationship
much more easily from this position than from one of accusation, and confession, apology, and forgiveness. She gives him a Saint Anthony medal to protect
him at the front, and Frederic leaves wearing Saint Anthony. As he says, intrud-
ing into the flow of the action, "after I was wounded I never found him. Some
one probably got it at one of the dressing stations" (p. 46).

Frederic does not see Catherine again until after he is wounded and is recov-
ering in the hospital in Milan. The plot leaves the romance story to focus on the
war until the two lovers are joined again through the coincidence of his wounding
and her assignment to the American hospital. That his first sight of her prompts
his feelings of affection had been foreshadowed by his growing involvement with
her in the earlier scenes:

> I looked toward the door. It was Catherine Barkley.
> She came in the room and over to the bed.
> "Hello, darling," she said. She looked fresh and young and very beauti-
> ful. I thought I had never seen anyone so beautiful.
> "Hello," I said. When I saw her I was in love with her. Everything turned
> over inside of me. (p. 95)

At the time of the telling, of course, even these memories of love and happiness
would have a poignant edge, a value quite distinct from those of the action.
Frederic's relation of this part of their romance continues to record the most
positive memories of Catherine coupled with some unflattering admissions on
his part.

For example, he remembers that after they had made love for the first time,
"the wildness was gone and I felt finer than I had ever felt" (p. 96). But this
sweet memory is linked to the awareness that at the time he had not wanted to fall
in love, not with her or with anyone (p. 97). In addition, he soon lies to her about
his having had previous love affairs (although he later confesses that he has had
gonorrhea [p. 309]) and, specifically, about having told prostitutes that he loved
them (pp. 108–09). In contrast, Catherine was almost entirely selfless in her
devotion: "I want what you want. There isn't any me any more," she says to him
(p. 118). Later, when they discuss the complexities of getting married under Italian law, she says that she could not be more married as it is and that "there isn't
any me. I'm you. Don't make up a separate me" (p. 119). Once again, Frederic's
emotions at the time of the telling must be very different from those of the time of
the events, when his success as lover would have given him great satisfaction.

Now, in the telling, he focuses on his equivocation and duplicity to counterpoint her total absorption in their emotional bond. In this sense, entertaining and relating these events would be more a means of expiating guilt than one of enjoying the pleasure of the past.

The final episode of their relationship that Frederic narrates deals with Catherine's pregnancy and the consequences that follow from it. Early in the romance Nurse Ferguson had warned Frederic that she did not "want her [Catherine] with any of these war babies" (p. 113), just as she had suggested that they would never get married (p. 112). These observations are obviously more meaningful to Frederic as he tells the story than at the time of the action, for there is no indication in what they do or say to each other that they take any precautions against pregnancy or even give the consequences of their behaviour the slightest thought. So it is not remarkable that Catherine soon reveals she is pregnant, although it is notable that she seems to suggest that she made an attempt to abort the child: " 'I took everything but it didn't make any difference' " (p. 144). This remark would be significant at the time of the telling because if she had aborted the child Catherine would, in all likelihood, still be alive. Similarly poignant for Frederic to remember would be her concern for him contrasted to his admission to her that " 'you always feel trapped biologically' " (p. 145). When she objects to the word "always," with its suggestion that he may have impregnated another woman previously, he can only offer apologies without denials: " 'I could cut off my tongue,' I offered."

The further development of this plot line is once again interrupted by the concerns of the war, as Frederic returns to the front in time for the disastrous retreat from Caporetto. When he arrives in Gorizia he finds Rinaldi disillusioned with the war but sensitive as ever to his friend's condition. Rinaldi sees at once that Frederic has changed: " 'You act like a married man,' he said. 'What's the matter with you?' " (p. 173). Frederic will admit only that he is in love with Catherine. Later, as he records the rambling thoughts of his dreams, he once again affirms his love: "Christ, that my love were in my arms and I in my bed again. That my love Catherine. That my sweet love Catherine down might rain. Blow her again to me" (p. 204). It is important to be aware that these are sentiments Frederic expresses not only at the time of the action, when they occur as part of a dream reverie, but also at the time of the telling when, in a more rational context, the feelings are recalled and formulated by a narrator who also wishes to have his love back again.

As Frederic flees the front by riding on an armaments train, hiding under a canvas tarp, he reveals more of the depths of his emotional dependence on her: "I could remember Catherine but knew I would get crazy if I thought about her when I was not sure yet I would see her. . ." (p. 240). This is another passage with profound implications on both levels of the novel. At the time of the action it suggests a situational vulnerability: Frederic has not yet recovered emotionally from the trauma of having shot a man, of having nearly been shot himself in his attempt to cross the Tagliamento, and is still in the act of desertion. If he is discovered and captured, without papers or orders, he may yet be executed. He cannot be sure he will make it back to Milan, or that Catherine will be there, and he is realistic in thinking that there is much uncertainty in his circumstances. At the time of the telling, however, the emotions are somewhat more deep: his suggestion of going crazy if he is unable to be with her would suggest an almost irremediable sadness in the present. A decade is a long time for a sense of loss to persist, especially with the intensity with which Frederic tells his story.

When he arrives in Milan he learns that Catherine has been transferred to Stresa, a convenient location, he learns from his friend Simmons, since they can row across the lake to safety in Switzerland. At the time of the action the value of this observation is simply part of the strategy of escape; from the time of the telling, there is a bitter irony. In planning to escape the dangers of Italy, Frederic and Catherine hasten to her death in Lausanne. When Frederic finally sees her in Stresa, it is clear that she is deeply in love with him: "Catherine looked at me all the time, her eyes happy," he says (p. 255). Here, too, there is pleasure in the past and pain in the present, in the memory of her devotion. Frederic then relates how accusatory Ferguson was about the pregnancy, and how Catherine came to his defense. But the emphasis is on how they were reunited in Stresa and how wonderful it was to be together.

The process of telling this part of his story leads Frederic to a series of generalizations about love that come not from feelings contemporaneous with the action, when the only thoughts would have been about the strategy of escape or the pleasure of love, but from the later period of loneliness and retrospective assessment:

> Often a man wishes to be alone and a girl wishes to be alone too and if they love each other they are jealous of that in each other, but I can truly say we never felt that. We could feel alone when we were together, alone against the others. It has only happened to me like that once. (p. 258)

The last comment, that such love has come only once, also suggests that Frederic has not replaced Catherine emotionally in the intervening years.

Linked to these reflections are Frederic's observations about the nature of the world and the status of the individuals in it. These thoughts are clearly from a later perspective as well:

If people bring so much courage to this world the world has to kill them to break them, so of course it kills them. The world breaks every one and afterward many are strong at the broken places. But those that will not break it kills. (pp. 258–59)

There would be no motivation for these sentiments prior to Catherine's death in Switzerland. As retrospective observations, they create the irony of two lovers fleeing joyfully toward their own disaster. Significantly, this passage is juxtaposed in Frederic's narrative to the billiard game with Count Greffi in which Frederic and the Count discuss death (p. 270). Count Greffi died six years after their conversation in Stresa, so Frederic's memories of the direction of their discussion have resonance for the Count as well as for Catherine.

But Frederic's recapitulation of the days immediately prior to the escape to Switzerland stresses his love for Catherine, the real subject of his narration. By going back over it all he can once again feel the emotions of that period at the same time he acknowledges what he has lost: " 'My life used to be full of everything,' I said. 'Now if you aren't with me I haven't a thing in the world' " (p. 266). It must be painfully evident to Frederic, as he tells his story, with Catherine long dead, that he has not "a thing in the world." This idea is reiterated a moment later when he says to her " 'I'm just so in love with you that there isn't anything else.' " As he remembers their lovemaking that afternoon, he recalls his emotions: " 'I felt faint with loving her so much' " (p. 268). He has come a long way from the cynical seducer who first met Catherine, who behaved only with calculation and brash assurance. Despite himself, he became a "lover" in every sense, one whose sense of being is engrossed in the beloved.

Frederic's telling of the escape across the lake that November night is largely an adventure story with relatively little reflection on the significance of the events or their later consequences. As always, however, there is resonance in the past for the present, as in the comment Catherine makes when he warns her to be careful not to allow the oar to hit her in the stomach when she takes her turn rowing: " 'If it did'—Catherine said between strokes—'life might be much simpler' " (p. 284). Once again Frederic remembers comments about causing an abortion which, from hindsight, could have saved her life.

The technicalities of entering Switzerland comprise a largely comic episode, despite the importance of the lovers' being admitted. But once that seems assured, what Frederic recalls is the regional rivalries among the guards and the extent to which Switzerland is a tourist business rather than a country. What is more important, however, is that as the story Frederic tells comes closer and closer to the ultimate tragedy, his interpretive comments diminish until at the end he is relating only events.

The fact that he does not intrude into the rendition of the action, however, does not mean that they do not have a deeply felt meaning for him. Frederic, as is the case with all narrators, must select material from memory to be told, and the events described may have a different meaning, or a deeper significance, for him as he tells them than as they happened. Throughout the early sections of Book Five, for example, Frederic describes the happiness he and Catherine had together the winter of 1918 in Montreux. The joy of the events is tinged with a sense of loss and tragedy from the time of the telling, however. Frederic mentions the close marriage of his landlords, Mr. and Mrs. Guttingen, who were "very happy together too" (p. 300). At the time it happened Frederic would have looked to them optimistically as a model of a good marriage; at the time of the telling he portrays them as a reminder of what he has lost. The distance between the two times is evident in the difficulty Frederic has in remembering certain details, ones not directly associated with Catherine: "There were three villages; Chernex, Fontanivent, and the other I forget" (p. 301).

There are other subtle touches with the narrative point of view. Now that Frederic can no longer see Catherine at all, he recalls how he could see her image in three mirrors simultaneously at the hairdresser's (p. 303). When she expresses her deep love for him, there is also a reminder that she is narrow in the hips and that the baby must be kept small (p. 304). At the beginning of the novel, when his relationship with Catherine was not at a crucial stage, he tended to narrate broad sweeps of time, using seasons as indicators of passing periods. As he tells about these crucial months, however, he becomes increasingly precise, specifying months, then days, and, finally, in the hospital, hours and minutes. He indicates that the snow in Montreux came on December 22, for example, since the snow will isolate them in their romantic haven. They were so happy together, that winter, that they felt no desire for the companionship of other people, as they discuss on two occasions (pp. 308, 313). The weight here is on how close they have become, how they seem to be one entity. Frederic once again makes the assertion to her that " 'I'm no good when you're not there. I haven't any life at all any more' " (p. 310). These sentiments may convey not only how he felt in Switzerland but how he feels at the time of narration.

Their happiness continues into the middle of January (by which time Frederic has grown a beard), through February, and into early March, when the rains come and ruin the landscape. From the calculations of their plan to go to Lausanne to have the baby, it would seem most likely that Catherine dies in early April, the cruelest month, since she is eight months pregnant in early March (p. 316). Frederic remembers that they stayed in one hotel for three weeks in Lausanne (p. 320), during which time she bought baby clothes and he boxed in the local gymnasium. It is "one morning" sometime later that Catherine experiences labor pains and the episode in the hospital began.

It is significant that Frederic's rendition of the trauma of labor and the death of Catherine is almost entirely free of retrospective observations. His comments about Catherine's suffering being the "price you paid for sleeping together" are his representation of his thoughts at the time of the action, since he does not yet know that she will die later that day (pp. 330–31). Similarly, his expectation that "now Catherine would die" is also a projection of the working of his mind at the time of the events, not a later assessment (p. 338). The famous "ants" passage, in which, in the past, Frederic observed ants coming out of a burning log and dropping off into the fire, most likely represents thinking at the time of the action when he would long for the ability to be a "messiah" and control death, thus saving Catherine. Frederic relates the events of this final episode without interpretation, suggesting that the facts speak for themselves and also, perhaps, that the recapitulation of the most painful episode of his life is almost too much for him, that his emotions can be controlled only in restraint. In this sense he is much less moved by his own physical wounding, about which he seems free to assess and evaluate without fear of the feelings involved; it is Catherine's death that he handles with emotional caution.

In his memory, it is Catherine who conducted herself bravely, and he retains only the most positive recollections of her fortitude and sensitivity. From the beginning of labor she regarded the worst pains as the best (pp. 323–24) and expressed concern not for herself but for him and any inconveniences that her problems might cause him. While she struggles through a prolonged labor, he goes for breakfast and then lunch and later dinner. He remembers the day, understandably, with great precision, giving the hours of key developments, the minutes between contractions (p. 327). There is irony, of course, in the reassurances he receives that Catherine is all right, that the baby is healthy, that he should not worry. His emotion of the time is told without apology: when he hears that she has begun to hemorrhage, he says that everything was gone inside of him. Rather than comment about his emotions, he captures his thinking in a stream of consciousness passage:

> Dear God, don't let her die. Please, please, please don't let her die. God please make her not die. I'll do anything you say if you don't let her die. You took the baby but don't let her die. That was all right but don't let her die. Please, please, dear God, don't let her die. (p. 341)

When he is finally admitted to her bedside, he leans over her and starts to cry. Catherine knows that she has very little time to live. Rather than descend into a false religiosity, as had Frederic earlier, Catherine does not want a priest and asks only to spend her last moments with him. Characteristically, she is concerned for him: she wants him to have the companionship of other women after she has died; she says she will come stay with him nights, since she knows he has insomnia and suffers from loneliness; she reassures him that she is not afraid of death and sees it only as a "dirty trick" (p. 342). In a passage Hemingway deleted from the manuscript, Frederic thinks: "And if it is the Lord that giveth and the Lord that taketh away, I do not admire him for taking Catherine away. . . ."[5] His rendition of the events after her death is abbreviated and unemotional: nothing after her death seems to matter, and the language is restrained because the emotion would be too much to bear, too painful for the telling.

But Frederic has told his story, and the honesty of his telling suggests that he is now ready to face the truth of the early stages of their relationship and implies that he has grown a great deal, emotionally and morally, in the years after her death. Frederic is not glossing over his behavior; the most he could hope for at the time of the narration is the theraputic value of a full accounting, of an honest assessment of his feelings throughout their relationship. The contrasting pattern in what Frederic reveals of Catherine's attitudes is most acute: she, as he chooses to recall and relate, was selfless from the start, open in her feelings, willing to give far more than she received from him, and soon became totally fused with him. At the time of the telling it is these sentiments that Frederic would remember: a man who finds the memory of his lost love too precious to surrender, even after a decade, is not going to dwell on petty points; he would, of course, subordinate any deficiencies in her nature to concentrate on what is of moment to him now, the quality of his loss, the death of a love he has not replaced.

It is understandable that the story he tells is rendered in language that is controlled and understated, since the pain of the memories is almost too much to bear even after a decade. In another passage that Hemingway excised from the manuscript, Frederic reflects that "the position of the survivor of a great calamity is seldom admirable."[6] Especially acute must be the emotions of telling what he said to Catherine in Stresa: " 'My life used to be full of everything,' I said. 'Now if you aren't with me I haven't a thing in the world' " (p. 266). *A Farewell to Arms* is a novel told by a man who feels he has nothing left in the world, nothing but the memories of the most painful and yet meaningful episode of his life.

It is important, however, as it is for all first-person narratives, to attempt to assess the motivation for revealing such intimate details. One impulse might be the desire to come to terms at last with the true nature of the events: as Robert W. Lewis, Jr., has suggested, "Henry has undergone an initiatory and learning experience that he is now ready to interpret."[7] Another impulse might be for Frederic to change his condition at the time of the telling. Frederic's story is one of progressive isolation. He begins as a member of the Italian army, with a primary identification with his own unit, moves to a union with Catherine, secluded within their transcient home in Switzerland, and ends without connection, alone in the rain.[8] But after a decade of reflection, his act of telling his story is fundamentally one of relating, of speaking to others about the intimate moments in his life, and this act implies the beginning of a movement into the world once again. Before doing so he seems to feel the need to evaluate his experiences and his younger self, however painful the process might be.[9] Although his observations stress the indifference of the universe, the perversity of fate, the vanity of human wishes, Frederic's comments also prepare him to move beyond his loss.[10]

What is clear is that although his motives and attitudes were not always noble in the early stages of his romance with Catherine, through his love for her he grew to be a better man, one who could love fully and assess himself truly.[11] There seems to be no justification for concluding, as Gerry Brenner does, that having told his story Frederic has little reason to go on living and will soon commit suicide.[12] Rather, the suggestion is that he is now prepared to resume living once again, to seek new relationships and new commitments, and to end his fixation on loss and pain, a process that has taken him a decade.

Before he does so, however, he apparently feels the need to think it all through once again and to tell his story from the beginning. What he tells is more a eulogy than a realistic account, particularly with regards to the portrait of Catherine.[13] Indeed, it is clear from the nature of the telling of *A Farewell to Arms* that she cannot be judged apart from the recognition that she exists in the novel only in Frederic's memories, that she is a projection of his thinking a decade after she has died. Far from "wanting" or "needing" her to die, Frederic has clearly been unable to reconcile himself to her loss during the intervening years and only now, through the act of the telling, does he come to terms with his sense of emptiness through the story he tells. The story he tells about Catherine, despite the fact that she dies at the end of it, shows her moving from a condition of psychological desolation to one of balance and love.[14] He now needs to find his own way through that process. His reflections and philosophical speculations reveal a man who knows much about what he must live without and what he will always live with, with the memories of the war and the love and loss of Catherine Barkley.

1. Ernest Hemingway, *A Farewell to Arms* (New York: Scribner's, 1957).

2. See Judith Fetterley, "*A Farewell to Arms*: Ernest Hemingway's 'Resentful Cryptogram,' " *The Authority of Experience: Essays in Feminist Criticism*, ed. Arlyn Diamond and Lee R. Edwards (Amherst: University of Massachusetts Press, 1977), pp. 258, 270.

3. For the information on the career of Babe Ruth and its role in dating the time of the narration of the novel, I am indebted to Dale Edmonds, "When Does Frederic Henry Narrate *A Farewell to Arms*," *Notes on Modern American Literature*, 4 (1980), Item 14.

4. Sheldon Norman Grebstein, *Hemingway's Craft* (Carbondale: Southern Illinois University Press, 1973), p. 76.

5. Quoted in Scott Donaldson, "Frederic Henry's Escape and the Pose of Passivity," *Hemingway: A Revaluation*, ed. Donald Noble (Troy, N.Y.: Whitston Publishing Co., 1983), p. 181.

6. Quoted in Donaldson, p. 181.

7. Robert W. Lewis, Jr., *Hemingway on Love* (Austin: University of Texas Press, 1965), p. 39.

8. See Michael S. Reynolds, *Hemingway's First War: The Making of* A Farewell to Arms (Princeton: Princeton University Press. 1976), p. 271.

9. See Arnold E. Davidson, "The Dantean Perspective in Hemingway's *A Farewell to Arms*," *Journal of Narrative Technique,* 3 (1973), 123, for a comment on Frederic's isolation.

10. See Davidson, pp. 123–24.

11. I am indebted here to the insights of Arthur Waldhorn, *A Reader's Guide to Ernest Hemingway* (New York: Farrar, Straus, and Giroux, 1972), p. 130.

12. See Gerry Brenner, *Concealments in Hemingway's Works* (Columbus: Ohio State University Press, 1983), p. 41.

13. Joyce Wexler, "E.R.A. for Hemingway: A Feminist Defense of *A Farewell to Arms*," *Georgia Review*, 35 (1981), 121, develops a similar logic.

14. I am indebted here to Roger Whitlow, *Cassandra's Daughters: The Women in Hemingway* (Westport: Greenwood Press, 1984), p. 22.

A TÉSSERA FOR FREDERIC HENRY: IMAGERY AND RECURRENCE IN *A FAREWELL TO ARMS*

GWEN L. NAGEL

IN AN EARLY DRAFT of *A Farewell to Arms,* Frederic Henry, after he deserts, makes arrangements with the proprietor of a wine shop in Milan to acquire a false identity card. Their conversation, which Ernest Hemingway eventually deleted, is inspired by Frederic's altered uniform. Frederic speaks first:

> "I have no need for papers. I have papers. As for the stars, they never wear them at the front."
> I thought a minute.
> "I will be back."
> "Only you must tell me now."
> "A Téssera," I said, "and leave papers."
> "Write the name."
> "Give me a pencil." I wrote a name on the edge of a newspaper. "Someone will call for them."
> "Who?"
> "I don't know. He will bring a photograph for the Téssera. You will know me by that."[1]

As Michael Reynolds and Sheldon Grebstein have noted, by deleting this passage Hemingway tightened the plot.[2] Scott Donaldson further observes that the deletion "also functions in two other ways: to avoid a lapse in credibility and to flesh out the character of the protagonist." Frederic's illegal attempt to purchase false papers would not only be out of character for him, it would "only exacerbate" his already considerable guilt.[3]

Given at the 1986 Italian Hemingway Conference, and published here for the first time with the consent of the author.

187

These are sensible reasons for Hemingway to have deleted the passage, but Hemingway's celebrated iceberg theory, and his aesthetic that calls for the elimination of redundancy, that eschews explication for implication, might suggest other reasons why the passage was eliminated. What has been pruned needlessly complicates the plot, and Frederic's conversation about the téssera and his gesture of writing a false name on the edge of his newspaper have been discarded from a manuscript that is filled with images of identity, both real and counterfeit. Details involving clothing, names, repeated scenes of mistaken or ambiguous identity, and interrogation scenes pervade the novel, and these incidents, along with Hemingway's deft use of personal pronouns, serve to underline the dual focus of Frederic Henry's identity in war (his public or national role) and in love (his private or familial role). The pervasiveness of identity scenes contribute much to the irony of the book, by exposing the gap between pretense or sham and what is real. And too, the ambiguity augments the emotional tone of the novel, that sense of confusion and disaffiliation which finally culminates in separation for both threads of the novel: Frederic's desertion from the Italian army and his sense of isolation at Catherine's death.

In the deleted passage, Frederic signs "a name," probably false, on the newspaper; a matter of continuing interest through the novel is the number of different names the protagonist is called. Frederic does not actually use his name until nurse Gage asks him who he is in the hospital in Milan.[4] Until that point others refer to him as Tenente, Tenente Enry, Enrico, Henry, Fred, Fredi, and Federico (pp. 77, 97, 172, 123, 175). The Italian major jokes about Frederic's name in the mess scene, asking him if he is Frederico Enrico or Enrico Fedrico (p. 40). On the simplest level these different names indicate that some of the speakers do not deal easily with English, but they also suggest that Frederic has an identity problem, that he is in the process of defining himself as a person.[5] "Having been christened with two first names" as Gerry Brenner has commented, "befuddles one's self-concept."[6]

Added to the confused names are a variety of appellations that others apply to Frederic which define the ways in which they perceive him. Rinaldi, for example, affectionately refers to Frederic as "Baby" (pp. 32, 40–41) and "brother" (pp. 65–67), terms that reveal his affection and familial identification with his friend. In the mess hall, when Rinaldi encourages Frederic to visit his family in Amalfi while on leave, he promises that "They will love you like a son" (p. 8). Similarly, almost from the beginning of their relationship Catherine refers to Frederic as "boy" (p. 31). Frederic does not protest her use of this affectionate diminutive, nor does he protest when the other nurses and some of the doctors cajole him to behave and "be a good boy,"[7] but he rejects the sham maternalism of Mrs. Meyers when she refers to a group of soldiers as her "dear boys" (p. 119). All of these appellations suggest familial relationships, a part of Frederic's identity that is missing in the novel except for a reference to a stepfather and a grandfather who pays the bills (p. 154) and Catherine's directive to "think about your people" when he goes under the anaesthetic (p. 103). The priest, with his strong sense of identity, of regional pride in the Abruzzi, and his firm familial roots, is, ironically, never named. But he is not immune to confusion and disorientation, which he expresses in part in a conversation about his identity. When Frederic compliments him by saying "You are a fine boy," the priest exposes his wonder at the irony of his title when he says to Frederic: "I am a boy,. . . But you call me father" (p. 72).[8]

Another way Hemingway suggests the confusion of Frederic's identity is through a number of scenes in which he is misidentified by other characters. In the first instance, Catherine, grieving over her lost fiancé, mistakes Frederic for her dead lover. It is interesting to note, however, that among Catherine's first words to Frederic are, "You're not an Italian, are you?" (p. 18). Her question, posed in the negative, is an attempt to clarify his nationality by stripping him of his relationship to Italy, a process that culminates with Frederic's defection. Later, when Frederic is wounded, the astute but pragmatic British soldier attempts to speed up the bureaucracy by identifying Frederic first as the son of President Wilson and later as the son of the American ambassador (pp. 58–59). Rinaldi insists Frederic is really Italian and only pretends to be American, he calls Frederic the American Garibaldi once, and greets him after his return from the hospital as "the fine good Anglo-Saxon boy" (pp. 66, 76, 168). The surgeon thinks Frederic is French and the proprietor of the bar in Milan inquires if he is South American (pp. 58–60, 238). While in the hospital in Milan, Frederic is shaved by a reticent but surly barber who mistakes him for an Austrian officer (pp. 90–91). During the retreat Frederic is worried that he will be mistaken for a German in Italian uniform, and in Stresa Fergy calls him an American Italian (pp. 224, 247). As these examples indicate, Frederic is a case of ambiguous nationality. As an American in the Italian uniform he is an oddity and because his background is obscure others project onto him values that express *their* needs, interests, fears, and anger. He is a chameleon for the convenience of the people around him.

In contrast to these instances, there is a series of interrogation scenes in the novel (at the front, in the hospitals in both Italy and Switzerland, and at the border in Switzerland) in which Frederic is required to provide information about himself. Such scenes not only lend realistic texture to the novel and provide a pattern of Frederic's repeated confrontations with officialdom, but they also highlight the split between Frederic's vacillating public role and that emergent private self that finds stability in union with Catherine.

Three interrogation scenes need comment. It is, of course, an interrogation scene that provides the motivation for Frederic's desertion, for when he overhears the battle police questioning the lieutenant colonel before they shoot him, Frederic anticipates he will be determined to be an enemy in Italian uniform and executed (pp. 224–25). It is perhaps ironic that it is in neutral Switzerland that both Frederic and Catherine "officially" misrepresent themselves, Catherine when she checks into the hospital as Catherine Henry (p. 313), a name that is psychologically true and in accord with her assertion that she and Frederic are "married privately" (p. 116), and Frederic when he presents his real documents at the border (not a forged *téssera*), but lies about his purpose in entering the country. He says he is a sportsman and tourist and then deflects the attention of the Swiss guards in an action worthy of Huck Finn. Like Huck, who demonstrates an uncanny ability to anticipate and judge the motives of his audience and then disguises himself repeatedly, Frederic, too, not only misrepresents himself,[9] but makes an astute judgment on the nature and vulnerabilities of his audience. He, a fugitive who feels little loyalty to any country, can take advantage of the regional affinity of his Swiss interrogators to save himself.

That split between public and private self, the self that can make a separate peace with a war, is most clearly indicated by clothing. Clothing denotes status and rank, occupation, region of origin, even number of wounds.[10] Except for the steel helmets and the pistol, which he feels were "too bloody theatrical," Frederic is at first comfortable wearing the uniform of the Italian army. When, for example, he stops on the street to have his portrait made, he declines to take off his army cap, prompting the man who is cutting the silhouette to say that the image will be more military as a consequence (p. 135). Here his uniform expresses Frederic's public allegiance, but it serves other more practical purposes as well. His uniform gets him into the races for free and, as Catherine notes, it allows them to dine at the better restaurants (pp. 125, 128). More seriously, when he is wounded Frederic begins to tear his shirt to use as a tourniquet for Passini, but he is too late to save him. Further, Frederic's army cape temporarily shields Catherine from the rain in Stresa; the tent Catherine creates with his cape fuses them into a unit, which is a manifestation of Catherine's later words: "There isn't any me. I'm you. Don't make up a separate me" (p. 115). In the retreat, when Frederic shoots the sergeant and strips him down to his "dirty long-sleeved underwear" and uses the dead man's coat to try to get the ambulance out of the mud, the Italian uniform, which had earlier provided Frederic with his sense of identity, has become an expedience. Finally, when Frederic dives into the river, he loses his military cap and notes that his uniform is valuable because it helps him sink out of the sights of the officers' rifles: "It was easy to stay under with so much clothing and my boots" (p. 225). Although he wants to remove his uniform when he reaches shore (p. 232), he only cuts off the stars until he arrives in Milan where he buys a new hat and puts on the clothes of Ralph Simmons, who sings under the name Enrico Del Credo, "Henry of the Creed" (p. 120). Throughout the episode of his escape to Switzerland, Frederic Henry is dressed as "Henry of the Creed," an ironic twist in that his only commitment at that point is to Catherine. The movement from military portrait to mufti parallels Frederic's progressive disillusionment with the military and his deepening involvement in his private life, which is imagistically exemplified by the tent Catherine makes of her hair when they are naked in bed.

In Switzerland, when Catherine and Frederic see the foxes, clothing becomes an issue again. Frederic asserts "I always wanted to have a tail like that. Wouldn't it be fun if we had brushes like a fox?" to which Catherine replies, "It might be very difficult dressing." Frederic's response, "We'd have clothes made, or live in a country where it wouldn't make any difference" (p. 303), has a serious side. He expresses a wish for a place to live free of the complications implied by the uniforms of the state, a place where their allegiance to each other is all that is needed.

Hemingway ends the novel with three strong images that are also a part of the iconography of identity. In the hospital Frederic dons the white gown and, seeing himself in the mirror (one of several mirror scenes), he feels he looks like "a fake doctor with a beard" (p. 319), a realistic reaction, given his inability to aid Catherine in her suffering. In the celebrated ants passage Frederic remembers a time when he was a potential messiah for some ants frying on a burning log. He recalls that he did nothing to save them but only watched the ants, and then hastened some of their deaths by emptying his coffee cup on them. His memory of these ants while Catherine is in the hospital suggests Frederic's final sense of identity in relation to Catherine as well: As a lover, posing as husband (and imagistically as doctor), he is no messiah and cannot save Catherine. Finally, when Frederic recoils from the goodbye in the hospital, he thinks of Catherine as a statue. By relating Catherine to this particular object (as she had thought of her dead lover with the riding crop) Frederic evokes death, burial, the loss of individuality, for the statue is like the marble busts he had seen in the hospital in Gorizia which he had speculated about: "I tried to make out whether they were members of the family or what; but they were all uniformly classical. You could not tell anything about them" (p. 28). In Gorizia Frederic had noted that "marble busts all looked like a cemetery. . . ." In one sense, however, and a final irony,

Frederic can more closely relate to Catherine in death, for he is now in a position that Catherine was in when they first met: he is alone, and he is shattered by the loss of a lover.

Besides these repeated motifs, Hemingway's use of pronouns also delineates Frederic's identity. Personal pronouns, of course, are inescapable in a first-person narrative, but they are a subtle means by which Hemingway reveals the changes in Frederic. It is by a pronoun that Hemingway first presents his narrator: "In the late summer of that year we lived in a house in a village that looked across the river and the plain to the mountains" (p. 3). On first reading the "we"[11] could suggest a happy domestic situation, but, ironically, this "we" links Frederic with the Italian army, not with any conventional domestic situation. There is another odd identification for Frederic when he jumps into the Tagliamento: "We passed the brush of an island above the water. I held onto the timber with both hands and let it take me along" (p. 225). The "we" is repeated four more times in the two paragraphs that describe the scene. Frederic is essentially merging with the log that carries him to the relative safety of the river bank. (Frederic here has better luck with *his* log than the ants do with *theirs*.) His relief at being delivered from death may have inspired Frederic's linguistic flight of fantasy (the "we"), but another way of reading this curious passage is that Frederic, cut off from his military group, is at this point unwilling or incapable of perceiving himself a self-reliant, autonomous human being. On the most literal level, Frederic and the log journey together; in another sense, however, when he jumps into the Tagliamento he is a man set adrift, a fugitive severed from other men, wearing a uniform that literally weighs him down.

Pronouns also suggest the progress and nature of his relationship with Catherine, their separateness as they first meet, a predominance of the plural "we" during the stay in Milan, the very interesting tension between the "we" and the "I" in the conversation between Frederic and Catherine in Switzerland (pp. 298–301). In this scene Catherine tries through talk about cutting her hair, of being "all mixed up" with each other (p. 300), and the wishing to go to sleep "at exactly the same moment" (p. 301), to reassure herself of their union, in effect, of their fused and single identity. Catherine's desire to lose herself in their love has been viewed by many as problematic, of course, but however one interprets this phenomenon of the merging of the two lovers (as a healthy merging or indication of pathology), the fact remains that despite his progression toward his merging with Catherine, Frederic does not achieve that fantasy of perfect union exemplified by falling asleep "at exactly the same moment" because he is distracted by other things in the night (p. 301).

In the final scene in the novel, Frederic returns to the use of the first-person pronoun to suggest his loss and isolation. Hemingway generally did not provide many references to the speaker in his dialogues, but in four of the six lines of conversation Frederic Henry delivers on the last page of *A Farewell to Arms*, he indicates that Frederic is the speaker with "I said." This repetition underlines the sense of separateness he feels at Catherine's death. It is not a confused Frederic Henry who writes his memorial to a lost time and a dead woman; rather it is an isolate who, to add to Michael Reynolds' list of what Frederic is not,[12] is a non-father and non-husband who has been unable to find any other woman who means as much to him as Catherine had.

Hemingway did not need the téssera passage. As others have pointed out, for Frederic to suddenly avail himself of counterfeit papers would needlessly complicate the plot. But a téssera would have given Frederic too literally a sham identity. What is pruned from the novel is there by implication. In the course of the novel Frederic moves from an involvement with the military that proves false toward one with Catherine that gives him meaning, and, ultimately, in her death, to complete isolation. Through his narrative Frederic reveals the complex nature of his identity, the tragic private life.

1. See MS 64, pp. 470–71, at the John F. Kennedy Library, Boston, Massachusetts.

2. Michael S. Reynolds, *Hemingway's First War: The Making of* A Farewell to Arms (Princeton: Princeton University Press, 1976), p. 36; Sheldon Norman Grebstein, *Hemingway's Craft* (Carbondale: Southern Illinois University Press, 1973), pp. 211–12.

3. Scott Donaldson, "Frederic Henry's Escape and the Pose of Passivity," in *Hemingway: A Revaluation*, ed. Donald R. Noble (Troy: Whitston, 1983), pp. 168–69.

4. Ernest Hemingway, *A Farewell to Arms* (New York: Scribner's, 1957), p. 84. All further references to the novel are to this edition and are made in the text.

5. Robert W. Lewis, Jr., in *Hemingway on Love* (Austin: University of Texas Press, 1965), pp. 41–42, and Earl Rovit, in *Ernest Hemingway* (New York: Twayne, 1963), pp. 100–01, both discuss the masquerade or disguise motif in the novel and its relationship to the identity theme.

6. Gerry Brenner, *Concealments in Hemingway's Works* (Columbus: Ohio State University Press, 1983), p. 53.

7. See *A Farewell to Arms*, pp. 87, 98–99.

8. The false name motif is not limited to Frederic alone. For example, the two tenors from San Francisco, Edgar Saunder (Eduoardo Govanni) and Ralph Simmons (Enrico Del Credo or "Henry of the Creed"), sing under Italian names, and the most blatant example of false identity in the novel is the horse Japalac, the ringer imported from France that has been dyed to disguise its identity.

9. Philip Young, in *Ernest Hemingway: A Reconsideration* (University Park: Pennsylvania State University Press, 1966), pp. 211–41 and Robert W. Lewis, Jr., pp. 40–41, discuss Frederic Henry's relationship to *Huckleberry Finn*.

10. See *A Farewell to Arms*, pp. 7, 18, 33, 44, 47, 100, 121.

11. Bernard Oldsey in *Hemingway's Hidden Craft: The Writing of* A Farewell to Arms (University Park: Pennsylvania State University Press, 1979), pp. 66–67, discusses this special narrative viewpoint, as does Michael Reynolds, who notes the revisions of the passage (p. 55), and discusses it as a way Hemingway "effaces" his narrator early in the novel (p. 59).

12. Reynolds, pp. 256–57.

HEMINGWAY AND THE AMBULANCE DRIVERS IN *A FAREWELL TO ARMS*

ROBERT A. MARTIN

IN MUCH THE SAME WAY THAT HEMINGWAY used Jake Barnes and the bullfighters in *The Sun Also Rises* and the Pilar-Pablo band of guerillas in *For Whom the Bell Tolls*, he used the ambulance drivers in *A Farewell to Arms* as a microcosm of the macrocosm within the larger events of the story. My purpose in the following pages will be to suggest that (1) the two groups of ambulance drivers assigned to Frederic Henry before and after his wounding both reflect and foreshadow the course of the Frederic-Catherine love affair from beginning to end; and (2) the names of the individual ambulance drivers have a greater significance within the structure of events than has been previously recognized.

Hemingway's own brief experience as an ambulance driver in Italy during World War I and his subsequent wounding, recovery, and love affair with Agnes von Kurowsky have been admirably and exhaustively documented by Bernard Oldsey in *Hemingway's Hidden Craft: The Writing of* A Farewell to Arms and by Michael Reynolds in *Hemingway's First War: The Making of* A Farewell to Arms.[1] While both these works reveal with striking clarity the extent to which Hemingway altered many of his wartime experiences to accommodate the fictional chronology, geography, and personal relationships within the novel, in general several facts remain unaltered in their fundamental authenticity and historical objectivity. First, Hemingway was an ambulance driver in the American Red Cross Ambulance Section at Schio, Italy for one month during June and early July in 1918. Second, he was seriously wounded at Fossalta di Piave when an Austrian trench mortar exploded on July 8 while he was on canteen duty. Third, he did have a love affair with his nurse, Agnes von Kurowsky, while he was recuperating from his wounds during the late summer and fall in a Milan hospital. In his biography, *Ernest Hemingway: A Life Story*, Carlos Baker describes the ambulance headquarters at Schio as being located in "an abandoned factory building":

> It had a paved courtyard with open sheds for the ambulances, seventeen large Fiats and half a dozen smaller Fords. . . . During his three weeks of driving for Section Four, Ernest took turns at the wheel of a lumbering Fiat. It was a clumsy vehicle, painted battleship gray with a large red cross on top. The road up Pasubio was a wilderness of hairpin turns, closely flanked with barbed wire which scraped and screeched against the sides of the cars. Two thirds of the work was done in daylight, and the three ambulances on call each made one run a day, evacuating wounded to the *smistamenti*, or distributing stations.[2]

If Philip Young is correct in assuming that Hemingway's wounding at Fossalta produced a permanent trauma that could be exorcized only by writing about the event again and again,[3] it would seem to follow that Hemingway's most vivid memories of his war experience would be not of his traumatic moment of a near-death experience, but of the three weeks he spent at Schio driving wounded Italian soldiers from the front lines to the first-aid stations. This may, in fact, account for the numerous references to ambulances that are scattered throughout *A Farewell to Arms*, but which seemingly have no specific point of reference or purpose other than forming a part of the background. For example, in Chapter 3, Frederic returns from his leave and notices that "there were some new hospitals. . ." and that "an ambulance was waiting by the side door" of his house in Gorizia, the same house that "looked across the river and the plain to the mountains."[4] His first meeting with Catherine Barkley takes place shortly after Frederic has inspected the ambulances in the garage, which "were lined up side by side under the long shed. They were top-heavy, blunt-nosed ambulances, painted gray and built like moving vans" (p. 15). In Chapter Five, at their second meeting, Frederic remarks that he has just returned from the front lines after inspecting a new road that would "go over the mountain and zig-zag down to the bridge. . . . The cars [ambulances] would be all right with their good metal-to-metal brakes, and anyway, coming down, they would not be loaded" (p. 24).

Against the background of a distant war, Frederic and Catherine meet in the garden of the hospital in between his trips to the front in Chapter Six. When they begin to talk seriously about loving each other, the conversation quickly turns to lies and illusion—a game like bridge, Frederic says, "in which you said things instead of playing cards." When Catherine insists that he tell her he loves her, Frederic tells us that he answered " 'Yes,' I lied. 'I love you.' " While she believes that Frederic is her dead lover who has "come back to Catherine in the night," he believes that she is "probably a little crazy," but does not care: "I knew I did not love Catherine Barkley nor had any idea of loving her" (p. 30). Although Frederic at this stage clearly has no interest in Catherine beyond a physical conquest, he is nevertheless engaged in a war in which he tells us twice in one paragraph that "Evidently it did not matter whether I was there or not," and after another trip to the mountain posts: "The whole thing seemed to run better when I was away" (pp. 16–17). Frederic's sense of disengagement from the war is further emphasized when he relates that his side-arm, an Astra 7.65 caliber pistol, jerks too sharply when fired to hit anything. "The ridiculousness of carrying a pistol at all came over me and I soon forgot it and carried it flopping against the small of my back with *no feeling at all* except a vague sort of shame when I met English-speaking people" (p. 29, italics added).

The above passage, while revealing, is buried within the two paragraphs that open Chapter Six in which he lies to Catherine and tells us he does not love her. Catherine, however, recognizes the charade and refuses to be fooled: "This is a rotten game we play, isn't it?. . . You don't have to pretend you love me. . . . Please let's not lie when we don't have to" (p. 31). Frederic is hardly disillusioned with the war at this point, and he certainly isn't in love with Catherine. He is instead acting out of a soldier's simple boredom and disinterest, with Catherine as the object of an intended sexual diversion until he moves on to another post in another town. Frederic sees no purpose in his work, he has no interest in the military aspects of the war, and he has no pride in being in uniform with a pistol he cannot shoot flopping against his back. Frederic is, indeed, playing "a rotten game" and with no feeling at all both toward Catherine and his role in the war. He has, in fact, announced his disinterest in an earlier conversation with Catherine: "Why did you join up with the Italians?" she asks. "I was in Italy," he answers, "and I spoke Italian" (p. 22). The only thing missing from this sentence is Frederic's unspoken, but clearly implied qualifier, "I don't know. It seemed like a good idea at the time."

Chapter Seven opens with another trip to the mountain post with Frederic sitting in the hot sun waiting for the wounded to be processed at the *smistamenti*. "I sat in the high seat of the Fiat and thought about nothing," he tells us (p. 33). Although he has just delivered an ambulance full of wounded men, and although an entire regiment is passing by, Frederic says he can only think of "nothing." This is certainly a reflection of Hemingway's sense of his personal ennui during the few weeks he drove up and down the mountains before his wounding. But the tone and attitude, the disengagement and disinterest in his immediate surroundings mark Frederic as an existential spectator almost completely up to the moment he is wounded and brought down another mountain in someone else's ambulance.

In what may be Hemingway's version of T. S. Eliot's "objective correlative," Frederic is assigned to two groups of ambulance drivers during the course of the novel—one group of four before he is wounded and a second group of three after he has recuperated and returned to the front. The first group of drivers appears in Chapter Seven, the same chapter in which Frederic is wounded, and are identified specifically by their names for the first time in his narrative. The names of the drivers in the first group are all derived from Italian words denoting social or impersonal qualities and characteristics. Their names—Manera, Passini, Gordini, and Gavuzzi—reflect their respective roles and relationships, and are quite literally an identification with their actions and conversations.[5] Given their collective impersonal qualities in names and deeds, they are correlated with Frederic's similar qualities and attitudes toward the war and toward Catherine in this early stage of their relationship.

The first driver is Manera whose name means "farmer or worker of the land" with its root in the Latin *manus* (hand) and *opera* (work). When Frederic returns to the dugout to be with the drivers, he tells us that Manera has a cigarette lighter that was shaped like a Fiat radiator (p. 47), as if to remind us that Manera is indistinct from his identity as a driver of a Fiat ambulance. Frederic tells them the attack will begin soon and that the road they will have to drive on will be heavy with bombardment. "That road will be a dirty mess," Manera replies (p. 47). Manera's comments and questions to Frederic are all practical and factual. He comments that "the granatieri are tall," that the enlisted men should not talk so other officers can hear, and that there is too much talk going on: "We must shut up. We talk too much even for the Tenente" (pp. 49–50). Once the attack begins and their area is being shelled, Manera's first concern is for the equipment: "How are the cars?" he asks Frederic as if to emphasize once again his nearly total identification and function as a mechanic and driver.

The second driver is Gavuzzi whose name is an Italian derivative meaning common man. Gavuzzi says very little to anyone, and asks Frederic only one question directly: "Do we eat yet, Tenente?" (p. 51). His question, however, is calculated to express his name as the common man who has little interest in the war beyond staying alive from moment to moment. His few other comments are direct and practical matters of survival. When Frederic and Gordini return with the food, Gavuzzi immediately hands Frederic the basin of macaroni and says "Start in to eat, Tenente," presumably so that he can also begin once Frederic as the officer-in-charge has been served first. When a shell lands near their dugout, Gavuzzi's only concern is for the technical aspect of its size, commenting that the shell was a "Four hundred twenty or minnenwerfer" (p. 54).

The third driver is Passini. His name derives from the Latin root of *pati*, which means to suffer, experience, or submit to. Although Passini is passive in his ability to act, he is also the most talkative of the four. When Frederic comments that "we should get the war over," and "It would only be worse if we stopped fighting" (p. 49). Passini replies, "It could not be worse. There is nothing worse than war." "Defeat is worse," Frederic says. "I do not believe it," Passini answers. "What is defeat? You go home" (p. 50). Passini's view of the advantages of defeat for the common soldier presumably reflects the attitude of all four drivers since none of them challenges Passini's assertion. They do not believe in the war and do not trust the officers who are commanding them. "We think. We read," Passini says. "We are not peasants. We are mechanics. But even the peasants know better than to believe in a war. Everybody hates this war" (p. 51). Passini—although articulate—is not by nature active enough to make any effort to stop a war he does not believe in. He accepts what he sees as his inevitable lack of choice in refusing to serve, but he knows, as Hemingway makes clear, that the enlisted men have nothing to lose or gain no matter which side wins. "There is no finish to a war," he says. "There is nothing as bad as war," (p. 50), all of which is, of course, precisely why his name and role are appropriate to his actions. He is disinterested and detached sufficiently to represent thought without emotion, which parallels Frederic Henry's relation with Catherine during the first part of the book before his wounding.

The fourth driver, Gordini, is the only one about whom Frederic comments directly: "He was the quietest one of the four." Although Gordini gets medical help for Frederic after the shell explodes, and is injured himself, he says almost nothing in the dugout. When Frederic leaves to get food, it is Gordini who goes with him while Manera, Passini, and Gavuzzi allow the food to be brought to them. "Is there anything I can do, Tenente? Can I help in any way?" (p. 51), he asks, and then helps Frederic carry the food back to the dugout. After the explosion, Gordini locates the English officer to whom Frederic turns over his remaining two ambulances before he is himself taken to the hospital.

Unlike the other three drivers, Gordini's name does not derive from Latin or Italian. It is apparently from a place name with a diminutive ending, but is so unusual for an Italian name in Hemingway's manuscripts and notes as to suggest that he was well aware of the departure. Gordini is the only one of the seven drivers with a proper name, and the only one of the first four Hemingway primarily identifies by a quality ("he was the quietest one of the four"). Gordini represents, both in thought and in action, the more thoughtful class of soldier that one encounters in any group of military men, those very quiet participants who are finally revealed as more complex mentally than they appear to be. His name, then, can be taken circumstantially as Hemingway's inversion on the Gordian knot in Greek legend, which involves the dilemma connected with any perplexing problem as well as a quick and efficient solution to a problem. In the Greek legend, Alexander the Great, failing to untie the knot tied by King Gordius, cut the knot with his sword to fulfill the prophecy that only the future master of Asia would be able to undo it. Gordini's two brief but efficient solutions to Frederic's need for assistance suggest a link between the names as well as with Hemingway's known knowledge of Greek mythology.

After the shell explodes, Frederic discovers that Passini has been killed, Gordini is wounded, but all right, and that Manera and Gavuzzi (the two most common and least thoughtful) have escaped without injury. Passini, like Frederic, is wounded in the legs, but dies almost immediately: "His legs were toward me and I saw in the dark and the light that they were both smashed above the knee. One leg was gone and the other was held by tendons. . ." (p. 55). By indirection, Passini's death from his leg wounds serves to place Frederic's leg wound into perspective and to suggest why Frederic is afraid of the surgeons in the Milan hospital (pp. 95–99).

None of the first group of drivers has any political or social convictions, and like Frederic are without personal characteristics or emotions. "They were all mechanics," Frederic comments, "and hated the war" (p. 48). They are also abstractions in one sense, representative classes of workers in another. In their association with Frederic, they point up his similar lack of interest, conviction, and purpose to an amazing degree. In one of their conversations in the dugout, Manera tells the story of how the Carabinieri had shot some troops that refused to attack: "They lined them up afterward and took every tenth man. Carabinieri shot them" (p. 49). This brief anecdote by Manera clearly serves as a foreshadowing of the later episode at the Tagliamento when Frederic watches the Carabinieri question and execute officers who were caught in the retreat. These two events provide an interesting example of Hemingway's ability to foreshadow a major event by use of a minor one, and prepare us for Frederic's decision to desert at the Tagliamento when he realizes that the Carabinieri have "shot every one they had questioned" (p. 224).

In Chapter Eleven, Frederic is in the field hospital waiting to be evacuated to the American hospital in Milan when he is visited by the priest. When the priest tells Frederic, "What you tell me about in the nights. That is not love. That is only passion and lust. When you love you wish to do things for. You wish to serve" (p. 72), he is also defining the course of the love affair with Catherine and the real meaning of love for Frederic. The priest's definition of love is thus the focus of a transition from an impersonal game of lust to a personal religion of love and service. He further establishes a technical problem for Hemingway in that if a change from lust to love is to occur, we as readers need some more compelling evidence of the change than is available from Frederic's first person testimony. During his long recuperation, nothing is more obvious in the love affair than Frederic's realization that he does love Catherine in the priest's terms, and that—structurally at least—his change in attitude toward her from lust to love is paralleled by the contrast between the two groups of ambulance drivers.

When Frederic returns to active duty in Book Three after his recuperation, it is fall again and the impersonal world of love as a game and war as a casual adventure have vanished along with Manera, Gavuzzi, Passini, and Gordini. Now he is truly in love with Catherine and the second group of ambulance drivers have names and qualities that correlate with the priest's definition of love. This time Frederic is assigned three drivers—a more spiritual number—rather than four, a secular number. The three—Aymo, Bonello, and Piani—have names that reflect moral and spiritual qualities that the first group of drivers lacked. In short, Frederic is associated symbolically with the three new drivers who are objectively correlated with his own altered beliefs and attitudes toward love and life. They appear as individuals with names, however, only after the retreat has started in Chapter Twenty-Seven following the Austrian break through at Caporetto.

The first driver is Aymo whose name derives from the Latin root *amor* (to love) reduced to the first person singular *amo* or "I love." Aymo helps Frederic and takes care of him, he fixes food for the other drivers and Frederic with considerable attention and care for their well-being: "Something hot will be good for those two anarchists," Aymo tells Frederic after preparing some *pasta asciutta*, "You go to sleep, Tenente" (p. 191). During the retreat, Aymo offers a ride to two young girls who are identified as virgins after he frightens them by making indecent remarks and gestures. When he discovers why the girls are so frightened, he tells them, "That's all right, that's all right" (p. 196), and protects them during the retreat as long as he can. Aymo appears as a kind, decent, and loving individual who is trapped in a war he does not believe in.

The second driver, Bonello, has a common name that derives from the Italian *buono* or Latin *bonus*, meaning "good" or "kind." Bonello is usually cheerful, makes a joke about sleeping with the queen (p. 192), and offers a ride to two sergeants during the retreat who have become separated from their unit. They were left to do something to a bridge, he explains to Frederic. "They can't find their unit so I gave them a ride" (p. 195). Bonello is the only one of the seven drivers who becomes actively involved in combat when he shoots one of the sergeants who refuses Frederic's order to dislodge the ambulance when it became mired in the mud. Frederic tells us that he shot at the sergeants as they were running away "three times and dropped one." Bonello, who is unfamiliar with side arms, offers to "finish him." Although Frederic has to cock the pistol for him before he can shoot, Bonello "finishes" him as a compensation for giving a ride to untrustworthy soldiers. He later says, "I killed him. I never killed anybody in this war, and all my life I've wanted to kill a sergeant" (p. 207). Bonello is, as his name implies, a good soldier who nevertheless can act forcibly if forced to do so. As he later tells Piani in reference to the war, "If I had any brains I wouldn't be here" (p. 210).

The third driver is Piani whose name means "soft" or "gentle." Of the three drivers, Piani is the most fully developed, and it is clear from the manuscript version that Hemingway intended at one point to do more with him. As they near the bridge over the Tagliamento, Piani tells Frederic, "I don't know anything about this kind of war," and, like Gordini from the first group, Piani is the only one in his group about whom Frederic comments directly: "Alone he was much gentler. When he was with the others he was a very rough talker" (p. 220). It is also Piani who explains to Frederic that "We're Socialists. We come from Imola" (p. 208), and who later pleads with Frederic not to report Bonello as a deserter because if the war went on they would make bad trouble for his family (p. 219).

Even as Aymo, Bonello, and Piani serve and respect Frederic in many ways that make them embodiments of the priest's definition of love, by the end of the book Frederic is also serving Catherine as she is dying by attempting to make her more comfortable: "Do you want me to do anything, Cat? Can I get you anything?" he asks her (p. 331). Of the second group, Aymo is killed gratuitously by the rear guard of the Italian army who mistake him for a German infiltrator. His death in the rain serves to foreshadow Catherine's death in the rain while in childbirth through a process of indirect parallelism. As Frederic will later futilely attempt to help Catherine as she is dying, Piani attempts to help Aymo: "Piani laid his head down, wiped at his face, with a piece of emergency dressing, then let it alone" (p. 213). A few lines later Frederic tells us:

> Aymo lay in the mud with the angle of the embankment. He was quite small and his arms were by his side, his puttee-wrapped legs and muddy boots together, his cap over his face. He looked very dead. It was raining. I had liked him as well as anyone I ever knew. (p. 214)

Not only does Hemingway's precise wording suggest a child at rest or in death, once Aymo is dead he is as much a statue as Catherine is after her death. The medical atmosphere of both scenes with their "emergency dressing" and the emergency of the "operating room" at the foreground of each provides a somber link between the two scenes and the two deaths. Bonello surrenders to the Austrians even before they reach the bridge at the Tagliamento because, as Piani tells Frederic, "He wanted to be a prisoner. . . . You see we don't believe in the war anyway, Tenente" (p. 217). Piani, conversely, joins the main retreat and passes safely over the bridge at the same time that Frederic is being arrested by the Carabinieri (p. 221).

In the original conclusion, Hemingway has Frederic comment that "I could tell how Piani got to be a taxi-driver in New York," while, as Oldsey has noted, "a variant of this conclusion places Piani in Chicago instead of New York and hints that something unpleasant happened to the socialist-deserter Bonello in his home town of Imola."[6] And in much the same way that Manera's story of the Carabinieri shooting troops anticipates the Carabinieri's hasty executions at the Tagliamento after the retreat, and Aymo's death in the rain anticipates Catherine's death in the hospital during the rain, Bonello's desertion during the retreat directly anticipates Frederic's desertion at the Tagliamento.

Although circumstantial, the names and events associated with the two groups of drivers and Frederic can hardly be coincidental. The names themselves—Passini (to suffer, submit to), Manera (farmer or worker of the land), Gavuzzi (common man), and Gordini (the dilemma posed by the Gordian knot myth) of the first group are entirely consistent with Frederic's indifferent and impersonal relationship and attitude toward Catherine before he is wounded. The names of the second group of ambulance drivers—Aymo (I love), Bonello (kind, good), and Piani (soft, gentle) form a contrast with the first group so distinct as to suggest a symbolic codification of names, events, and characters that parallel Frederic's transformation from lust to love. Nor have I attempted to illustrate every case in which such a symbolic codification is to be found in *A Farewell to Arms* in the dialogue of the ambulance drivers. To do so would be redundant if not superfluous, but numerous examples exist to add supporting evidence.

It is, of course, not unusual in Hemingway to find a system of shorthand symbols and associations that function on both private and public levels of meaning. On the more concrete level of manuscript evidence, Michael Reynolds has reproduced nine first draft examples of names he cites as later undergoing changes in subsequent revisions in *Farewell*. Of the nine examples, four are names of the ambulance drivers that were revised in subsequent drafts.[7] Hemingway studied Latin in high school for three years, and—according to Carlos Baker—by the time he returned from Italy in January 1919, he could speak and sing passably in Italian with Italian friends in Chicago.[8] By the time he was writing *A Farewell to Arms* nine years later in 1928, there is little reason to question Hemingway's ability to construct seven Italian names with their appropriate symbolic meanings. For a writer whose reputation was built solidly on the foundations of fact and accuracy, Hemingway's use of the ambulance men as reflectors of Frederic Henry's changing attitudes and as a means of foreshadowing later events would of necessity require a careful planning within the framework of T. S. Eliot's principle of the "objective correlative," with Hemingway was familiar.

Thirty years after he wrote *A Farewell to Arms* Hemingway still remembered the ambulance drivers when he was writing *A Moveable Feast*. In recounting the afternoon on which Gertrude Stein told him, "All of you young people who served in the war. You are all a lost generation," Hemingway recalls thinking to himself as he walked home later that night:

> I thought about the boy in the garage and if he had ever been hauled in one of those vehicles when they were converted to ambulances. I remembered how they used to burn out their brakes going down the mountain roads with a full load of wounded and braking in low and finally using the reverse, and how the last ones were driven over the mountain empty, so they could be replaced by big Fiats with a good H-shift and metal-to-metal brakes. I thought of Miss Stein and Sherwood Anderson and egotism and mental laziness versus discipline and I thought who is calling who a lost generation?[9]

1. Bernard Oldsey, *Hemingway's Hidden Craft: The Writing of* A Farewell to Arms (University Park: Pennsylvania State University Press, 1979) and Michael Reynolds, *Hemingway's First War: The Making of* A Farewell to Arms (Princeton: Princeton University Press, 1976).

2. Carlos Baker, *Ernest Hemingway, A Life Story* (New York: Scribner's, 1969), pp. 41–42.

3. Philip Young, *Ernest Hemingway: A Reconsideration* (University Park: Pennsylvania State University Press, 1966).

4. Ernest Hemingway, *A Farewell to Arms* (New York: Scribner's, 1929), pp. 3 and 10.

5. I am indebted to Professor Oscar Budel of the University of Michigan's Department of Romance Languages for confirming and refining the name derivations and meanings in modern Italian of the seven ambulance drivers in *A Farewell to Arms*.

6. Oldsey, p. 79.

7. Reynolds, p. 54.

8. Baker, pp. 58 and 60.

9. Ernest Hemingway, *A Moveable Feast* (New York: Scribner's, 1964), pp. 22–30.

III: The Work, The Thirties to the Nobel Prize

HEMINGWAY: WORK IN PROGRESS

MALCOLM COWLEY

CHIEF AMONG HEMINGWAY'S VIRTUES AS A WRITER is his scrupulous regard for fact, for reality, for "what happened." It is a rare virtue in the world of letters. Most writers want to please or shock, to be "accomplished craftsmen" or to be "original"; in both cases their work is determined by literary fashions, which they either follow or defy. From the very first, Hemingway did neither, since his aim was simply to reproduce the things he had seen and felt—"simply," I say, but anyone who has tried to set down his own impressions accurately must realize that the task is enormously difficult; there is always the temptation to change and falsify the story because it doesn't fit into a conventional pattern, or because the right words are lacking. Hemingway himself had to find a whole new vocabulary, one in which old or popular words like "good," "nice" and "rotten" are given fresh values. But it always makes me angry to hear people speaking of his "lean, hard, athletic prose." Sometimes his prose is beautiful, poetic in the best sense, in its exact evocations of landscapes and emotions. Sometimes it is terse and efficient. Sometimes, with its piling up of very short words, it gives the effect of a man stammering, getting his tongue twisted, talking too much but eventually making us understand just what he wants to say.

During the last ten years Hemingway has been imitated more widely than any other American or British writer, even T. S. Eliot. You find his influence everywhere from the pulp-paper true-detective-story weeklies to the very little magazines making no compromise with the public taste. You find it in newspapers and the movies, in English highbrow novels and even in this weekly journal of opinion. Partly it has been a bad influence. It has made people copy the hard-boiled manner of "The Killers" and "Fifty Grand"—this latter being the

Reprinted with permission from *The New Republic*, 20 October 1937, pp. 305–06.

205

cheapest story that Hemingway ever signed. It has encouraged them to boast in print of their love affairs and drinking bouts—though God knows they needed little encouragement. Worst of all, it has caused many young writers to take over Hemingway's vocabulary and his manner of seeing the world—thereby making it impossible for them to be as honest as Hemingway. But in general I think that his influence has been excellent. It has freed many writers—not only novelists but poets and essayists and simple reporters—from a burden of erudition and affectation that they thought was part of the writer's equipment. It has encouraged them to write as simply as possible about the things they really feel, instead of the things they think that other people think they ought to feel. Critics in particular owe a debt to Hemingway; and many of them, including myself, have been slow to acknowledge it. So let me put the record straight. I don't think he is as great as Tolstoy or Thomas Mann, but I do think that he is perhaps as good as Mark Twain, and that is saying a great deal. In our generation, he is the best we have.

His new novel I found easy to read, impossible to lay down before it was finished, and very hard to review. It contains some of the best writing he has ever done. There are scenes that are superb technical achievements and other scenes that carry him into new registers of emotion. As a whole it lacks unity and sureness of effect.

Part of its weakness is a simple matter of plot structure, a department in which Hemingway was never strong. The book falls apart at the beginning and the end. It begins with two long stories about Harry Morgan—both of them, I think, were first published in the *Cosmopolitan*—and it ends with a fine soliloquy by Harry Morgan's widow. In the intervening pages, Hemingway deals with his principal theme, which is really two themes in counterpoint—on the one side, the life of the Have-Nots, that is, the Key West fishermen and relief workers who surround Harry Morgan; on the other side, the life of the Haves, that is, the wealthy yachtsmen and the drunken writers who winter in the Key West bars. These two themes never quite come together.

But a more serious weakness lies in the characters themselves, or rather in the author's attitude toward his characters. Some of them—the writers for example—are the same sort of people, leading the same sort of lives, as he described in *The Sun Also Rises*. In those days Hemingway was unhappy about the lives they were leading, yet he approached the people with real sympathy, going to great pains, for example, to explain to himself why Robert Cohn was really a villain in spite of all his admirable qualities. But this time Hemingway really hates the people; he pictures them not as human beings but as the mere embodiments of lust or folly, as wolves or goats or monkeys disguised with little mustaches and portable typewriters. "All right," Helen Gordon says to her husband. "I'm through with you and I'm through with love. Your kind of pick-nose love. You writer." It is the final insult. But since Hemingway is a writer himself, this aversion is also a self-aversion, and prophesies a change in his own career not from literature to fishing, for example, but rather from one kind of writing to another kind. And that change, that transition, is already foreshadowed in his characters. Among the very few that he portrays sympathetically are two Catholics[1] and a Communist war veteran. Harry Morgan himself begins as a tough guy capable of killing people in cold blood, either to get money or to save his hide; but he dies as a sort of proletarian hero.

There is a story behind this novel perhaps more interesting than the story that Hemingway has told. Some day we may know the whole of it; at present I have to reconstruct it from word-of-mouth information and from internal evidence. Hemingway has been working on the book for several years—at the very least, since 1933. It was practically finished a year ago, before he left for Spain. At that time it was a longer novel than in its present version, and it ended in a mood of utter discouragement. When Hemingway returned, full of enthusiasm for the Spanish Loyalists, he must have felt dissatisfied with what he had written; at any rate he destroyed large parts of it. It may have been then that he wrote a death scene for Harry Morgan—the scene in which he stammers out with his last few breaths: "One man alone ain't got. No man alone now. . . . No matter how, a man alone ain't got no bloody f——g chance." This might be the message that Hemingway carried back from Spain, his own free translation of Marx and Engels: "Workers of the world unite, you have nothing to lose. . . ."[2] The whole scene is beautifully done, but it doesn't grow out of what has gone before.

There are other scenes that are even stronger, and better integrated with the story—for example, the phantasmagorical drinking and slugging bout of the veterans on relief, and the quarrel between Helen Gordon and her husband, and Mrs. Morgan's last soliloquy. Almost all the women in the novel are portrayed with subtlety and sureness. As a whole, *To Have and Have Not* is the weakest of Hemingway's books except perhaps *Green Hills of Africa*—but it is by no means the least promising. For some years now the literary hyenas have been saying that Hemingway was done for, but their noses have betrayed them into finding the scent of decay where none existed. From the evidence of this book, I should say that he was just beginning a new career.

1. Hemingway became a temporary Catholic during his marriage to Pauline Pfeiffer (1927–40).
2. ". . . but your chains," *The Communist Manifesto* (1848).

HEMINGWAY'S WOMEN'S MOVEMENT

CHARLES J. NOLAN, JR.

HEMINGWAY'S TROUBLES WITH WOMEN ARE LEGENDARY. Beginning with his quarrels with his mother—that "all-time, All-American bitch," as he once called her[1]— and running throughout his relationships with his four wives and with others, Hemingway's sometimes public disagreements helped to create his popular image as woman-hater. As if biographical detail were not enough, stories like "The Short Happy Life of Francis Macomber," with its unforgettable depiction of five-letter Margot and, by extension, of all of American womanhood, worked to solidify the portrait. But for all the clamor, recently joined by feminist critics,[2] there is another side to this major if troubled artist. Whatever his personal idiosyncrasies (and there were many), as a writer he saw more clearly than perhaps even he knew. Throughout his work up to the late thirties, there runs a strong sympathy for the plight of women, a sympathy that at one point, in fact, is expressed in feminist rhetoric and rage[3] (as I will eventually show).

Such sympathy begins early—in one of Hemingway's first stories, "Up in Michigan" (written in 1921), a story that Gertrude Stein warned was *"inaccrochable"* because of its frankness in depicting seduction.[4] The story, telling of a young woman's first and unsatisfactory sexual experience, makes obvious use of stereotypes. Liz Coates is a diffident and inexperienced woman in the thrall of what is apparently her first grand passion. Her thoughts of Jim Gilmore, the local blacksmith, become obsessive, she cannot sleep when he leaves on a hunting trip, and she feels weak and sick upon his return. Jim, on the other hand, sees Liz, when he thinks of her at all, as mere sexual object. A manly but insensitive lout, he seduces Liz, after a good meal and a number of drinks, upon his return from deer hunting. The seduction itself shows how clumsy and selfish Jim is: he hurts

Reprinted with permission from *The Hemingway Review*, 3, No. 2 (Spring 1984), 14–22.

her. But it is the aftermath of this brutish coupling that most clearly demonstrates Hemingway's sympathy for Liz:

> Jim was asleep. He wouldn't move. She worked out from under him and sat up and straightened her skirt and coat and tried to do something with her hair. Jim was sleeping with his mouth a little open. Liz leaned over and kissed him on the cheek. He was still asleep. . . . Liz started to cry. . . . She was cold and miserable and everything felt gone. She walked back to where Jim was lying and shook him once more to make sure. She was crying.
>
> "Jim," she sad, "Jim. Please, Jim."
>
> Jim stirred and curled a little tighter. Liz took off her coat and leaned over and covered him with it. She tucked it around him neatly and carefully. Then she walked across the dock and up the steep sandy road to go to bed. (*SS*, pp. 85–86)

Though the story is told in the third person, much of the focus is on the feelings of Liz Coates; Hemingway puts us inside Liz's consciousness, making us experience her pain. But unlike Liz, we feel angry at and disgusted with Jim. What finally emerges is a strong sympathy for the plight of all women like Liz who are exploited at the hands of the insensitive and grasping men in their lives.

"Out of Season" (1923) is similarly sympathetic. In *In Our Time* (1925), the story is part of Hemingway's marriage group—a series of three tales demonstrating the failure of relationships between men and women in modern life.[5] Though the title refers specifically to illegal fishing, it suggests symbolically a marriage in the process of collapse.

In the story a young American couple in Italy have quarreled about something rather serious, and their disagreement, not fully resolved, has carried over into their fishing trip. Initially, the wife's sullenness seems mere petulance, but, as the story progresses, we gradually take her side against her husband, who shows his basic weakness of character in his dealings with and capitulation to their drunken guide. Though the day's excursion is clearly illegal, the husband, in his wife's words, hasn't "got the guts to just go back" (p. 176). Eventually, she returns to the hotel; the husband and the guide go on. When they discover they have no lead for sinkers, the husband seizes the opportunity to turn back, promising the guide that they will go again tomorrow: "The young gentleman felt relieved. He was no longer breaking the law" (p. 178). After getting the guide even more drunk and allowing him to become too familiar, the American "lends" the guide money, preparatory to breaking his promise about fishing next day. The sleaziness of his backing out is suggestive of his character: " 'I may not be going,' said the young gentleman, 'very probably not. I will leave word with the padrone at the hotel office' " (p. 179).

Though Hemingway is working here with traditional, male-role definitions—men should be courageous and decisive—the feeling of compassion he engenders for a woman married to such an unappealing man predominates. Even the husband's apology for the couple's earlier disagreement comes off as weakness: "I'm sorry I talked the way I did at lunch. We were both getting at the same thing from different angles"—a comment to which his wife appropriately replies, "It doesn't make any difference. . . . None of it makes any difference" (p. 175).

Another story in that marriage group, "Cat in the Rain," also documents Hemingway's sympathetic treatment of women.[6] Here again is a young American couple apparently travelling through Italy. Because of the rain, their sightseeing this particular day is postponed, and they are left with a rainy day to get through. The husband settles down to read, but the young woman is clearly restless and, before the story is over, gives a rather sharp focus to what is causing her dissatisfaction.

Looking out the window, she sees a cat crouching under one of the outdoor tables, "trying to make herself so compact that she would not be dripped on" (p. 167). (Hemingway makes the cat female.) Something in the forlornness of the cat's situation stirs the woman to action, and she announces that she is going to retrieve the animal. Though her husband makes a perfunctory offer to do the chore for her, she is intent upon saving the cat herself. When she reaches the lobby, the hotel-keeper bows to her graciously and engages her briefly in conversation about the weather. "The wife liked him," Hemingway tells us. "She liked the deadly serious way he received any complaints. She liked his dignity. She liked the way he wanted to serve her. She liked the way he felt about being a hotel-keeper. She liked his old, heavy face and big hands" (p. 168).

When she gets ready to get the cat, a maid with an umbrella suddenly appears—sent, the woman recognizes, by the hotel-keeper. After a fruitless search for the cat, the woman returns to the lobby and, when the padrone bows to her again, she feels, like the cat, "very small and tight" (p. 169) yet at the same time very important. "She had," Hemingway observes, "a momentary feeling of being of supreme importance" (p. 169). With such a feeling, she returns to her reading husband, telling him how much she wanted "that poor kitty. It isn't any fun to be a poor kitty out in the rain" (p. 169). George, her husband, goes on reading, the contrast between him and the hotel-keeper becoming painfully clear. Looking at herself in the mirror, the woman asks if she shouldn't let her hair grow out; she is tired, she says, "of looking like a boy" (p. 169). But George, who "like[s] it the way it is" (p. 169) and who is beginning to be sexually stimulated by watching her, replies. "You look pretty darn nice" (p. 169).

At this point, some of the woman's dissatisfactions with her life emerge:

> "I want to pull my hair back tight and smooth and make a big knot at the back that I can feel. . . . I want to have a kitty to sit on my lap and purr when I stroke her."
>
> "Yeah?" George said from the bed.
>
> "And I want to eat at a table with my own silver and I want candles. And I want it to be spring and I want to brush my hair out in front of a mirror and I want a kitty and I want some new clothes."
>
> "Oh, shut up and get something to read," George said. He was reading again. (pp. 169–70)

If she can't have long hair or any fun, she continues, she at least wants a cat; but George isn't listening. It is at this point that the maid shows up with a cat that the padrone has secured and sent up for her.

Though it is true that the young woman with her close-cropped hair shows a clear preference for the traditional feminine role instead of the role she has adopted (this is 1924, after all), Hemingway's focus is on the boorishness of the husband. George is insensitive to his wife's deepest needs. In fact, he treats her outburst as he would that of a petulant child: he ignores her.[7]

"The End of Something," also part of *In Our Time*, brings us to the mainstream of Hemingway's fiction. Here, too, Hemingway's sympathy for women is evident. In the story, the something to which there is an end is teenage love: out fishing with his girlfriend, Marge, Nick breaks up with her. That is, however, no spontaneous decision, as we see at the end of the story when Nick's friend Bill arrives at the campsite, wondering if Marge has left without a scene. Nick has planned to end his romance, has, apparently, talked everything over with Bill beforehand in typical teen-age fashion—Marge is the last to know.

The way in which Nick precipitates the break is also typically adolescent: he tries to start an argument. When Nick observes that there will be a moon and Marge responds, "I know it," Nick suddenly changes the tone of their conversation: "You know everything," Nick says (p. 110).

> "Oh, Nick, please cut it out! Please, please don't be that way."
>
> "I can't help it," Nick said. "You do. You know everything. That's the trouble. You know you do." (p. 110)

After a few more exchanges, Marge tells him: "You don't have to talk silly. . . . What's really the matter?" Nick fumbles around for a while but eventually, even a bit brutally, makes himself clear: "It isn't fun any more. Not any of it. . . . I feel as though everything was gone to hell inside of me. I don't know, Marge. I don't know what to say" (p. 110). When Marge asks, "Isn't love any fun?" Nick bluntly replies, "No" (pp. 110–11). Marge leaves without a scene or even a tear, her dignity simple but evident. Nick lies down "with his face in the blanket" (p. 111), absorbing what has just happened. We see his own pain when Bill asks him how he feels and he replies, "Oh, go away, Bill! Go away for a while" (p. 111).

Hemingway means the story, I think, to show how things go wrong for his hero—for all of us—in our time: here love ebbs away. And though in the following story, "The Three-Day Blow," Nick believes that nothing is "irrevocable" (p. 124), that he can always "go into town on Saturday" (p. 124) and start all over again with Marge, Hemingway, and we his readers, know better. War will teach Nick that people in our time can't keep things "in reserve" (p. 125).[8] But in "The End of Something," Nick has not learned that lesson yet. In his own adolescent way, he has sent Marge packing merely because "It isn't fun anymore" (p. 110). More mature than Nick, we recognize that Marge is lucky to be rid of him. In this story, as in others, our sympathies are with Marge, not Nick, with the woman, not the man.

Though such a claim cannot really be made for the characters in *The Sun Also Rises* (1926), Lady Ashley—Brett—deserves more consideration than many readers have given her. It is true that what she is now, in the present time of the novel, is not the most admirable. But what she has become is, in large part, the result of what has happened to her. The initial blow comes when her first love dies of dysentery in the war. Traumatized by his death, Brett volunteers her services as a nurse's aide—a V.A.D. like Catherine Barkley—more, we suspect, out of shock than from anything else. Presumably on the rebound from her pain, she marries Ashley. The novel suggests that she marries him offhandedly, capitulating to life. Certainly, as Jake makes clear, she hadn't loved him when she married him (*The Sun Also Rises*, p. 39).[9] At this point, apparently, she meets and falls in love with Jake, whom she tends in the hospital after his horrible wounding. Incapable of expressing their love physically, they go their separate ways after the war. As we later learn, Brett's way has been almost as difficult as Jake's. Mike Campbell provides the details of Brett's marriage to Ashley: "When he came home [from the war] he wouldn't sleep in a bed. Always made Brett sleep on the floor. Finally, when he got really bad, he used to tell her he'd kill her. Always slept with a loaded service revolver. Brett used to take the shells out when he'd gone to sleep. She hasn't had an absolutely happy life, Brett" (p. 203).

Now, cut off by fate from Jake, whom she still loves, and by choice from Romero, whom she will only harm if she continues to live with (pp. 241, 243), she will marry Mike Campbell, who is, in her own words, "so awful" but "my sort of thing" (p. 243). The fact that Hemingway treats one of his "bitches" so compassionately, detailing the many reasons for her being destructive, suggests a sympathy for women not usually noted.[10]

"Hills Like White Elephants" (1927), which seems to be rapidly replacing "The Killers" as the required Hemingway piece in many anthologies, comes next, chronologically, in this specialized survey of Hemingway's art.[11] No doubt the story's subject matter—abortion—accounts in part for its current popularity, but its unmerciful exposure of male selfishness and female long-suffering also contributes to the contemporary anthologists' interest in it.

In the story an American couple, travelling this time through Spain, has reached a point of impasse in their relationship. Though we're not sure initially just what the source of conflict is, it soon becomes evident that the woman, Jig, is pregnant and that her lover wants her to have a abortion: " 'It's really an awfully simple operation, Jig,' the man said. 'It's not really an operation at all' " (p. 275). There follows a series of exchanges that make clear that the male character wants their essentially shallow relationship to continue as it has and that Jig wants to move it to firmer ground.

As her lover keeps up the pressure on her "You know how I get when I worry," he tells her (p. 275)—Jig becomes increasingly aware of how he is killing her love for him. "[W]e could have everything," she notes, "and every day we make it more impossible" (p. 276). But he blunders on:

> "You've got to realize," he said, "that I don't want you to do it if you don't want to. I'm perfectly willing to go through with it if it means anything to you."
> "Doesn't it mean anything to you? We could get along."
> "Of course it does. But I don't want anybody but you. I don't want anyone else. And I know it's perfectly simple." (p. 277)

Finally, she asks him: "Would you please please please please please please please stop talking?" (p. 277).

Though Jig is in some ways the typically submissive Hemingway woman—at one point, she tells her lover that she will go through with the risky abortion "Because I don't care about me" (p. 275)—Hemingway's focus here is on her victimization by her immature lover. There is little doubt that Hemingway highlights Jig's maturity and superiority as he excoriates the selfishness and insensitivity of her companion.

The much discussed "The Snows of Kilimanjaro" (1936), one of Hemingway's best stories, is often read as dramatizing the evil inherent in a writer's marrying money. His wife's wealth, the argument goes, makes Harry soft, and, as a result, he never fulfills his promise.[12] But such a pat interpretation is true neither to the complexity of the story nor to the portrait of Helen, Harry's wife, in it.

It is easy enough to see why critics have been misled. Harry's musings, as he dies rotting of gangrene in Africa, seem to justify the usual interpretation. He reminds himself that if he "kept from thinking," everything was all right. Because he had "good insides," he wouldn't ruin himself with liquor; and, though he pretended that he no longer cared about his work, he told himself that eventually he would write about the "very rich." Almost immediately, however, he realizes that he would never keep that promise, because each day of comfort and of being what he detested sapped his will to work until finally he did no writing. When his thoughts turn to Helen, "this rich bitch," he thinks of her as the "kindly caretaker and destroyer of his talent" (pp. 59–60).

But that's playing the game of selective quotation. What's omitted is material that makes clear that the reason for Harry's failure lies within, not without—that Helen, not Harry, is the one victimized. Observing that, in order not to disturb him, Helen has gone away from the camp to kill game, Harry remarks on her thoughtfulness. He notes too that it wasn't her fault that he had given up before he met her. How could she know that he wasn't sincere? He reflects that he was more successful with women when he lied to them than when he told them the truth. "It wasn't this woman's fault," he reminds himself. "If it had not been she it would have been another" (pp. 59–60).

And just after he thinks of Helen as the "destroyer of his talent" (p. 60), he corrects himself: "Nonsense. He had destroyed his talent himself. Why should he blame this woman because she kept him well?" (p. 60). He goes on to reflect that he had destroyed his talent in a number of ways: by not writing, by betraying himself and his ideals, by excessive drinking, by laziness, and by snobbery. In addition, he thinks, he had traded on his talent and "chosen to make his living with something else instead of a pen or a pencil" (p. 60). It is "strange," too, he notes, that each woman he had taken up with was richer than the previous one and that when he was "no longer. . . in love" but only "lying," he gave his companions more than when he had loved (p. 60). Such is the case with Helen, "who had the most money of all. . . who loved him dearly as a writer, as a man, as a companion and as a proud possession" (p. 60).

Far from being a mere "rich bitch," Helen is a good woman who has suffered her share of earthly calamity, as Hemingway soon makes clear. After her husband had died, leaving her a young widow, she had devoted herself to a variety of things, including her children, who were "embarrassed at having her about" (p. 61). For a while, liquor was an anodyne, enough of a one at any rate so that she was drunk enough after dinner to sleep. Next came lovers, but they "bored" her. Then, after one of her children was killed, she didn't want the lovers, and liquor no longer had its effect. Terrified of loneliness, she began to look for someone to be with whom she respected. Unfortunately for her, she chose Harry, whom she had first acquired and then fallen in love with, to build a new life around. She had gotten herself mixed up, that is, with an utterly loathsome person who, several hours before, had made a mockery of her love and kindness by telling her, savagely, that he had never loved her (p. 55).

In reality, she is, as she tells Harry, "only a middle-aged woman who loves you and wants to do what you want to do. I've been destroyed two or three times already. You wouldn't want to destroy me again, would you?" (p. 63). Badly used, Helen has just claim on our sympathies. Hemingway sees to that, in linking her to such a disagreeable lover and in very carefully providing her with a painful past.

Another Helen for whom Hemingway has real sympathy is Helen Gordon in *To Have and Have Not* (1937), Hemingway's protest novel. Easily one of his weaker performances, the book makes claims other than artistry on our attention.[13] Part of a subplot designed to show by contrast the vitality of Hemingway's common man hero (Harry Morgan), the Richard-and-Helen-Gordon section of the novel depicts a failing marriage. Richard Gordon is a bad writer and a bad man who justifies his infidelity on the grounds that a writer "can't restrict his experience to conform to Bourgeois standards" (*To Have and Have Not*, p. 140). When the inevitable confrontation between the Gordons comes, Hemingway gives Helen a speech dripping with feminist rage:

> "Everything I believed in and everything I cared about I left for you because you were so wonderful and you loved me so much that love was all that mattered. . . . Slop. Love is just another dirty lie. Love is ergoapiol pills to make me come around because you were afraid to have a baby. Love is quinine and quinine and quinine until I'm deaf with it. Love is that dirty aborting horror that you took me to. Love is my insides all messed up. It's half catheters and half whirling douches. I know about love. Love always hangs up behind the bathroom door. It smells like lysol. To hell with love. Love is you making me happy and then going off to sleep with your mouth open while I lie awake all night afraid to say my prayers even[,] because I know I have no right to any more. Love is all the dirty little tricks you taught me that you probably got out of some book. All right. I'm through with you and I'm through with love. Your kind of picknose love. You writer." (pp. 185–86)

Though the charge here is against one man, it is hard to read the passage without hearing in the background the condemnation of all men.

As if to make the point about male selfishness even clearer, Hemingway provides, near the end, a more general excoriation. Once more working by way of contrast, Hemingway presents in Chapter 24 a stinging portrait of the idle and jaded rich, the "haves" of the novel. Taking us aboard various yachts in the Havana harbor, he shows us all manner of degeneracy—sexual, financial, social—and the effects of that corruption on the "have nots." The rich are despicable: that's the point of the chapter. But in one of the vignettes presented comes a passage of feminist rhetoric, surprising by its modernity. On one of the yachts, Hemingway tells us, "a professional son-in-law of the very rich and his mistress, named Dorothy, the wife of that highly paid Hollywood director, John Hollis, whose brain is in the process of outlasting his liver. . . are asleep" (p. 241). Actually, only Eddie, the male of this twosome, is asleep; Dorothy lies awake because Eddie drank too much and nodded off before he could satisfy her. Dorothy, Hemingway makes clear, has her failings: she drinks too much and cuckolds her husband, though her behavior results, we gather, more from the fact that her husband has "drunk so much he isn't any good" anymore (p. 244) than from anything else. Once again, Hemingway creates a basically good, if sexually needy, woman, destroyed by the men in her life.[14]

As Dorothy lies awake, despite the luminol she has taken to sleep, she thinks about her fate and its cause—clearly, male inadequacy. The perspective and the rhetoric are recognizably feminist:

> I suppose I'll end up a bitch. Maybe I'm one now. I suppose you never know when you got to be one. Only her best friends would tell her. You don't read it in Mr. Winchell. That would be a good new thing for him to announce. Bitchhood. Mrs. John Hollis canined into town from the coast. Better than babies. More common I guess. But women have a bad time really. The better you treat a man and the more you show him you love him the quicker he gets tired of you. I suppose the good ones are made to have a lot of wives but it's awfully wearing trying to be a lot of wives yourself, and then some one simple takes him when he's tired of that. I suppose we all end up as bitches but who's [sic] fault is it? The bitches have the most fun but you have to be awfully stupid really to be a good one. Like Helene Bradley. Stupid and well intentioned and really selfish to be a good one. Probably I'm one already. They say you can't tell and that you always think you're not. There must be men who don't get tired of you or of it [intercourse]. There must be. But who has them? The ones we know are all brought up wrong. Let's not go into that now. No, not into that. Nor back to all those cars and all those dances. I wish that luminol would work. Damn Eddie, really. He shouldn't have really gotten so tight. It isn't fair, really. No one can help the way they're built but getting tight has nothing to do with that. (pp. 244–45)

The scene ends with her having to masturbate to put herself to sleep; the other choice is more luminol, which has unpleasant side effects and which may not work.

There are, no doubt, a number of reasons why the legendary Hemingway is anti-woman—biography and critical tradition not the least among them. But Hemingway the writer is much more sympathetic to women and their plight than readers have generally recognized. From the very beginning, Hemingway saw the difficulties that women faced with their men and saw too that, often, the men were to blame. Though his perception may not always have found their way into his life, they surely had a impact on his a＜ :. The challenge for us is to see beyond the legend as we continue to reevaluate Hemingway's place in our literary tradition.

1. Carlos Baker, *Ernest Hemingway: A Life Story* (New York: Scribner's, 1969), p. 465. See also Carlos Baker, ed., *Ernest Hemingway: Selected Letters 1917-1961* (New York: Scribner's, 1981) for other derogatory comments Hemingway made about his mother—e.g., "my bitch of a mother" (p. 594).

2. See, for instance, Judith Fetterley, "*A Farewell to Arms*: Hemingway's 'Resentful Cryptogram,' " *Journal of Popular Culture,* 10 (1976), 203-14, as a recent, specific example or such surveys as Katherine M. Rogers, *The Troublesome Helpmate: A History of Misogyny in Literature* (Seattle: University of Washington Press, 1966), especially pp. 247-51, for general remarks.

3. Alan Holder, "The Other Hemingway," *Twentieth Century Literature,* 9 (1963), 153-57, rpt. in *Ernest Hemingway: Five Decades of Criticism,* ed. Linda Welshimer Wagner (East Lansing: Michigan State University Press, 1974), pp. 103-09, was the first to document Hemingway's sympathetic treatment of women. He sees this "other Hemingway," however, only in the minor works. Though in four instances we overlap, I discuss works that he does not examine, and I exclude five stories that he believes fit his thesis. Footnotes indicate where we agree. More recently, Abdel-Ghani Ahmed Hasanain, "Women in Hemingway" (Diss. University of Toledo 1981), has argued that "Hemingway's women characters are 'real,' yet are governed by Hemingway's idealism; that Hemingway is more sympathetic toward women than has hitherto been admitted; that his criterion is conservatism, evident in his attitude toward lesbians and other women who act or look like men; that women are not sex objects but active participants in a male-female mutual experience; and that to Hemingway the best wife and mother is the woman who knows the real world, not the so-called free but promiscuous woman, or the ignorant and narrow-minded but 'genteel' woman" (p. 18). I have indicated in the footnotes where readers can find Hasanain's analyses of the works I discuss. In addition to those cited in the notes below, see also Leon Linderoth, "The Female Characters of Ernest Hemingway," Diss. Florida State University 1966; Naomi M. Grant, "The Role of Women in the Fiction of Ernest Hemingway," Diss. University of Denver 1968; Delbert E. Wylder, *Hemingway's Heroes* (Albuquerque: University of New Mexico Press, 1969); S. T. Kallapur, "Ernest Hemingway's Conception of Love and Womanhood," *Banasthali Patrika,* 19 (1972, pub. 1974), 37-47; Pamela Farley, "Form and Function: The Image of Woman in Selected Works of Hemingway and Fitzgerald," Diss. Pennsylvania State University 1973; Sunita Jain, "Of Women and Bitches: A Defense of Two Hemingway Heroines," *Journal of the School of Languages,* 3, No. 2 (1975-76), 32-35; Mona G. Rosenman, "Five Hemingway Women," *Claflin College Review,* 2, No. 1 (1977), 9-15; William K. Spofford, "Beyond the Feminist Perspective: Love in *A Farewell to Arms*," *Fitzgerald/Hemingway Annual, 1979,* pp. 307-12; Linda W. Wagner, " 'Proud and Friendly and Gently': Women in Hemingway's Early Fiction," *Ernest Hemingway: The Papers of a Writer,* ed. Bernard Oldsey (New York: Garland, 1981), pp. 63-71; and Joyce Wexler, "E.R.A. for Hemingway: A Feminist Defense of *A Farewell to Arms*," *The Georgia Review,* 35, No. 1 (1981), 111-23.

4. Though McAlmon published it in *Three Stories and Ten Poems* (1923), Liveright refused to reprint it in *In Our Time* (1925); Hemingway replaced it with "The Battler." Holder discusses this story, p. 104; Hasanain, p. 44.

5. The other two are "Mr. and Mrs. Elliot" and "Cat in the Rain." Hasanain discusses this story, pp. 50–52.

6. Though the story precedes "Out of Season" in the collection, it was most likely written later, probably in 1924. Holder discusses the story, pp. 105–06; Hasanain, pp. 52–53.

7. But see Gertrude M. White, "'We're All 'Cats in the Rain,'" *Fitzgerald/Hemingway Annual, 1978*, pp. 241–46. In the course of showing that "The story. . . seems less like the drama of a particular crisis in a particular relationship than a paradigm of man's plight," White argues that there is "no evidence that Hemingway likes or sympathizes with his heroine" (p. 245).

8. Though in his edition of *The Nick Adams Stories* Philip Young sees the events of "The End of Something" as occurring after the war, the story is almost certainly pre-war. See Robert M. Davis, *"The Nick Adams Stories:* A Review Essay," *Southern Humanities Review,* 7 (1973), 215–19, and Douglas Wilson, "Ernest Hemingway, *The Nick Adams Stories,*" *Western Humanities Review,* 27 (1973), 295–99. Recently, in "Hemingway Papers, Occasional Remarks" *(Ernest Hemingway: The Papers of a Writer,* ed. Bernard Oldsey, pp. 139–47), Young has conceded "that the decision on where to put 'The End of Something,' 'The Three-Day Blow,' and very likely 'Summer People' probably went the wrong way" (p. 147). See also Young's original introduction to this edition of the stories in *Novel,* 6 (1972), 5–19, rpt. in Jackson J. Benson, *The Short Stories of Ernest Hemingway: Critical Essays* (Durham, N.C.: Duke University Press, 1975), pp. 29–45. Hasanain discusses this story, pp. 46–47.

9. Hasanain discusses the novel, pp. 110–22.

10. See Delbert E. Wylder, "The Two Faces of Brett: The Role of the New Woman in *The Sun Also Rises,*" *Kentucky Philological Association Bulletin* (1980), 27–33. Wylder suggests that the Victorian attitude of many male critics has, in part, clouded "the subtlety with which Hemingway treats some of the deeper aspects of Jake's and Brett's rather complicated relationship, and particularly the characterization of Lady Brett Ashley" (p. 28).

11. Holder discusses the story, p. 105; Hasanain, pp. 53–55.

12. See, however, Roger Whitlow, "Critical Misinterpretations of Hemingway's Helen," *Frontiers,* 3, No. 3 (1978), 52–54, who shows, as I do, that critics have misread the story. Whitlow believes that Helen is "the most unfairly treated victim of the party-line criticism on Hemingway's 'bitch women'" (p. 52). Hasanain discusses the story, pp. 63–68.

13. Holder discusses the novel, p. 105; Hasanain, pp. 83–89.

14. John S. Hill, *"To Have and Have Not*: Hemingway's Hiatus," *Midwest Quarterly,* 10 (1969), 349–56, sees Dorothy Hollis as one of "three bitches [in the novel] used by Hemingway to reveal his own [negative] view of the American woman" (p. 353). Hill does note, however, that Helen Gordon is a "worthwhile woman" but one who "plays a very minor role" (p. 352).

FOR WHOM THE BELL TOLLS
AS MYTHIC NARRATIVE

JOHN J. TEUNISSEN

As *FOR WHOM THE BELL TOLLS* BEGINS, a young man lies on the pine-needled floor of a forest high in the mountains; the wind blows through the treetops; the young man is with "a solid old man in a black peasant's smock" and "rope-soled shoes" whose name is Anselmo.[1] The young man is an American, the old man a Spaniard. They discuss the strategy of destroying a bridge over a gorge, and the young man remembers that a man named Golz had said to him: "To blow the bridge is nothing. . . . Merely to blow the bridge is a failure" (p. 4).

As the narrative ends, it is three days later; the young man, whose name is Robert Jordan, lies on the pine-needled floor of a forest high in the mountains; the wind blows through the treetops; he is alone, for the old man is dead; his left thigh is broken; he is protecting the retreat of his friends, among whom is a woman named Maria to whom he has said: "I am with thee. . . . I am with thee now. We are both there. Go!" (p. 465) The bridge is destroyed, but its destruction has accomplished nothing; the young man is about to die. The narrative occupies the sixty-eight hours between "Saturday afternoon and Tuesday noon of the last week of May 1937."[2]

When *For Whom the Bell Tolls* appeared in 1940 the Spanish Civil War was well on its way to becoming a World War. Literary criticism through the '30's had demanded that fiction recognize its social responsibility. It is small wonder, then, that a novel about the Spanish Civil War should be subjected to the tests of realism and proper values. Hemingway's stock rose and fell with the critical brokers, those who on the one hand praised the verisimilitude of setting, dialogue, characterization, and event, and on the other with those who damned Hemingway's flagrantly romantic falsification of historical fact.

Reprinted with permission from *Dalhousie Review*, 56 (1976), 52–69.

221

The latter attitude has remained prevalent among historians and historically-oriented critics. Hugh Thomas, in his 1961 history of the Spanish Civil War, for example, expresses some concern that during the period of the action of the novel "Hemingway himself, oddly enough," rather than being involved directly in the conflict in Spain was "back in New York, campaigning to raise funds for the Republic. His old friends in America thought that they were seeing the transformation of a previously uncommitted writer."[3]

A central document in the controversy, and one that has since become a classic of its kind, is Arturo Barea's indignant but incisive review, "Not Spain but Hemingway."[4] Barea takes issue with several reviewers who have argued that "Hemingway knows his Spain profoundly" (p. 81). Barea, on the contrary, argues that Hemingway's vision of Spain is very far from being realistic and that it is really peculiarly his own. He concludes that "as a novel about Spaniards and their war, it is unreal and, in the last analysis, deeply untruthful." Some of Barea's quarrels with Hemingway are trivial, but he makes several important—and subsequently seldom successfully challenged—points: first, that persons like Pablo and Pilar would never have emerged as the leaders of a band of *guerrilleros*; second, that the scenes of mass murder and rape are grossly exaggerated and "contrary to Spanish psychology" (p. 85); third, that the love encounter between Robert and Maria is "pure romanticizing," primarily because Hemingway does not understand the psychology of a Spanish girl of the rural middle class; and fourth, that his rendering of the language of the Spanish peasants into English is a "curious translation, which is no real translation" at all (p. 87).

I have no quarrel with Senor Barea, for he is right. And ironically, it is exactly such attacks upon the "realism" of *For Whom the Bell Tolls* which provide most fruitful points of departure for readers who feel the greatness of Hemingway's art but who seem to be left with only the tattered remnants of what was supposed to be a socially responsible work of fiction. For it is precisely this lack of realism, this tendency to romanticize—Robert Jordan continually reminds himself not to "go romanticizing" the Spanish peasant—which labels the book as American and which places it in an old tradition; and, understandably, it is precisely this traditional element—the mythic element—which the European critics have been slow to recognize. To cite a more recent example, these are the words of Nemi D'Agostino:

> The utter uselessness of the attempt on the bridge, upon which the future of the
> human race might depend, is made clear from the start, as is the uselessness of
> the pathetic heroism of that group of solitary eccentrics which Hemingway
> selects as his chief characters. The sky overhanging the Sierra is without depth

and beyond the mountains there is no crusade but only the confused movements of the heterogeneous crowds, a massacre in a betrayed land. Jordan is a new Frederic Henry, who finds a code of behavior by which to endure life in the exact fulfillment of his mission, and in the end is driven to "sacrifice" more by desperation than by any certainty. Even his improbable sentimental idyl (and those scenes of love in the face of death are among Hemingway's most inadequate, naturalistic, and yet abstract writing) only serves to emphasize the self-centeredness and irresponsibility of his character. His drama is too oppressive and restricted to reflect the so much wider and more complex tragedy of Spain.[5]

Barea, then, argues that Hemingway's vision of the Spanish Civil War is too subjective, and Barea might very well have written a review of *Moby-Dick* called "Not Whaling but Melville." D'Agostino argues that the vision is too restricted and idiosyncratic, and he fails to recognize the fact that there is a tragedy, if one likes, which is much larger and more complex even than that of Spain.

Still, the European critics, it seems to me, are finally more seminal in their attacks upon Hemingway than are the Americans in their defenses of him.[6] Because *For Whom the Bell Tolls* is not a historical novel. It is not even an *a*historical novel: it is in its very essence antihistorical. Nonetheless, in the same way that it is possible—if one wants to—to chart the progress of Ahab's *Pequod* through the Sea of Japan in his pursuit of the Whale, so is it possible to locate and isolate the time sequence and the geographical area in which the action of *For Whom the Bell Tolls* takes place. The chronometer and the topographical map are indexes to the temporal and spatial, but in *For Whom the Bell Tolls*, as in other great mythic works of literature, topography becomes, to use Theodor Gaster's word, *topocosm*.[7] Time and place are as important to the mythic novel (or romance) as they are to the sociological novel; if they serve no other function they provide us at least with the temporal and spatial relations traditionally thought to be necessary to coherent narrative.[8] In the romance, however, time, place, and character are subsumed and apotheosized into the archetype, into the arrangement of archetypes which is myth, where time (for my present purposes) becomes *tempus* and place becomes *locus*. The mountains of Spain and a northwestern American state are both called *Montana*: "In your country there are mountains? With that name surely there are mountains," Robert Jordan is asked by a young Spaniard called Primitivo (p. 206).

Or to use Mircea Eliade's terms, time and place (i.e., history) are profane, *tempus* and *locus* sacred. In *Cosmos and History* Eliade has described for us how myth and ritual are seen to be primitive man's attempt to escape from the prison of time and history into the timeless through the repetition of primordial gestures, of the archetypal creative act, of the sayings and makings of the ancestors. The successful repetition holds back chaos in an essentially heroic way.[9] All rites of passage, all initiation rituals, are for Eliade the attempts of primitive man to share in the creativity, the fertility, of the great ancestor, the archetypal hero. The essential pattern is that of the "eternal return" because time is linear while *tempus* is cyclical. This is why, of course, so many mythic narratives like *For Whom the Bell Tolls* seem to begin and end in the same place.

Thus it is also that often the temporal individual who re-enacts the role of the great ancestor is sacrificed, like the great ancestor, so that the community can be assured of the transcendent reality and security of the archetype. Often too, a regenerative kind of epiphany will occur at one of the auspicious geographical locations (*loci*). The ritual repetitions of the primordial gestures are arduous ones, but their re-enactment is necessary if contemporary man is to awaken into the "dream time," into the mythic vision which can redeem him and make him one with his ancestors.

In this connection, much has been written about Hemingway's obsession with war and the other forms of ritualized violence like the bull fight. Philip Young in particular has pointed out the private symbolic and psychological significance for Hemingway of Nick Adams' ritual exorcism of the Wound.[10] I believe, however, that Hemingway's well known obsession is so far from being a personal idiosyncracy based upon neurosis as to make it shamanistic in Andreas Lommel's definition of the term.[11] The shaman, the primitive artist, takes upon himself the blood guilt collective neurosis of the tribe, and through certain specifically artistic (i.e., both graphic and poetic, spatial and temporal) ritual narratives exorcises those neuroses brought on by the tribe's time and place, its human condition. As I shall attempt to point out later, Hemingway's artistic response is, in the foregoing sense, primitivistic if not completely primitive. To illustrate the point let me here suggest that the basic theme of *For Whom the Bell Tolls* is not a political one;[12] it is contained in the lyrics of the song the gypsy sings early on in the narrative: *"I had an inheritance from my father"* (p. 59). So has Robert Jordan.

We recall that Robert Jordan's father was a henpecked coward and finally a suicide. In symbolic terms, however, his inheritance from his father is not just the consciousness and guilt of parental failure, it is also the modern world (i.e., the Spanish Civil War), the profaneness of which the father has handed down to the son as his temporal burden. Since in mythic terms history is decline, the more immediate the ancestor the more profane must be his influence upon his descendant, it is not surprising that in the background we feel with Robert Jordan the presence of the great ancestor, the grandfather, in the "dream time" of nineteenth-century America with *its* Civil War and its great Indian fighters. The Spanish Civil War with its physical and psychic violence is also an inheritance of Maria's. Echoing Stephen Dedalus' comment about history, she says of the omnipresent bombers which "move like mechanized doom" over the mountains: "it seems as though they were a dream that you wake from" (p. 87). Nonetheless, in her background too is the great ancestor with his simple yet potent beliefs and ways, the old bear hunter Anselmo.

Now when Golz argues that to blow the bridge is nothing, he is of course speaking in terms of the larger military offensive and of topographical reference points; it is my contention, however, that Hemingway is thus emphasizing the symbolic nature of the act to which Robert Jordan is committed. He is committed to it at first, naturally, because of his political ideals;[13] later on, after his two days or so of intimate contact with Maria, Pablo, Pilar, Anselmo and the other guerrillas, he will blow the bridge truly in the name of humanity—his descendants and his ancestors—and not at all for politics. And paradoxically his blowing of the bridge must be regarded as a creative act because the bridge is a profane thing, it is of this time and place, it is made of steel; it is the viaduct by which time and place can enter the timeless and placeless *topocosm* of these Spanish mountains.

James Baird, in his Jungian *Ishmael: A Study of the Symbolic Mode in Primitivism*, has given us the language with which to describe this primitivistic movement in the American writer and in his fictional protagonist.[14] Baird's prime example is Melville and his Tommo in *Typee*, but Hemingway and his Robert Jordan would have served as well to illustrate Baird's thesis. Indeed, in his introduction Baird speaks of "Hemingway's. . . preferences for elemental Spain" (p. 6). For Baird, the American writer sensing cultural failure in his contemporary America makes a physical journey to the Orient where he discovers viable symbols to replace the inherited and impoverished religious symbolism of his own culture. The Orient, of course, is itself a symbolic complex which may be—as in Melville's case—Polynesia, but from the present point of view could as easily be Hemingway's La Granja or the Wounded Knee of contemporary American mythology. For this journey is as much into the collective unconscious as it is to far away and primitive places. In Hemingway's fiction we find this archetypal journey already having begun in Nick Adams' summer trips from Oak Park, Illinois, to the Indian camps of the upper Michigan fishing country.

The Orient as symbol reservoir, however, involves both a landscape and the eternal interaction between it and the People—our ancestors—and it is therefore regarded as a sacred place. Conveniently we can turn at this point from Baird to Gaster in our attempt to define exactly what this Spanish place and people signify for Hemingway and his hero in *For Whom the Bell Tolls*. In *Thespis* Gaster points out that the ancient mythic rituals are specifically assigned to places made sacred by their association with the ancestors, divine and human. To such places he assigns the name already mentioned above, *topocosm*, and he makes the following comment: "Basic to the entire procedure is the conception that what is in turn eclipsed and revitalized is not merely the human community of a given area or locality but the total corporate unit of all elements, animate and inanimate alike, which together constitute distinctive character and 'atmosphere'." And he goes on to point out that this *topocosm* includes within itself both the here and now and the there and then which I have termed *locus* and *tempus*: "The essence of the topocosm is that it possesses a two-fold character, at once real and punctual, and ideal and durative, the former aspect being necessarily merged in the latter, as a moment is merged in time. If it is bodied forth as a real and concrete organism in the present, it exists also as an ideal, timeless entity, embracing but transcending the here and now in exactly the same way that the idea America embraces but transcends the present generation of Americans" (p. 24).

It is significant that Gaster, even though discussing the myth and drama of the ancient Near East, should introduce the example of America as topocosm. Moreover America seems to lend itself very well to the expounding of such a concept. Jacques Maritain, for example, also speaks pointedly to the same issue when he describes a landscape which is not topo*graphical* but topo*cosmic*: "When you drive along the Hudson River or through the hills of Virginia. . . imagine for a moment that the country you contemplate is still populated with Indian warriors and tents: then the beauty of Nature will awake and make sense all of a sudden, because the relationship between Nature and Man has been re-established; modern inhabitants have not yet had the time to permeate the land with the form of man."[15] One could suggest, to simplify the above discussion and to bring it into more obvious relation to *For Whom the Bell Tolls*, that, modern real estate jargon aside, the profound psychological contrast between topographical place and topocosm is available in our very different emotional responses to the words "house" and "home". It is obviously much easier to return to a house than it is to a home. And so I wish now to argue that Robert Jordan's physical uprooting from Montana actually becomes in the course of the narrative a spiritual replanting into his native rocky soil as he finds it in the mountains of Spain at a particularly traumatic period in Spain's history and his own psychological "development", his de-individuation.

Central to my concern here is Chapter 30 in which Robert Jordan, now near the end of his three days, remembers his grandfather and the American Civil War and the Indian fighting while he muses to himself: "I wonder what Grandfather would think of this situation. . . Grandfather was a hell of a good soldier, everybody said. They said if he had been with Custer that day he never would have let him be sucked in that way. How could he ever not have seen the smoke nor the dust of all those lodges down there in the draw along the Little Big Horn unless there must have been a heavy morning mist? But there wasn't any mist. I wish Grandfather were here instead of me" (pp. 337–38).[16] But the image of the suicide twentieth-century father intrudes itself, and Robert Jordan concludes: "It's a shame there is such a *jump in time* between ones like us" (emphasis mine). What Robert Jordan has *almost* been able to discover at this stage is that the "jump in time" is only an illusion and that the ancestor is always present in the unconscious of his descendants or, as the New England Primer once so quaintly put it: "In Adam's fall / We sinned all."

The clue to this, and (among other things) what enables Robert Jordan to make his final sacrifice, is the archetypal icon of General George Custer in his last stand at the Little Big Horn. Robert Jordan's memory moves from the wife-bullied father to what his grandfather had said about Custer:

> "George Custer was not an intelligent leader of cavalry, Robert," his grandfather had said. "He was not even an intelligent man."
>
> He remembered that when his grandfather said that he felt resentment that anyone should speak against that figure in the buckskin shirt, the yellow curls blowing, that stood on that hill holding a service revolver as the Sioux closed in around him in the old Anheuser-Busch lithograph that hung on the poolroom wall in Red Lodge.
>
> "He just had great ability to get himself in and out of trouble," his grandfather went on, "and on the Little Big Horn he got into it but he couldn't get out. . . ." (p. 339)

It is of the utmost significance that at this point Robert Jordan should remember Custer's Last Stand in iconographic terms and that the icon should have found its way into a beer advertisement. For it is one of the measures of the power of a national myth that it should remain with the people in their art. The poolroom wall in Red Lodge is as much a museum of archetypes as is the Louvre.

As John Steinbeck tells us: "I don't suppose there is an American who doesn't carry Remington's painting of the last defense of the center column of the 7th Cavalry in his head."[17] In historical terms the battle of the Little Big Horn was, of course, a rather miserable and humiliating skirmish in the last phase of the "pacification" of the plains Indian. As the result of a tactical error (or series of errors) by a story-seeking commanding officer 250 or so men died on and around a hill at the junction of two small rivers in the shadow of the Rocky Mountains. But if ever an action has occurred which makes it evident that certain historical events and characters are essentially mythic (and *not* later mythicized) it is the battle of the Little Big Horn. To build for a moment upon G. E. Lessing's analysis of the iconography of the *Laocoön*[18] the inherently mythic action freezes itself in art just before its archetypal climax, freezes itself graphically in space, perpetuates itself narratively in time. Whether Custer made errors or not, in temporal-spatial military terms, ceases to matter. He has numerous prototypes in epic, among them Byrchtnoth in his last stand at Maldon and Roland in the pass at Roncesvalles. The archetypal action demands iconographic representation, and the icon makes no historical judgments. Custer and the Sioux and Cheyenne are locked topocosmically together forever in the landscape, the memory, and the collective unconscious. That Laocoön in the *Aeneid* was being punished for impiety does not matter; nor does it matter whether the victory at the Little Big Horn was Sitting Bull's or Crazy Horse's. These are judgments for historians, not for artists. They are not even judgments for art critics.

Before we get back to Spain permit me one more, somewhat quaint, example of the iconographic process at work. That Custer's Last Stand demanded such representation is borne out by the famous pictograph of the battle by the warrior Kicking Bear. In the centre of the pictograph we have not Custer, as understandably with Remington, but four Indian warriors: Crazy Horse, Sitting Bull, Rain-in-the-Face, and Kicking Bear himself. And like Hemingway much later, poor Kicking Bear has been taken to task by the historians for falsifying the facts of the battle; because Sitting Bull was not at the battle, he was guarding the Indian village "and directing the packing up of the lodges by the squaws in case they had to move away."[19] Myth, however, does not care that Sitting Bull was not really directly involved in the battle any more than it cares that Hemingway was in New York in May of 1937.

Now in order to understand the mythology which informs *For Whom the Bell Tolls*, it is necessary to move from the central icon to its constituent symbolic elements. The first of these is the all-pervasive presence of the machine in the Spanish landscape, and with Maritain I would argue that the machine has not yet had time to impress itself upon that topocosm. No one can discuss this aspect of *American* mythology, however, without being greatly indebted to Leo Marx for *The Machine in the Garden*.[20] There have been few quarrels with Hemingway's historical treatment of machines as used in the Spanish Civil War, for it is a fact of history that never before had a war been so mechanized, partly because the great European powers were using Spain as a proving ground for the most up-to-date and sophisticated weaponry.[21] Nevertheless, little attention has been paid to Hemingway's technique in revealing the machine to us more through the eyes of the Spanish peasants than through the consciousness of Robert Jordan. Here, for example, is a Spaniard's description of the attack on the train during which Maria was rescued:

> "Then it came chu-chu-chu-chu-chu-chu steadily larger and larger and then, at the moment of the explosion, the front wheels of the engine rose up and all of the earth seemed to rise in a great cloud of blackness and a roar and the engine rose high in the cloud of dirt and of the wooden ties rising in the air *as in a dream* and then it fell on to its side like a great wounded animal and there was an explosion of white steam before the clouds of the other explosion had ceased to fall on us and the *maquina* commenced to speak ta-tat-tat-ta!" went the gypsy shaking his two clenched fists up and down in front of him, thumbs up, on an imaginary machine gun. . . . "Never in my life have I seen such a thing, with the troops running from the train and the *maquina* speaking into them and the men falling." (p. 29, emphasis mine)[22]

The speaker is a Spanish gypsy; and the American Indian, unfortunately, did not have the assistance of Russian dynamiters in their attacks upon the Iron Horse, but the gypsy's exultation, his "excitement so great that I cannot tell it," are calculated by Hemingway to bring to the surface in both Robert Jordan and his readers a primordial image from America's mythic past which is once again iconographic and which expresses the icon, like Kicking Bear's pictograph, not from the civilized white man's point of view but from the Indians'.

Moreover, while the gypsy's language may not be a direct enough translation from the Spanish to suit our historians, it is through such archaic idiom that Hemingway is able to lead us into the primitive mind.[23] The American Indian and the Spanish gypsy express the machine in animistic terms: the engine of the train rises up on its hind wheels like a wounded horse and falls like one; the machine gun speaks lethal words at the enemy. There are many other examples of this primitive animistic reaction to the machine, among them Agustin's description of the whippet tank's appearance: "It seems like a mouse coming out of its hole. . . . This is the big insect Pablo has been fighting" (p. 453). Thus an evidence of Robert Jordan's gradual atavistic reversion is his learning to speak this primitive language:

> "Watch me break the windshield in the truck," the gypsy said happily.
> "Nay. The truck is already sick," Robert Jordan said. (p. 448)

If these Spaniards then can understand the Iron Horse only in animistic terms, their relationship to the horse itself goes back and down to the most profound depths of totemistic psychology.[24] Pablo has killed a pair of Guardia Civil and stolen their horses. What he is proud of is that "we were able to kill them without injuring the horses" (p. 14). When Pilar first meets Robert Jordan she asks him:

"Do you come for us to do another train?"

"No," said Robert Jordan, trusting her instantly. "For a bridge."

"*No es nada,*" she said, "A bridge is nothing. When do we do another train now that we have horses?" (p. 31)

And while the series of confrontations between Robert Jordan and Pablo might strike us as a stereotype drawn from the pre-*High Noon* western film (and why should it not?), the two are nonetheless brought spiritually together through their horsemanship. At their first meeting Pablo boasts regarding his five horses: "All these I have taken. . . ":

"That," said Robert Jordan, pointing to one of the bays, a big stallion with a white blaze on his forehead and a single white foot, the near front, "is much horse."

He was a beautiful horse that looked as though he had come out of a painting by Velasquez.

"They are all good," said Pablo. "You know horses?"

"Yes,"

"Less bad," said Pablo. "Do you see a defect in one of these?"

Robert Jordan knew that now his papers were being examined by a man who could not read. (p. 13)

These representative passages convince one that this little band of guerrillas with their women and horses finds its prototype in the hunted American Indian of the 1870's. Nevertheless, there are ironies present. For we know that while the Sioux and Cheyenne were regarded in the nineteenth century as among the finest light cavalry in the world, their horses of course traced their ancestry back to those of the Spanish *Conquistadores* and Spain itself. The Spaniards are among the finest horsemen of western Europe. Hemingway's reader will remember too that the leaders of many of the last Indian guerrilla bands of the American Southwest bore Spanish names—Geronimo, Cochise, Mangas, Coloradas. And finally while Robert Jordan's Spaniards fear the Moors more than any other enemy, so the American Indian feared the regiments of black soldiers sent against them after the Civil War, men whom they called "Buffalo Soldiers" because of their dark colour. The weight of this kind of mythology makes Hemingway's continuing references to the Indian attributes of the Spanish guerrillas almost superfluous. One cannot resist drawing attention, however, to the character and fate of El Sordo, "a man of few words," with "a thin-bridged, hooked nose like an Indian's," who speaks Tontoese prose—"when blow bridge?"—who drinks not wine but firewater, and who dies on top of a hill outnumbered and outgunned, sheltered at last behind the body of his dead horse (pp. 140, 141, 198, 307ff).

Pablo and El Sordo are two more of Robert Jordan's male ancestors. The third—and perhaps the most important because in him the ancestry is even more basically primitive—is Anselmo. He, like Pablo, cannot write, but he is a great hunter:

> "After we have won you must come to hunt."
> "To hunt what?"
> "The boar, the bear, the wolf, the ibex—"
> "You like to hunt?"
> "Yes, man. More than anything." (p. 39)

Then follows a long conversation about bear totemism:

> "So is the chest of a man like the chest of a bear," Robert Jordan said. "With the hide removed from the bear, there are many similarities in the muscles."
> "Yes," Anselmo said. "The gypsies believe the bear to be a brother of man."
> "So do the Indians in America," Robert Jordan said. "And when they kill a bear they apologize to him and ask his pardon. They put his skull in a tree and they ask him to forgive them before they leave it."
> "The gypsies believe the bear to be a brother of man because he has the same body beneath his hide, because he drinks beer, because he enjoys music and because he likes to dance."
> "So also believe the Indians."
> "Are the Indians then gypsies?"
> "No. But they believe alike about the bear." (p. 40)

Anselmo's totemism is somewhat atavistic, however, since he does not believe—or at least he *says* he does not believe—with the gypsies in the brotherhood of bear and man, nor does he believe in killing men. His atavism, nonetheless, fills him full "Of pride of remembrance of the encounter with the bear on that hillside in the early spring" (p. 40). It reminds him of his many trophies and particularly that "On the door of the church of my village was nailed the paw of [the] bear that I killed in the spring, finding him on a hillside in the snow, overturning a log with this same paw" (p. 30). Anachronism that he is, Anselmo misses God, "having been brought up in religion" (p. 41), the very religion which has attempted to stamp out his primitive totemistic beliefs—the nailing of the paw to the church door of course being the Christian version of leaving the skull in the tree—but, be it added, not his profoundest feelings. Christianity—historically—has replaced totemism, and Communism has replaced Christianity. Small wonder then that with nothing left to believe in, Anselmo, who does not know a Staff car from a regular army motorcar, should as a result of his primitive naiveté die wounded by a piece of steel from the profane bridge, as blown it falls into the gorge. For, as Robert Jordan knows, "Spain has never been a Christian country" (p. 355).

Then there is Pilar, who has "gypsy blood" (p. 28), who is "almost as wide as she is tall" (p. 30), who is a seeress, reading Robert Jordan's fate in his palm, who has been loved by many men, among them bullfighters, who is so "simple" that she is "very complicated" and who is "gross" but also "very delicate" (p. 156).[25] It is she who recognizes the affinity between Robert and Maria and who educates Maria in the ways of love; it is she who counsels and guides the pair, and not always gently:

> Pilar did not even speak to him. It was not like a snake charming a bird, not a cat with a bird. There was nothing predatory. Nor was there anything perverted about it. There was a spreading, though, as a cobra's hood spreads. He could feel this. He could feel the menace of the spreading. But the spreading was a domination, not of evil, but of searching. I wish I did not see this, Robert Jordan thought. (p. 173)

Nowadays when novelists such as Doris Lessing (*The Golden Notebook*) and Robertson Davies (*The Manticore*) have made such skillful use of the figure of the female Jungian analyst, the Wise Old Woman, we will perhaps take for granted Robert Jordan's conclusion that Pilar is a psychiatrist (p. 137). What we might need to be reminded of, however, is the degree to which Jungian analysis is essentially shamanistic, the degree to which archetype and icon are used in leading the way back and down to the dark gods within the individual and group psyche, in preparing the way for the "naming." This explains, I think, why Hemingway has Pilar choose the seemingly incongruous time and place of Robert and Maria's pastoral idyl to tell them the terrible story of the massacre of the fascists. Before she starts her story she warns that it may give Robert Jordan "bad dreams" (p. 99); Maria has of course already been *in* the dream; and when the story is finished Robert Jordan thinks to himself: "Pilar had made him see it in that town. If that woman could only write. He would try to write it and if he had luck and could remember it perhaps he could get it down as she told it. God, how she could tell a story" (p. 134).[26]

Were Pilar's story simply about a massacre, were it told artlessly about an artless—i.e., randomly historical—occurrence, it could have no efficacy, no more efficacy than any newspaper story; it could not have made Robert Jordan react the way he did. In many respects it is a story not of how it was but of how it ought to have been. The story is a simple one, though; it is of how Pablo had the village fascists "beaten to death with flails" (p. 103); but the naming process makes us go deeper and, with Pilar, recognize both the archetype and the icon. It was dusty that day "and we were all powdered with dust. . . as powdered as men are at a threshing. . . but each one [of the dead *guardia civil*] was now moistening with his blood the dry dirt by the wall where they lay" (p. 102). Pablo has organized the execution very well indeed. The peasants form up in two lines facing each other as the fascists are made to walk or run between the lines; most of the peasants have flails, "And those who did not have flails had heavy herdsman's clubs, or ox-goads, and some had wooden pitchforks. . . . Some had sickles and reaping hooks. . . " (p. 105). And when a peasant comments that he does not think the weapons adequate to the job, another replies: "That is the beauty of it. . . . There must be many blows" (p. 105).

Because this is a festival in the true and ancient sense of the word. The archetypal content of ritual killing for the renewal of the land is inherent to this particular festival, and it seems to me much more important in context than the historical fact that sometimes Republicans massacred Loyalists, or vice versa. The Republicans are peasants, primitive man, while the Loyalists are petty bourgeoisie, modern man. This is why the icon which emerges would strike particularly the American reader as that of "running the gauntlet," one of the more dramatic rituals in the myth of the American Indian. Thus by the time that Pilar's story is over we really do not have to be reminded that Pilar has "high Indian cheekbones" (p. 298) or that her bed smells "the way an Indian's bed does" (p. 360).

In the impulse toward mythic renewal which informs *For Whom the Bell Tolls* the hierogamy, the sacred marriage, counterpoints both ritual killing and military murder. We can rely once more upon Eliade to enlighten us about the place of hierogamy in the primitive cosmic order (pp. 23–27), so let it suffice for the present to suggest that human sacred marriage is an imitation, a re-creation, of the original marriage of earth and sky, of god and goddess, or of god and human.[27] This divine union once ensured the renewal of terrestrial fecundity and its imitation in the month of *May* by young human couples is thought among primitive peoples to accomplish the same thing. Thus in China Eliade records that "young couples went out in spring and united on the grass in order to stimulate 'cosmic regeneration' and 'universal germination' " (p. 25). "Their union coincides with that of the elements; heaven embraces its bride, dispensing fertilizing rain" (p. 24). So one would wish to argue, machismo aside, that the impulse to seek union with Maria in a sleeping bag under the stars is in Robert Jordan a primitive and religious one. For Maria, whose cropped hair is like a beaver pelt or a field of grain and who walks like a colt *is* Robert Jordan's America, his new found land.

This hierogamous union has great efficacy for the lovers who "feel the earth move" (p. 160) and as a result of which they pass into *"la gloria"* (p. 379). The earth's moving is what for Pilar sets the sacred seal upon the union: for it never moves more than three times in any lifetime, and for most people—the profane ones—it moves not at all. This evidence of hierogamy is gypsy knowledge and, as Pilar makes clear, it is not a primitive euphemism for orgasm. Finally, and as a direct result of this conversation with Pilar on the subject, Robert Jordan comes to new understanding: "Nobody knows what tribes we come from nor what our tribal inheritance is nor what the mysteries were in the woods where the people lived that we came from. All we know is that we do not know. We know nothing about what happens to us in the nights. When it happens in the day though, it *is* something" (p. 175).

It does not rain as a result of this hierogamous union, however; it snows instead, as if the gods were demonstrating that for modern man the times really are out of joint. Personal fulfillment in the union with the archetypes of the Great Past seems still possible, but the possibility for communal revitalization, Hemingway tells us, is gone. Robert Jordan has already sensed this when, even in the midst of hierogamy he watched time in the form of a machine moving on his wrist; the omen of the two hares killed while making love in the snow confirms it. Nevertheless he has been able to go home again, to *locate* himself in the mythic sense of that word. At the beginning of the narrative he was the young man who said: "I would rather have been born here" (p. 15). At the end, because he has been enabled through contact with the truly primitive to make the journey back and down, he can conclude: "I have been all my life in these hills since I have been here. Anselmo is my oldest friend. I know him better than I know Charles, than I know Chub, than I know Guy, than I know Mike, and I know them well. Agustin, with his vile mouth, is my brother, and I never had a brother. Maria is my true love and my wife. I never had a true love. I never had a wife. She is also my sister, and I never had a sister, and my daughter, and I never will have a daughter. I hate to leave a thing that is so good (p. 381)." This is not political and it is not sentimental. It emerges from and strikes back down into the most basic and primitive yearnings of mankind, yearnings which primitive man seeks to realize through myth and ritual and which the modern artist occasionally expresses through his art. At the very end Robert Jordan says to himself: "I'd like to tell grandfather about this one" (p. 469). What he fails to realize (and why would he as twentieth-century man?) is that he has redeemed the grandfather who was so critical of Custer; he has redeemed the father who rejected life; he has reasserted the value of Custer's lost battle and of Sitting Bull's victory; he has learned that you can go home again but that once you are there you have to stay.

1. Ernest Hemingway, *For Whom the Bell Tolls* (New York: Charles Scribner's Sons, 1940), p. 1. Future references are in the body of the essay. This essay is based upon a paper read at the annual meeting of the Association of Canadian University Teachers of English, University of Toronto, 28 May 1974.

2. Carlos Baker, *Hemingway: The Writer as Artist* (Princeton: Princeton University Press, 1956), p. 238. It was pointed out to me by David Williams that I read the original of this essay thirty-seven years later on the last Tuesday in May at 2:00 p.m. The superstitious reader of Hemingway will no doubt want to make something of the coincidence.

3. Hugh Thomas, *The Spanish Civil War* (London: Eyre & Spottiswoode, 1961), p. 444.

4. Arturo Barea, "Not Spain but Hemingway," in Sheldon Norman Grebstein, ed., *The Merrill Studies in* For Whom the Bell Tolls (Columbus: Charles E. Merrill, 1971), pp. 80–90 (first printed 1941). A number of excellent essays have been here reprinted by Grebstein.

5. Nemi D'Agostino, "The Later Hemingway," in *Hemingway: A Collection of Critical Essays,* ed. Robert P. Weeks (Englewood Cliffs, N.J.: Prentice Hall, 1962), pp. 152–60.

6. See for example Allen Guttmann, "Mechanized Doom: Ernest Hemingway and the Spanish Civil War," in Grebstein, pp. 71–79; Keneth Kinnamon, "Hemingway, the *Corrida,* and Spain," *Texas Studies in Language and Literature* 1 (Spring 1959), 44–61; and Robert O. Stephens, "Language Magic and Reality in *For Whom the Bell Tolls,*" *Criticism,* 14 (Spring 1972), 151–64.

7. Theodor H. Gaster, *Thespis: Ritual, Myth and Drama in the Ancient Near East* (New York: Schuman, 1950). There will be further reference to his discussion of topocosm.

8. See Earl Rovit, *Ernest Hemingway* (New York: Twayne, 1963), who in his chapter "Of Time and Style," pp. 126–46, discusses the narrative technique from the novelistic point of view of isolation in time and space.

9. Mircea Eliade, *Cosmos and History: The Myth of the Eternal Return,* trans. Willard R. Trask (New York: Harper and Row, 1970). See also Gerry Brenner, "Epic Machinery in Hemingway's *For Whom the Bell Tolls,*" *Modern Fiction Studies,* 16 (Winter 1970–71), 491–504, who fairly exhausts Carlos Baker's earlier suggestion (pp. 245–50) that Hemingway was very consciously engaged with the epic genre in *For Whom the Bell Tolls.*

10. Philip Young, *Ernest Hemingway: A Reconsideration* (University Park: Pennsylvania State University Press, 1966), especially pp. 106–11.

11. Andreas Lommel, *Shamanism: The Beginnings of Art* (New York: McGraw Hill, 1966), the introductory section.

12. For recent political approaches see John M. Muste, *Say That We Saw Spain Die* (Seattle: University of Washington Press, 1966), pp. 95–119; Leonard Lutwack, *Heroic Fiction: The Epic Tradition and American Novels of the Twentieth Century* (Carbondale: Southern Illinois University Press, 1971), who argues, for example, that Maria is a "symbol of the cause for which Jordan and the partisans are fighting" (p. 73). David Sanders argues that the novel is nonpolitical, "Ernest Hemingway's Spanish Civil War Experience," in Grebstein, pp. 32–42, and especially p. 39; Warren French, in a fine piece of novelistic criticism, maintains that it is political, but insofar as it is "a poignant piece of antiwar propaganda"; "A Troubled World—'You'd Like Malindi,' " from *The Social Novel at the End of an Era* (Carbondale: Southern Illinois University Press, 1966), rpt. in Grebstein, pp. 56–70.

13. Muste argues that Jordan's and Hemingway's ideological "difficulties" contribute to a degree of artistic failure (pp. 114–19); see also Stanley Cooperman's somewhat spurious discussion of Robert Jordan's "ideology without intellect": "Hemingway's Blue-eyed Boy: Robert Jordan and 'Purging Ecstasy,' " *Criticism,* 8 (Winter 1966), 87–96.

14. James Baird, *Ishmael: A Study of the Symbolic Mode in Primitivism* (Baltimore: The Johns Hopkins Press, 1956), Part I.

15. Jacques Maritain, *Creative Intuition in Art and Poetry* (New York: World, 1954), p. 7. See also Leo Gurko, *Ernest Hemingway and the Pursuit of Heroism* (New York: Thomas Y. Crowell, 1968), who insists that "Hemingway dramatizes nature; he does not merely describe it. The Spanish landscape, the Spanish earth are central to the novel and not just its panoramic scene" (p. 127); Michael J.

B. Allen, "The UnSpanish War in *For Whom the Bell Tolls,*" *Contemporary Literature*, 13 (Spring 1972), 204–12, presents Hemingway as "mythmaker" in the realm of allegory and suggests that here "Spain is an abstract landscape. . . " (p. 212). I wish to emphasize my position that Hemingway's kind of myth is about as far from allegory and abstraction as a writer of fiction can get.

16. Brenner, in his somewhat mechanical application of the machinery of epic to the novel, stresses the heroic stature of the "Chiron-like grandfather" (p. 498). As I shall attempt to point out below, the grandfather strikes me as heroic in everything but his mistaken assessment of George Custer.

17. John Steinbeck, *Travels with Charley* (New York: Bantam, 1961), p. 159. That Hemingway had found the Custer myth useful to his art is also borne out by the "picture of Custer's Last Stand on the wall" which Harry Morgan looks at "as though he'd never seen" it, and this just prior to Morgan's last stand. See *To Have and Have Not* (New York: Charles Scribner's Sons, 1937), p. 123.

18. Gotthold Ephraim Lessing, *Laocoön: An Essay Upon the Limits of Painting and Poetry* (Boston: Little, Brown, 1910).

19. John A. Hawgood, *America's Western Frontiers* (New York: Knopf, 1967), p. 293. Hawgood reproduces Kicking Bear's pictograph. It is perhaps not strange that Emily Stipes Watts makes no reference to the Remington painting or the Anheuser-Busch lithograph in her *Ernest Hemingway and the Arts* (Urbana: University of Illinois Press, 1971), although she does discuss Hemingway's affinity for Goya and Carlos Baker's suggestion that *For Whom the Bell Tolls* has a great deal in common pictorially with Picasso's famous *Guernica* (p. 64). *Guernica* indeed might be just such another inevitable iconographic representation as I have discussed above. But it is not really a *representation;* it is an *impression*, nightmarish and allegorical. One might develop the argument that the less personally involved man becomes in his warfare the less representational and the more mechanical will become his depictions of it. This began in the American Civil War with Matthew Brady, perhaps, and found its supreme iconographic embodiment in the famous photograph of the raising of the flag on Iwo Jima. For our own interpretations of the impact of archetype and icon upon culture see the following essays by Evelyn J. Hinz and me: "The Pieta as Icon in *The Golden Notebook,*" *Contemporary Literature*, 14 (Autumn 1973), 457–70; "The Attack on the Pieta: An Archetypal Analysis," *Journal of Aesthetics and Art Criticism* 33 (Fall 1974), 43–50; "Saviour and Cock: Allusion and Icon in Lawrence's *The Man Who Died,*" *The Journal of Modern Literature*, 15 (April 1976), 279–96.

20. Leo Marx, *The Machine in the Garden: Technology and the Pastoral Ideal in America* (New York: Oxford University Press, 1964).

21. From the purely historical point of view Allen Guttmann clearly defines the central issue: "for Hemingway the Spanish Civil War was dramatized as, among other things, a struggle waged by men close to the earth and to the values of a primitive society against men who had turned away from the earth, men who had turned to the machine and to the values of an aggressive and destructive mechanical order" (p. 76). What Guttmann fails to take into account is that the Spanish peasants are absolutely delighted with the *machine* gun, human nature being what it is.

22. One might point out that there is a distinct change in diction in the quoted passage. Down to the first use of *maquina* Hemingway's own voice seems to intrude, and that we see the same kind of passionate involvement with the material here as in the famous Colonel Sherburne speech in *Adventures of Huckleberry Finn* requires additional study.

23. John J. Allen admits that "the English of Hemingway's Spaniards is anything but" an accurate rendition of the original but he insists nevertheless that it is an accurate reflection of the "author's impressions both of the people and of their language": "The English of Hemingway's Spaniards," in Grebstein, p. 93. Brenner finds the language "consonant with epic characteristics" (p. 495).

24. Using what one might term the "Golden Bough approach," Stephens sees "imitative and contagious magic" in operation in the world of Robert Jordan (p. 155).

25. Delbert E. Wylder describes Pilar as one of Jung's "dual mothers": *Hemingway's Heroes* (Albuquerque: University of New Mexico Press, 1969), p. 160. A thoroughgoing Jungian analysis of the book, which I have not had the space to undertake here, would discover many other archetypal counterparts for Hemingway's characters.

26. Again following his particular Frazerian bent, Stephens describes the power of Pilar's stories of the bullfighters and the massacre in terms of "phatic communion" (p. 161).

27. Critical opinion is almost unanimous that Maria's characterization is the weakest in the book. Again one must stress the fact that Hemingway was not striving for phenomenal realism; he was profoundly after the numenal. M. Esther Harding, a Jungian psychologist, in her discussion of the role of the hierodule in primitive religion can perhaps be of help: "The term virgin, then, when used of the ancient goddesses, clearly has a meaning not of today. It may be used of a woman who has had much sexual experience; it may be even applied to a prostitute. Its real significance is to be found in its use as contrasted with 'married.' " See *Woman's Mysteries Ancient and Modern: A Psychological Interpretation of the Feminine Principle as Portrayed in Myth, Story, and Dreams* (New York: Bantam, 1973), p. 121. Her entire chapter, "The Moon Mother," is of interest in terms of the hierogamy of Robert and Maria.

THE MASK OF DEATH, THE FACE OF LIFE: HEMINGWAY'S FEMINIQUE

ROBERT D. CROZIER, S.J.

AS LATE AS THE NOBEL PRIZE, Ernest Hemingway was being given star billing for his style. His own mockery of irony and pity had gotten him nowhere. A critic here and there tentatively pointed at a few ideas or insisted that with the great short stories of 1938 he was becoming a thinker. Again in 1940 he satirized the idea with the claim that Robert Jordan was no thinker but a bridge blower. The irony of that statement was lost and is still lost upon the critical community. So was the fury of the query possibly aimed directly and vengefully at Edmund Wilson: "I wonder how they will like Maria in Missoula, Montana?" When he died, he knew; and he died with his triumphant last laugh. He had had a few modest thoughts, a few theories and critiques. Perhaps he was not aware of Longinus's requirements for the sublime, but in reaching it in 1940, he provided not only the passion but the thought required, even as he had much earlier—in fact from the beginning. Among these great thoughts is his own feminine mystique, his feminique.

The symbolic structure of the later works is a combination of realistic action reinforced by symbolic allusion and interpretation. Pilar, Maria, and Renata are not just didactic figures. They do live the reality suggested by their symbolic sources and associations. The qualities they possess as women and share with, reproduce, or draw out of men can be reduced to six: (1) a way of seeing, hearing, and knowing; (2) a special sense of time; (3) an ability to love truth and, therefore, to face death squarely; (4) an exceptional understanding of the possible and with it a capacity for tenacious fidelity and endurance; (5) a hope for a better world and a desire to create and raise children for that world; and (6) a subtle,

Reprinted with permission from *The Hemingway Review*, 4, No. 1 (Fall 1984), 2–13.

realistic sense of human brotherhood. These are the basic feminine characteristics seen by Hemingway as distinctive in themselves and yet communicable to and needed by men. All of them, taken together, are also essentially religious, and religion, therefore, for Hemingway is essentially feminine.

Pascal put it well concerning belief when he said: "to deny, to believe, and to doubt well, are to man what running is to the horse" (*Pensées*, Ch. XXV, xlvii). Pascal did not comment on any distinction here between men and women. Hemingway emphasized the difference even at the risk of dignifying mere credulity and superstition. Nevertheless, he is serious. Women have a greater ability than men to see, hear, smell, and know mysteries that men notice not at all or, like Jordan, regard as nonsense. Pilar abounds in these capabilities and suffers much for it in her efforts to explain what she knows about life, love, death, and God in this mystical way. But this kind of understanding is shown to be very practical. It can measure character, courage, resolution, and the real limits of human possibility. Such is the meaning of her story of the short-statured, always fearful, yet extremely courageous bullfighter, Finito (finite, limited), a story which once again fails to reach the mark of her constant effort to educate:

> "If he was so short he should not have tried to be a matador," Primitivo said.
> Pilar looked at Robert Jordan and shook her head. Then she bent over the big iron pot, still shaking her head.
> What a people they are, she thought. What a people are the Spaniards, "and if he was so short he should not have tried to be a matador." And I hear it and say nothing. I have no rage for that and having made an explanation I am silent. How simple it is when one knows nothing. *Que sencillo!* Knowing nothing one says, "He was not much of a matador." Knowing nothing another says, "He was tubercular." And another says, after one, knowing, has explained, "If he was so short he should not have tried to be a matador." (*For Whom the Bell Tolls*, pp. 188–89)

Pilar describes herself as being both very simple and very complicated. Robert Jordan is neither. But Hemingway had commented in *Death in the Afternoon* how difficult it is to master the truly simple. There, too, he is contemplating the multiple dimensions possible to prose and the serious writer:

> There are some things which cannot be learned quickly and time, which is all we have, must be paid heavily for their acquiring. They are the very simplest things and because it takes a man's life to know them the little new that each man gets from life is very costly and the only heritage he has to leave. (p. 192)

Using such knowledge with her "little *Ingles*," Pilar forces him to declare his limited belief in work. But she promises him that they will come to understand each other and that there is "a commencement of caring for everyone" (pp. 30, 92). These are the results of such knowledge at its very best. The word itself is transcendent in its ability to communicate these transcendental realities: "I like to talk. It is the only civilized thing we have. How otherwise can we divert ourselves?" (p. 98). This is a lesson Jordan masters when he later discloses his new belief that last words can last (p. 355).

Maria also has such knowledge, less spectacular, perhaps, but even more deep, more subtle, more spiritual, and more abiding. In her first sharing of bed with Robert Jordan, she says, "I loved you when I saw you today and I loved you always but I never saw you before. . ." (p. 73). And she knows the meaning of *la gloria*, the profound mystical and metaphysical experience of love, which even Jordan, though he denies that he is a mystic, has come to understand in two stages through her, and which he recognizes as a kind of knowing which even he cannot deny: "I am no mystic, but to deny it is as ignorant as though you denied the telephone. . ." (p. 380). He, who had denied the existence of luck, also comes to acknowledge its existence after this experience when he admits their indebtedness to that mysterious source.

Renata is graced with this kind of sensing and knowing in the lightest, most delicate way of all. She is even gifted with a mildly deprecating sense of humor about it all. She dances on the edges of its uncertainty, and yet she is as profoundly convinced by it and true to it as Pilar or Maria. Referring to the hopeless obsessiveness of their love and wondering if everyone suffers so much from that, she says of its "badness," "I know now. I know now and for keeps and for always. Is that the correct way to say it?" (*Across the River and into the Trees*, p. 89).

Renata's most profound experience of this kind of consciousness is expressed in the following passage:

> "Are there five corners to the world?"
> "I don't know," she said. "It sounded as though there were when I said it.
> And now we are having fun again, aren't we?" (p. 99)

This is certainly Hemingway's brightest and most cheerful expression of the superbly feminine theme of unknowing knowing derived from the Western metaphysical tradition. The tone only intensifies its conviction. It relates to women's sense of time, and of truth, and a similar but emotionally more sober expression of it will later illustrate how and why women, according to Hemingway, face death so openly and courageously.

Renata, too, is aware of and grateful for the luck and the sense of luck which is a part of this kind of human experience and knowledge:

> "We've had some luck."
> "Yes," the Colonel said. "Good and bad."
> "But it was all luck." (p. 232)

Her extraordinary percipience here easily embraces the merely apparent negative of the "bad."

Colonel Cantwell responds strongly to this kind of sensitivity and knowledge in Renata. By the end of the novel he has assimilated it, at least in part and imperfectly, as a control over his own impulsiveness and bitterness. On several occasions he describes his awareness of it in her: ". . . she is younger and older than hell; which is quite an old place" (p. 176). Talking to the portrait, he asks, "How do girls like you and she know so much so damn young and so beautiful?" (p. 178).

What he calls the static element in painting provokes in him that strange insight alloying him with her. A bit earlier, and long before his own assimilation of this quality in the act of sexual fondling, the first wrestling, the dark night of sense, the part of the Jacob vision in which the angel wounds the thigh of the manly wrestler, he plunged deeply into awesome recognition of this mode of perception:

> "My darling," he said. "My well beloved. Please."
> "No. Just hold me very tight and hold the high ground, too." (p. 153)

That strange moment in which she expresses the kind of knowledge which has assimilated his interest in the metaphysics of warfare to their own situation, loading it with the most profane and the most sacred meanings of love, draws from him a limited but progressive awareness of belief:

> The Colonel said nothing, because he was assisting, or had made an act
> of presence, at the only mystery that he believed in except the occasional brav-
> ery of man. (p. 153)

It is not necessary to treat each of the six qualities of Hemingway's feminique in detail. It is important to realize that given the first quality the others follow in a chain of cause and effect. They are metaphysical qualities and therefore often distinguishable in the same experiential phenomenon—an action, a statement, dialogue, or description. For that reason, some of the examples already given can be employed again in illustration of the other qualities. Some elaboration, however, of two of the most important qualities is necessary for completeness and conviction. These are the ability to face death, or truth, and the capacity for the possible.

With a sense of time or duration which goes beyond death, a sense which links woman's "always" with man's "now," the "now and at the hour of our death" of the Hail Mary, Hemingway's women have a dedication to truth which strips the mask of death from the face of life in order to free life and to strengthen and vitalize it. In the later novels this quality is developed not only in the descriptions and direct comment of the women but also, and perhaps most of all, in the assimilative reactions of the men in thought, word, and action.

Pilar's clairvoyance about the immediate presence of death is not to be confused with this quality. Even though she possesses foreknowledge with some anxiety, it does not diminish her ability to act courageously in the face of mortal danger. She will not push Jordan to acknowledge and accept what she knows in that exceptional way. To protect him, she even denies her own knowledge as "gypsy nonsense" (*For Whom the Bell Tolls*, p. 387). She strongly advises Maria that prudence is the better part of valor in this matter. But from her ordinary kind of knowledge of death comes her doctrine of acceptance, a kind of controlled surrender to the worst as well as the best of reality. Maria tells Jordan,

> "She [Pilar] said that nothing is done to oneself that one does not accept
> and that if I loved someone it would take it all away. I wished to die, you see."
> (p. 73)

After the first experience of *la gloria*, Jordan immediately faces the prospect of death. He discovers a concept of a full life in seventy hours which he tries to reject as nonsense, but he does not reject it because of further reflection on this previously unknown experience with Maria. A bit later he also acknowledges that this kind of love is not merely a reaction to the obvious dangers of guerrilla warfare: "But he did not believe that Maria had only been made by the circumstances" (p. 169). In fact, he discovers what she already knows, that death viewed in this way is a kind of hindrance, a mere obstacle to the continuity and intensity of life. "But when I am with Maria I love her so that I feel, literally, as though I would die and I never believed in that nor thought that it could happen" (p. 166). He is, of course, giving his own perception of the *"petite mors"* tradition and interpreting it in a unique understanding of its relationship to a sense of immortality. So he does again later, somewhat less perceptively, backing away from his own bitter thought about actual death when, after a less intense, more ordinary experience of the sexual relationship, he says: "With a man there is a difference" (p. 263).

In the lull after the climax of the avoided confrontation with El Sordo's pursuers and just before El Sordo's final engagement, Jordan admits that life has never meant much to him, but now he repents of joking about Kashkeen and himself and begins to insist with himself on truth before death:

> "I am alive and he is dead," Robert Jordan said. Then: what's the matter with you? he thought. Is that the way to talk? Does food make you that slap happy? What are you, drunk on onions? Is that all it means to you, now? It never meant much, he told himself truly. You tried to make it mean something, but it never did. There is no need to lie in the time that is left. (p. 289)

In the final night before the second experience of *la gloria*, when, because of her pain, Maria has to deny sex to Jordan, when he seeks the false surrender of make believe rather than the true surrender of acceptance, Maria forces him to face death with utter coolness and courage. Her first approach is oblique, asking him merely to talk about his work as a demolitions expert. She is rebuffed by his assertion that that would not be "intelligent" (p. 342). It is important to realize that her effort is cutting across the time of Jordan's nervous thinking generated in the loneliness of having finished all there was to do before dawn before joining Maria in the robe. Then he had thought of death, trying to buck himself up, led to it by the thought of his grandfather and of his father's suicide. He had even faced the possibility of a "hereafter" and denounced it: "Well, maybe we will all be together by tomorrow night. If there should be any such damn fool business as a hereafter, and I'm sure there isn't, he thought" (p. 338).

Maria will not long allow Jordan the luxury of his make believe. She begins indirectly again, cunningly putting him into the position of asking for the painful truth by teasing his curiosity and concern for her. Then she lets him have it with no holds barred:

> "I will not keep it from you then. The Pilar told me that we would all die tomorrow and that you know it as well as she does and that you give it no importance." (p. 345)

Jordan is shocked. The sweat of clammy fear erupts from him, and he curses Pilar and even Maria when she tries to continue. She allows him to retreat a bit into make believe, but now it is just lying for him and "all the luxury of acceptance was gone" (p. 345). That, of course, is false acceptance not founded on reality.

Soon Maria goes further and finally engages his attention fully in the real acceptance of the final stage of her brave strategy, making it clearly known that in the conduct of this healing provocation she has been steadily going against the advice of Pilar, the seemingly conventional wisdom of pretense. So that he might be proud of their marriage, she tells him of the brave deaths of her parents and of their courageous and profound last words. She tells the brutal story of her own treatment by the Fascists, she who could not listen to Pilar's earlier story of her worst day. Jordan is stirred to rage and tries to stop her, but she goes on to the possibility that they may never have children and to chide his contentment with this, to the hope of children for a better world, and to try to direct the energy of his rage at the true enemy. Only then, in the full blossom of truth, does she stop and accept him in marriage as he now does her.

What is the final effect on Jordan of this encounter with Hemingway's feminine ideal? He acknowledges the value of mystical knowledge. He also realizes that it creates a kind of brotherhood which gives importance to every human life, an importance of the individual he had never known before. He sums it all up in an important phrase of Spanish understatement which he had earlier admired when spoken by Anselmo. Now it verifies the great gift of a education given him by a woman: "I find life very interesting," he said to Maria (p. 381). He is now like Anselmo, and Pilar, and Maria, all very simple and very complicated—and very feminine.

Under the bridge several hours later, while laying the charges to destroy it and hearing Pilar and the others fighting, he, who could have no women with him in his work, is struck by a ironic thought which reveals much about what has happened to him:

> You're shaking like a Goddamn woman. What the hell is the matter with you? You're trying to do it too fast. I'll bet that Goddamn woman up above isn't shaking. That Pilar. Maybe she is too. She sounds as though she were in plenty trouble. She'll shake if she gets in enough. Like everybody bloody else. (p. 437)

It is, however, in his final moments that the feminine in him comes out fully. Then he makes that surrender he had often wished were possible in war, the final true acceptance. In the presence of an unknown being greater than he or Maria, he gives up the choice of suicide. In awareness of this presence as a voice within him and in full awareness of Maria and that her "always" and their "now" is one and will continue, he foregoes his own self-destruction and lives that life which is truly worth dying for. His surrender, the act of woman possible in all men, is a prayer:

> All right, he said. And he lay very quietly and tried to hold onto himself that he felt slipping away from himself as you feel snow starting to slip sometimes on a mountain slope, and he said, now quietly, then let me last until they come. (pp. 470–71)

That is why the last line of the book, the line which was also the first, and which has been twice repeated in the last few chapters, is now repeated for the last time with the significant addition of the word "heart": "He could feel his heart beating against the pine needle floor of the forest" (p. 471).

Toward the end of *Across the River and into the Trees*, Colonel Cantwell pronounces Renata champion. But long before that he has recognized and acknowledged her fighting spirit, her tenacious determination and endurance, and her gift of command. Not bad for one of the most *macho* of Hemingway characters.

Renata's approach to the moment of truth, to death, is, like Maria's, a three salient plan of attack: (1) to purge her Colonel of the frustration and bitterness of his long ministry of death; (2) to give him control and mastery of the latent talent of gentleness within him, a calm, quiet, but profoundly active acceptance of the mystery of man's apparently transient reality (and of his abuse even of that); and (3) to enlarge his sense of life before and beyond death. It is a battle of woman and man, youth and age, fought in the season of late fall and early winter when snow already covers the nearby mountains and the ducks fly south, fought in a city of a long tradition of fighters. It is a story which transforms the Christmas trees of Huertgen Forest and Passchendaele into a Christmas of the Colonel's own rebirth and an Easter resurrection, the "Pâques ou Trinité" which lies beyond this last, lost weekend. Neither her manner nor his submission to this campaign is as intense, or mystical, or marvelous as that of Maria and Jordan. But it is marvelous enough, and, perhaps, all the more marvelous for the restraint of its more relaxed understatement of realism in spite of the often noted and inescapable autobiographical blemishes.

If Cantwell is to accept and integrate in himself the mind and spirit of woman, then his teacher, Renata, as a woman must also integrate within herself the mind and heart of man. Her professed interest in war is, therefore, something more than merely a tactic or method of education. It is part of the education itself, its subject. Long after she has begun purging Cantwell of his bitterness about his personal defeats in the hierarchy of command, she insists on this educational approach of inferior and superior to encourage him to go on with the relief of his burden of a mind distorted by loss and evil. It is as if the angel of the Apocalypse sent to curse the world with the wormwood cast into its waters is also sent to cure the world by the very administration of that discipline of bitterness:

> "Will you tell me some happy things I can have for during the week and some more of war for my education?"
> "Let's skip war."
> "No. I need it for my education." (pp. 216–17)

The student now acknowledged as teacher also admits his need for education at this point, marking a significant step toward the humility necessary for the final stage of his enlightenment which begins at this point: "I do too," the Colonel said (p. 217). Soon he discovers that a crucial part of the lesson he is learning is that it is a lesson in penitence, in sorrow for sin, not just one's own personal sin but for the burden of sin shared by one's own humanity, a healing vision which paradoxically makes guilt bearable:

> "So we made the mucking breakthrough," the Colonel said, and now his
> head was turned to her head, and he was not lecturing; he was confessing.
> (p. 222)

Both the unusual semicolon and the ironic agreement of the detail under discussion, the "breakthrough," mark the importance in Hemingway's eyes of this development in his character's advance in self-awareness and wisdom. Later on, at the end of his account of war and its injustice on one's own side, he uses another peculiarly Christian word to identify finally the lesson he has learned and the healing he has received, if not perfectly yet, nevertheless in a continuing progression: "Then his contrition did not last" (p. 251). The lapse is only temporary and now insignificant.

Throughout this spiritual exercise of purging and controlling it is Renata's clear understanding and purpose in inducing it. She affirms her comprehension at two points early and late in the last stage of the process, clarifying it for the reader. Her first description of purpose also makes clear the importance of the early part of the process, part means, part end, which consists of the individual's and humanity's need to bring itself to terms with the truth, Hemingway's higher realism, Renata says:

> "Please don't be rough. Just tell me true and hold me tight and tell me
> true until you are purged of it; if that can be." (p. 225)

At that point Cantwell is still incapable of understanding the need for such a purgation: "I don't need to purge," he said (p. 225).

Later, when she is aware of his recognition and acceptance of this need, expressed to himself in terms of confessing and contrition, Renata delivers her most complete explanation of her esteem for this exercise. As part of the process she has implied that she is an intermediary in it, not a principal: "I am not an inquisitor; or whatever the female of inquisitor is" (p. 226). The emphasis here is squarely placed by Hemingway not only on the method of the process but on the feminine spirit of its administration and of its exercise. The final explanation makes clear Hemingway's sense of the femininity of method and purpose once again. It is for him essentially feminine to face the meaning of death. While women, as the passage points out, can fail to understand and appreciate men at war, his ideal woman can understand that in that failure or boredom lies a failure to understand that essential aspect of the spiritual life which John of the Cross has described as warfare. It is a failure in analogy, a failure in the masculinity essential to true femininity. The novel's references to the tragedy of Othello and the symbolism of Hemingway's choice of Venice as the locale of this novel are also clarified by this passage:

> "I'll tell you," the Colonel said. "But I don't want to hurt you."
>
> "You never hurt me. We are an old town and we had fighting men, always. We respect them more than all others and I hope we understand them a little. We also know they are difficult. Usually, as people, they are very boring to women."
>
> "Do I bore you?"
>
> "What do you think?" the girl asked.
>
> "I bore myself, Daughter."
>
> "I don't think you do, Richard. You would not have done something all your life if you were bored by it. Don't lie to me please, darling, when we have so little time."
>
> "I won't."
>
> "Don't you see you need to tell me things to purge your bitterness?"
>
> "I know I tell them to you."
>
> "Don't you know I want you to die with the grace of a happy death?"
> (pp. 239–40)

It is no easy task for the woman to teach this lesson. To teach it she must be as involved in that death of which she speaks as the student. But Hemingway's true woman is capable of paying that price. Neither his woman teacher nor the man who learns the lesson "go gentle into that good night."

The second salient point of Renata's strategy involves a discipline, a training in gentleness. There is no need to illustrate it here in detail. The book itself abounds with examples of her constant insistence on this trait. She knows that this discipline makes possible the achievement of the feminine goal and yet is paradoxically in its perfection part of the goal itself which is peace, a homely peace. Nor is she blind to the fact that harshness, or the opposite of gentility, is often needed, too, as a method, not a goal. She is sometimes very rough with her rough Richard, even rougher than he. The short months which she has, less than one year, are enough, however, to achieve her goal. At the end, after leaving her for the last time, when the less than satisfactory duck hunt moves Richard to rough, *macho* explosiveness in feeling and in thought, he restrains the normal bent he would have given to those ungentle impulses in thought, word, and deed: "But do not even think rough, he told himself. You have to be good now in every way until you say good-bye" (p. 268). Thus he had spoken at the beginning of their last meal together. But after the good-bye and after the hunt with the provocative guide when he starts to think of retaliation, he commands himself: "Stop that, he said to himself, and think about your girl. You do not want to kill anyone anymore; ever" (p. 291). Colonel Cantwell is finally absolved of Hemingway's greatest human sin.

Life is a series of spiritual ups and downs according to St. John of the Cross, like Jacob's ladder, a ladder of higher and higher forms of love. The thought of death is not a cheerful nor an easy thought even at its highest form. In pursuing her grand strategy of facing and preparing for death, Renata does not spare herself. Her intention is to convince Richard that death is not an end. The thought of death can expand the life before it and create the conviction in faith and hope of the life beyond it. It is man's and woman's most serious test of truth, but it is woman or a feminine attitude which best meets the test in surrender, acceptance, and hope.

Her first comment on death does not completely unmask it; it is cheerful and points to the enhancement of life by the possibility opened up by death. It is her comment on having five sons to send to the five corners of the world (p. 99). She amplifies the meaning of that statement later when she says that it is having this purpose of the five sons and the five corners of the world which truly excites woman, not the vanity and boredom of looking in mirrors, of making up, and of arranging hair. The vain life, she says,

> is not a life for a woman, or even a girl alone, who loves someone. When you want to be the moon and various stars and live with your man and have five sons, looking at yourself in the mirror and doing the artifices of a woman is not very exciting. (p. 118)

When Cantwell has made considerable progress under her tutelage and command, he returns to this thought, and it inspires him for a moment to challenge his own lack of faith, his agnosticism and fatalism:

> And why can't I have her and love her and cherish her and never be rude, nor bad, and have the five sons that go to the five corners of the world; wherever that is, I don't know. I guess the cards we draw are those we get. You wouldn't like to re-deal would you dealer? (p. 179)

He relapses into gloomy fatalism immediately, but even then his prayer is being answered. Life is being re-dealt to him—through Renata.

Another series of her comments on death contrast with the playful, mythopaic comment. They are rougher, more direct, more realistic, tougher, more suffused with pain and sorrow. But they also carry their own antidote, that of dedicated hope. We have already seen her comment about the goal of a happy death, the second of such comments. Earlier, pointing out that they cannot be married because of her Catholic belief in marriage, she had spoken of and he had replied to this far reaching concern of hers about the possibility created by the fact of death:

> "But I will love you, whatever that means, and you and I know what it means very well, as long as either of us is alive and after."
>
> "I don't think you can love very much after you, yourself, are dead," the Colonel said. . . .
>
> "I don't know whether you can either," the girl said. "But I will try. Don't you feel better to be loved?" (p. 128)

The Marvellian echo and flat contrast provide a ironic lightness for this heavy observation, adding to the lightness already present in the statement of Renata's brave spirit and probing curiosity and knowledge.

At his low point in these considerations, while Renata naps by his side, Cantwell invokes his recollection of a Bosch painting of death. He mocks death in his misery, but he also remarks that he, who had made a career of being able to mock anything of value, now feels strangely compelled to care about the regret and sorrow he now feels about his own approaching death (p. 254).

At their last meal Renata shares with him this dark side of death, but together they pull out of despondency with the resolve of hope, something he wouldn't have done before he truly knew that death had to be not only experienced but shared. This time he initiates the shared mood by asking a seemingly light question:

> "What happens to people that love each other?"
>
> "I suppose they have whatever they have, and they are more fortunate than others. Then one of them gets the emptiness forever."
>
> "I won't be rough," the Colonel said. "I could have made a rough response. But please don't have any emptiness."
>
> "I'll try," the girl said. "I've been trying ever since I woke up. I've been trying ever since we knew each other. . . ."
>
> "Keep on trying, daughter," the Colonel said. (pp. 271–72)

Without knowing it, he has joined her in the difficult journey of hope. Her low point has joined his, and an equal caring has lifted them both up the ladder of life, love, and hope.

Shortly thereafter in the course of the last supper or communion which comes after confession, they both reach a subdued summit in this spiritual and metaphysical process of unknowing knowing. The answer to all their questions is given in wry joke by both Richard and the *Gran Maestro* of the Gritti, the answer of Easter or Resurrection:

> "It is Saturday," she said. "And when is next Saturday?" (p. 273)

The wind is blowing in the wrong direction to bring cheerful odors from the kitchen, and as the next chapter will tell us, the trees are black and have lost their leaves early. Death is in the very physical atmosphere within which Richard responds to the question:

> "Next Saturday is a movable feast, daughter. Find me a man who can tell me about next Saturday."
> "You could tell me if you would."
> "I'll ask the *Gran Maestro*, maybe he knows. *Gran Maestro* when will next Saturday come?"
> "*A Paques ou à la Trinité,*" the *Gran Maestro* said. (p. 273)

Renata's encouragement to Richard to join her in belief and hope about the continuity of life is not completely answered, but it is to her satisfaction, for she presses no more, knowing Richard better than he knows himself.

The last good-bye keeps the questions open but sums up all her lessons in the mystical meaning of the word itself and in their unknowing knowing incantation of its inner meaning. Renata begins to cry, but she stops resolutely in her antipathy to the role of hysterical woman:

> "So now what?"
> "So now we stand up and kiss each other and say goodbye."
> "What's that?"
> "I don't know," the Colonel said. "I guess that is one of the things everybody has to figure out for themselves."
> "I'll try to figure it."
> "Just take it as easy as you can, Daughter."
> "Yes," the girl said. "In the vehicle without the shock absorbers."
> "You were tumbril bait from the start."
> "Can't you do anything kindly?"
> "I guess not. But I've tried."
> "Please keep on trying. That's all the hope we have."
> "I'll keep on trying. . . ."
> "I'd rather take the displaced engine boat if you don't mind."

"Mind?" the Colonel said. "Not me. I only give orders and obey orders.
I don't mind. Good-bye, my dear, lovely, beautiful."

"Good-bye," she said. (pp. 276–77)

Has Cantwell learned her lesson? From this point of view, he has. Most critics make a secular decision in their interpretation of Hemingway's meaning and intent. This view goes all the way with his early insistence that if, as an artist, one is going to paint Christ, then one had better believe in Christ. These last works are paintings of Christ and the Virgin. They must be interpreted in terms of their own vision which was one of faith. The trick lies in understanding how the apparently secular conceals in John of the Cross's unknowing knowing the gift of faith as it is sometimes given to modern agnostic man within the very trappings of his own agnosticism and disbelief, and in seeing the clues of ironic presentation which he so carefully provides. After Colonel Cantwell's departure from Renata, there are several of these critical secular-religious orientations. The man who did not believe in hell now believes in heaven. The fatalist who believed that life is biologically and statistically determined now believes in luck or Providence. This luck, he recognizes, has totally changed his life. A totally different view of life which reaches beyond death has been given him even though he cannot fully come to terms with it or even understand it.

He calls the whole sequence of events which make up his love for Renata a miracle:

> So that was that, and maybe it was that day or maybe it was another that made the miracle. You never knew, he thought. There was the great miracle and he had never consciously implemented it. Nor, he thought, you son of a bitch, did you ever oppose it. (p. 288)
>
> . . . .
>
> So he had no shooting and he thought without intention, trying to find what had made it at the first. He knew he did not deserve it and he accepted it and he lived by it, but he sought, always, to understand it. (p. 282)

Here he invokes the key word also used by Hemingway in the end of *For Whom the Bell Tolls* to signify the God or the Providence in his unknowing knowing way who gave him this luck or good fortune so miraculously at the very end of his life:

> Very rough trade, he thought. Loving and leaving. People can get hurt at it.
>
> Who gave you a right to know a girl like that?
>
> Nobody, he answered. But Andrea introduced me to her.
>
> But how could she love a sad son of a bitch like you?
>
> I do not know, he thought truly. I truly do not know.

> He did not know, among other things, that the girl loved him because he had never been sad one waking morning of his life; attack or no attack. He had experienced anguish and sorrow. But he had never been sad in the morning.
>
> They make almost none like that, and the girl, although she was a young girl, knew one when she saw one. (p. 289)

The *nobody* refers to the bodiless spirit known in the West as God. The repetition of that key word at the end of the novel is not accidental. In the moment before Richard's death, he recalls this last good-bye:

> You have said good-bye to your girl and she has said good-bye to you. That is certainly simple. (p. 306)

Cantwell is putting his last affairs in order with the clipped, methodical manner of the military man who has simplified so much of life, but Hemingway and his reader know that it is not that simple. We catch the allusion to the literal meaning of *good-bye*, as Hemingway intends, God be with you, and all that that means about world without end.

At the last moment, when the last attack begins, Richard, now truly the lion-hearted, the Griffin personification of Dante's Christ, confesses positively, in a concealed form of gratitude which denies all determinism and opens the heart, the great good luck or the God who, according to Christian theology, denies nothing to whoever does what is possible:

> Three strikes is out, he thought, and they gave me four. I've always been a lucky son of a bitch. (p. 307)

Between the second and final blows of the heart attack which follow, he recalls General Jackson's last words on the occasion of his death, "let us cross over the river and rest under the shade of the trees" (p. 307). Colonel Cantwell has what Renata had sought for him—peace and the grace of a happy death. The three attacks link him with the three hours of Good Friday which celebrate the death of Christ, the falls and risings of the Stations of the Cross, and the strange "now" of the Hail Mary linked with the "forever" of the Our Father. He closes the door of the car, and he gets into the back seat before the final blow, "carefully and well" (p. 307). The Cantwell who so often couldn't finally could. The man who regarded religion as cant finds his boat canting well on the last rough voyage over the last Grand Canal.

Some have pointed to the passage in which the Colonel seems to deny becoming a Christian in the end as verification of that position as a fact. But does that passage truly deny religion? In the light of all that has been said, one would think not. It is rather an ironic reflection on what he has already become. After

all, the initial "R.C." on the flask which Renata has given him means not only
Richard Cantwell but Roman Catholic:

> You going to run as a Christian? You might give it an honest try. She would like
> you better that way. Or would she? I don't know, he said frankly. I honest to
> Christ don't know.
>
> Maybe I will get Christian toward the end. Yes, he said, maybe you will.
> Who wants to make a bet on that?
>
> "You want to bet on that?" he asked the calling duck. But she was looking
> up at the sky behind him and had commenced her small chuckling talk. (p. 291)

Hemingway may be alluding here to Pascal's Great Wager, and he may be invok-
ing St. Paul who describes the Christian in terms which link him interiorly with
the feminine: "But the fruit of the Spirit is love, joy, peace, long-suffering, gentleness, goodness, faith, meekness, temperance: against such there is no law"
(Gal. v. 22–23).

What should be clear now is how profoundly Hemingway, the supposedly
macho author, is concerned about the nature, the meaning, and the complex but
simple relationship of both the feminine and the masculine in universal terms.
One cannot do or be without the other. The complement engrosses him.

His attention to the masculine is not precisely conventional, but his articu-
lated, detailed, theoretic, and schematic presentation of the feminine is new,
unconventional, and most of all rewardingly provocative and remarkably pro-
phetic. How many today are approaching and sharing elements of his vision of a
strong, new, and enduring unity of the sexes. Like the feminists, he knew that this
vision could only be achieved by an exceptional attention to and emphasis on the
feminine to discover its real and potential significance, not only in personal but in
public life. Just as the recent awareness of the self is graduating into a new
concept of community, so his study of the feminine preceded, though often muted
and misunderstood, the feminist awareness initiated by Betty Friedan. Like the
feminists he rejects any goddess on a pedestal notions in favor of a deeply chal-
lenging, frequent, and not painless approach to a genuine understanding of the
true reality and possibility of the feminine. No weak notions these, and certainly
not for the faint of heart either masculine or feminine. Contemporary psychological and social thought seem now to be taking great strides precisely along these
lines, strides that would never have been taken without the awareness generated
by the women's movement or the intellectual feminine strength explosively
released by that movement.

Perhaps the 20th Century owes to Hemingway, in part, what the 19th owed,
in part, to Ibsen, and in a lesser way to John Stuart Mill. It is a supportive role,

but its ultimate goal is a true, proportional equality, a participating feminine role before which older concepts of inferiority and superiority will be totally demolished. It is fascinating to think that one who enjoyed the universal endearment of the name "Papa" and who referred to Marlene Dietrich and Renata as "Daughter" might ultimately be seen as a David who slew the Goliath of patriarchism and paternalism. The man who wrote *In Our Time* is in but not of our time; he is a man for all times.

HEMINGWAY'S POETRY:
ANGRY NOTES OF
AN AMBIVALENT OVERMAN

NICHOLAS GEROGIANNIS

I seek another word for music, I always
find only the word Venice. . . .

My soul, a stringed instrument
sang to itself, invisibly touched,
a secret gondola song,
quivering with iridescent happiness,
—Did anyone listen to it?

Friedrich Nietzsche, Ecce Homo[1]

THERE IS ANGER IN HEMINGWAY'S POETRY, but it is not the anger of an individual voice; this is the voice of an author unleashing the anger that is inherently part of his literary heritage. The messages in the poems are concentrated notes, which are merely a part of the more persistent anger that characterizes the fiction.[2] At times, Hemingway's anger is turned upon himself, and the poems reflect the depression caused by the author's ambivalence. At other times, his anger is directed at the world in which he lives. The assumptions which motivate him are those of an egoist; the judgments are those of a Nietzschean overman.

James Joyce identified egoist writing by making an important distinction. In his biography of Joyce, Richard Ellmann recounts an exchange that took place in 1908 between the author and his brother Stanislaus. Joyce's outburst is aimed at the psychological mode of writing:

Reprinted with permission from *College Literature* special Hemingway issue, as published in book form as *Ernest Hemingway: The Papers of a Writer*, ed. Bernard Oldsey (New York: Garland Publishing, Inc., 1981), pp. 73–87.

257

"Psychologist! What can a man know but what passes inside his own head?" Stanislaus replied, "Then the psychological novel is an absurdity, you think? and the only novel is the egomaniac's? D'Annunzio's?" Joyce replied, "I said as much in my pamphlet."[3]

Joyce is referring to his 1901 essay "The Day of the Rabblement," which is a broadside against Irish parochialism. In this essay he lectures that until the artist "has freed himself from the mean influences about him," he is not an artist at all.[4] The examples that Joyce cites of the new literature are Flaubert's *Madame Bovary* and Gabriele D'Annunzio's *Il Fuoco* (*The Flame,* 1900).

A writer of egoist fiction employs many of the literary devices that the psychological novelist uses. However, there are distinguishing qualities. First, egoist writing is close in time and subject to the surface of life; this gives it a deceptive autobiographical quality. But to the egoist author experience is a fusion of the events of his own life with those things he has heard about, and those he has read. Thus his imagination places him within the living fictions created around his inspirations. Finally, following the precepts of Nietzsche, the literary goal of the egoist writer is not altruistic; although the egoist does seek to teach the community of sympathetic souls, his goal is to influence future generations. The egoist is an artist in the process of becoming, and he is usually a personality who impresses his legend upon his age. It is within this tradition that Hemingway belongs, along with Dante, Bryon, Stendhal, Flaubert, Turgeniev, Nietzsche, D'Annunzio, Joyce, and Pound.

Hemingway's path to Nietzsche is direct. Noel Fitch has documented the fact that on 4 May 1926 Hemingway left Shakespeare & Co. with James Gibbons Huneker's *Egoists: A Book of Supermen.* The central figures in Huneker's study are Stendhal and Nietzsche; Hemingway admired Stendhal, but on this occasion we must assume that he was interested in Nietzsche because, on 5 May, he returned to 12 rue de L'Odeon and checked out *Thus Spake Zarathustra.*[5]

Nietzsche scholar and translator Walter Kaufmann explains the idea of Nietzsche's hero: "The Overman is the man who has overcome himself; the passionate man who is the master of his passions; the creator who excels in both passion and reason and is able to employ his powers creatively."[6]

From this we see that there are many points where Nietzsche and Hemingway meet. Nietzsche built a powerful philosophy around the anger of his overman creator; Hemingway's work is an echo of that anger and that philosophy. Nietzsche and Hemingway would hardly have disagreed, for instance, on their feelings toward scholars. Hemingway probably approved of the martial quality with which Nietzsche imbued Zarathustra's aesthetics. Without question, Nietzsche's insistence on the idea of eternal recurrence was shared by Hemingway. He adopted Nietzsche's idea that a man and a woman could become one in a relationship—a sort of "over-couple." Most important, in his fiction and poetry, Hemingway dramatized and defended Zarathustra's insistence on the overman's right to "free death."[7]

All of this contains possibilities, but I would not presume to apply Nietzsche's philosophy to Hemingway's poetry, much less to his fiction and his life, if it were not for the discoveries which led me to consider Nietzsche in the first place.

By the time Hemingway encountered Zarathustra he had already been deeply influenced by a Nietzsche disciple, the Mediterranean overman—Gabriele D'Annunzio. Hemingway's poem "D'Annunzio" (p. 28) is a three-line verse that is meaningless when considered by itself; however, as I searched through Hemingway's writings, I was surprised to find that there are a number of overt and covert references to this Italian writer.

D'Annunzio was born in 1863, in Pescara, Italy. He established his reputation as a premier literary figure with a series of novels which particularly celebrated his relationships with aristocratic women. He was idolized. He became a figure very much like Lord Byron. In the mid 1890s he was deeply influenced by Richard Wagner and Nietzsche. He introduced the theme of the overman into Italy by adopting the principles of Nietzsche's creation to the Mediterranean man. In 1895, in Venice, he began his most celebrated love affair, with Eleonora Duse, the actress who was Sarah Bernhardt's only rival. D'Annunzio fused Nietzsche's philosophy, Wagner's influence, and the events of his relationship with Duse into his most famous novel, *The Flame*. Probably in 1918, but no later than 1920, Hemingway read *The Flame*.[8]

During the Great War D'Annunzio was the most famous man in Italy. In his critical biography *The Poet as Superman*, Anthony Rhodes summarizes D'Annunzio's military experience:

> His superiors soon lost trace of him and his exploits. . . . D'Annunzio delighted in a kind of individual enterprise in which, together with some chosen Ulyssean companions in a motor-boat, he would glide into an Austrian harbour by night, and fire off torpedoes, at shipping or at the shore. . . . Officially a commissioned officer in the army, he adopted on his own authority a naval title *Comandante*. . . . He fought in the air, on the sea, on the land. . . . His theory was that fear is natural to the body, and that courage to control it belongs to the mind.[9]

Obviously, there was much in D'Annunzio's style as a warrior for Hemingway to have admired, but there was also much about D'Annunzio that he rejected. In the four pages in *Across the River and into the Trees* that are devoted to D'Annunzio,[10] we find passages that lead to extraordinary relationships between the writings and lives of these two men. In Hemingway's Venetian novel, Colonel Cantwell acknowledges that with D'Annunzio "it was always the same appearances."[11] And the Colonel offers a qualified homage: ". . . Lieutenant Colonel D'Annunzio, writer and national hero, certified and true if you must have heroes, and the Colonel did not believe in heroes. . . ."[12]

As Hemingway moves Cantwell through Venice toward his rendezvous with Renata, he sends the reader an important message through his Colonel's thoughts and words. Cantwell is riding in a gondola past the house where D'Annunzio and Duse had lived. His remarks to his driver, Jackson, hold no qualifications for D'Annunzio as a writer:

> "Jackson," he said, "that small villa on the left belonged to Gabriele D'Annunzio, who was a great writer."
>
> "Yes, sir," said Jackson, "I'm glad to know about him. I never heard of him."
>
> "I'll check you out on what he wrote if you ever want to read him," the Colonel said. "There are some fair English translations."
>
> "Thank you, sir," said Jackson. "I'd like to read him anytime I have time. He has a nice practical looking place. What did you say the name was?"
>
> "D'Annunzio," the Colonel said. "Writer."
>
> He added to himself, not wishing to confuse Jackson, nor to be difficult, as he had been with the man, several times that day, writer, poet, national hero, phraser of the dialectic of Fascism, macabre egotist, aviator, commander, or rider, in the first of the fast torpedo attack boats, Lieutenant Colonel of Infantry without knowing how to command a company, nor a platoon properly, the great, lovely writer of *Notturno* whom we respect, and jerk.[13]

The key phrase is "the great, lovely writer of *Notturno* whom we respect."

D'Annunzio wrote *Notturno*[14] in 1916 at his home in Venice while he was recuperating from a serious eye injury received in an airplane crash. In this lyrical memoir the author recalls his relationship with Duse; he exhibits a rare sense of remorse over having lost this greatest of all his lovers. He sentimentally recounts his military exploits with his comrades, and he recalls the death during battle of his closest wartime friends. He reflects on his life.

Notturno is written by a man in his fifties, a writer-turned-warrior, in pain and preparing himself to die while remembering his past. In spirit alone, D'Annunzio's memoir is close enough to *Across the River and into the Trees* to be accepted as the prototype for Hemingway's novel. But there is more.

The central female figure in *Notturno* is D'Annunzio's daughter—Renata. She grew up adoring D'Annunzio, and prepared herself to serve him just as the heroines serve the heroes in his novels. Renata's sacrificing spirit pervades *Notturno* and constantly brings the author hope.

But Hemingway's Renata is not merely a fictional projection designed by the author to link himself to an old hero, and *Across the River and into the Trees* is not merely Hemingway's *Notturno*. Hemingway's heroine, like her namesake, nurses her wounded hero and guides him through his ordeal. But Hemingway created his Renata by fusing D'Annunzio's daughter to D'Annunzio's fictional representation of his most celebrated mistress; Hemingway's Renata possesses the wisdom, sacrificing spirit, and erotic personality of the heroine of *The Flame*, La Foscarina, who is a thinly-disguised persona for Eleonora Duse. Thus Hemingway achieved the satisfaction of entering a lyrical and erotic myth. Cantwell's thoughts reflect this romantic projection:

> But now he was passing the house where the poor beat-up old boy had lived with his great, sad, and never properly loved actress, and he thought of her wonderful hands, and her so transformable face, that was not beautiful, but that gave you all love, glory, and delight and sadness; and of the way the curve of her fore-arm could break your heart, and he thought, Christ they are dead and I do not know where either one is buried even. But I certainly hope they had fun in that house.[15]

Most of Cantwell's thoughts are of the woman, and his memory of Eleonora Duse is remarkable for its sympathetic insight.

The structure of *Across the River and into the Trees* parallels in many respects the structure of *The Flame*. It is important to note that the heroes of both novels define themselves through references to historical figures. (D'Annunzio's hero, Stelio Effrena, is imbued with the author's sense of himself as the heir to Dante; naturally, Dante is prominent in Hemingway's novel.) Both strong men, D'Annunzio's Stelio and Hemingway's Richard, are baptised in the font of experience and art—that font is Venice. In *The Flame*, Stelio pays homage to his spiritual master, Wagner, by stopping his gondola and placing flowers before the dying man's door; in *Across the River and into the Trees*, Cantwell rides in his gondola past D'Annunzio's door, remembers, and offers his best wishes across time.

There is an important turnabout between the characters of the two novels. D'Annunzio's novel is about a love affair between an older woman and a younger man; Hemingway's novel is about an older man and a younger woman. D'Annunzio's hero and Hemingway's heroine play similar roles in their respective novels; both are young people who learn from their older lovers, and they envy them their experience. Also, the roles of the two older characters,

D'Annunzio's Foscarina and Hemingway's Cantwell, are similar. Cantwell shares with Foscarina (Duse) a deep symbolic association with Venice, a history of pain and pleasure, and a majestic sadness.

Duse, or at least Foscarina of *The Flame*, must have left a deep impression on Hemingway's youthful imagination in 1918. Duse was six years older than D'Annunzio; the author of *The Flame* continuously reminds the reader of the age difference between Stelio and Foscarina in order to dramatize his hero's power over this erotic and experienced woman. Hemingway could not have missed applying this to his "affair" with Agnes von Kurowsky. His romantic remembrances of his time in Italy may have been influenced by *The Flame*.[16] Agnes was seven years older than Hemingway. Katy Smith, with whom he had an ambiguous relationship in Chicago, was also seven years older than he was. Hadley Richardson was eight years older. We must wonder whether the conquest of an older woman had not become a romantic ideal for him, a D'Annunzian ideal.

Foscarina (Duse) has qualities which remind us of Catherine Barkley and *A Farewell to Arms*. In 1929, F. Scott Fitzgerald suggested this same point in a letter to Hemingway:

> You are seeing him Frederic in a sophisticated way as now you see yourself then but you're still seeing her as you did in 1917 through a 19-year-old's eyes—in consequence unless you make her a bit fatuous occasionally the contrast jars— either the writer is a simple fellow or she is Elenora [sic] Duse disguised as a Red Cross nurse.[17]

Fitzgerald had read the typescript of *A Farewell to Arms*, and he sent Hemingway a not entirely welcome set of criticisms and suggestions. In this case, Fitzgerald made a rather fine critical leap with his insight about Catherine Barkley and Duse (one that possibly could have been made only by another novelist).

Foscarina (Duse) feels "a great solitude," a separateness from others. During moments when her terror of loneliness and death overwhelm her, she is driven further within herself and she struggles against her lover. Wherever the lovers go, Foscarina is associated with statues, which are "witnesses to her own decay."[18] Eventually, she attempts to lose herself in a sense of oneness with the hero.

Foscarina's past loves and mystery appeal to the hero of *The Flame*, who dreams of "extraordinary promiscuities."[19] Their affair begins quickly. But Foscarina draws Stelio close to her because she discovers "his secret need of believing and confiding."[20] The heroine's previous affairs and experiences have been annulled (although they occasionally seem to bother the hero). Through her love for Stelio, Foscarina recovers her "carnal power." She offers her lover her "girlhood's dream intact, the dream of Juliet."[21] Like Eleonora Duse, Foscarina had played the part of Juliet when she was fourteen, and from that mystical evening in her par* her "destiny seemed to be getting mixed up with the destiny of the Veronese maiden."[22] To consummate her love for Stelio she asks only one thing: "A child by you."[23]

D'Annunziᴑ defines the overman's woman as "a good and faithful instrument at the service of genius, a strong, willing companion."[24] This portrait of the overman's lover describes many of Hemingway's heroines; this idealized image— a sacrificing spirit linked to an erotic sensibility—caused him trouble. But I believe that Eleonora Duse's myth, through D'Annunzio's fictional heroine, was the inspiration for Hemingway's ideal woman. His romantic heroines— Catherine, Maria, Renata—are women with experience, and they are good sexual mates for his heroes, who have "a secret need for believing and confiding."

The poems which deal with Hemingway's relationships with women reveal a man who compromises his ideal of independence in order to satisfy his complex vulnerability and his needs for domesticity; repeatedly this leads him to personal failure and remorse. At first, a woman's sense of freedom appealed to Hemingway as it did to D'Annunzio. The Dionysian "Lines to a Young Lady on Her Having Very Nearly Won a Vögel" contains the D'Annunzian image of the "two sleepy birds" as background to the woman dancing with "pagan grace" (p. 33). But following the preliminary enticement, things become complex. The woman in "Bird of Night" (p. 36) is a predator/lover, much like Foscarina who is described as a "bird of prey." In this poem, the sense of erotic sanctuary is achieved through a D'Annunzian mixture of strong nature and sexual images. The man escapes from solitude beneath the "pinions" of his "bird of night" much like Frederic Henry seeks his sanctuary beneath the tent of Catherine's hair. There is pain in this kind of love. Colonel Cantwell feels "how close life comes to death when there is ecstasy."[25]

Hemingway dramatizes this intimately in "Killed Piave—July 8—1918," which links the date of his wounding to the image of a nocturnal lover who is described as "A dull, cold, rigid bayonet/On my hot-swollen, throbbing soul" (p. 35). However, in other poems written in Chicago during 1920–1921, the city inhibits sensuality. Hemingway's Dionysian dreams were complicated by his domestic impulses. In "Night comes with soft and drowsy plumes. . . " (p. 31) and "At night I lay with you. . . "(p.32) we sense a prelude to domesticity. In "On Weddynge Gyftes" (p. 38), an exaggerated and ironic statement on antiquated wedding rituals, he feels conformity and domesticity closing in on him. The voice in the facetious "I'm off'n wild wimmen. . . " (p. 57) is howling toward domesticity.

In a sharp brief scene early in *The Flame* D'Annunzio characterizes domestic bliss as an anesthetic condition for those who are unconscious and dumb.[26] His hero prefers the drama of his affair with his "carnal mistress." As D'Annunzio seems to interpret Nietzsche, after lovers achieve their sense of oneness, the man is free, carnally, to move on. This is what happens in *The Flame*, and this is what D'Annunzio did countless times throughout his life. Hemingway used death as a device to end the oneness achieved by his lovers in *A Farewell to Arms* and *For Whom the Bell Tolls*. At other times in his fiction, as in his life, matters were not so conveniently arranged. In the poem "Sequel," written about the time Ernest left Hadley, indecision has turned into self-pity: "So if she dies/And if you write about it/Being a writer and a shit/Dulling it so you sleep again at night" (p. 91). "We leave them all quite easily/When dislike overcomes our love" (p. 121), Hemingway writes in "Black-Ass Poem After Talking to Pamela Churchill." "Travel Poem" (p. 124) also reflects the dark side of a relationship when domesticity is felt to be an irritant. D'Annunzio consciously and successfully acted out his Dionysian roles; he left them all quite easily. Hemingway's rather fantastic bragging about his sexual exploits suggests that at times he may have envied D'Annunzio's erotic life.

Cantwell reflects on D'Annunzio as a warrior and a lover. D'Annunzio "had moved through the different arms of the service as he had moved in and out of the arms of different women. All the arms were pleasant that D'Annunzio served with and the mission was fast and easily over, except the infantry."[27] The repetition and double usage of the world "arms" should attract our attention, because by this point in *Across the River and into the Trees* Hemingway has made other plays on worlds. After all, Cantwell, through his memorial service at the spot where he was wounded in World War I, has been linked to Hemingway and to the hero of *A Farewell to Arms*. The Colonel's thoughts, through a reference to D'Annunzio, form another link between Hemingway's Italian novels:

> And the Colonel remembered one time when he had stood, commanding a platoon of assault troops, while it was raining in one of the interminable winters, when the rain fell always; or at least, always when there were parades or speeches to the troops, and d'Annunzio. . . looking thirty hours dead, was shouting, "Morire non è basta," and the Colonel, then a lieutenant, had thought, "What the muck more do they want of us?"[28]

This sounds like a scene which Frederic Henry describes in *A Farewell to Arms*:

> I was always embarrassed by the words sacred, glorious, and sacrifice and the expression in vain. We had heard them, sometimes standing in the rain

almost out of earshot, so that only the shouted words came through, and had read them, on proclamations. . . [29]

The patriotic oration delivered during an "interminable winter" sounds like the occasion in November 1917 when D'Annunzio addressed the army at Piave.[30] It was a memorable scene which Hemingway could have heard about when he arrived in the region seven months later. On that occasion D'Annunzio stirred the simple hearts of his audience by applying religious symbolism and images to the task that the soldiers faced. In June 1918 an American public information officer asked D'Annunzio to write a poem in salute to the Fourth of July.[31] To commemorate Americans' involvement in the war D'Annunzio wrote a sixty-stanza ode "All' America in Armi" ("To America in Arms"); the poem was translated into English by B. Harvey Carroll, American Consul at Venice, and it was published in Milan's *Corriere della Sera* on 4 July 1918, four days before Hemingway was wounded. This may be one of the "proclamations" that Frederic Henry had read. "To America in Arms" is filled with words that he finds "obscene." When Frederic says his farewell to arms, he is declaring his freedom from the sentiments contained in D'Annunzio's poem.

Hemingway's poem "To Good Guys Dead" also bitterly denounces the patriotic sentiments and heroic words that only resulted in dead soldiers: "Patriotism,/Democracy,/Honor—/Words and phrases,/They either bitched or killed us" (p. 47). "Champs d'Honneur" depicts a view of the Great War that is far different from D'Annunzio's heroic style: "Soldiers smother in a ditch;/Choking through the whole attack" (p. 27). "Shock Troops" (p. 43) defines the difference between jovial fresh recruits and veterans. "Riparto d'Assalto" (p. 46) presents a contrast between the sexual fantasies of a non-combatant lieutenant and an ambulance full of mortally wounded Arditi. "Arsiero, Asiago. . . " (p. 49) is about "all the places where men died that nobody ever heard about."[32] "All armies are the same. . . " (p. 42) describes the men who are entrapped by the war; there is little sense of D'Annunzian adventure in it for them.

Although Hemingway reacted against D'Annunzio's easy language of war, he evidently embraced D'Annunzio's legend and the forms he used to achieve it. Gabriele D'Annunzio was fifty-two years old when Italy entered the war. He was a free lance, a legendary figure who believed in himself. An impressionable eighteen when he arrived in Italy, Hemingway's youthful personality was influenced by D'Annunzio's style of martial romanticism. Much of D'Annunzio's poetry, like his "To a Torpedo-boat in the Adriatic,"[33] was written in honor of his military exploits and for the men who served with him in his often unauthorized adventures. But that was World War I, and D'Annunzio was in the Italian army.

In World War II, the American army in Europe had little patience with a middle-aged writer's extracurricular activities in the business of war. Hemingway was out of his time. His attempt at a D'Annunzian adventure in the Caribbean aboard the *Pilar* ended with a whimper. Before he dramatized the experience in *Islands in the Stream*, he lamented his fate in "First Poem to Mary in London": "His boat is in the faraway sea. His people are dispersed and his armaments surrendered to the proper authorities. Duly receipted and accounted for" (p. 103). Although Hemingway's heroes reject D'Annunzio's language, Hemingway embraces and defends the concepts of honor and courage in his World War II poems.

Long before Hemingway found himself out of time in his last war, he reacted to threats from other enemies—critics and scholars. He reacted sharply, in a typically Nietzschean fashion. In his story-essay "A Natural History of the Dead" Hemingway imagines "indecorous" deaths for Humanist critics, these "children of decorous cohabitation."[34] He had considered the same group in "Poem, 1928":

> They say it's over
> The need, now, is for order
> Not for substance
> For piety
> We must be full of grace, or on the way there,
> Our works must lead to something,
> Morally instructive, dull, but stemming from
> the classics
> Which mostly dealt, if I remember,
> With incest, rapes, and wars
> And dirty stories
> My Ovid, James, where is it got to—(p. 95)

Hemingway was reacting to what he sensed to be an academic attempt to reduce the experiences of his generation to an abstraction. Zarathustra's words on his enemies, the scholars, must have given Hemingway joy: "I have freedom and the air over the fresh earth; rather would I sleep on ox-hides than on their decorums and respectabilities."[35] Hemingway concludes "Poem, 1928" with a Nietzschean denunciation:

> We have something that cannot be taken from us by an
>   article
> Nor abolished by a critical agreement of Professors

> The searchers for order will find that there is a certain
> > discipline in the acceptance of experience.
> They may, that is;
> They rarely find out anything they cannot read in
> > books or articles
> But if we last and are not destroyed
> And we are durable because we have lasted. We do
> > not destroy easily.
> We'll write the books.
> They will not read them
> But their children may
> If they have children. (p. 96)

Hemingway's argument is weak and abstract because of its bluntness. In order to understand this clash between two systems of value we need the egoist voice of Ezra Pound:

> Christ follows Dionysius,
> Phallic and ambrosial
> Made way for macerations;
> Caliban casts out Ariel.[36]

Dionysius represents the highest form of faith for the egoist/overman. Kaufmann explains that to Nietzsche, Dionysius "represents passion controlled and creatively employed as opposed to the negation of the passions, of the body and of the world."[37] But self-overcoming is a challenge, not a prediction; whoever chooses the way of the overman creator chooses a lonely path. In *The Birth of Tragedy* and *Beyond Good and Evil*, Nietzsche explains that ambiguity is part of the very nature of the Dionysian artist. In a letter to his sister, he alludes to his own life, saying the overman must "strike new paths, fighting the habitual, experiencing the insecurity of independence and the frequent wavering of one's feelings and even one's conscience. . . ."[38] Like the character in "Chapter VII" of *In Our Time*, the persona in Hemingway's poem "Chapter Heading" seems to believe in Nietzsche during the day and Christ during the night:

> For we have thought the longer thoughts
> > And gone the shorter way.
> And we have danced to devils' tunes,
> > Shivering home to pray;
> To serve one master in the night,
> > Another in the day. (p. 34)

D'Annunzio announced the principle of self-reliance for the overman creator in his poem *Maia*:

> You must know you are the lone one of your species,
>   For in your march through life you are alone,
> Alone at the last supreme moment,
>   Alone you are the strongest friend you have.[39]

Hemingway passes on this idea to Adriana Ivancich in "Lines to a Girl 5 Days After Her 21st Birthday." His echo of Kipling—"She travels the fastest/Who travels alone" (p. 125)—underscores his message to Adriana that the artist's life is perverted and weakened by relationships; there is decay in contacts. What is important is the creator's sense of himself, of his overcoming through hard work. Hemingway challenges the young artist to "Live alone and like it/Like it for a day" (p. 125). When she misunderstands his meaning, his clarification defines the personal relationships of every true overman artist: "But I will not *be* alone, angrily she said, / Only in your heart, he said, Only in your head" (pp. 125–26). He accepts her right to be superior, but he urges her to go beyond argument to action—to work and to struggle. But above all, he tells her, "Please *do* it your own way" [emphasis Hemingway's].

> Trade bed for a pencil
> Trade sorrow for a page
> No work it out your own way
> Have good luck at your age. (p. 126)

He could have added Zarathustra's words to the creator: "But the worst enemy you can encounter will always be you, yourself; you lie in wait for yourself in caves and woods,"[40]

Zarathustra counsels us to "Remain faithful to the earth, and do not believe those who speak to you of otherworldly hopes."[41] "Eternal recurrence," writes Kaufmann, ". . . is an antithesis to the Christian conception of time and history."[42] Nietzsche teaches us that for man, to overcome his human self, to become overman, he must have the guidance of a model, an "educator." The passing on, from generation to generation, of the challenge to become overman is part of what Nietzsche calls "eternal recurrence." Nietzsche looked to Wagner; D'Annunzio looked to Wagner and Nietzsche; Joyce looked to Flaubert and D'Annunzio; Hemingway looked to D'Annunzio, Pound, and Joyce. D'Annunzio concludes *The Flame* with Wagner's death and a speech by his hero that sounds like a modern sequel to *Ecclesiastes*; immediately following, Stelio leaves to accompany the hero's casket back to Germany. Hemingway's faith in the earth is legend; however, it is still surprising to many people that he was an "educator." He was well aware of his role. No other writer of this century, except Pound perhaps, set out as consciously as Hemingway did to influence the sensibilities of the children in the coming generations. I know only that in May 1926 Hemingway walked out of Shakespeare and Company carrying *Thus Spake Zarathustra*, and that he kept the book until September; however, the more I learn about Nietzsche's book the more I am convinced that Hemingway's fictions are dramatizations of Zarathustra's teachings, and Hemingway's life was that of an ambivalent overman.

Now we must recall Zarathustra's final lesson to his children: get along without me.

After the flame has been passed, all that is left is the wish for "a worthy end."[43] "Many die too late, and a few die too early. The doctrine still sounds strange: 'Die at the right time!' "[44] Thus, Zarathustra counsels us on "free death." In *The Flame*, the dying of Wagner casts a spell over the entire story. D'Annunzio's hero is established as Wagner's spiritual disciple; after an encounter with the stricken hero, Stelio is inspired to an epiphany of his highest aesthetics and concludes with a consideration of Wagner: "He has conquered; he may die."[45] The words reflect the belief Hemingway expresses in his "Poem to Miss Mary": "If your dues are paid/You carry, always, your own spade" (p. 119).

The notion of heroic suicide, or "free death," is central to some of Hemingway's more important poems, as it is to much of his prose. "Montparnasse" contrasts the lonely suicides of transients with the histrionics of "the people one knows" (p. 50) who spend their afternoons in Paris cafes. Dorothy Parker, who "always vomitted in time" (p. 87), is attacked in "To a Tragic Poetess" for her sham suicide attempts and for her using the occasions as material for her poems. Hemingway characterizes her as being devoid of sympathetic imagination:

> To sit one day in the Luticia
> and joke about a funeral passing in the rain
> It gave no pain
> because you did not know the people. (p. 87)

For real tragedy, Hemingway turns to the "suicides of sunny Spain" (p. 89). He recounts the delirious despair suffered by the bullfighters Litri (Manuel Baez) and Maera (Manuel Garcia) before they died. The poetic anecdote of the methodical suicide of an eighty-year-old man in Miguelete sounds like the truth that was left out of "A Clean, Well-Lighted Place":

> An old man named Valentin Magarza
> climbed in his eightieth year the tower of Miguelete
> and was, the Valencian paper said,

> destroyed completely on the pavement.
> His granddaughter had said he was a bother
> and he was getting old. (p. 88)

It took Nietzsche eleven years to die following the destruction of his mind. D'Annunzio tempted death repeatedly during the Great War; however, his fate was to sink into old age and silence behind dark veils of privacy at his villa which had belonged to Wagner's daughter. Hemingway's last true heroic gesture was the wartime adventure aboard the *Pilar*. Following that he joined the world war in Europe. In "First Poem to Mary in London" he writes: "No, it is not a good ending. Not the ending we had hoped for. . . . Not as we thought it should be each time we took her from harbour" (p. l04).

The lassitude remained when he began to write again. In the last 1940's, Hemingway returned in his imagination and in his fiction to the Italy of his youth. He revisited old places and old fictions. After the Great War, when it had seemed to him that D'Annunzio placed personal glory before the deaths of 500,000 Italian soldiers, he had called him a "son of a bitch" (p. 28). D'Annunzio got mixed up in politics (which is anathema to an overman creator), but Hemingway still believed in 1923 that the old hero would topple Mussolini. He prophesied in "Mussolini: Biggest Bluff in Europe": "A new opposition will rise, it is forming already, and it will be lead by that old, bald-headed, perhaps a little insane but thoroughly sincere, divinely brave swashbuckler, Gabriele D'Annunzio."[46] D'Annunzio disappointed him and Italy. Thus, Cantwell calls him a "jerk,"[47] which he later defines as "a man who has never worked at his trade (oficio) truly, and is presumptuous in some annoying way."[48] In 1950, to vent his frustration over the critical and public reception of *Across the River and into the Trees*, Hemingway recorded "In Harry's Bar in Venice."[49] This tale of an eighteen-year-old colonel who is in love with an eighty-six-year-old Venetian countess, but who finally falls for a Venetian maiden, is for the most part a parody of *The Flame*, not of *Across the River and into the Trees*. Just before recording this extemporaneous concoction, he told A. E. Hotchner: "The parody is the last refuge of the frustrated writer."[50] In this case I am not sure whether Hemingway was denying an old story he had loved, and thus denying the influence of its author, by mocking them, or whether he was using a crude form to send a message to anyone who was listening—the same message he had tried to send in his Venetian novel. Or, perhaps, supported by the wine, Hemingway was just weaving a nocturnal entertainment for himself.

But I am sure that for more than thirty years of Ernest Hemingway's life Eleonora Duse was his muse, and that at least for his Italian novels, his true Penelope was D'Annunzio.

1. Friedrich Nietzsche, *Ecce Homo*, in *Basic Writings of Nietzsche*, trans. and ed. Walter Kaufmann (New York: Modern Library, 1968), p. 708.

2. Ernest Hemingway, *88 Poems*, ed. Nicholas Gerogiannis (New York: Harcourt Brace Jovanovich/Bruccoli Clark, 1979). All subsequent references to Hemingway's poems will be to this edition.

3. Richard Ellmann, *James Joyce* (New York: Oxford University Press, 1959), p. 275.

4. James Joyce, "The Day of the Rabblement," in *The Critical Writings of James Joyce*, ed. Ellsworth Mason and Richard Ellmann (New York: Viking, 1964), p. 71.

5. Noel Fitch, "C/O Shakespeare and Company," *Fitzgerald/Hemingway Annual, 1977*, p. 176.

6. W[alter] K[aufman]n, "Friedrich Nietzsche," *Encyclopaedia Britannica*, 1966, Vol. 16, p. 496. For the sake of brevity and directness I have selected to cite Kaufmann's *Britannica* entry. His introductions and notes to *The Portable Nietzsche* (cited below) and to *Basic Writings of Nietzsche* (cited above), as well as his classic study *Nietzsche: Philosopher, Psychologist, Antichrist* (Princeton: Princeton University Press, 1950), contain the same definitions in more detailed form.

7. Friedrich Nietzsche, *Thus Spoke Zarathustra*, in *The Portable Nietzsche*, ed. and trans. Walter Kaufmann (1954; rpt. New York: Penguin, 1978), pp. 183–86.

8. Carlos Baker, *Ernest Hemingway: A Life Story* (New York: Scribner's, 1969), p. 69. Baker writes that in March 1920, Hemingway gave an inscribed copy of *The Flame* to Dorothy Connable. More information on this and related readings of D'Annunzio's works is forthcoming in Michael Reynolds' *Hemingway's Reading, 1910–1940* (Princeton University Press).

9. Anthony Rhodes, *The Poet as Superman: A Life of Gabriele D'Annunzio* (London: Weidenfeld and Nicolson, 1959), p. 157. For my account of D'Annunzio's life I have relied on Rhodes and the following biographies: Tom Antongini, *D'Annunzio* (London: Heinemann, 1938). Reynolds reports that in May 1938 Hemingway ordered this biography from Scribner's bookstore. Phillipe Julian, *D'Annunzio*, trans. Stephen Hardman (New York: Viking, 1973). Frances Winwar, *Wingless Victory: A Biography of Gabriele D'Annunzio and Eleonora Duse* (New York: Harper and Brothers, 1956).

10. Ernest Hemingway, *Across the River and into the Trees* (New York: Scribner's, 1950), pp. 49–52.

11. *Across the River and into the Trees*, p. 50,

12. *Across the River and into the Trees*, p. 50.

13. *Across the River and into the Trees*, pp. 51–52.

14. Gabriele D'Annunzio, *Notturno* (Milano: Presso I. Fratelli Treves, 1922). Since Hemingway refers to the book by its Italian title, I assume that he read the above edition or a later reprint; however, he could have read the French translation: Gabriele D'Annunzio, *Nocturne* (Paris: Calmann-Levy, 1923).

15. *Across the River and into the Trees*, p. 51.

16. Catherine Barkley's emotional and erotic personality cannot be explained away by comparing her to Agnes von Kurowsky. The Agnes that Michael Reynold reveals in *Hemingway's First War: The Making of* A Farewell to Arms (Princeton: Princeton University Press, 1976), and in "The Agnes Tapes: A Farewell to Catherine Barkley," *Fitzgerald/Hemingway Annual, 1979*, pp. 251–276, is not essentially the sexual Catherine of *A Farewell to Arms*. Hadley may be closer in that respect. Perhaps Foscarina (Duse) is closest of all.

17. *Hemingway's First War*, pp. 18–19.

18. Gabriele D'Annunzio, *The Flame of Life*, trans. Baron Gustavo Tosti (New York: Collier, n.d.), p. 267. I have found three English translations of *The Flame* (sometimes translated as *The Flame of Life*). All are quite similar. I have selected this edition for reference purposes because it may be the easiest to locate.

19. *The Flame of Life*, p. 107.

20. *The Flame of Life*, p. 176.

21. *The Flame of Life*, p. 328.

22. *The Flame of Life*, p. 320.

23. *The Flame of Life*, p. 326.

24. *The Flame of Life*, p. 396.

25. *Across the River and into the Trees*, p. 219.

26. *The Flame of Life*, pp. 116–20.

27. *Across the River and into the Trees*, p. 49.

28. *Across the River and into the Trees*, p. 50.

29. Ernest Hemingway, *A Farewell to Arms* (New York: Scribner's, 1929), p. 196.

30. *Wingless Victory*, pp. 287–88.

31. *Wingless Victory*, p. 290. Also see Carl A. Swanson, "D'Annunzio's Ode 'All America in Armi' (4 Luglio 1918)," *Italica* (September 1953), 135–43.

32. Quoted from *Hemingway's First War*, p. 14.

33. George R. Kay, ed., *The Penguin Book of Italian Verse* (1958; rpt. Middlesex, England: Penguin, 1968), p. 338.

34. Ernest Hemingway, "A Natural History of the Dead," in *Death in the Afternoon* (1932; rpt. New York: Scribner's, 1972), p. 139. A reference to Humanists was cut in an early draft of "Poem, 1928"; see *88 Poems*, p. 94.

35. *Thus Spoke Zarathustra*, p. 237.

36. "Hugh Selwyn Mauberley," *Personae: The Collected Shorter Poems of Ezra Pound* (New York: New Directions, 1926), p. 189.

37. Kaufmann, "Friedrich Nietzsche," p. 496.

38. *The Portable Nietzsche*, p. 29.

39. Quoted in *The Poet as Superman*, p. 52.

40. *Thus Spoke Zarathustra*, p. 176.

41. *Thus Spoke Zarathustra*, p. 125.

42. Kaufmann, "Friedrich Nietzsche," p. 496.

43. *The Flame of Life*, p. 195.

44. *Thus Spoke Zarathustra*, p. 183.

45. *The Flame of Life*, p. 222.

46. Ernest Hemingway, "Mussolini: Biggest Bluff in Europe," *The Toronto Daily Star* (January 27, 1923), rpt. in *By-Line: Ernest Hemingway*, ed. William White (New York: Scribner's, 1967), p. 65.

47. *Across the River and into the Trees*, p. 52.

48. *Across the River and into the Trees*, p. 97.

49. *Ernest Hemingway Reading*, Caedmon (TC 1185).

50. *Ernest Hemingway Reading*, quoted on back cover.

REVIEW OF *THE OLD MAN AND THE SEA*

WILLIAM FAULKNER

HIS BEST. Time may show it to be the best single piece of any of us, I mean his and my contemporaries. This time, he discovered God, a Creator. Until now, his men and women had made themselves, shaped themselves out of their own clay; their victories and defeats were at the hands of each other, just to prove to themselves or one another how tough they could be. But this time, he wrote about pity: about something somewhere that made them all: the old man who had to catch the fish and then lose it, the fish that had to be caught and then lost, the sharks which had to rob the old man of his fish; made them all and loved them all and pitied them all. It's all right. Praise God that whatever made and loves and pities Hemingway and me kept him from touching it any further.

Reprinted with permission from *Shenandoah*, 3 (Autumn 1952), 55, and from *Essays, Speeches and Public Letters* by William Faulkner, ed. James B. Meriwether, 1952, by permission of Random House, Inc.

THE POEM OF SANTIAGO AND MANOLIN

LINDA W. WAGNER

> *I sometimes think my style is suggestive rather than*
> *direct. The reader must often use his imagination or lose*
> *the most subtle part of my thought.*

> —*Ernest Hemingway, "A Man's Credo"[1]*

SOME RECENT CRITICISM of Hemingway's work[2] indicates that readers might now—ten years after his death—be more open to his posthumously published comment. Hemingway as *suggestive*, as poet of the American novel, is a new portrait for many readers. Yet if we can let ourselves see him as the craftsman he was, teeth cut on Pound's Imagist-Vorticist energies and Ford's Impressionist anxieties in the *Transatlantic Review* office, then perhaps we can more accurately read his writing. In the same way that paraphrasing poems is dangerous, since no one-to-one equivalent exists for the compression inherent in a poem, so a simple distillation of Hemingway's writing is often misleading.

I do not intend in this essay to trace the relationships between the Imagist and Vorticist poets and Hemingway. We know that the younger writer first wrote poems, and then moved cautiously to the stories and prose vignettes that comprised *In Our Time*. By his own account, when Hemingway began *The Sun Also Rises*, he was "still having a difficult time writing a paragraph"[3]—precisely because he was, from the beginning, so terrifically conscious of "getting the words right."[4] And although his first novel was a masterpiece, as were *A Farewell to Arms* and *For Whom the Bell Tolls*, Hemingway could never rest on laurels. Yet, after *The Old Man and the Sea*, he tended to be more at peace; in fact he wrote in August of 1952 about the Santiago story, "It's as though I had gotten

Reprinted from *Modern Fiction Studies*, 19, No. 4 (Winter 1973–74), 517–30, with the permission of the author.

finally what I had been working for all my life."[5] The focus in this essay, then, is on Hemingway's last great satisfaction, the lyric novel that may be his greatest because in it all segments of the book—structure, imagery, word choice, characters, plot—create a single organic whole. Hemingway began as a poet and so he ended—and, well aware of Dylan Thomas' remark that the greatest poems have in them both love and death, he captured in *The Old Man and the Sea* several great loves, and a truly noble death.

T. S. Eliot may have been thinking of Hemingway's writing as well as Djuna Barnes's when he commented in his introduction to *Nightwood*, "it is so good a novel that only sensibilities trained on poetry can wholly appreciate it. A prose that is altogether alive demands something of the reader that the ordinary novel-reader is not prepared to give."[6] With Hemingway's fiction (as with the Imagist poems that preceded it by a decade) each word counts. Years before he created the iceberg theory, he operated under its premises but with perhaps even more attention to making each word do several things. In this, Hemingway's admiration for Joyce and Pound was no doubt of greater influence than his shorter-lived friendship with Gertrude Stein.[7]

In considering each word's significance, the writer was also constrained to create an active, moving focus. Literature could never exist as a static picture. Verbs were prized; adjectives made useful. The Imagists had initially made these suggestions and Pound's work with Chinese ideograms intensified their interest. For Hemingway, the principle of active writing operated at a double level in *The Old Man and the Sea.* There are many verbs and surprisingly few adjectives, considering that much of the novel is description. And, in a broader sense, Santiago's struggle is always a dynamic one. There is movement, verve—even when only the stars are moving. The book's original title *(The Sea in Being)* suggested this dynamism, reflecting the source of Hemingway's later pride as he commented that "the emotion was made with the action."[8] Had Santiago not cared so much, he would not have gone out so far; had he not revered the fish, he would have cut the line and come home; had he not come to love it, he would not have struggled so valiantly to save little more than its carcass. Just as every word in the book is there for a purpose, so is Santiago's every act. His dialogue with his left hand is a vivid reminder of the importance of each gesture, each movement.

By focusing on the immediate action, Hemingway follows Imagist doctrine and also avoids the sentiment inherent in his choice of hero. Santiago is pure pathos—alone except for an unrelated boy, poor, comfortless, unlucky, and old; yet because Hemingway presents him as proud and courageous, aligned with the arch young lions, that is the way we see him. (As Pound commented, the poet can at least partially control his readers' reactions, as the journalist cannot.)[9]

Perhaps this is one of the most difficult of the Imagist tenets to employ, the fact that the author controls without interfering. He presents, he renders the story; but his control is limited to the selection of details. Pound had discussed (in a 1914 essay on Joyce) the dangers of both realism and impressionism:

> There is a very clear demarcation between unnecessary detail and irrelevant detail. An impressionist friend of mine talks to me a good deal about "preparing effects," and on that score he justifies much unnecessary detail, which is not "irrelevant," but which ends by being wearisome. . . .
>
> [Joyce] excels most of the impressionist writers because of his more rigorous selection, because of his exclusion of all unnecessary detail.[10]

Pound's summary tone suggests that anyone can tell when detail is irrelevant, but only the master craftsman—here, Joyce; later, Hemingway—knows the line between necessary (and superfluous) detail. It becomes a matter of both quantity and kind.

Hemingway's choice of the singular noun *shirt* in his brief opening description of Santiago is one such essential detail:

> Once there had been a tinted photograph of his wife on the wall but he had taken it down because it made him too lonely to see it and it was on the shelf in the corner under his clean shirt.[11]

The reader is led quickly through the impressions—a photo, and colored at that, must have been a great tribute to his love; then Hemingway recreates his sadness, in removing the photo; then he reinforces Santiago's poverty: *the* shelf may well have been the only shelf, just as the single shirt was his only change. In one sentence Hemingway has conveyed both Santiago's passion and his poverty.

The same care with detail is even more evident once Santiago is in action, fishing. Many of Hemingway's paragraphs follow the pattern of (1) large narrative statement, then (2) accumulation of reinforcing details, and finally (3) the summary statement that gives the otherwise objective paragraph its determination. When Santiago baits his hooks, Hemingway leaves no question that the old man is expert.

> (1) Before it was really light he had his baits out and was drifting with the current. (2) One bait was down forty fathoms. The second was at seventy-five and the third and fourth were down in the blue water at one hundred and one hundred and twenty-five fathoms. Each bait hung head-down with the shank of the hook inside the bait fish, tied and sewed solid and all the projecting part of the hook, the curve and the point, was covered with fresh sardines. Each sardine was hooked through both eyes so that they made a half-garland on the

projecting steel. (3) There was no part of the hook that a great fish could feel which was not sweet smelling and good tasting. (p. 30)

The final tone, established through the adjectives "sweet smelling and good tasting," comes as no surprise to the reader, even though he has been reading about baits, because earlier in the description, Hemingway had used the words *solid, fresh,* and particularly *half-garland.* The reader is thus viewing the entire process as Santiago would—the fish are beautifully fresh, the act of fishing is a ritual.

Working in a nearly poetic condensation, Hemingway turns frequently to figures of speech—often patterned in a series—as a way of giving extra meaning to his seemingly simple descriptions. Our initial picture of Santiago depends largely on this use of connected images. We first see his patched sail, looking when furled "like the flag of permanent defeat" (p. 9). Then Hemingway gives us Santiago's scars, "as old as erosions in a fishless desert" (p. 10). *Defeated, fishless*—the images are rapidly taking us one direction until the author moves, quickly, to Santiago's eyes: "Everything about him was old except his eyes and they were the same color as the sea and were cheerful and undefeated." The identification with the sea, coupled with the direct contradiction of "undefeated," establishes the tone Hemingway wants. But we also have the facts—and it is not because of the existing facts that Santiago is whole, but rather because of his spirit.

Operating throughout the writing in *The Old Man and the Sea* is a kind of rhythmic identity, evident in this excerpt, which William Gass has recently described in his discussion of Gertrude Stein:

Her success in uniting thought and feeling in the meaning and movement of speech showed that rhythm is half of prose, and gave it the power of poetry without the indecency of imitation. . . . Sometimes she brings prose by its own good methods to the condition of the lyric. [12]

As his experiments with language in his earlier novels had shown, Hemingway was also concerned with this rhythmic identity as an integral part of the whole effect. The rhythm of *The Sun Also Rises* is laconic, abrupt; of *For Whom the Bell Tolls*, moderately smooth, with much longer sentences. Hemingway's attempts to use the Spanish language, and the more personal pronoun forms, were ways of attaining the flavor—at least partially a rhythmic concern—of the Spanish people (the duration of the word *thee* is longer than *you* no matter how slowly the latter is said). Even Richard Cantwell's crudities help create the disjointed, even staccato measures of *Across the River.* But nowhere does Hemingway match so well the language of his persona with the narrative voice of the novel. Santiago's tranquillity sets the pace for *The Old Man and the Sea,* in keeping with his slow, chary, and deceptively uncomplicated speech.

The passage describing Santiago's baits also illustrates the somewhat idio-syncratic use Hemingway makes here of the compound structure, particularly the connective *and*. In its simplest position, the *and* coupling suggests that there is no judgmental relationship between the clauses connected: "He was an old man who fished alone in a skiff in the Gulf Stream and he had gone eighty-four days now without taking a fish." It is not *because* he fishes alone that Santiago has caught nothing. The simple statement of apparent fact does what it purports to do, puts down the facts, with no causation or blame.

Hemingway achieves the same kind of objective tone when he uses the struc-ture in more emotional situations, "The old man had taught the boy to fish and the boy loved him." Perhaps Manolin did love Santiago partly because of his having taught him, but rather than oversimplify the relationship, Hemingway again uses the simple coupling which leaves more to the reader's own insight. The structure—for all its apparent simplicity—is thus suggestive.

At times several of these compound sentences must work together as a unit to help reinforce the impression the reader will probably draw from the first sentence. In his description of Manolin and Santiago stopping for a beer, Hemingway sketches the milieu of the fishing village in two such connected sentences:

> They sat on the Terrace and many of the fishermen made fun of the old man and he was not angry. Others, of the older fishermen, looked at him and were sad.

That Santiago was not angry is a bit ambivalent—is he beaten or indifferent, or has he "the peace that passeth understanding," the wider tolerance? The follow-up sentence shows that the latter interpretation is the one Hemingway intends to reinforce.

It is one matter to look at single words and sentences and nod sagely, think-ing, "Yes, that's Hemingway's 'one clear sentence,' and there is the 'no ornament except good ornament' "; it is more impressive to see all these single elements joined into a longer passage which works, and conveys surprising richness. The page of dialogue between Santiago and Manolin essentially presents their past relationship, their present love for each other—and the effect that love has on Santiago—all amid more commonplace detail about the village and the fishing process.

> "How old was I when you first took me in a boat?"
> "Five and you nearly were killed when I brought the fish in too green and he nearly tore the boat to pieces. Can you remember?"
> "I can remember the tail slapping and banging and the thwart breaking and the noise of the clubbing. I can remember you throwing me into the bow

where the wet coiled lines were and feeling the whole boat shiver and the noise
of you clubbing him like chopping a tree down and the sweet blood smell all
over me."

"Can you really remember that or did I just tell it to you?"

"I remember everything from when we first went together."

The old man looked at him with his sun-burned, confident loving eyes.

"If you were my boy I'd take you out and gamble," he said, "But you are
your father's and your mother's and you are in a lucky boat."

"May I get the sardines? I know where I can get four baits too."

"I have mine left from today. I put them in salt in the box."

"Let me get four fresh ones."

"One," the old man said. His hope and his confidence had never gone.
But now they were freshening as when the breeze rises. (pp. 12–13)

In Manolin's comparatively long memory of the fish, Hemingway writes his
usual active prose, relying on the many -*ing* words, but he more importantly
resolves the boy's memories happily. Even though Santiago is "clubbing" the
fish, his action seems as natural to the boy as "chopping a tree down," and the
heavy blood smell he recalls as "sweet." That a five-year-old child had such a
reaction to what must have been a gory and frightening scene shows clearly the
trust he had in Santiago. Hemingway gives us further proof of the old man as
trust-inspiring in his description of his "sun-burned, confident loving eyes," and
then goes on to show in turn the power of Manolin's love on him, with the closing
image. By placing the descriptions of Santiago throughout the section,
Hemingway keeps the old man before us, even when Manolin carries most of the
dialogue. And by establishing tone through nature images, he reinforces the
impression of Santiago as sea-like, old, strange, proud, and unbeaten.

The relationship between Manolin and Santiago is poignantly done, particularly when one considers that the boy appears in only one-fifth of the novel—in
the first eighteen pages and the last six. The structure of the book is thus like that
of *The Sun Also Rises*, with Jake and Brett together in Parts I and III, as are
Manolin and Santiago. Yet when Santiago is alone, he thinks often of the boy, and
his thoughts of him become a kind of refrain.

It begins, "I wish I had the boy," (p. 51) and then modulates into "If the boy
were here" (pp. 56, 62, 83); finally reaching its climax in a threefold repetition,
as the coils of line tear Santiago's hands,

If the boy was here he would wet the coils of line, he thought. If the boy
were here. If the boy were here. (p. 83)

Santiago has no time to pray, he tells God in his humorous attempt to bargain, but
his thoughts of Manolin come at points of crisis and—structurally—seem to sub-

stitute for the prayers another man might be saying. That this effect is intentional—Manolin as Santiago's only hope, only love—is restated later when Santiago justifies killing the marlin.

> Besides, he thought, everything kills everything else in some way. Fishing kills me exactly as it keeps me alive. The boy keeps me alive, he thought. I must not deceive myself too much. (p. 106)

Using structure as well as immediate presentation, Hemingway drew this all-encompassing love relationship, perhaps the most convincing of those in any of his novels. When Manolin says, "I remember everything from when we first went together," we accept his exaggeration, as Santiago does, as evidence of his selfless love for the old man. His willingness to bargain, to beg, to steal for food and supplies for him—and to go against his parents' wishes—is further evidence of that generous relationship. With Hemingway's definition of love as generous giving, the similarities between Manolin's devotion to Santiago and Maria's to Jordan and, to an even greater degree, Renata's to Cantwell, are evident. Sex aside, much of each of these relationships exists in the near-reverence of youth for the enduring wisdom of age. In *Across the River*, Renata wants to learn from Cantwell; true, she thinks his talking about war will in some way exorcise his bitterness, but her thirst for information must have some basis in interest as well. The closest parallel to the love between Manolin and Santiago, of course, is that between Jake and Brett. Also sexless, that love was proven chiefly in Jake's desire to give whatever he could toward Brett's happiness—and only because society finds bullfighters more objectionable than cups of coffee did Hemingway's first novel fail to have its appropriate effect.

Manolin wants everything good for Santiago; there is no jealousy between competing fishing boats here. He is confident in his position with the old man; there is no timidity or artifice. One of the best evidences of the latter is the fantasy Santiago and the boy create about the yellow rice and fish. Only very confident lovers joke (as Santiago does with God).[13] Such scenes create the aura of tranquillity, of surety, that this novel maintains throughout. Like Shakespeare in *The Tempest*, Hemingway has realized the value of humor in the midst of the life-and-death struggle that the book really is, and he uses it well: the old man's thoughts about Joe DiMaggio's bone spur, and his childlike wondering about it, occur at some of the highest peaks of action. And the comic dialogue between Santiago and Manolin about fear is a skillful touch of the raspberries to any former Hemingway reader. To come from Robert Jordan's near-obsession with fear, fear as an index of manliness, to Santiago's mocking comments on the base-ball teams is progression indeed:

"The Yankees cannot lose."

"But I fear the Indians of Cleveland."

"Have faith in the Yankees my son. Think of the great DiMaggio."

"I fear both the Tigers of Detroit and the Indians of Cleveland."

"Be careful or you will fear even the Reds of Cincinnati and the White Sox of Chicago." (p. 17)

Santiago—and Manolin in his tutelage—seems to be almost beyond man's usual concerns with mortality—hence, his "strangeness"[14] and perhaps his complete resolution (Cantwell's ability to spit might be an intermediate stage in this progression). Yet Hemingway includes enough detail to show that Santiago is a realist, not a romantic; he knows he will have to use "tricks" on the fish because his strength is not what it was when he was young. And he accepts his fate realistically, too, knowing that he "went out too far." The fish—though an impossibility—was not impossible to catch; it was only bringing it back such a long distance, unscathed, that was impossible.

Admittedly, Santiago shares many traits with the best of Hemingway's heroes, Jake Barnes and Robert Jordan. He does not admit to a limited set of hopes for man; there are no impossibilities. The central image occurs near the center of the story when Santiago, bemused at the size of the marlin, considers man's "luck":

"I have never seen or heard of such a fish. But I must kill him. I am glad we do not have to try to kill the stars."

Imagine if each day a man must try to kill the moon, he thought. The moon runs away. But imagine if a man each day should have to try to kill the sun? We were born lucky, he thought. (p. 75)

This is the same kind of reversal in our normal perception of events that Hemingway emphasizes as Santiago sits cramped all night in the cold boat, "The sack cushioned the line and he had found a way of leaning forward against the bow so that he was almost comfortable. The position actually was only somewhat less intolerable; but he thought of it as almost comfortable" (p. 47).

Calling it optimism is too pale. Santiago's outlook is stoicism at its best, somehow infused with a living, growing hope. And the presentation of it is amazingly effective, partly because of the author's shifting point of view.

Trying to categorize Santiago's philosophy makes one eager for generalities, and we tend to summarize all the Hemingway heroes, noticing how few suicides there are in any of the fiction, although nearly every character at some moment has a right at least to contemplate the act. One of the difficulties with identifying with Jake Barnes was our sparse knowledge about his real feelings, the restrictions of using first-person point of view with a laconic and rather tough-sounding narrator. By the time of *The Old Man and the Sea*, Hemingway had learned not only to move easily between first person and omniscient (and here to include dialogue for more necessary insights); he had also learned to give the reader didactic help at crucial moments. Rather than have us believe what Santiago says—that the pain is nearly comfortable—Hemingway tells us how it really was. And rather than have us slide over the moon-sun passage, he adds a summary image a few pages earlier, so that Santiago's position is crystallized in our minds. It is all hopeless.

> The old man had seen many great fish. He had seen many that weighed more than a thousand pounds and he had caught two of that size in his life, but never alone. Now alone, and out of sight of land, he was fast to the biggest fish that he had ever seen and bigger than he had ever heard of, and his left hand was still as tight as the gripped claws of an eagle. (p. 63)

Soon after this, we have one of the few flashbacks in the book, as Santiago thinks of his Indian wrestling with the strongest man on the docks. They had gone one night and one day, and, for no rational reason, Santiago had won. So Hemingway tells us, in effect, that spirit can go a long way. It cannot, however, overcome everything.

Santiago is never broken, but then Hemingway has also told us that "man is not made for defeat. . . . A man can be destroyed but not defeated" (p. 103). What is new in this novel is the explicit injunction to think. Contrary to the earlier admonitions of Barnes, Henry, Morgan, Jordan, Thomas Hudson, and Cantwell that they not think—because, we suppose, Hamlet-like, they would be too fearful to act—Santiago in all his wisdom admits, "But I must think. . . . Because it is all I have left." Then he improvises the weapons he has lost, and later repeats, "Think of what you can do with what there is." In this synthesis of thought and action, Santiago works just as Jordan surely has, to the best of his ability, using what he has but never mourning, as Cohn might have, for what he did not have and could not hope to obtain. Hemingway's theme has changed little throughout his writing, but his method of expressing that theme has been modified toward greater directness and greater emphasis on the final effect. The latter part of *The Old Man and the Sea* is the most didactic of any of Hemingway's writing.

The "Cuba" and "Sea" sections of the posthumously published *Islands in the Stream* run a close second, however, and in the Thomas Hudson story is found the same emphasis on endurance. By depriving Hudson of his three sons, two at the close of the "Bimini" section and the third during the "Cuba,"

Hemingway has set up a different kind of endurance test, a torture of the heart rather than the body. Hudson, describing life as a series of tests, thinks to himself that all will be well "if we can get by this one and the next one and the next one."[15] As he summarizes his own position, "Get it straight. Your boy you lose. Love you lose. Honor has been gone for a long time. Duty you do." Again Hemingway gives us a man who has known love—like Santiago—but is now bereft of it all. (The first part of *Islands* works largely to establish how great his devotion to his sons is and how lost he is in their absence.) Unwieldy as some parts of the novel are, and unfinished, the book is still a moving study of man's bereavement. Just as Santiago loses parts of the fish to the sharks, so Hudson loses parts of his own life until finally, as his behavior in the "chase" section suggests, that life means little. His actions show that all he has left is duty. (Once injured, in another reasonless aberration of fate, Hudson does think of his painting—"life is a cheap thing beside a man's work"—but it seems to be a definite afterthought.)

The transfer of emotion from this mass of writing, loosely connected as the "sea novel," to *The Old Man and the Sea* is evident. Whereas Hudson is concerned with his love for his sons and his first wife, Santiago has Manolin. The somewhat inarticulate conversations between Hudson and his boys seem stilted (one exception is young Tom's reminiscence of his early days in Paris) compared with the direct expressions of Manolin and Santiago. But then these characters are simpler, and their laconic language is borne out by substantiating actions. In *Islands*, so many people are involved that giving any one of them sufficient emphasis is difficult. The situation may have been closer to the author's own, but it was much harder to achieve artistically than the single man-single boy of *The Old Man and the Sea*. Only once in *Islands* does Hemingway achieve a similar concentration, when David tries to land the fish. There also the action is meaningful: it is focused on only several characters (with Hudson's position as separate, yet horribly involved, clearly drawn), and the scene moves quickly. Like Santiago's feeling for the marlin, David's reaction to his fish is compelling—his injured hands and feet, his feeling of union with the fish, his reticence, and his love for it. The boy's experience is, however, finally less effective than Santiago's because of the constant interruptions from the other six people on the boat and also because Hemingway uses third person point of view to convey the boy's reactions.

In *Islands,* too, the fishing experience is primarily an initiation process giving us greater insight into Hudson's fears for his sons—fears that the novel shows, perhaps too quickly, were well founded. The scene ends when the fish breaks away. In *The Old Man and the Sea,* by extending the story much further, by taking us past the excitement of the catch, the fight, and the possession, Hemingway emphasizes what a man can endure (just as in *Islands,* the successive two parts of the novel do this for Hudson). By shifting emphasis from catching the fish to staying with it, Hemingway changes the nature of the story. In the course of *The Old Man and the Sea,* he shows repeatedly Santiago's doing what he as man "had to do," and much more, until he finally waits, unarmed, for the last sharks, wondering "what can a man do against them in the dark without a weapon?" (p. 117).

It has been called existential, the fact that Hemingway gives his hero this dilemma, and makes him face it. But how similar the whole situation is to that of the scene in Faulkner's *The Unvanquished* when Bayard Sartoris asks, "How can you fight in the mountains, Father?" and the answer comes, "You can't. You just have to." [16] *The Old Man and the Sea* is the novel Faulkner admired. For it is the first one Hemingway had written in thirty years in which the hero stood it all. And lived.

The catharsis here, in this spent resolution of Santiago's struggle, must remind any reader of the effects of Greek tragedy. The classic intensity of focus is evident in the limitation to three characters, the nearly single setting (village, ocean, village), the three-day time span (unified by the single action), and the resolution of that single action. So tightly unified is the story, in fact, that some of the telescoping of time is so heightened that it creates irony. As Santiago pulls on the line, for example, Hemingway writes,

> This will kill him, the old man thought. He can't do this forever. But four hours later the fish was still swimming steadily out to sea. (p. 45)

The juxtaposition of time information with Santiago's incorrect "knowledge" does more than convey fact; it also foreshadows the falsity of many of Santiago's expectations. And we are reminded again of the Hemingway thesis: even the greatest of men can seldom be in complete control of all circumstances.

Structurally, too, Hemingway emphasizes this axiom. It takes Santiago ninety-four pages to get the fish and only eighteen to lose it to the various sharks. The concentration, even in terms of space and detail, falls on Santiago's purely voluntary exposure to danger. For the first time in twenty years, the hero of a Hemingway novel was not chafing under "orders." (As Hudson said, in the passages written immediately after *The Old Man and the Sea,* "There are worse places to be than on your own" [*Islands*, p. 343].) Santiago could not complain about the higher powers—except the highest fates of all, those that willed him toward his destiny. Like Jake Barnes, Santiago's duty is only to himself and his ideals; similarly, only those who know him well, who understand him, can judge him. Therefore, Hemingway concludes the novel by letting Manolin give his reaction to Santiago's experience, fittingly, in actions as well as in words: crying, warming and rewarming Santiago's coffee, and keeping guard as the old man sleeps. Here love is a secure and confident relationship.

The actual ending of *The Old Man and the Sea* works perfectly to complement the rest of the book. It is no deliberate Christian ploy to have Santiago carry the mast up the hill (on page 26 he carried it down), and then lie face down on his bed (this is the falling action of an exhausted man, not a person going to bed). For those who read these last ten pages as evidence of Hemingway's Christ symbolism, one must suggest that Santiago's not saying the promised prayers provides an antidote to that interpretation. Instead, we must view the last few passages as (1) summation of the theme that runs, obviously and yet skillfully, throughout the book—man's incredible ability to survive, and more, to dare; to make it, whole in spirit and body; (2) a return to the enduring love that Manolin gave and Santiago lived for; (3) a necessary ending to the apparent "plot"—Santiago alive, his reputation vindicated, and the marlin skeleton disposed of; and (4) one of the most masterful of Hemingway's exercises in juxtaposition.

Once Santiago is asleep, focus shifts again to Manolin whose tears of joy and sorrow, occurring three distinct times, are the best single testimony to Santiago's courage. Then the last few pages of the novel shift setting kaleidoscopically: Manolin watching Santiago, going for coffee, talking with the crowd gathered near the skeleton, talking with Santiago, and then again returning to the village. As the boy hurries back and forth, we sense the reactions of the entire village and even of the outsiders—those uninitiated observers who usually appear in a Hemingway novel, but often to the detriment of any total effect. Here, however, after the laconic dialogue of Manolin and Santiago, with even his evident suffering described only as "Plenty," the ending image of the tourists' ignorance has a triple-edged effect. The evidence of Santiago's greatest catch is now garbage and, as such, has no meaning for any but the initiated. Even when the waiter tries to explain what has happened ("Tiburon." "Eshark"), the tourists hear him incorrectly. In the vapid "I didn't know sharks had such handsome, beautifully formed tails," Hemingway has caught the tone of facile indifference he despised. Yet in this novel—rather than belabor the ignorance, or admonish, or let Manolin comment—he instead moves quickly back to the sleeping Santiago, strangely at peace with his pain, the pain which signifies life, dreaming once again of the lions, as Manolin stands watch. We are given Santiago's peace in the envelope of Manolin's concern.

The relationship between Santiago and the marlin has been made much of, and rightly so, for the sense of wonder, the immensity, the brotherhood is beautifully conveyed. But, as the structure and imagery of *The Old Man and the Sea* prove, it is the love between imperfect human beings that lies at the core of Santiago's experience. It is that love that redeems Santiago; and it is that love to which he returns.

1. *Playboy,* 10 (January 1963), p. 124.

2. See particularly Julian Smith's essay, "Hemingway and the Thing Left Out," *Journal of Modern Literature,* 1 (1970-71), 169-82; Robert O. Stephens' *Hemingway's Nonfiction* (Chapel Hill: The University of North Carolina Press, 1968); and Nicholas Joost's *Ernest Hemingway and The Little Magazines: The Paris Years* (Barre, Mass.: Barre Publishers, 1968).

3. From Hemingway's *Paris Review* interview in *Writers at Work,* Second Series, ed. Malcolm Cowley (New York: The Viking Press, 1963), p. 231.

4. *Interview,* p. 222.

5. In a letter to the Editors of *Life,* 25 August 1952, p. 124.

6. Introduction to *Nightwood, The Selected Works of Djuna Barnes* (New York: Farrar, Straus, and Cudahy, 1962), p. 228.

7. See his note in the *Paris Review* interview (p. 226) that he was influenced by "Joyce, Ezra, the good of Stein"; and the accounts of Hemingway's friendships with these older writers as described in George Wickes' *Americans in Paris* (Garden City, N.Y.: Doubleday, 1969); Joost's book (note 2); and K. L. Goodwin's *The Influence of Ezra Pound* (London: Oxford University Press, 1966).

8. Quoted in Carlos Baker, *Ernest Hemingway, A Life Story* (New York: Charles Scribner's Sons, 1969), p. 504.

9. Ezra Pound, *Literary Essays of Ezra Pound* (Norfolk, Conn.: New Directions Press, 1968), p. 227.

10. *Pound,* pp. 401-02.

11. *The Old Man and the Sea* (New York: Charles Scribner's Sons, 1952), p. 16. Hereafter cited in text.

12. William A. Gass, *Fiction and the Figures of Life* (New York: Alfred A. Knopf, 1970), pp. 95-96.

13. See Joseph Waldmeir's discussion of Santiago's relationship with God in "Confiteor Hominem: Ernest Hemingway's Religion of Man" in *Ernest Hemingway, Critiques of Four Major Novels,* ed. Carlos Baker (New York: Charles Scribner's Sons, 1962), pp. 144-49.

14. Hemingway is himself the "strange" old man in conversations. His use of the adjective here has the connotation of private joke as well as of allusion.

15. *Islands in the Stream* (New York: Charles Scribner's Sons, 1970), p. 326. Hereafter cited in text.

16. William Faulkner, *The Unvanquished* (New York: Vintage Books, 1938), p. 19.

IV: Hemingway's Death and Posthumous Publications

THE HEMINGWAY OBITUARY

JOHN WAIN

IF THE WORD "CLASSICAL" still has any meaning except just as the opposite of "romantic," then we can say that Ernest Hemingway was a classical writer. He was terse, lucid, economical; he pared life down to what he took to be the essentials, and then worked with great care and concentration to embody these essentials in imaginative form. He had neither the romantic interest in the untypical nor the adventure-story writer's interest in action for its own sake.

His characteristic form is the heroic fable. If Homer (assuming one single person of that name to have existed) could return to earth and read modern literature, he would find very little in it that was congenial to him until he got to Hemingway. There, in *A Farewell to Arms*, in "Fifty Grand," in "The Undefeated," in *The Old Man and the Sea,* he would find himself back in his own world, of heroic simplicities that are not simple, of unreflective action that is yet more action of the mind than of the body.

Except for Macaulay, no writer in the English-speaking world has been so widely imitated as Hemingway. Even Byron was not copied by so many, nor for so long. At any given time since the late twenties there has been a huge tribe of would-be Hemingways who have taken from the master the little they could use and left the much they could not. They have imagined that all one had to do to be a Hemingway was to write about violence and use short sentences. Yet, to a thoughtful reader, it is clear that hunting and fighting are important to him only secondarily. His vision of life embodied itself in fables concerning physical activity and the outdoor world, but there is never any doubt that for Hemingway, as for all sensitive men, the real battleground is inward.

Reprinted with permission from *The Observer*, 9 July 1961, p. 21.

289

Hemingway's soldiers, hunters, boxers and bullfighters are all men who have to face their personal testing-time in isolation, drawing strength, if they are fortunate enough to have strength, from the resources of their innermost being. So does every man; the same laws that apply to these picturesque men of action apply equally to curate or bank clerk; and this, so far from banishing Hemingway to the triviality of the adventure-story writer, is precisely what gives him his universality and greatness. It is nowhere suggested in his work that men who do not kill wild animals, or risk their lives in the bullring, are less real and significant than men who do. It is simply that his imaginative vision was able to refract itself through these tales of courage, fear, hunger, sweat, loneliness and death.

Hemingway is a very physical writer; the "objective correlative,"[1] in Eliot's famous phrase, is always to him a matter of the concrete, the seen and touched and experienced. Happiness is the kick of a salmon on one's line, or a glass of cold beer in the hot spring sunshine, or making love to a girl in a sleeping-bag. Tragedy is death, bereavement or mutilation. We all know that every Hemingway story has a Wounded Hero—a roll-call of his principal characters would hardly produce a whole man—but I think there is a danger of making too much of this. Serious fiction has always dealt with the Wounded Hero; its chief characters are all people who have to struggle against some blemish or deficiency in themselves. Hemingway, following his bent, expressed this in directly external terms, by lopping off an arm, or making his hero impotent or afflicting him with heart disease. But this does not mean that he exalted the external matter over the inward essence.

Hemingway's heroes are wounded because his view of life is a tragic stoical pessimism. It is the losing fight, or the fight carried on under some cruel disadvantage, that interests him. He sees life as essentially a losing battle, but instead of reasoning from this that nothing matters much he takes the attitude that is, in fact, normal among lofty tragic writers: that a defeat, if it is faced with courage and endured without loss of one's self-respect, counts as a victory. If a man can dig down to his own deepest springs, and find something good there, he can go ahead and die, because the most important business of his life is completed.

Another feature of Hemingway's work which his imitators failed to take over is his deep compassion. He has a large-hearted sympathy for those who carry impossible burdens or whose luck has failed them. One sees this at its simplest level in his writing about poverty. Much of his life was spent in countries where the poor were very poor, as indeed they were for most of his lifetime in the United States. His books abound in sketches of simple, dignified people who face without complaint a life of unending hardship; in these sketches, his respect for men who earn their living with their bodies was able to merge with his sense of tragic stoicism.

There is no blinking of the facts, no sentimentalisation of poverty as something ennobling. Being poor does bring out some godlike attributes in people, and also some savage animal ones. The first chapter of *To Have and Have Not* shows how Harry Morgan, bilked by the rich summer visitor who ruined some expensive fishing equipment and then left without paying, is thrown back on the necessity to use his fishing-boat in an illegal emigration voyage which involves him in murder and cruelty; what makes the story so magnificent is that Hemingway has sympathy for Morgan, for the murdered go-between, and for the desperate emigrants who fail to make their getaway, in about the same proportion; this, he is saying, is what life has done to these people: the only moral outcast is the swindling vacationer.

It is this all-embracing tragic and compassionate vision that sets Hemingway so firmly apart from the action writers who aped his style. But there is an equally evident separation on the plane of art. Hemingway was one of those writers to whom language matters. He had a passionate fastidiousness about words and rhythms, a contempt for imprecision, and the wholeheartedness of a Flaubert. Though there were many imitators there was never truly a "school of Hemingway," because the standard he set was too severe.

On this side, Hemingway belongs with the poets. And it was from the poets that he learnt to write. His training started in a newspaper office, but it was completed in the Paris days when he was associated with the group of experimental, expatriate writers presided over by Ezra Pound.

"Nothing can please many, or please long, but just representations of general nature."[2] Dr. Johnson's remark gives the classicist's position in one sentence. Most modern literature is "romantic" in that it explores the possibilities of the extreme; it eagerly pursues madness, eccentricity, the solitary and the perverse. Where it is not romantic, it becomes gregarious, concerning itself with the social questions which men face all together. Ionesco and Genet on the one side, Arthur Miller and C. P. Snow on the other.

Hemingway's attitude was exceptional because classical art, nowadays, is exceptional. He took men singly, not forgetting the collective world they belonged to, but seeing them as individuals, amid the individual's ultimate loneliness, within that world. He placed them in positions of extreme stress. And he showed them behaving under that stress as men behave: not as civil servants behave, or factory workers, or Americans, or lepers, or bohemian intellectuals. His aim was to get below the skin and present the universal, underlying truth to experience that Johnson had in mind when he spoke of "just representations of general nature." In my submission, he succeeded. And for that reason his books please many, and will surely please long.

1. T. S. Eliot, "Hamlet and His Problems (1919)," *Selected Prose,* ed. Frank Kermode (London, 1975), p. 48: "the only way of expressing emotion, in the form of art, is by finding an 'objective correlative'; in other words, a set of objects, a situation, a chain of events, which shall be the formula for that poetic emotion."

2. Johnson makes the same point in chapter 10 of *Rasselas* (1759) when Imlac says: "The business of the poet is to examine, not the individual, but the species; to remark general properties and large appearances."

HEMINGWAY: THE DYE THAT DID NOT RUN

NELSON ALGREN

THE VITAL DIFFERENCE BETWEEN THIS YOUTHFUL American in love with his wife, his writing, food, wine and racehorses, was that the others had arrived at the Moveable Feast directly from a picnic in Kansas City or St. Paul, but he had come to his place by way of death.

Paris to the Fitzgeralds was only a farther place on a meadow of endless sun. But Hemingway had so narrowly missed having no place at all—"I'd felt my life flutter like a handkerchief in the wind"—that he knew how swiftly all good days are taken away. Hemingway was a young man learning how to sleep again.

But his hold on life having once been loosened, it now became all the more tenacious for that. The tension that began to pervade his writing derived from this tenaciousness, and lent him a perspective larger than that indicated by a phrase like "lost generation." When Gertrude Stein tried to pin it on him he rejected the label.

A French garage owner, impatient with a young mechanic who was goofing on Miss Stein's car, reproached him: "You are all a lost generation." Whereupon Miss Stein turned her irritation onto the nearest American—"All you young people who served in the war are a lost generation, you drink yourselves to death"—who happened to be Hemingway.

"Don't argue with me, Hemingway," she added firmly. "It does no good at all. You're all a lost generation exactly as the garage keeper said."

She wasn't prophesying the destiny of a generation; she was merely expressing the irritation of a car owner who finds the car isn't ready.

And Hemingway, having disputed her reluctantly and still feeling salty, walking home alone and catching a view of a heroic statue of Marshal Ney,

Reprinted with permission from *The Nation*, 1 June 1964, pp. 560-61.

293

turned his own irritation on the Marshal. "What a fiasco you made of Waterloo!" Who was calling who lost? "All generations were lost by something and always had been and always would be—the hell with her lost generation and all the dirty, easy labels."

Hemingway wasn't lost. He would have been an expatriate even if he had never left Oak Park. His exile, like Villon's, was not from a land, but from the living. His need was not for a country, but for the company of men. Spiritually, therefore, he was closer to Villon than to Scott Fitzgerald. And, for a fact, Villon understood Hemingway better than have any of the critics:

> In my own country I am in a far-off land
> I am strong but have no force nor power
> Well-received, rebuffed by all
> I win all yet remain a loser
> At break of day I say goodnight
> When I lie down I have a great fear of falling.[1]

If we consider that Hemingway, like Villon, was forging a style not out of literature, but out of his need, we see not only what style is, but what Hemingway was.

The man and the style were one: the style was the instrument by which his need was realized; and the need was for light and simplicity. Thus, in achieving this for himself, he touched multitudes enduring a murky complexity.

A critic who can discover that Hemingway was nothing more than an innovator is scratching in the wrong barnyard. Dependence upon the catch phrase "lost generation," in lieu of insight into a writer's work, is of no use at all. One must distinguish between a man who represents his time, like John Dos Passos, and one who, like Hemingway, made his time represent him.

Multitudes saw the Spanish Civil War by Hemingway's light, because the light was true. When we consider how many novels have been turned out in imitation of him as a writer, we can only surmise how many Americans have tried to be Hemingway, because the image felt true. This was the image of the man or woman who felt that to become aware of life's precariousness was to become more alive. He caused the complacent man, standing content in his own well-lit door, suddenly to sense the precipitous edge where life drops off into utter dark. The woman counting her hours slowly dragging down, was troubled by the death of Catherine Barkley: lest no tragic hour ever strike for her.

Hemingway's own tragedy was that the light didn't hold. The present reminiscence is pleasant, humorous and evasive. "For reasons sufficient to the writer," he advises the reader, "many places, people, observations and impressions have been left out of this book. . . there is always the chance that such a book of fiction may throw some light on what has been written as fact."

The light he throws here is upon others. It is the harsh light of exposure: he reserves a soft, blurring glow for himself. Reporting a dialogue between two raving dikes, overheard accidentally thirty-five years before, is a bit the book could have done without. He might have let the poor brutes be. But the spotlight is useful when he recalls Fitzgerald's relationship to Zelda, because it reveals the fashion in which Fitzgerald was cut down. It does not have that justification with Gertrude Stein.

Fitzgerald appears to have been a sorry stiff, too disturbed about his wife's threat that "you can never make any woman happy." The washroom incident in which Hemingway assures Fitzgerald that he (Fitzgerald) could make any woman happy, by taking his measurement, is both comical and ominous. That a woman, failing to find her own femininity, may conceal that failure by attributing it to lack of manliness in her husband, is a trick we've all caught onto by watching TV. But Fitzgerald, with nothing to tune in but a radio, turned to drink.

Hemingway was a tolerant opponent and a mean competitor, both. Henry Strater, the artist whose portrait of Hemingway illustrates the back cover of *A Moveable Feast,* and who was close to Hemingway in Paris because he could knock Hemingway down as often as Hemingway could knock him down, remembers that their friendship ended on a fishing trip in a quarrel over a marlin. "I hated his guts for twenty years over that," Strater now recalls their feud, "I never hated any man so much in my life." Then he added: "But of all the friends I've had, now dead, the one I most wish were alive today is Hemingway."[2]

---

1. François Villon, "Ballade-VI (c. 1460)," *The Complete Works of Francois Villon,* trans. Anthony Bonner (New York, 1960), p. 143.
2. Henry Strater, "Hemingway," *Art in America,* 49 (1961), 84–85.

ARE WE GOING TO HEMINGWAY'S *FEAST*?

GERRY BRENNER

"Nobody including me would be permitted to put his cotton-picking typewriter to work on Ernest's prose to 'improve' it. Except for punctuation and the obviously overlooked 'ands' and 'buts' we [Charles Scribner's Sons and I] would present his prose and poetry to readers as he wrote it, letting the gaps lie where they were. Where repetitions and redundancies occurred, we would cut. We would not add anything."

—*Mary Hemingway, on the second "principle of procedure" that would guide her as executor of her husband's literary estate.*[1]

GRAY BOXES FILL SEVERAL SHELVES along the northeast wall of the fourth-floor Hemingway Room in the recently opened John F. Kennedy Library on Columbia Point. Two of those many boxes of holographs, typescripts, letters, notes, photographs, and miscellany contain Items 121–89, the drafts, revisions, fragments and miscellaneous notes of *A Moveable Feast*. Any careful study of the materials in those Items must call into question the 1964 edition that Charles Scribner's Sons issued under Mary Hemingway's authority as executor. The materials show that contrary to her "Note" in the book, Hemingway had not "finished" it "in the spring of 1960 in Cuba."[2] They also show that she altered, cut and added significant material. Those changes affect emphases Hemingway had sought and modify his discernible intentions in shaping the book and in trying to guide an understanding of them. As might be expected, the drafts not only disclose problems Hemingway had in writing and revising various sections, but also allow glimpses

Reprinted with permission from *American Literature*, 54, No. 4 (December 1982), 528–44.

into personal concerns simmering deep in the work. Mary Hemingway's substantial changes in the materials that went into *Feast* raise at least two ethical questions. Short of adding a disclaimer to the "Note," alleging that Hemingway had finished the novel, should Scribner's consider issuing a revised edition, one that might represent more accurately the book that Ernest Hemingway, not his widow, had prepared for publication? And can Hemingway scholars continue teaching a bastard text?

Before discussing the *Feast* materials, I should make it clear that I do not wish to impugn Mary Hemingway's editorial skills.[3] Like all Hemingway scholars, critics, students, and general readers, I am deeply grateful for her midwifery in bringing *Feast* to print. The book may not give us the "real gen on the old days in Paris," as Hemingway thought it would.[4] Indeed, it may only have let loose a salvo to redress old grudges, one that rallied literary historians to the trenches. Or it may only contribute, as memoirs, to his image as a "compleat" man of letters. Still, any study of Items 121–89 will find vexing problems that Mary Hemingway had to solve when she and Charles Scribner Jr. agreed to publish the book embedded in those items.[5]

I

Mary Hemingway's declaration that her husband "finished the book in the spring of 1960 in Cuba" misrepresents the facts. Although the 1960 dating of Hemingway's "Preface" seems to confirm her declaration, as does a statement by her eventual daughter-in-law,[6] yet as early as 1972 the scrupulous Carlos Baker commented, "I have not seen the original of this prefatory note."[7] His scruples give reason to suspect the composition and the date of the "Preface." Indeed, no such "Preface" in Hemingway's handwriting exists among the *Feast* items. There are, of course, various drafts with expressions that could be collated into a "Preface." For instance, several times in Item 122, the source of some materials for an "introduction," almost the exact phrasing of the last sentence of the "Preface" turns up: "But there is always the chance that such a book of fiction may throw some light on what has been written as fact." Yet nowhere in the holographs or typescript does the first sentence of that two-sentence, last paragraph exist: "If the reader prefers, this book may be regarded as fiction." Rather on several sheets in Item 122 Hemingway writes more assertively, "This book is fiction."[8] And over one-half of the second paragraph, considerably edited, comes from a section catalogued under Item 124 as "Endings." Hemingway varyingly refers to this set of drafts as both a last chapter and an introduction. On several sheets he notes that this material should be inserted into chapter twenty-one, that it should be put into the last paragraph of the intro-duction, that as the last chapter it is not yet right, that it is not successful, that he should try to improve upon it. Only in typescript as Item 125, then, can the pub-lished "Preface" be found. And that typescript has "Ernest Hemingway" typed at the bottom, not signed. Most tellingly, that typescript is dated 1959, not, as repre-sented in the published text, 1960.

To conclude that the holograph for that "Preface" got lost is tempting. But anyone familiar with the Hemingway Collection knows that virtually nothing got lost, that Hemingway kept nearly every scrap of paper he put his hand to. It can be argued that the holograph has been misplaced or withheld,[9] but I think is is more likely as the rest of my essay should show—that Mary Hemingway collated and, in places, created the "Preface."

Other evidence proves that she, not her husband, finished the book. Fore-most is the "finished" typescript of the 19 chapters that Hemingway had com-posed, completed, and corrected, Item 188.[10] This "finished" typescript has one less chapter than the published version. To his 19 chapters Mary Hemingway added, as the tenth chapter, "Birth of a New School," in which the young Hemingway sarcastically urges a pestering young writer to become a critic. Hemingway had worked on the chapter enough to bring it from holograph to typescript. But he had not included it in his "finished" typescript.

II

A more significant change that Mary Hemingway made in the *Feast* manu-scripts was in the ordering of the chapters. How to sequence his 19 chapters understandably troubled Hemingway. The various drafts show many strike-overs and renumberings of the sequence. But by the time of his "finished" typescript, he had resolved the problem, a resolution that Mary Hemingway, for "continui-ty's sake," as she acknowledges,[11] altered in two places.

One alteration concerned placing the chapter *"Une Génération Perdue."* In Hemingway's "finished" typescript it stands as "Chapter Seven." In the pub-lished version it became chapter three. By moving it forward, Mary Hemingway obscured two fine patterns that Hemingway weaves—carefully, I think—into his text. One is the pattern of despotic women, a pattern that Gertrude Stein's recur-ring image strengthens. That is, had Mary Hemingway deferred to the "finished" typescript and left out "Birth of a New School," it would be clear that the book loops back to Gertrude Stein twice, highlighted as she is in Hemingway's "Chap-ter Two," "Chapter Seven," and "Chapter Twelve" of Item 188. Her recurring image at those five chapter intervals lessens the impression of the book as a randomly arranged gallery of portraits. Even more, it better emphasizes, through delayed repetition, her role as adversary, as the "bad mother" of Hemingway's Paris years. Five chapters after the last Gertrude Stein material he brings his thematic momentum against destructive women to its crescendo, for the last three chapters of his "finished" typescript focus indirectly, then directly, upon Zelda Fitzgerald, in his eyes a predatory hawk.

The second pattern that Mary Hemingway's rearranged sequence obscured was the contrast that Hemingway achieves by juxtaposing chapters on Gertrude Stein and Sylvia Beach. In his "finished" typescript "Shakespeare and Company" (his "Chapter Three") follows "Miss Stein Instructs," and "Hunger Was a Good Discipline" (his "Chapter Eight") follows *"Une Génération Perdue."* This alternation silently contrasts two mother images, the dogmatic, highhanded and imperious Gertrude Stein against the tolerant, nurturing and modest Sylvia Beach. The rearranged chapters simply blur this pattern.

Mary Hemingway shuffled the chapter sequence a second time by putting the chapter on Schruns and the breakup of Ernest and Hadley's marriage at the end. In contrast, Hemingway's "finished" typescript has this as "Chapter Sixteen," set between the chapter on Dunning and the three chapters on Fitzgerald. Part of Hemingway's plan, I think, was to conclude with the last of these three chapters, "Chapter Nineteen," now titled "A Matter of Measurements." That chapter would have ended the book adroitly by providing a double rationale for writing it. It would have informed Georges, bar chief at the Ritz Hotel, about "this Monsieur Fitzgerald that everyone asks. . . about" (p. 191). It would also have made good Hemingway's promise to himself to write "about the early days in Paris" (p. 193).

Certainly the last chapter of the published edition provides a satisfying climax, ending the book as it does with the sense of what Hemingway lost because of the seductions of the "pilot fish," John Dos Passos, and of the rich, Pauline Pfeiffer and the Murphys, Gerald and Sara. There is good reason to admire Mary Hemingway's ending to her husband's "Chapter Nineteen." But that change alters considerably the emphases that Hemingway gave his materials, as I will discuss presently at some length.

But first, one of Mary Hemingway's more curious alterations needs comment: she changed the epigraph to the F. Scott Fitzgerald chapters. Except for one deleted sentence, the published version on p. 147 copies verbatim the text of what seems to be the earliest holograph of that foreword, Item 170.[12] The deleted sentence follows sentence two about how Fitzgerald's talent "was brushed or marred." It reads, "He even needed some one as a conscience and he needed professionals or normally educated people to make his writing legible and not illiterate."[13] Item 171, the typescript of his holograph, allows this sentence to stand. But in Item 172, a heavily corrected typescript, Hemingway revises his headnote, lining through the just-quoted sentence. However, he also lines through the last two clauses that Mary Hemingway kept in the published headnote; "and could not fly any more because the love of flight was gone and he could only remember when it had been effortless." Then he adds a sentence about *The Great Gatsby*, commenting that Fitzgerald was "thinking well" and was "fully conscious of its worth" when he had written it. A second sentence commends *Tender Is the Night* as a "better book written in heroic and desperate confession." He begins a third sentence, "It was the failure of these." But then he strikes through all three sentences and drafts, instead, a single sentence: "He was flying again and I was lucky to meet him just after a good time in his writing if not a good one in his life." On the last, an unnumbered, page of Item 172 Hemingway drafts the following revision, one that appears also in his "finished" typescript: "Later he became conscious of his damaged wings and of their construction and he learned to think. He was flying again and I was lucky to meet him just after a good time in his writing if not in his life."

Hemingway, then, had second, if not third, thoughts about the concluding clauses of the published headnote, judgmental and condescending as they are. And while the published version reads more smoothly and eloquently than the "finished" typescript version, the latter expresses a note of genuine gratitude, a note that warmly contravenes the scorn in Hemingway's three-chapter portrait of Fitzgerald.

III

While Mary Hemingway's alterations change *Feast* in ways not intended by her husband, her cuts more significantly affect it. Some of her cuts show good judgment, even though they go beyond her principle of cutting only "where repetitions and redundancies occurred." For example, she cut several explicit references to Pauline Pfeiffer where mention of her would have required information that Hemingway had not provided. Items 175 and 188, the penultimate and the "finished" typescripts of the Chapter "Hawks Do Not Share," include such references. The closing paragraph begins by noting that no one besides Pauline gave any thought to Zelda Fitzgerald's "great secret" that "Al Jolson is greater than Jesus." Because *Feast* elsewhere omits reference to Pauline, Mary Hemingway wisely kept specific mention of her out of the text.

Another cut was equally judicious. Hemingway's draft of the chapter on Ralph Cheever Dunning, "An Agent of Evil," ends in Item 169 and 188 with a sentence about Evan Shipman. Because, Hemingway explains, he has never read anything on Shipman or on his unpublished poetry, including him in the book is very important. Mary Hemingway correctly saw the inconsistency of Hemingway's explaining here—but nowhere else—his reason for writing about any person. And because Hemingway writes of Shipman in the chapter before this one, his concluding sentence is irrelevant. That the sentence survived into the "finished" typescript once again indicates the unfinished state of that typescript.

Other cuts Mary Hemingway made in the "finished" typescript are, I think, protective. One such cut is in the chapter "Hawks Do Not Share." How to comment on Fitzgerald's "editorial" or advisory role clearly troubled Hemingway. On the question of when he showed Fitzgerald the manuscript of *The Sun Also Rises* (pp. 184–85), he writes two sentences in the pencil manuscript, Item 173. First he says that not until after he had sent the manuscript to Scribner's did he show it to Fitzgerald. But he then adds that he *thinks* he first showed Fitzgerald the first proofs, which he had already cut in several places. In the corrected typescript, Item 175, he strikes through this second sentence, perhaps because its "I think" acknowledges uncertainty. And to the first sentence he adds the details that we now have on p. 184: "Scott did not see it until after the completed rewritten and cut manuscript had been sent to Scribner's at the end of April." But in that same typescript Hemingway adds four sentences, ones cut from the published version, even though they were in his "finished" typescript. In them he admits that he forgets both when he first let Fitzgerald look at his fair copy and when Fitzgerald first looked at the proofsheets of the shorter, revised version. He goes on to acknowledge that he discussed the proofsheets with Fitzgerald but that any decisions were his own. Then he dismisses the entire episode by remarking that it didn't matter anyway.

Surely Hemingway's admission of forgetfulness here, more than a "repetition or redundancy," does not warrant excision. Perhaps Mary Hemingway felt that it would be inconsistent for him to confess forgetfulness. After all, Hemingway prides himself on his memory throughout the book, nowhere more clamorously than in that litany of "I remember" that swells to a coda near the end of the Schruns material. But to conceal a gap in his virtually seamless memory by cutting the passage is protective.

Mary Hemingway's most significant cut was in the ending of Hemingway's "Chapter Sixteen," the Schruns material that she used for her twentieth chapter, "There is Never any End to Paris." Without question the task of writing about the breakup of his and Hadley's marriage had to be the most painful section he wrote.

Confirming its painfulness are the pages and pages of drafts and revisions of that material, assembled in Items 121, 123, 126 and 127. They reveal a different thrust to the book. In them Hemingway stops projecting himself as that responsible young artist or as an innocent victim of the rich. Instead he exposes himself, tries to deal honestly with complex emotions and guilt.

The earliest draft of the events behind the breakup may be the unnumbered last page of Item 121. It is worth noting that Hemingway's first try at writing about these events comes as an addendum to writing about the more easily remembered pleasures of the Schruns winters. The addendum, an unnumbered twentieth page that follows the 19 page pencil holograph, suggests that initially he was reluctant to stir up dormant pools of guilt. It also suggests that he realized the falseness of his idyllic recollections, were he to shy away from the calamitous "nightmare winter." In his addendum, then, he avoids identifying the destroyers of his and Hadley's happiness. But he says that they were rich infiltrators whose relentless determination yet good intentions overran him and Hadley, whom he characterizes as a carelessly confident young couple. Interestingly, he magnanimously declares that the blame for the breakup belongs only to himself, acknowledges that he lived with that blame all his life, and then asserts that only one person was blameless and came out of the experience well. Of course he refers, albeit indirectly, to Hadley.

Hemingway reworked this ending several times. In an unnumbered page of the penciled drafts that are gathered together in Item 123 he notes that the story of that breakup is complicated and has no place in this book. Even more, rather than disparage the woman who contributed to the breakup as an evil woman, he insists that she helped shape a new happiness that yielded good work, here alluding to Pauline. Again he still blames only himself for what happened and is grateful that the one person who bore no culpability was not permanently harmed.

More interesting versions of this ending are the pair of page numbered, penciled drafts in Item 123, which, regrettably, I can only summarize here. On pages 5 and 6 of one of them, Hemingway details the particulars of his bad luck, of the destructiveness of loving two women simultaneously, and of the trusting wife with whom he has shared many hardships. He continues by remarking on the new woman's incredulousness that he can love her and his wife at the same time. He observes, though, that she says this only after their own relationship has developed, after the "murder" has been done. He finishes with a half-dozen sentences that admit to his lying to everyone, to doing unbelievable things, to breaking promises, to Pauline's immediate victory—because of her ruthlessness—and to the eventual victory of the one who apparently had lost—Hadley. Of all the things that ever occurred in his life, he calls Hadley's victory the luckiest.

Displeased, I must assume, with this recapitulation, Hemingway describes the *menage à trois* on pages 6 and 7 of yet a second, more sustained draft, still in Item 123. He says that in the beginning he tries to live each day as it comes, not worrying, but trying to enjoy what he has. Yet he admits that this triangle is destroying him, that he hates it, that each day becomes more dangerous and impossible, and that it is like a war-time existence, living for one day at a time. While the two women are happy, or so he believes, he wakes at night and realizes his deep internal strife. Still he cannot get over the strange fact that he truly loves both women whether he is with one or the other or both, and that he, too, is happy. Then he realizes that the new woman is unhappy because she wants his love all to herself and is unwilling to believe that he can love both her and the other woman at the same time. He writes of the care he takes not to mention his wife's name when he is with the new woman, hoping to help her and himself, even though, as he sees, he is beyond help. Then he senses that by mid-winter the new woman has resolved to stalk him for marriage. But she is ever so careful to keep on friendly terms with his wife, guaranteeing her advantageous position. So she maintains her image of innocence, goes away at times to protect that appearance, but goes away only long enough to make him miss her and want her strongly. He equates the "winter of the avalanche," 1924–25, to a "happy day in childhood" when contrasted to the winter of the *menage à trois*, 1925–26. He finishes by declaring that the new woman made one serious error when she decided to get him to marry her. She failed to appreciate the power of remorse that would haunt him and eventually spoil their own relationship.

Both of these drafts are in the typescript of the Schruns material, Item 126. Interestingly, the paragraph that had formed the first of the two penciled drafts I have just summarized is very lightly lined through, obedient to Hemingway's instruction on the left margin of p. 5 of that draft that "Val" type the material but strike lightly over it in pencil.[14] To the typescript of the second penciled draft he made only two additions. Above the second line of p. 6 he inserts that the new girl was fine. And at the end of that same paragraph he exonerates her by asserting that her intentions are not evil, that she's got an aim, that she loves him truly, and that the two of them are happy, both in their heads and hearts.

Item 127, clearly his last version of the Schruns material, summarizes the breakup abruptly, reworking material from those earlier drafts. At the bottom of p. 14 of the 15-paged typescript, he strikes through the last line. In ink he instructs "Betty," the typist, to go on to the following page of penciled holograph. But before looking at that penciled page, I think it is worth spending a few moments on this corrected p. 15 of the *typescript*. Here Hemingway explains that he and Hadley were susceptible to infiltration because they were excessively confident in one another and had become too careless in their pride and confidence. He claims both that others overran them but that the story of the destruction of one couple's happiness and the forging of another's can be quite instructional. Next he magnanimously asserts, as in earlier drafts, that never did he try to divide up the blame for these events, accepting only his own blame, which he says he saw with clarity all his life. To conclude, he ambiguously remarks that that year produced but one good, and he is grateful for his recognition that from all of this he learned the complexity of loving two women simultaneously, learned that there is nothing more instructional and complex for a man to learn.

This typescript p. 15, as I noted, is not the penciled one that Hemingway instructs "Betty" to go on to. Instead he asks her to type out a second p. 15 in Item 126, a page of penciled holograph that, again, I can only summarize. The first two sentences are almost identical to the first two that begin the first paragraph on p. 207. But the published version has a phrase not in the penciled holograph or in any of the available materials I have seen. So rather than leave the second sentence to read, "The winter of the avalanches was like a happy and innocent winter in childhood compared to that winter and the murderous summer that was to follow," Mary Hemingway inserted as an appositive after the third "winter" the phrase, "a nightmare winter disguised as the greatest fun of all." Hemingway proceeds, declaring that his and Hadley's self-confidence made them carelessly proud, that except for his own share he has never apportioned anyone else's blame for the violation of their happy relationship. He declares, too, that though three hearts were "bulldozed" and one happy relationship destroyed, yet another was built. The love and good work that came from this second happy relationship, however, are separable from this book. Indeed, he has written about it, he says, but has chosen to omit it, for it is a complex, worthwhile and instructional story whose own end is also irrelevant. He accepts any blame for the "bulldozing," contritely admitting that it is his to own and to come to terms with. He concludes by exonerating Hadley of any blame and expressing gratitude for the single, durable good that resulted: that Hadley finally fared well, married a man far superior to himself, is and deserves to be happy. This penciled holograph, then, concludes Hemingway's Schruns chapter. Indeed, in one circled note at the top of it, Hemingway designates it the final version, dating it "March 15." And in ink at the bottom of the page he instructs "Betty" to "please end here." It is this text that ends his "Chapter Sixteen," pp. 10 and 11 of Item 188.

IV

This shows, of course, that Mary Hemingway chose to withhold this ending from publication. Perhaps she realized it would leave several questions dangling for readers. Who were the new people who came deep into Ernest and Hadley's lives? What made the following summer "murderous?" Why not go into the details of the complex, worthwhile and instructional story about three bulldozed hearts? Even more than the questions, the passage has a finality about it that makes it read like a coda, like the book's climax. The following chapters on Fitzgerald, then, would be anticlimactic. Justifiable or not, Mary Hemingway's deletion of this ending violates her principle for making cuts in her husband's work.

The above ending to the Schruns material shows something else, too. It shows that Hemingway intended to exclude from his book all the material about the "pilot fish" (John Dos Passos) and the rich. Yet his executor grafted large portions of it onto the Schruns ending. There is some fine writing in that material, and it would be hard to resist adding it somehow, somewhere. While Mary Hemingway chose to add it, she did not add it as her husband had left it.

Here I must backtrack to Item 126, the most interesting of the *Feast* Items. This 26-page, corrected typescript of Item 123 has two parts. The 15-page second part, which covers the first winter in the Vorarlberg and becomes pp. 197–207 of *Feast*, poses no problems. But the first part does, even though it fails to become part of the typescripts of either Items 127 or 188. This 11-page section (a 9-page text with a second set of pp. 8 and 9) about the second winter in the Vorarlberg provides the text for the last five pages of *Feast*. Mary Hemingway heavily edited this material, in several places cutting more than "repetitions and redundancies." Five cuts especially warrant remark.

The first of these was in the segment about Hemingway's trip to New York and his return to Paris. The last sentence of the second full paragraph of the published text, p. 210, reads, "But the girl I was in love with was in Paris then, and I did not take the first train, or the second or the third." The next paragraph begins, "When I saw my wife again standing by the tracks as the train came in. . . ." But in Item 126, pp. 6–7 of the typescript, Hemingway writes that the girl he loved was in Paris now, still corresponding with his wife, and he makes no mention of a first, second or third train. Instead, he tells where he and the girl he loved went and what they did, and says that everything they did made them feel unbelievably, wrenchingly, killingly happy, selfish and treacherous. Continuing, he adds that the dreadfulness and strangeness of their happiness brought on remorse so black that he hated their evil but felt no contrition until he saw the wife he loved, standing by the tracks. The answer to why Mary Hemingway would keep the factual rind of such a sentence but discard its confessional, perhaps over-ripe fruit may lie in her second cut.

That cut was in the ending of the next-to-last paragraph of the book. We now have only the sentence, "We never went back to the Vorarlberg and neither did the rich." But Hemingway actually concludes that paragraph with a sentence (drafted on p. 9 of Item 123 and copied out in typescript on p. 7 of Item 126) about how good a thing remorse was, about how—were he luckier and a better human being—remorse could have reserved for him something worse than to be, for the next several years, a constant, genuine companion. As with the first cut, then, Mary Hemingway seems intent upon striking from the record any impression that Hemingway suffered either guilt or remorse for his conduct.

Cut three was in Hemingway's long conclusion to this material in Item 126. She lifted several sentences from it and conflated them with material from a brief passage in Item 124 about "There is never any ending to Paris. . . ." But she deleted one long typescript paragraph on pp. 7 and 8 of Item 126 that deals fair-handedly with the rich, partly excusing their role in his and Hadley's breakup. In this paragraph Hemingway concedes that perhaps the rich were good, that the "pilot fish" was truly a friend, that they were never opportunists who used others to serve their own aims, that they collected people in much the way that others collected or bred horses. More, he acknowledges that they supported his own ruthless decisions, but only, he pencils in, after he had already made them. And he admits that deceit—whether his or theirs is unclear—had made all occasions seem natural, rational, and good. Then he comments that the decisions he had made turned out poorly not because of the rich but because of bad luck and his own character flaws. He sees that anyone who lies and deceives people once will do so again. He next remarks that he hated the rich people who had supported and encouraged his wrongdoing. But he corrects himself, saying that he had once hated them, indicating thereby that he has gotten over that hatred. And he reiterates that they had supported him only after he had made his decisions, that his life with Pauline had been as good for quite a few years as his life with Hadley had been in their early years in Paris. Even more, he owns that the rich could not know all of the circumstances that lay behind his decisions, that they had no way of knowing that the decisions would be wrong and would go sour. Then he acknowledges that nothing was their fault except for involving themselves in other people's lives. And while they brought bad luck to those people whose lives they did enter, their own lives suffered even worse luck and they ended up having the worst luck imaginable.

Hemingway valued this lengthy paragraph, as seems confirmed by the existence of a corrected copy of it, typed out on a second p. 8 of this first typescript in

Item 126. But then at this point in the typescript he strikes through two paragraphs about his remorse and its lasting until Hadley remarried. In blue ink he boldly lines through them again on the second set of pp. 8 and 9.[15] Then on their heels finally emerges the line, "That was the end of the first part of Paris." But once again Mary Hemingway cut, this time Hemingway's ending. She followed his typescript through the sentence, "We never went back to the Vorarlberg and neither did the rich" (p. 211). But then she stopped. His typescript continues, saying that even the "pilot fish" never returned, that there were other spots for him to guide the wealthy to, and that eventually he too became wealthy. Hemingway then adds that the "pilot fish" suffered worse luck than anyone else. On the second typed p. 9 of this ending he strikes out the words that compare the "pilot fish's" bad luck to others, leaving just the thought that the "pilot fish" had bad luck, too.

By ending his commentary on the rich with the note that fate eventually dealt harshly with Dos Passos, Hemingway adds a measure of compassion absent from the published text, backs away from the harsh portrait he had sketched. That compassion, added to the previously cut expressions of remorse and of forgiveness toward the rich, contributes to a less judgmental, more tolerant Hemingway.

Hemingway finished this section with one last, corrected paragraph, making a few changes to the first typescript version of p. 9 and adding to the second typescript of p. 9 two long last sentences. Yet Mary Hemingway cut this entire paragraph, the last I call attention to. It begins by remarking that no one climbs up slopes to ski down them now, that nearly everyone breaks a leg skiing, but that breaking a leg is probably easier in the long run than breaking a heart, even though "they" say that some people sometimes are strong, later, where the breaks have been. Coyly, Hemingway admits he is not sure about that, but recalls who expressed the idea. Then he declares that this was the way Paris had been during his early years when he and Hadley were quite poor and quite happy. He owns that he has not included a lot of other things about Paris, but feels that he has written enough, perhaps, for one book. He has written, he says, another book that deals with the parts he has not included, and he remembers, too, the stories that Hadley lost.

V

Mary Hemingway's many changes in the endings of the Schruns material make it clear that she faced a difficult decision. She could have taken the easy solution. She could have had Scribner's publish the "finished" typescript, Item

188. Many scholars and students will frown at her failure to abide by her duty as executor—to publish only her husband's "completed" work—or at least to be loyal to her own second "principle of procedure." But she chose the more difficult and questionable task of salvaging some excellent writing that might otherwise have ended up as miscellany, were it ever to see print at all.

Nevertheless, her ending to *Feast* does not read like vintage Hemingway. Some of what she kept, her husband, with better judgment, discarded. She kept his disingenuous self-deprecation. After so many chapters in which young Ernest's ruthlessness or sarcasm stands out in high relief, it rings false at the end to read his self portrait as a clown or a fond, unsuspecting dog that wags its tail for the scraps of approval doled out by the rich: "Under the charm of these rich I was as trusting and as stupid as a bird dog who wants to go out with any man with a gun, or a trained pig in a circus who has finally found someone who loves and appreciates him for himself alone. . . . I wagged my tail in pleasure. . ." (p. 209). Even more, she kept the melodrama of the happy, young, inexperienced Hemingways overrun by the cunning, irresponsible rich "who, when they have passed and taken the nourishment they needed, leave everything deader than the roots of any grass Attila's horses' hooves have ever scoured." She kept the sentimentality, too. I cannot look easily at the garnished image of the susceptible young Hemingways, so easily taken advantage of by the rich, particularly after Hemingway has demonstrated so often his skill with satiric rapier. Indeed, by leaving out the material in Item 126 in which he excuses the rich and accepts the blame for what happens, Mary Hemingway further sentimentalizes Hemingway's view of what had happened and who was to blame. His revision of that material shows more maturity in him than does her version, which portrays him as the adolescent, whimpering over the ashes of his and Hadley's happiness, torched by the rich.

Perhaps most of all, Mary Hemingway's version deletes Hemingway's apologies to Hadley. In draft, revision, and "finished" typescript he insists that she was in no way responsible for what happened, expresses gratefulness that she remarried and came out of the entire experience well. It may be that we should quibble most with this omission. Perhaps Mary Hemingway was wise to omit, for most readers conclude that Hadley is the book's heroine, as he expressed overtly in many of the drafts of beginnings and endings.[16] Mary Hemingway may have seen that her husband's "finished" typescript ending of "Chapter Sixteen" blubbers a bit in his gratitude that Hadley lived and fared well after that "nightmare winter" and the "murderous summer" that followed. But it is as likely that she took umbrage at the inferior position his praise of Hadley put her in. After all, Hadley comes away from Hemingway's writing, once again, as the undisputed, central woman in his life. Yet that first wife never faced the hard task and all its attendant problems of seeing into print an important, all-but-finished work. The last wife did. For that she deserves, again, gratitude and respect.

Perhaps my discussion expresses little respect. It may seem, for example, that I rely too heavily upon documents and so overlook the likelihood that Hemingway discussed his plans for *Feast* with his wife. It is appealing to think that Mary Hemingway's private knowledge of her husband's intentions gave her access to the kinds of changes he would have made before he would publish these memoirs. But his silence about his own work is well known, projected early onto Jake Barnes: "You'll lose it if you talk about it." And as Mary Hemingway herself has acknowledged, she was not privy to his private world of authorship, having declared that never did her husband discuss his writing with her in the seventeen years they were together.[17]

1. *How It Was* (New York: Knopf, 1976), p. 520. I wish here to thank the University of Montana for a travel and research grant that enabled me to do the preparatory work for this article. For assistance at the John F. Kennedy Library I also thank the staff and especially Jo August Hills, model curator of the Hemingway Collection. Because I was refused permission to quote directly from the unpublished manuscripts, I am forced to paraphrase several key passages.

2. In my text I parenthesize subsequent quotations from this edition (New York: Scribner's).

3. It is erroneous to single out Mary Hemingway as the person responsible for every change made in *Feast*, for she and L. H. Brague at Scribner's "worked together" on the book, as she records in *How It Was*, p. 520. When I remark, then, her decisions or her additions, alterations or cuts, I may well be in error: they may have been Harry Brague's. But as executor she had to approve any changes, making her ultimately accountable for them.

4. Carlos Baker, *Hemingway: The Writer as Artist*, 4th ed. (Princeton: Princeton University Press, 1972), p. 350.

5. For a preliminary assessment see Jacqueline Tavernier-Courbin, "The Manuscripts of *A Moveable Feast*," *Hemingway Notes*, 6 (1981), 9–15.

6. In "Reminiscences of Hemingway," *Saturday Review*, 9 May 1964, Valerie Danby-Smith, Hemingway's secretary during the summer of 1959, remarks that she read "several chapters" of the Paris sketches "one day in August" (p. 30). She adds that the following spring Hemingway resumed working on the manuscript, preparing it "for publication that fall or the following spring" (p. 57). But none of the dates on any of the *Feast* manuscripts vouch for those May 1960 additions or corrections. The "history" of the composition of the book is contradictory, as Baker noted long ago, *Writer as Artist*, p. 353; and Jacqueline Tavernier-Courbin more recently, "The Mystery of the Ritz-Hotel Papers," *College Literature*, 7 (1980), 289–303.

7. *Writer as Artist*, p. 355.

8. Tavernier-Courbin, "The Manuscripts," p. 13.

9. An argument for its being misplaced or withheld could be made on the grounds that it met with the same fate as another holograph that seems intended as part of the *Feast* materials. I refer to Hemingway's 8-page "word-portrait of his son Bumby," to which Baker refers in *Writer as Artist*, pp. 353, 358. My inquiries have yielded no clue to that manuscript's whereabouts.

10. There are, in fact, two "finished" typescripts of the book that Hemingway had settled on. But Item 189 is an uncorrected carbon of the typescript in Item 188.

11. *How It Was,* p. 520.

12. It is difficult to fix the date of the composition of this headnote. As long ago as 1969 in *The Hemingway Manuscripts: An Inventory,* (University Park: Pennsylvania State University Press), p. 19, Philip Young and Charles W. Mann had described it as "considerably older than the rest of the manuscript." See also Tavernier-Courbin, "The Mystery," p. 300.

13. Tavernier-Courbin, "The Manuscripts," p. 12. The other quotations I cite on the epigraph are also available in this article.

14. "Val" is Valerie Danby-Smith, the typist for this material, for whom Hemingway felt adulterous desire—as he had for Adriana Ivancich a decade earlier. This material, then, had its contemporary relevance for Hemingway. After all, his discussion of the difficulty of loving one's wife and a new woman applied as much to Valerie's presence among the Hemingways during the summer of 1959 and, later, in the Hemingway household during much of 1960 as it had applied to Pauline's presence during the winter of 1925.

15. Tavernier-Courbin, "Manuscripts," p. 13, quotes part of this "revealing passage."

16. Item 122, a 9-page, undated, unnumbered set of penciled "Starts and Incompletes" with some ink and red pencil corrections, contains most of the tributes to Hadley.

17. MH to GB, 4 August 1975.

"BIMINI" AND THE SUBJECT OF HEMINGWAY'S
ISLANDS IN THE STREAM

JOSEPH M. DeFALCO

IN HIS 1970 REVIEW of Ernest Hemingway's *Islands in the Stream*, Irving Howe suggests that Hemingway underwent a "creative crisis" during the period he was at work on the book. Howe attributes the cause of the crisis to Hemingway's loss of a "firm and disciplined vision of life." Since such a vision is considered to be the *sine qua non* of Hemingway's best work, Howe's assessment raises the question of just how seriously we should take this work as part of the Hemingway canon. Most of the early reviewers expressed similar reservations over the purpose and artistry of the work, and the critical appraisals have changed little since 1970. Edmund Wilson's 1971 prophecy that "in the long run, the book will appear to be more important than seems to be the case right now" suggests that he detected elements in the work that redeem it from its present condition as a kind of autobiographical curiosity.[1]

Wilson had a strong feel for the darker elements in Hemingway's work, and along with Malcolm Cowley who responded to the archetypical and mythical resonances gave us an early perspective from which to engage the more puzzling elements of *Islands in the Stream*.[2] The primary matter of the three published segments insists that we take the secondary mythic structures as important components of the larger thematic structure. Hudson's self-created "Eden" of the "Bimini" segment, the "long, dark night of the soul" of "Cuba," and the Homeric *Nekuia* of the final "At Sea" part of the novel invite us to respond to the work as a unified structure rather than as a disjointed trilogy. New Testament matter inherent in the names Thomas, Andrew, and David provides the hint of allegory as another unifying structure. In particular, David, whose name suggests

Reprinted with permission from *Topic*, 31 (1977), 41–51.

313

the House of David among other possibilities, undergoes a Christ-like *agon* in the episode with the swordfish that results in the iteration of the Biblical themes of love and suffering.

Hemingway never submitted to the temptation to beggar his fictive details by limiting their suggestivity to the *sensus literalis* of easy allegorizing, and he does not do so in *Islands in the Stream*. If flashes of his best writing appear in this work, these occur because Hemingway employed his time-proven but never shop-worn method that he described in his well-known "tip of the iceberg" comment. Whatever that comment may mean, what it stresses is the importance of meta-phor to the craft of fiction. Almost from the beginning, Hemingway's method of developing suggestive meaning was based upon the premise that subject is meta-phor and that metaphor is subject. From this elementary premise, Hemingway maneuvered simple details of objective reality into positions that generated meta-phorical pressures of an extremely complex order. The unfinished character of *Islands in the Stream* is easily visible in the many instances of trivial dialogue and tedious expositions, but the exploitation of metaphorical possibilities inher-ent in the subject matter rarely falters.

Even if the novel were a finished product, the likelihood of its having received critical acclaim is remote. There are many reasons, but chief among them seems to be the subject itself. Indeed, the novel itself raises the question: What is the subject? It is nearly impossible for any reader of the novel to identify sympathetically with Thomas Hudson and his peculiar *Weltanschauung* and self-generated *angst*. Those who choose to read the novel as author-biography find it distasteful because it seems to be Hemingway doing again what so many had faulted him for doing in the past: fictionalizing his own real-life experiences. The most persuasive proponent of this position is Carlos Baker in his *Hemingway: The Writer as Artist*. He views the work as an extreme extension of what he calls "The Narcissus Principle": "To his original impulse to transform his personal past into material for art was added an ulterior and perhaps mainly subconscious determination to exploit it as a means of justifying himself and his actions in the eyes of the world." Baker follows this line of argument to account for "episodes and anecdotes, held together by the ligatures of Thomas Hudson's history and personality" in the first two parts of the novel.[3]

As Baker's analysis reveals, the stumbling blocks en route to an appreciation of the novel as an artistic whole are formidable. Principally, though, they are biographical. From the same source, however, there is another perspective avail-able, and it does provide an alternative conclusion. Aside from his remarks about icebergs, putting down "what really happened in action," trying to write "clas-sics," and the like, Hemingway told us and often demonstrated that he was an experimentalist with fictional materials and form. For example, he told us in the "Foreword" to *Green Hills of Africa* (1935) of his attempt there "to write an absolutely true book to see whether the shape of a country and the pattern of a month's action can, if truly presented, compete with a work of the imagination."[4] Earlier, in *Death in the Afternoon* (1932), he had experimented with a mixed-genre approach to give dramatic force to factual matter about bullfighting. After the critical debacle following the publication of *Across the River and into the Trees* in 1950, he tried to explain to hostile ears that the work was "experimental."

We may dismiss Hemingway's remarks as defensive or as authorial bravado, but there is the achievement of *The Old Man and the Sea* (1952). The importance of that achievement to *Islands in the Stream* lies in the near-relationship (organic, for Hemingway, if not for his critics) the works share in the time of conception. Both are parts of what Hemingway termed in another context "the whole genesis" of an ambitious plan for a series of interlinking works. In *Ernest Hemingway: A Life Story*, Carlos Baker reports that both were parts of a work in which the story of Santiago was entitled *The Sea in Being*, followed by "Parts 2 and 3, the story of Thomas Hudson from before the war until his death at sea." Once he had dropped *The Old Man and the Sea* from the work that evolved into the present *Islands in the Stream*, Hemingway referred to the opening sections as *The Island and the Stream*. A part of the Hudson story also had the title of *The Sea When Absent*. At one time Hemingway indicated that he was writing a trilogy about the sea, described then by the tentative titles of *The Sea When Young, The Sea When Absent*, and *The Sea in Being*. Putting aside the even more complex and somewhat mysterious citations of a "Land, Air, and Sea" novel, and other permutations, the common element in the "whole genesis" is the sea. As Baker points out, the generic title for the various phases of *Islands in the Stream* was "The Sea Book."[5]

Hemingway's intention to use the sea in a metaphorical way to suggest time, life, and experience seems overt in light of the various contexts in which he employed the image in the shifting titles. The formulaic progression from youth to age in the early conception hints at the magnitude of the design, and the metaphysical implications of the *Sea in Being* title indicate the philosophical import Hemingway envisioned for the whole. Most readers have recognized these claims in the transformed segment published as *The Old Man and the Sea*, but few would be willing to grant *Islands in the Stream* the status of a fiction of the same order.

No amount of synthetic critical manipulation can change an unfinished work into a completed work, but knowing the genesis of *Islands in the Stream* and knowing Hemingway's unique method of maneuvering metaphor does give us a first-rank of fiction writing. The sea-as-image is the key to the metaphorical and thus the imaginative dimensions of the work. Placing a character such as Thomas Hudson at the center of the entire metaphorical complex posed a difficult problem for Hemingway. Initially, he postulated in "Part I: Bimini" a central character not intended to be liked by the reader. The tone of the narrator supports the authorial character-premise and often goes out of its way to distance reader from material. The only sympathy evoked in the narrative presentation is that which is produced by scenic descriptions—in particular, those of the sea. Description had been Hemingway's mainstay for a long time, but here he deliberately pits it against character and situation. The tension among the fundamental constituents of fiction results in something very near to a new order of fictional *praxis*.

When character, situation, and setting no longer function in a mutually supportive way, the traditional ends of fictionalizing are no longer served. The reception of any experiment in fiction cannot be predicted, of course, and the unenthusiastic reception of *Islands in the Stream* when compared to Hemingway's private expressions of enthusiasm suggests how far apart the artist and his audience had drifted. Hemingway had taken such risks before, but never quite so daringly in the realm of *praxis*. The magnitude of the metaphor of the sea and of the thematic concerns it was to serve accounts for the need to shift the focus away from character—the usual concern of the literary realist—to setting. Thomas Hudson is a painter, and we expect him to respond with both an inner and outer vision to the phenomena of reality. But he disappoints us at every turn. To be sure, he has the eye of the artist in superficial matters of color and detail. But his artistic imagination has mortified, and his responses to the sea measure the extent of his enervation.

Emily Stipes Watt's observation in *Ernest Hemingway and the Arts* leads us close to an understanding of what Hemingway was attempting in the characterization of Hudson: "Hemingway's own creation of Thomas Hudson is the culmination of the increasing intellectualization of his protagonists."[6] Such an insight assists us insofar as we recognize that Hemingway needed an element in his characterization that would communicate the extent of the character's alienation from nature. The sea as symbol of all of cosmos that man can know and of the only arena of action where man can define himself is the foreground of Hemingway's presentation; for Hudson, it is the background against which his contracted ego deludes itself into believing that it knows itself. Hudson's intellectualizing of art and life is simply a self-serving defense of the ego.

When the artist divorces himself from the source of his artistic power and falls back upon the meager resources of his own ego, he has ceased to be an artist in Hemingway's view. Disenchanted with existence, Hudson disengages himself.

In the process, he cuts himself off from the only source of imaginative power available to the individual imagination. Without that power man cannot create structures or artifacts of whatever order out of the flux of reality. "Bimini" is not a presentation of a troubled Eden in which a lonely father manages to garner a degree of joy from the visit of his three sons. It is self-created Eden in which a deluded Hudson recapitulates the Fall, and the end result is equally disastrous. The true state of affairs is that joys are no longer possible for Thomas Hudson. Hemingway signals this predicament in many ways but never so vividly as in the casual remark of the narrator at the beginning of the calamitous celebration of the Queen's birthday: "Thomas Hudson could not sing, so he sat back in the dark and listened."[7] What passes for joy in Hudson's life are the palliatives of work and "moderate" drinking. The arrival of his sons presents the opportunity for passage back into an existence where joys are possible, but he is incapable of freeing himself from his obsession with his self-created abstraction.

The two key incidents which involve David in "Bimini" serve to portray Hudson as an emotional cripple. At times, Hudson is aware of the extent of the disintegration of his moral personality, but he consistently refuses to expose his ego to further anguish—the only possible course open to him if he is to find joy in this world. Hemingway, in the dock incident, had pointed to the kind of effete piety Hudson has accepted in lieu of painful engagements with reality. Although the moral context is ambiguous, Hemingway forces us to attend to the implications of Frank Hart's accusation that Hudson and Roger Davis are playing the role of "reformed bastards," who are "christing around," and who are "spoiling any fun" (p. 37).

When David is attacked by "the biggest hammerhead shark Hudson had ever seen" (p. 86), the implication of Hart's accusation that the moral pose is empty is validated through the dissolution of another of Hudson's—and to a lesser degree, Roger's—poses. Although Hudson fancies that his role as "father-protector" is legitimate, his actions during the shark attack reveal how helpless he has become. His armament for the confrontation with the forces generated from the literal sea complements that with which he faces the metaphorical sea: four bullets and a light-calibre and short barrelled .256 Mannlicher Shoenauer. Further, where once he had "confidence shooting it, as to being able to place his shots at close and moderate range" (p. 82), now "feeling sick at his stomach" (p. 85) he misses the shark three times. While Hudson attempts to "think" his last shot, his mate, Eddy, kills the shark with a heavy-calibre submachine gun. The episode alerts the reader to Hudson's inadequacies and points to one consequence of facing the contingencies of existence armed with the light weaponry of a dissolving moral personality.

Hudson's careful preservation of his role as a spectator-artist, observing the struggles of those who are willing to go "too far out," as David remarks of himself after the shark incident, occasions his loss of another significant opportunity to reverse the processes of spiritual decay. In the incident in which David hooks his "big fish" and undergoes his Christ-like spiritual *agon*, Hudson remains on the bridge and aloof from the action, "trusting the boy and the fight to Roger. As he saw it there was no other thing to do" (p. 124). The narrator has subtly informed us at the beginning of the novel that Hudson is not a great artist but a financially successful "good painter." His responses here and throughout the section suggest that, as a life-artist in the life-stream, he is considerably less than successful or "good."

The character of the sea in its representation of all-time, all-experience, and all-human history is of the same order as that sea out of which Santiago caught his "big fish" in *The Old Man and the Sea*. Rooted in the same imaginative complex, these fictive seas are generative in nature. Hudson's resistance to ontological reality, in spite of his protestations to the contrary, so blurs his vision that he is incapable of perceiving that existence emits not only pain and anguish but beauty and joy as well. Thus Hemingway equates Hudson's physical vision of the events of David's ordeal with the "broadbill" and Hudson's inner vision of reality. In an earlier vignette, Hemingway portrays this reluctance to relinquish the posture assumed in the name of objectivity as a visual distortion of reality. Watching Roger and the three boys swimming "out with the wind," Hudson is impressed by the easy adaptation of the human form to the sea. When he enters the sea his whole perspective alters; "With his head on the same level theirs were on, it was a different picture now, changed too because they were swimming against the breeze coming in and the chop was bothering both Andrew and David, who were swimming raggedly. The illusion of them being four sea animals was gone. . . . It was just enough to take away any illusion of being at home in the water as they had looked going out" (pp. 70–71). Although he realizes that altered perspectives alter perceptions, his choice of the actual over the illusion is qualified: "perhaps the second was the better one" (p. 70).

His responses to the affair of David's ordeal with the swordfish are similar. In terms of figurative revelation, Hudson's responses reflect his resistance to a reality that implies struggle and agony. After David has fought the fish for five hours and fifty minutes, and after having assisted only in the mechanical operation of the boat from the remoteness of the flying bridge, and after observing in his aloofness the tutelage of David by Roger, the ministrations of Eddy, the soothing services of young Tom, and the kibitzing of Andrew, Hudson finally descends to the level of the deck. Hemingway records Hudson's thoughts, and their signification is suggested both directly and through the simile: "It was strange to be on the same level as the action after having looked down on it for so many hours, he thought. It was like moving down from a box seat onto the stage or to the ringside or close against the railing of the track. Everyone looked bigger and closer and they were all taller and not foreshortened" (p. 136). Rounding out the implications of the extended simile, Hemingway tells us that from the near-perspective Hudson can now see "David's bloody hands," his "oozing feet," the "welts," and the "almost hopeless expression on his face." Even "the sea looked different now that he was so close to it" (p. 136). Finally, the altered perspective produces a view of the fish different in order: "Now he was really huge, bigger than any swordfish Thomas Hudson had ever seen. All the great length of him was purple blue now instead of brown" (p. 137).

Hudson's deficiency of "vision" allows us to entertain the possibility that the impressiveness of life-in-the-large reality as opposed to "foreshortened" and illusory views obtained from distancing life will convert Hudson into an enthusiastic devotee of metaphorical immersions, of living "life all the way up," as Jake says of bullfighters in *The Sun Also Rises*. Hudson, though, has made his "separate peace," as a deluded Frederic Henry had attempted in *A Farewell to Arms*. Hudson's "protective routine" of work, order, meals, drinks, and books has been disturbed by the arrival of his sons. If the disturbance has given him the opportunity to redeem his ego from the self-protective insulation of emotional contraction, the effort entails too great a strain upon his capacity for love and its correlative, anguish, and here, too, he demurs.

Hemingway tells us as much at the end of the episode with the swordfish. Roger has told David something just after the loss of the fish, but "Thomas Hudson never knew what it was that Roger had said to him" (p. 143). It is more than words that Hudson misses at this point; it is that kind of secret-sharing that can take place only when one is willing to discard the protective mantle of personal egoism and surrender the self totally to the pain and suffering of others. The God-pursued and bedeviled Roger Davis who has "seen" the Deity "crowd the plate" before his arrival on Bimini, whose life Hudson has a difficult time thinking of without a touch of scorn, is capable of that degree of spiritual empathy necessary to free the self from the tortures of personal egoism. Roger understands David's report that "when I was the tiredest I couldn't tell which was him and which was me" (p. 142). The reported experience is tantamount to "translation," or as near to one as possible in Hemingway's ontological view. The empathetic Roger in sharing the ordeal of the experience has shared what the aficionado shares with the matador in Hemingway's early fiction; both are conveyed into a realm where individual egos have no role. Hudson "never knew" because he is incapable of that degree of empathy which would allow him to drop his reserve and assimilate the meanings of what seems to be needless and futile suffering.

Hudson's moral and emotional acrobatics cannot save him from the fluctuating exigencies of the metaphorical sea of existence. The delusion that he can order reality by exercising "discipline" in his own life-style, by "absenting" himself from those engagements which demand that the desires of the ego and its defense against further battering be subordinated to engagements by the will, is abruptly shattered near the end of "Bimini" when he receives the news of the death of David, Andrew, and their mother. Throughout "Bimini" he has attempted to forestall the pain of engagement in on-going reality through a variety of defensive evasions. His life-plan and his artistic-plan are of the same order. He has built his emotional house to resemble his actual house on the island: "The house was built on the highest part of the narrow tongue of land between the harbor and the open sea. . . and on the ocean side you could walk out of the door and down the bluff across the white sand and into the Gulf Stream" (p. 3). Typically, the literal details generate metaphorical meanings of considerable magnitude. The Gulf Stream epitomizes the life stream of the larger sea imagery. In its aloofness from the Gulf Stream, the house figures Hudson's defensive postures. He literally believes that he too can "ride out storms" (p. 4) of an emotional order through his rationally contrived regimen of work and sensual pleasures. Hemingway makes it clear, however, that emotionless postures are inhuman postures. Hudson's delusive contrivances do not "save" his ego from human vulnerability, and the contingencies of existence do not offer the balm of going "with the house," as he had wished, when emotional storms of hurricane velocity destroy that house. At the end of "Bimini," Hudson's "Edenic" delusion collapses; it is, in Hemingway's figure, "the end of a man's own world" (p. 194).

Throughout the "Bimini" section, Hemingway's use of literal and metaphorical details has given us ample instruction for the understanding of Hudson's plight after he has lost his two sons. Through the governing metaphor of the sea, through the function Hemingway ascribes to the three sons and Roger, Mr. Bobby and even Audrey Bruce, we see various ways that individuals engage and respond to the life-stream. The boys, in their immaturity, respond with vigorous inquisitiveness to the dangers and the beauties of life symbolized in the fishing episodes and in their eager inquiries about life, love, art, and the past. The long discussions of Paris, artists, and their work, and "the way it was" for a younger Thomas Hudson and for his son Tom as an infant and child provide a contrast to the characterization of Hudson in the dramatic present by opposing his aloofness from present realities to his enjoyments in the past. For him, the past is another secure haven. It is like the island and the house, a place where the vicissitudes of life may be viewed without threatening the ego. It is a "known" quantity, and what Hudson fears most is the risk involved in the unknown outcomes of emotional encounters.

In the character Roger Davis, Hemingway employs the Conradian motif of "one of us" that he had used through Brett in *The Sun Also Rises*, and variously in his later fiction. Here, however, it is used as a fictive gambit that provides an alternative to Hudson's despairing ways. Both characters have bruised and battered psyches as a result of past physical and emotional *agons* and both are perilously close to the edge of a complete disintegration of their moral personalities. The difference lies in Roger's ability to respond emotionally and thus humanly to human situations. He, too, recognizes that there are no reasonable explanations for what they both term "evil" in the world. But Roger is still capable of resisting that evil when it is encountered. He reveals his humanness in making resolutions ("I'm not going to fight and I'm going to be some good and quit writing junk" [p. 76]), breaking them, when he fights with the man on the deck, and in suffering remorse afterward; "So I wasn't feeling so good about tonight. There's a lot of wickeds at large. Really bads. And hitting them is no solution" (p. 47). Hudson's resolutions, however, are passionless, intellectual contrivances which allow no tolerance for human deviations: "just made up my mind I wouldn't fight" (p. 76). Avoidance props Hudson's dictum of "Take it easy." Roger shares this belief, and both repeat it a number of times before the fight on the deck. The difference lies in the tenacious way Hudson holds to the precept in order to avoid making another error of judgment that will place him in a "foolish" position and cause regret. As he rather smugly concludes, he is "through with remorse" (p. 97). The intensity of the dramatic irony that is evoked by the statement approaches the existentially comic.

Roger's "union" with Audrey Bruce signals another major difference in the responses he and Hudson make to human situations. For Hudson, she represents another instance of his former engagement in the life-stream. She is the past brought forward in the form of physical beauty, and she invites emotional involvement in the present. She represents pleasant memories that have survived emotional calamities and should function to revive the emotionally sterile Hudson. For Hudson, however, pleasant memories are just that. Having screened out the anguish of the past to avoid remorse in the present, he sees Audrey more as an artifact of past joy than a reality in the joyless present. Roger is willing to risk "love" once again in the hope of becoming part of life. Hudson's "island" ways demand loyalty to the cult of "one of us," but Roger's understanding of David and affection for Audrey give him hope in his writing and effect his escape towards a life with meaning.

Although Mr. Bobby's function in "Bimini" seems to be mainly comic, Hemingway uses him early in the section to comment on Hudson's artistic vision. Through Mr. Bobby we learn the subjects of Hudson's paintings: ". . . pictures of Uncle Edward. Pictures of Negroes in the water. Negroes on land. Negroes in boats. Turtle boats. Sponge boats. Squalls making up. Waterspouts. Schooners that got wrecked. Schooners building" (p. 17). Later he tells Hudson, "You've just been painting these little simple pictures" (p. 18). Although his notion of subject for great painting is full of comic exaggeration, it modifies our view of Hudson's capacities as an artist. The narrator had referred to Hudson through understatement as a "good painter," but Mr. Bobby wants him to be a "big painter" (p. 19). Mr. Bobby's insistence that "You got to have vision," is, in fact, precisely Hemingway's major motif for the entire section. The narrowness of Hudson's subjects reflects just how much he has allowed his limited personal experiences to govern his artistic imagination. In spite of the comic context, the "movement and grandeur" of Mr. Bobby's conception suggest the historical role of the artist as one who rises above his own experiences and captures the universal griefs and aspirations of all mankind.

Hemingway emphasizes the point and allows us to see in a more serious way the extent of Hudson's imaginative impairment when he rationalizes his decision to remain in his protective Eden: "Now when he was lonesome for Paris he would remember Paris instead of going there. He did the same thing with all of Europe and much of Asia and Africa" (p. 7). His justification for what amounts to moral cowardice is exacted from a revealing comparison he makes between Renoir and Gauguin: "He remembered what Renoir had said when they told him that Gauguin had gone to Tahiti to paint. 'Why does he have to spend so much money to go so far away when one paints so well here at the Batignolles?'. . . and Thomas Hudson thought of the island as his *quartier*" (p. 7). Carlos Baker sheds some light on this passage in the biography. Unhappy over the illustrations for an edition of *A Farewell to Arms* in 1948, Baker reports of Hemingway: "If Ernest wrote a book about the Bahamas, he would like it to contain pictures—not illustrations—by Winslow Homer; if he were Guy deMaupassant, pictures by Toulouse-Lautrec or Renoir would suit the book he wrote" (p. 466). Hemingway seems to be thinking of Maupassant as the "father" of the modern commercial short story. Lumping Toulouse-Lautrec and Renoir together in this way disparages Renoir. Hemingway likely refers to Renoir's lyrical appeal to the eye, as opposed to the vibrancy and vitality of Gauguin's colors. Hudson celebrates Renoir in the commentary, but Hemingway links Hudson's rationalization with Renoir's complacency. The irony is finally Hemingway's. It does not imply complete disparagement of Hudson's skill as a painter, but it does serve to amplify other elements in the characterization that reveal Hudson's artistic and moral weaknesses.

In Chapter XV of "Bimini" when Hudson is forced to leave his *"quartier"* by the deaths of his two sons, Hemingway reveals through the narrator how little prepared Hudson is to comprehend an *angst* grounded on the substantial fact of death: "He thought that on the ship he could come to some terms with his sorrow, not knowing, yet, that there are no terms to be made with sorrow. It can be cured by death and it can be blunted or anesthetized by various things. Time is supposed to cure it, too. But if it is cured by anything less than death, the chances are that it was not true sorrow" (p. 197). The comment by the narrative voice invites the comparison between Hudson's present situation and his earlier excessive reaction to divorce and separation from his children. The escalation of personal tragedy demands a response of the same magnitude, but at the end of "Bimini" Hemingway saturates Hudson's response with connecting qualities. At the verge of insight, Hudson responds with understatement that is as much self-pity as it is self-irony: "You see, he said to himself, there's nothing to it" (p. 200). Hemingway leaves Hudson with a vast emotional expanse over which he must travel in the remaining segments of the novel. Hudson does travel it, but in the end his final "vision" remains a qualified, "I think I understand" (p. 466).

The critical judgment of *Islands in the Stream* as a work riddled with defects is largely correct. But Hemingway's attempt to shift his emphasis to the subject of the "sea" and away from character in order to engage themes larger than the human personality was an impressive experiment. That it could work when the nature of the characterization did not effect a disjunction that would destroy aesthetic unity, was amply demonstrated by *The Old Man and the Sea*. Hudson's overwhelmingly negative responses so dominate his story that the metaphorical subject loses its force and is often submerged. Recognizing its defects does not necessarily lessen the value of the enterprise. Hemingway may be criticized for producing a work that fails to engage our interest, but the fault lies more with the subject matter than with the subject. *Islands in the Stream* and *The Old Man and the Sea* share the same subject, and our interest or lack of interest in one over the other may say as much about ourselves as it does about Hemingway.

---

1. Irving Howe, "Great Man Going Down," *Harper's*, October 1970, p. 123; Edmund Wilson, "An Effort at Self-Revelation," *The New Yorker,* 2 January 1971, p. 62. For a thorough digest of the early reviews, see William R. Anderson, Jr., *"Islands in the Stream—*The Initial Reception," in *Fitzgerald/Hemingway Annual, 1971*, pp. 326–32.

2. Malcolm Cowley, "A Double Life, Half Told," *The Atlantic Monthly,* December 1970, pp. 105–06, 108.

3. Carlos Baker, *Hemingway: The Writer as Artist* (Princeton, 1972), p. 392.

4. *Green Hills of Africa* (New York, 1937).

5. Carlos Baker, *Ernest Hemingway: A Life Story* (New York, 1969), p. 494 ff. The "whole genesis" appears on p. 497.

6. Emily Stipes Watts, *Ernest Hemingway and the Arts* (Urbana, 1971), p. 181.

7. Ernest Hemingway, *Islands in the Stream* (New York, 1970), p. 28. Subsequent references are to this edition, and page numbers of excerpts are given parenthetically in the text.

BRAVER THAN WE THOUGHT

E. L. DOCTOROW

EARLY IN HIS CAREER Ernest Hemingway devised the writing strategies he would follow for life: when composing a story he would withhold mention of its central problem; when writing a novel he would implant it in geography and, insofar as possible, he would know what time it was on every page; when writing anything he would construct the sentences so as to produce an emotion not by claiming it but by rendering precisely the experience to cause it. What he made of all this was a rigorous art of compressive power, if more suited to certain emotions than others. He was unquestionably a genius, but of the kind that advertises its limits. Critics were on to these from the very beginning, but in the forward-looking 1920s, they joined his readers to make him the writer for their time. His stuff was new. It moved. There was on every page of clear prose an implicit judgment of all other writing. The Hemingway voice hated pretense and cant and the rhetoric they rode in on.

The source of his material and spring to his imagination was his own life. Issues of intellect—history, myth, society—were beside the point. It was what his own eyes saw and heart felt that he cured into fiction. Accordingly he lived his life to see and feel as much as possible. There was no place on earth he was not at home, except perhaps his birthplace. His parents' Middle Western provincialism made independence an easy passage for him. He married young and fathered a child—the traditional circumstances for settling down—and took his family with him to Europe in pursuit of excitements. He skied in the Austrian Alps, entrained to Paris for the bicycle races or prizefights, crossed the Pyrenees for the bullfights and made urgent side trips to mountain villages for the fishing or shooting. In America too, he drove back and forth from Idaho or Wyoming to Florida, never

Reprinted with permission form *The New York Times Book Review*, 18 May 1986, pp. 1, 44–45.

renting a place to live in for more than a season. He was divorced and remarried, with more children, before he bought a place of his own in Key West. But there was better fishing in Cuba, and a woman he secretly wooed there who was to become his third wife—and so on. It was Flaubert who said a writer has to sit quietly in one place, rooted in boredom, to get his work done. Hemingway lived in a kind of nomadic frenzy, but the work poured out of him. The stories and pieces and novels were done in longhand in the mornings, at whatever makeshift table he could find in a room away from his family.

As his fame grew he was able in this or that remote paradise he had found to demolish his solitude by summoning friends or colleagues from other parts of the world. And they came, at whatever inconvenience to themselves, to fish or hunt or ride with him, but most importantly to drink with him. He had sporting friends, military friends, celebrity friends, literary friends and friends from the local saloon. He was forever making friendships and breaking them, imagining affronts, squaring off in his heavy-weight crouch. Most people are quiet in the world, and live in it tentatively, as if it is not theirs. Hemingway was its voracious consumer. People of every class were drawn to this behavior, and the boasting, charming or truculent boyishness of his ways, and to his ritual celebration of his appetites.

By and large he worked from life on a very short lead time. He wrote *The Sun Also Rises* while still seeing many of the people in Paris on whom he modeled its characters, and though it took him 10 years to use his World War I experiences for *A Farewell to Arms,* by the time of the civil war in Spain he was making trips there knowing he was collecting the people, incidents and locales for *For Whom the Bell Tolls,* a novel he completed in 1939, within months of the war's end. Only illness cut down his efficiency, or more often physical accidents, of which he had a great many; he ran cars into ditches and broke bones, or cut himself with knives, or scratched his eyes. But with the Second World War his ability to work quickly from life declined, and with it the justification of his techniques. Though he was prominently a correspondent in that war, the only novel he produced from it was the very weak *Across the River and into the Trees,* and that not published until 1950. People noted his decline and attributed it to the corruption of fame, but in the last decade of his life he wrote *A Moveable Feast,* a memoir of his early days in Paris (published posthumously in 1964), and *The Old Man and the Sea,* and seemed to have found again what he could do.

Hemingway talked of suicide all his life before he committed it. In 1954 his proneness to accident culminated in not one but two airplane crashes in East Africa where he had gone to hunt, and which left him with the concussion, crushed vertebrae, burns and internal injuries that turned him, in his 50s, into an old man. From a distance the physical punishment his body received during his lifetime seems to have been half of something, a boxing match with an invisible opponent, perhaps. His mind was never far from killing, neither in actuality as he hunted or ran off to wars, nor in his work. He went after animals all his life. He shot lion and leopard and kudu in Africa, and grizzly bear in the Rockies, he shot grouse in Wyoming and pigeon in France; wherever he was he took what was available. And after he killed something it was not necessarily past his attention. His biographer, Carlos Baker, tells of the day, in Cuba, when Hemingway hooked and fought and landed a 512-pound marlin. He brought it to port in triumph, receiving the noisy congratulations of friends and acquaintances. But this was not, apparently, enough. After a night of drunken celebration, at 2 or 3 that morning, he was seen back at the dock, all alone under the moon; the great game fish hanging upside down on block and tackle, he was using it for a punching bag.

Since Hemingway's death in 1961, his estate and his publishers, Charles Scribner's Sons, have been catching up to him, issuing the work which, for one reason or another, he did not publish during his lifetime. He held back *A Moveable Feast* out of concern for the feelings of the people in it who might still be alive. But for the novel *Islands in the Stream* he seems to have had editorial misgivings. Even more deeply in this category is *The Garden of Eden,* which he began in 1946 and worked on intermittently in the last 15 years of his life and left unfinished. It is a highly readable story, if not possibly the book he envisioned. As published it is composed of 30 short chapters running to about 70,000 words. A publisher's note advises that "some cuts" have been made in the manuscript, but according to Mr. Baker's biography, at one point a revised manuscript of the work ran to 48 chapters and 200,000 words, so the publisher's note is disingenuous. In an interview with *The New York Times* last December, a Scribner's editor admitted to taking out a subplot in rough draft that he felt had not been integrated into the "main body" of the text, but this cut reduced the book's length by two-thirds.

The hero of this radically weeded *Garden of Eden* is David Bourne, a young novelist and veteran of World War I, who is traveling with his wife, Catherine, through Spain and France in the 1920s. The couple are on their honeymoon. In their small black Bugatti, they drive from the seaport village of Le Grau-du-Roi, where their stay has been idyllic, to Madrid, where the first shadows appear on their relationship. Catherine evinces jealousy of his writing. At the same time she demands experimentation in their lovemaking—she wants them to pretend that she is the boy and he is the girl. At Aigues-Mortes, in France, she has her hair cut short, and later she insists that he have his cut by the same hairdresser in a match to hers, so that he will look like her. David complies in this too, though not without some resistance and a foreboding of the ultimate corruption of the marriage.

Going on to La Napoule, near Cannes, they engage rooms in a very small hotel, where it is quiet because it is summer, the off-season in the south of France. One of the rooms is for David to write in. He has just published his war novel in America and received in the forwarded mail the press clippings and publisher's letter telling him he is a success. This news disturbs Catherine. The differences between them sharpen as she presumes to tell him the only subject worth writing is their life together on their honeymoon.

One day drinking at the cafe terrace of their hotel, they attract the attention of a beautiful young woman named Marita, who is very impressed by this darkly tanned couple with their newly dyed, almost white hair, and French fisherman shirts and linen trousers and espadrilles. She moves to their hotel. Catherine fulfills David's forebodings by commencing an affair with Marita. In further sign of her instability, she encourages David to embark on his own erotic relationship with the woman, who makes it easy by privately confessing to him that she has fallen in love with both of them. He succumbs. The ménage swims from the deserted beach coves of the area and sunbathes nude. David sleeps with one or the other as they designate in their time-sharing with him. Every day consists of a good deal of drinking, of martinis, which David himself mixes and garnishes with garlic olives at the small hotel bar, or absinthe, or Haig pinchbottle and Perrier, or Tavel, or carefully prepared Tom Collinses. The mixing and consuming of drinks is the means they seem to have chosen to adjust to the impact of their acts and conversation on one another.

It is Catherine who begins spectacularly to come apart under the strain. Becoming, in turn, bitter or remorseful, she either excoriates David for his relationship with Marita, or condemns herself for making a mess of everything. As a defense against the situation, and what he perceives as his wife's clearly accelerating mental illness, he begins to write the story he has been resisting for years, the "hard" story, he calls it, based on his life as a boy in East Africa with his white-hunter father. This story gradually intrudes on the main narrative as the boy David sights the bull elephant with enormous tusks that his father and an African assistant are looking for; he reports his sighting and lives to regret it, as the father tracks down the great beast and destroys it. The climax of the novel has to do with Catherine's reaction to this story, which David has written by hand in the simple cahiers used by French schoolchildren. A disaster then occurs which is the worst that can befall a writer as a writer, and the ménage breaks up forever, two to stay together and one to leave.

At first reading this is a surprising story to receive from the great outdoor athlete of American literature. He has not previously presented himself as a clinician of bedroom practices. Even more interesting is the passivity of his writer hero who, on the evidence, hates big-game hunting, and who is portrayed as totally subject to the powers of women, hapless before temptation and unable to take action in the face of adversity. The story is told from David Bourne's masculine point of view, in the intimate or pseudo-third person Hemingway preferred, but its major achievement is Catherine Bourne. There has not before been a female character who so dominates a Hemingway narrative. Catherine in fact may be the most impressive of any woman character in Hemingway's work, more substantive and dimensional than Pilar in *For Whom the Bell Tolls,* or Brett Ashley in *The Sun Also Rises.* Even though she is launched from the naïve premise that sexual fantasizing is a form of madness, she takes on the stature of the self-tortured Faustian, and is portrayed as a brilliant woman trapped into a vicarious participation in someone else's creativity. She represents the most informed and delicate reading Hemingway has given to any woman.

For Catherine Bourne alone this book will be read avidly. But there are additional things to make a reader happy. For considerable portions of the narrative, the dialogue is in tension, which cannot be said of *Across the River and into the Trees*, his late novel of the same period, and for which he looted some of the motifs of this work. And there are passages that show the old man writing to the same strength of his early work—a description of David Bourne catching a bass in the canal at Le Grau-du-Roi, for example, or swimming off the beach at La Napoule. In these cases the strategy of using landscape to portray moral states produces victory.

But to be able to list the discrete excellences of a book is to say also it falls short of realization. The other woman, and third main character, Marita, has not the weight to account for her willingness to move in on a marriage and lend herself to its disruption. She is colorless and largely unarticulated. David Bourne's passivity goes unexamined by the author, except as it may be a function of his profession. But the sad truth is that his writing, which we see in the elephant story, does not exonerate him: it is bad Hemingway, a threadbare working of the theme of a boy's initiation rites that suggests to its own great disadvantage Faulkner's story on the same theme, "The Bear."

In David's character resides the ultimate deadness of the piece. His incapability in dealing with the crisis of his relationship does not mesh with his consummate self-assurance in handling the waiters, maids and hoteliers of Europe who, in this book as in Hemingway's others, come forward to supply the food and drink, the corkscrews and ice cubes and beds and fishing rods his young American colonists require. In fact so often does David Bourne perform his cultivated eating and drinking that a reader is depressed enough to wonder if Hemingway's real achievement in the early great novels was that of a travel writer who taught a provincial American audience what dishes to order, what drinks to prefer and how to deal with the European servant class. There are moments here when we feel we are not in France or Spain but in the provisional state of Yuppiedom. A reader is given to conclude that this shrewdest of writers made an uncharacteristic mistake in not finding a war to destroy his lovers, or some action beside their own lovemaking to threaten their survival. The tone of solemn self-attention in this work rises to a portentousness that the 70,000 words of text cannot justify.

But here we are led back to the issue of editing a great writer's work after his death. As far as it is possible to tell from biography, and from the inventory of Hemingway manuscripts by Philip Young and Charles W. Mann, Hemingway intended *The Garden of Eden* as a major work. At one point he conceived of it as one of a trilogy of books in which the sea figured. Certainly its title suggests a governing theme of his creative life, the loss of paradise, the expulsion from the garden, which controls *The Sun Also Rises* and *A Farewell to Arms*, among other books and stories. Apparently there is extant more than one manuscript version for scholars to choose from. Carlos Baker mentions the presence of another married couple in one of the versions, a painter named Nick, and his wife, Barbara. Of the same generation as David and Catherine Bourne, Nick (is Adams his last name?) and Barbara live in Paris. And there may be additional characters. Presumably the material involving them is in a less finished state and easily stripped away to find the spare, if skimpy, novel we have now in print. But the truth about editing the work of a dead writer in such circumstances is that you can only cut to affirm his strengths, to reiterate the strategies of style for which he is known; whereas he himself may have been writing to transcend them. This cannot have been the book Hemingway envisioned at the most ambitious moments of his struggle to realize it, a struggle that occupied him intermittently for perhaps 15 years. And it should have been published for what it is, a piece of something, part of a design.

For there are clear signs here of something exciting going on, the enlargement of a writer's mind toward compassion, toward a less defensive construal of reality. The key is the character of Catherine Bourne. She is in behavior a direct descendant of Mrs. Macomber, of "The Short Happy Life," or of Frances Clyne, Robert Cohn's emasculating lover in *The Sun Also Rises*, the kind of woman the author has before only detested and condemned. But here she has grown to suggest in Hemingway the rudiments of feminist perspective. And as for David Bourne, he is unmistakably the younger literary brother of Jake Barnes, the newspaperman wounded to impotence in that first expatriate novel. But David's passivity is not physical and therefore more difficult to put across. He reminds us a bit, actually, of Robert Cohn, whom Jake Barnes despised for suffering quietly the belittling remarks of women in public. Perhaps Hemingway is learning to dispense his judgments more thoughtfully. Or perhaps David Bourne was not designed as the hero of the piece at all.

With a large cast and perhaps multiple points of view, something else might have been intended than what we have, a revised view of the lost generation perhaps, some additional reading of a kind of American life *ex patria* with the larger context that would earn the tone of the book. There are enough clues here to suggest the unmistakable signs of a recycling of Hemingway's first materials toward less romance and less literary bigotry and greater truth. That is exciting because it gives evidence, despite his celebrity, despite his Nobel, despite the torments of his own physical self-punishment, of a writer still developing. Those same writing strategies Hemingway formulated to such triumph in his early work came to entrap him in the later. You can see this beginning to happen in his 1940 novel, *For Whom the Bell Tolls*, where implanting the conception of the book in geography, and fixing all its action in time and relentlessly understating the sentences, were finally dramatic strategies not formally sufficient to the subject. I would like to think that as he began *The Garden of Eden*, his very next novel after that war work, he realized this and wanted to retool, to remake himself. That he would fail is almost not the point—but that he would have tried, which is the true bravery of a writer, requiring more courage than facing down an elephant charge with a .303 Mannlicher.

INDEX

333